Shojo Beat

OTOMEN

Story & Art by
Aya Kanno

Volume
SEVEN

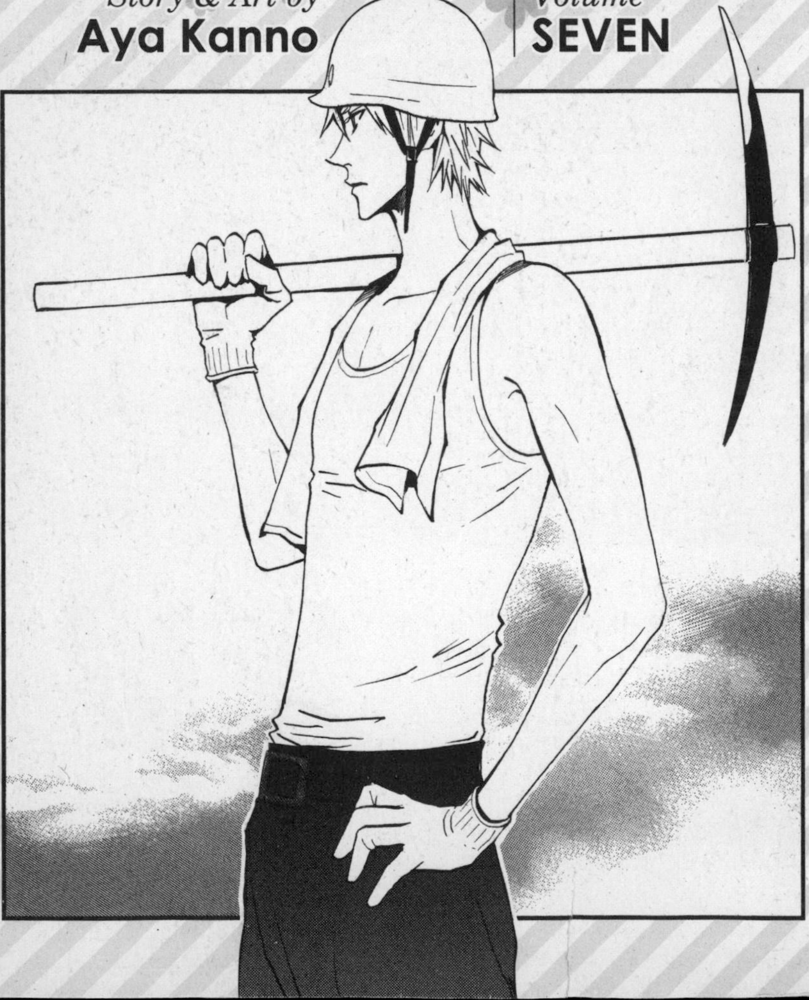

OTOMEN CHARACTERS & STORY

What is an OTOMEN?

O•to•men [OH-toe-men]
1) A young man with girlish interests and thoughts.
2) A young man who has talent for cooking, needlework and general housework.
3) A manly young man with a girlish heart.

Asuka Masamune

The captain of Ginyuri Academy High School's kendo team. He is handsome, studious and (to the casual observer) the perfect high school student. But he is actually an *otomen*, a man with a girlish heart. He loves cute things ♥, and he has a natural talent for cooking, needlework and general housekeeping. He's even a big fan of the shojo manga *Love Chick*.

STORY

Asuka Masamune, the kendo captain, is actually an *otomen* (a girlish guy)— a man who likes cute things, housework and shojo manga. When he was young, his father left home to become a woman. His mother was traumatized, and ever since then, he has kept his girlish interests a secret. However, things change when he meets Juta, a guy who is using Asuka as the basis for the female character in the shojo manga he is writing (—top secret). Asuka also starts having feelings for a tomboy girl who is good at martial arts. Because of this, he's slowly reverting to his true *otomen* self!

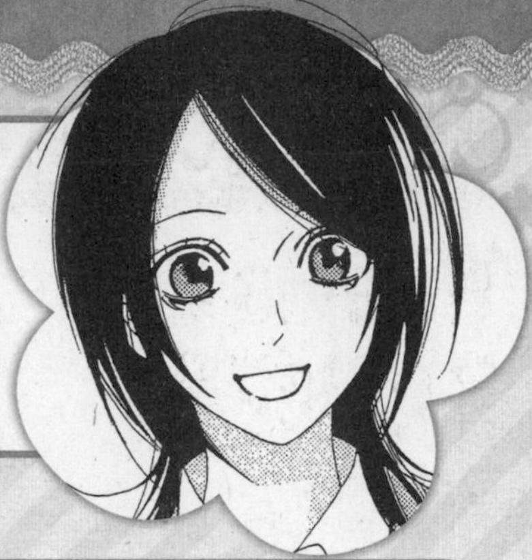

Ryo Miyakozuka

Asuka's classmate for whom he has feelings. She has studied martial arts under her father ever since she was little, and she is very good at it. On the other hand, her housekeeping skills are disastrous. She's a very eccentric beauty.

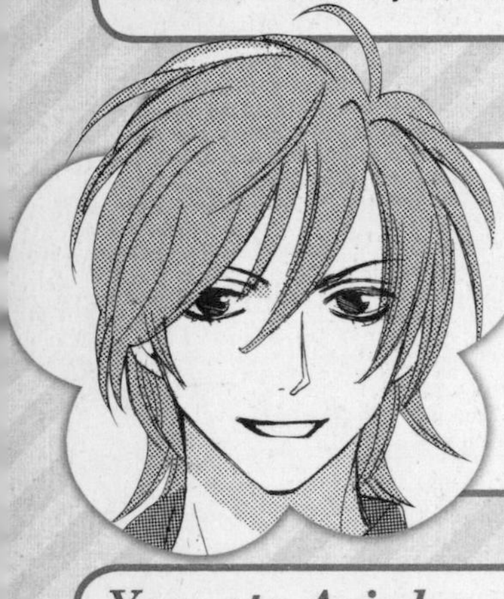

Juta Tachibana

Asuka's classmate. He's flirtatious, but he's actually the popular shojo manga artist Jewel Sachihana. He is using Asuka and Ryo as character concepts in his manga *Love Chick*, which is being published in the shojo magazine *Hana to Mame*. His personal life is a mystery! He also has ten younger sisters!!

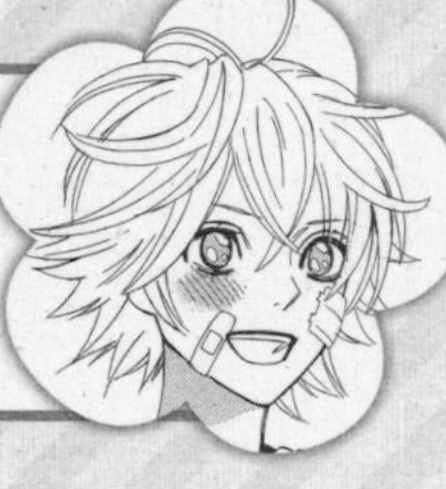

Yamato Ariake

Underclassman at Asuka's school. He looks like a girl, but he admires manliness and has long, delusional fantasies about being manly...

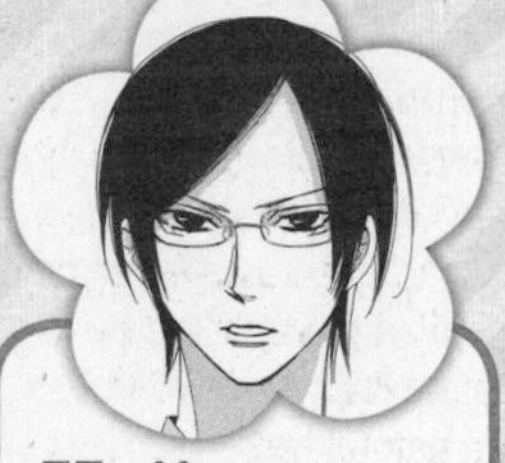

Hajime Tonomine

The captain of Kinbara High School's kendo team, he sees Asuka as his lifelong rival. He is the strong and silent type but is actually an *otomen* who is good with makeup. A *Tsun-sama*.

("Tsun-sama" © Juta Tachibana.)

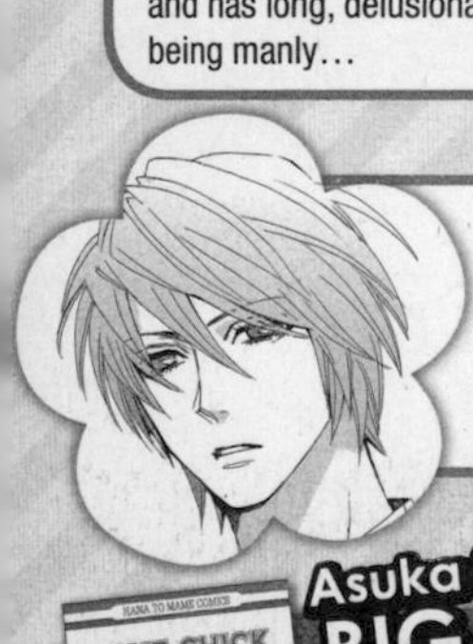

Kitora Kurokawa

Asuka's classmate. He is obsessed with the beauty of flowers. He is an *otomen* who refers to himself as the Flower Evangelist.

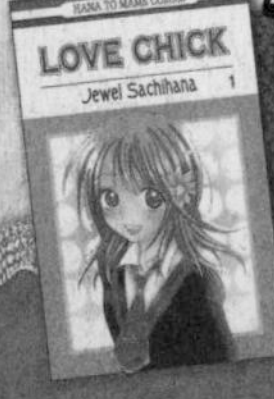
HANA TO MAME COMICS
LOVE CHICK
Jewel Sachihana
1

Asuka is also a BIG FAN!

Hana to Mame Comics

LOVE CHICK by Jewel Sachihana

(Now serialized in *Hana to Mame*)

The very popular shojo comic that Juta writes (under the pen name Jewel Sachihana).

OTOMEN
volume 7
CONTENTS

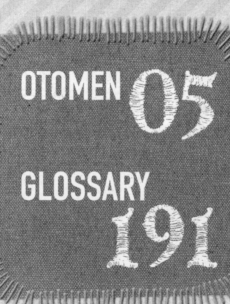

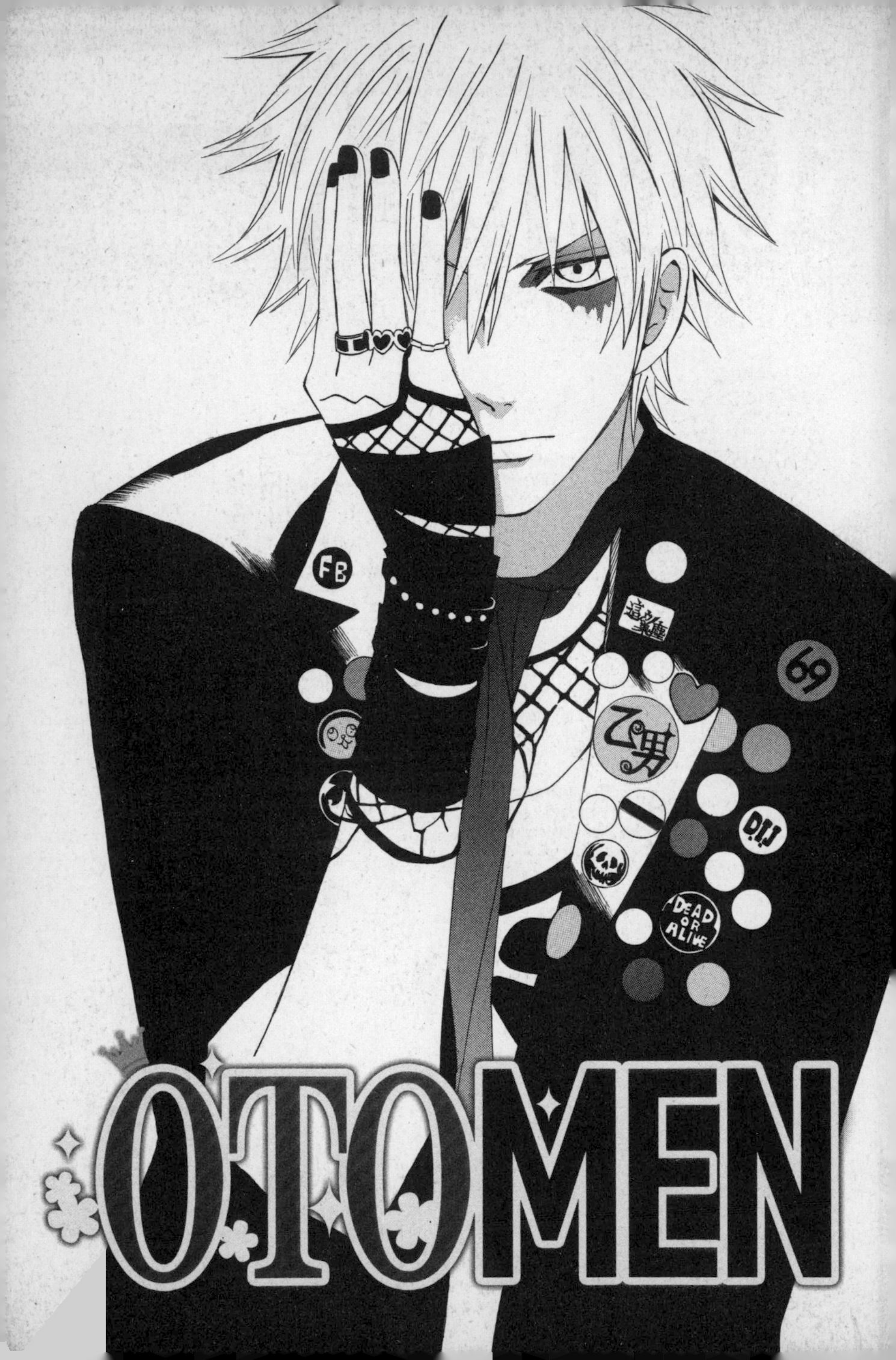
FB
69
乙男
DEAD OR ALIVE
OTOMEN

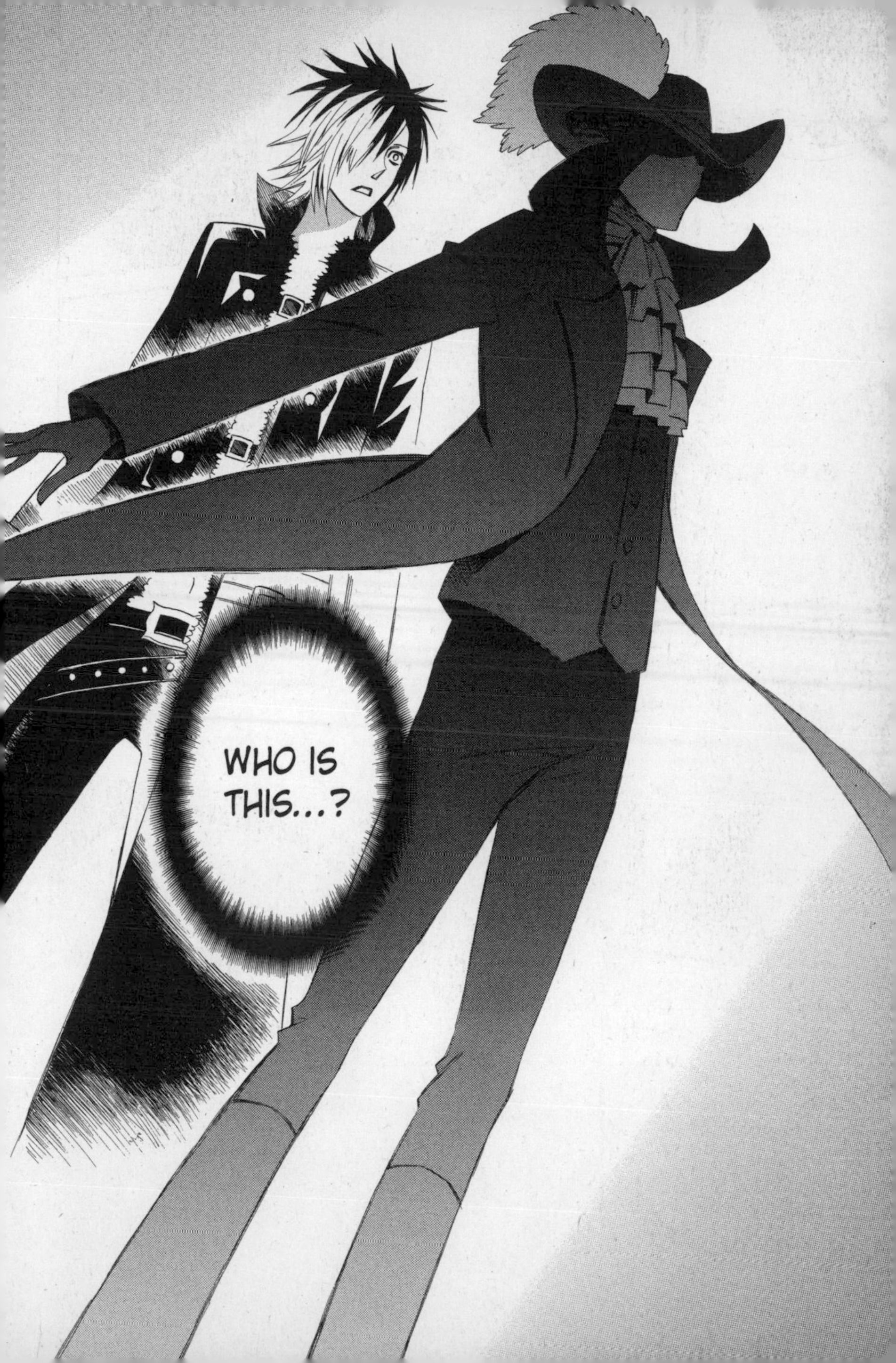
WHO IS THIS...?

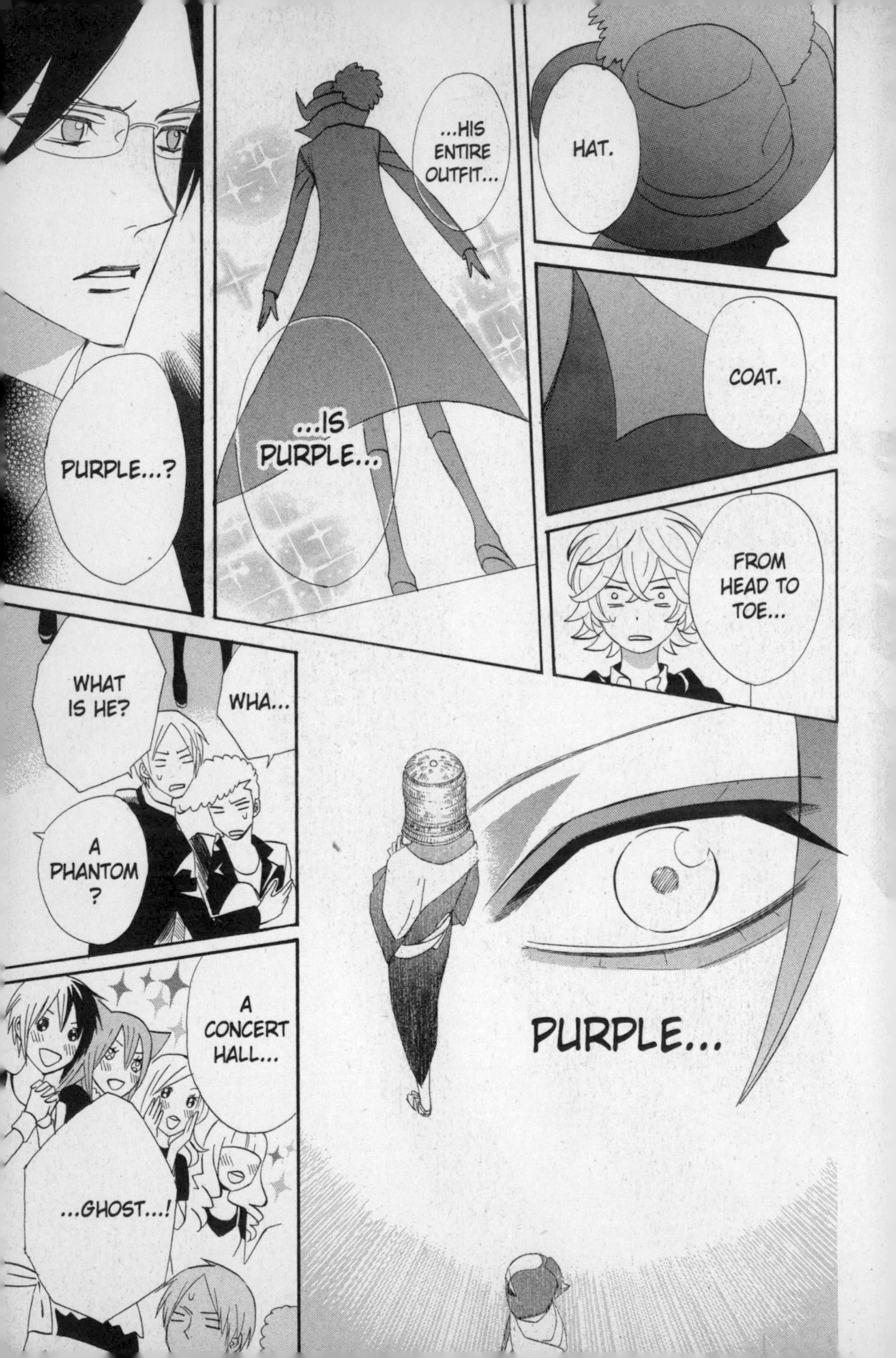
HAT.
COAT.
FROM HEAD TO TOE...
...HIS ENTIRE OUTFIT...
...IS PURPLE...
PURPLE...?
PURPLE...
WHA...
WHAT IS HE?
A PHANTOM ?
A CONCERT HALL...
...GHOST...!

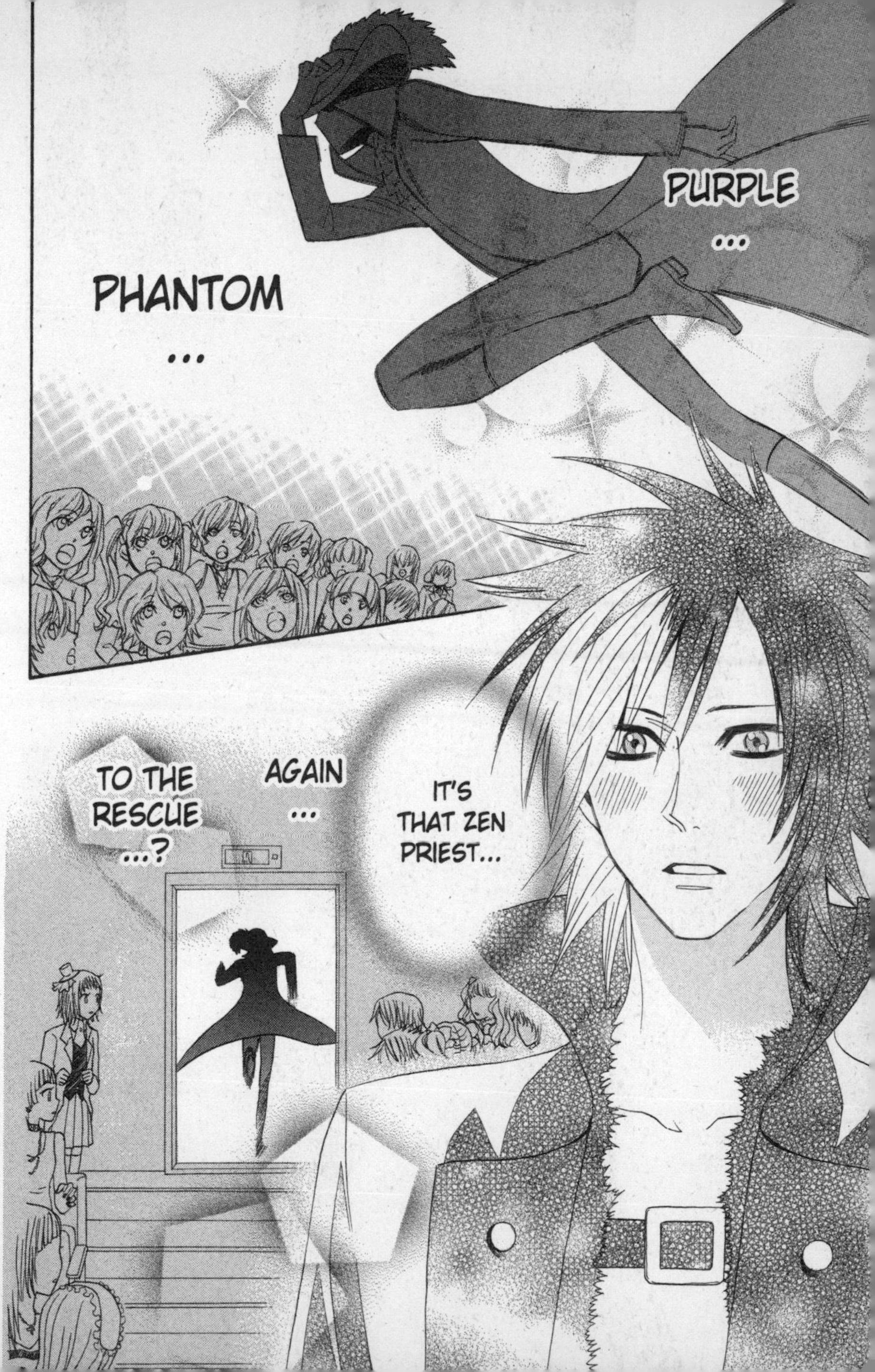
PURPLE ...
PHANTOM ...
IT'S THAT ZEN PRIEST...
AGAIN ...
TO THE RESCUE ...?

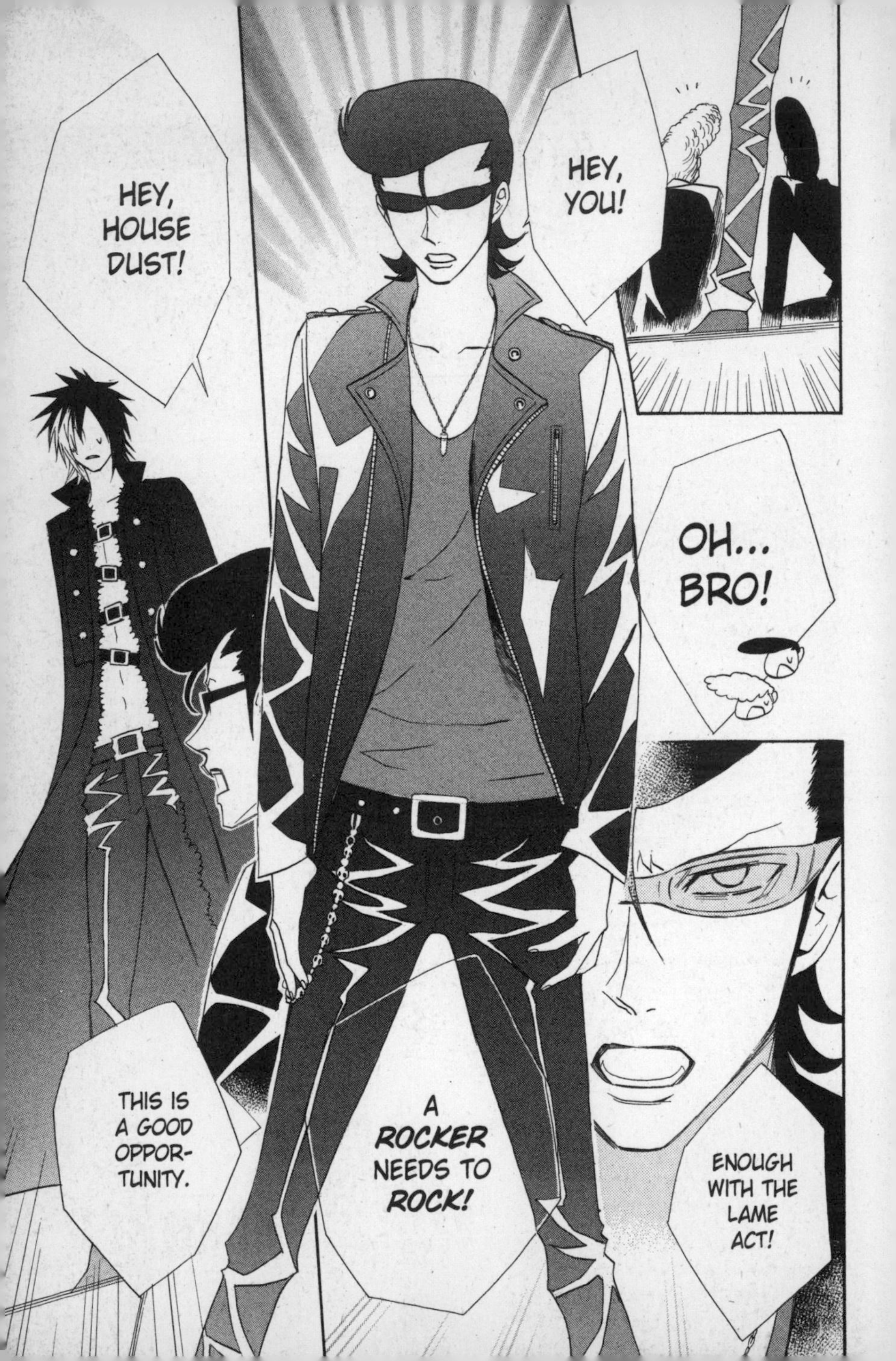
HEY, YOU!
OH... BRO!
HEY, HOUSE DUST!
ENOUGH WITH THE LAME ACT!
A ROCKER NEEDS TO ROCK!
THIS IS A GOOD OPPORTUNITY.

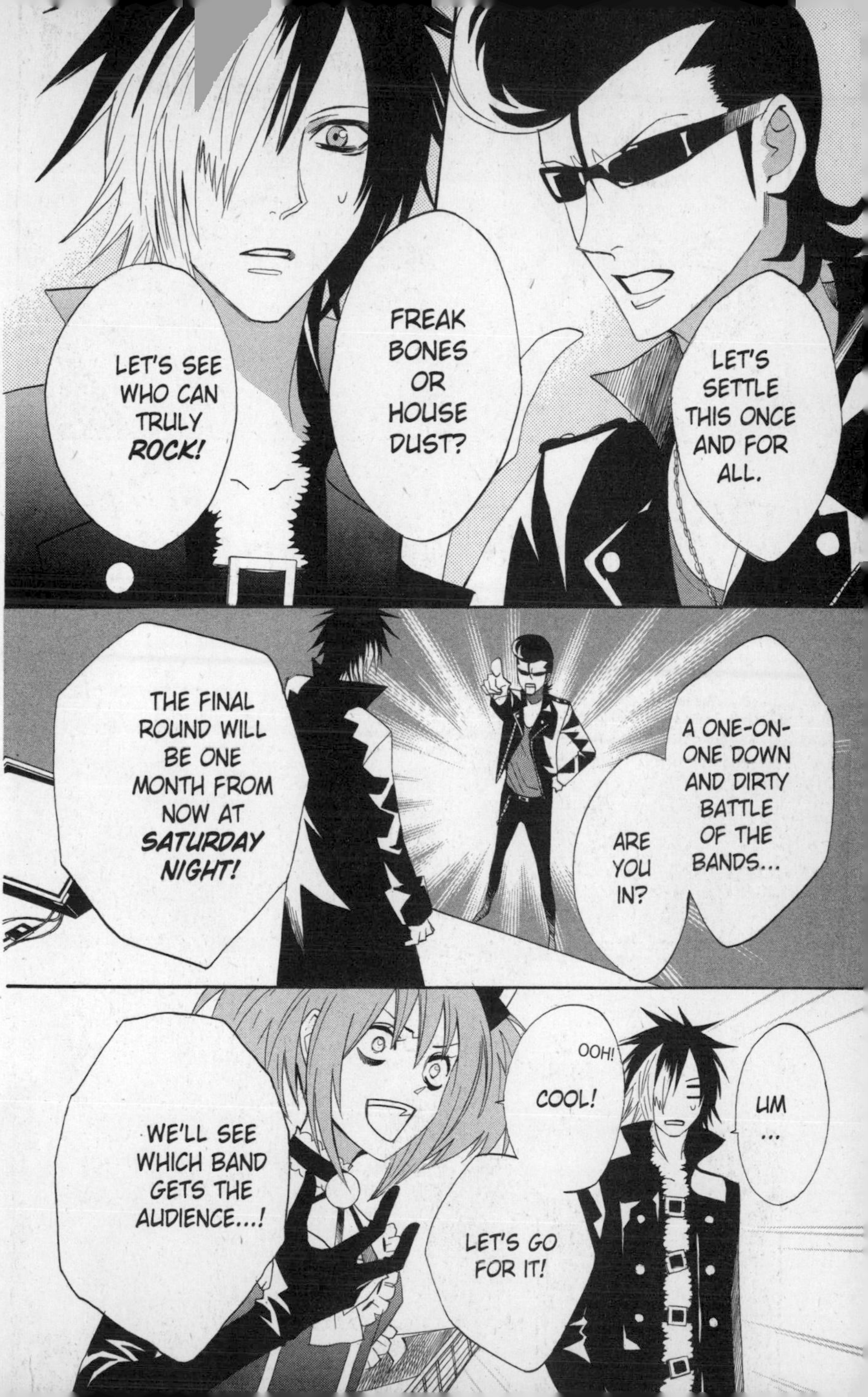
LET'S SETTLE THIS ONCE AND FOR ALL.
FREAK BONES OR HOUSE DUST?
LET'S SEE WHO CAN TRULY ROCK!
A ONE-ON-ONE DOWN AND DIRTY BATTLE OF THE BANDS...
ARE YOU IN?
THE FINAL ROUND WILL BE ONE MONTH FROM NOW AT SATURDAY NIGHT!
UM ...
OOH!
COOL!
LET'S GO FOR IT!
WE'LL SEE WHICH BAND GETS THE AUDIENCE...!

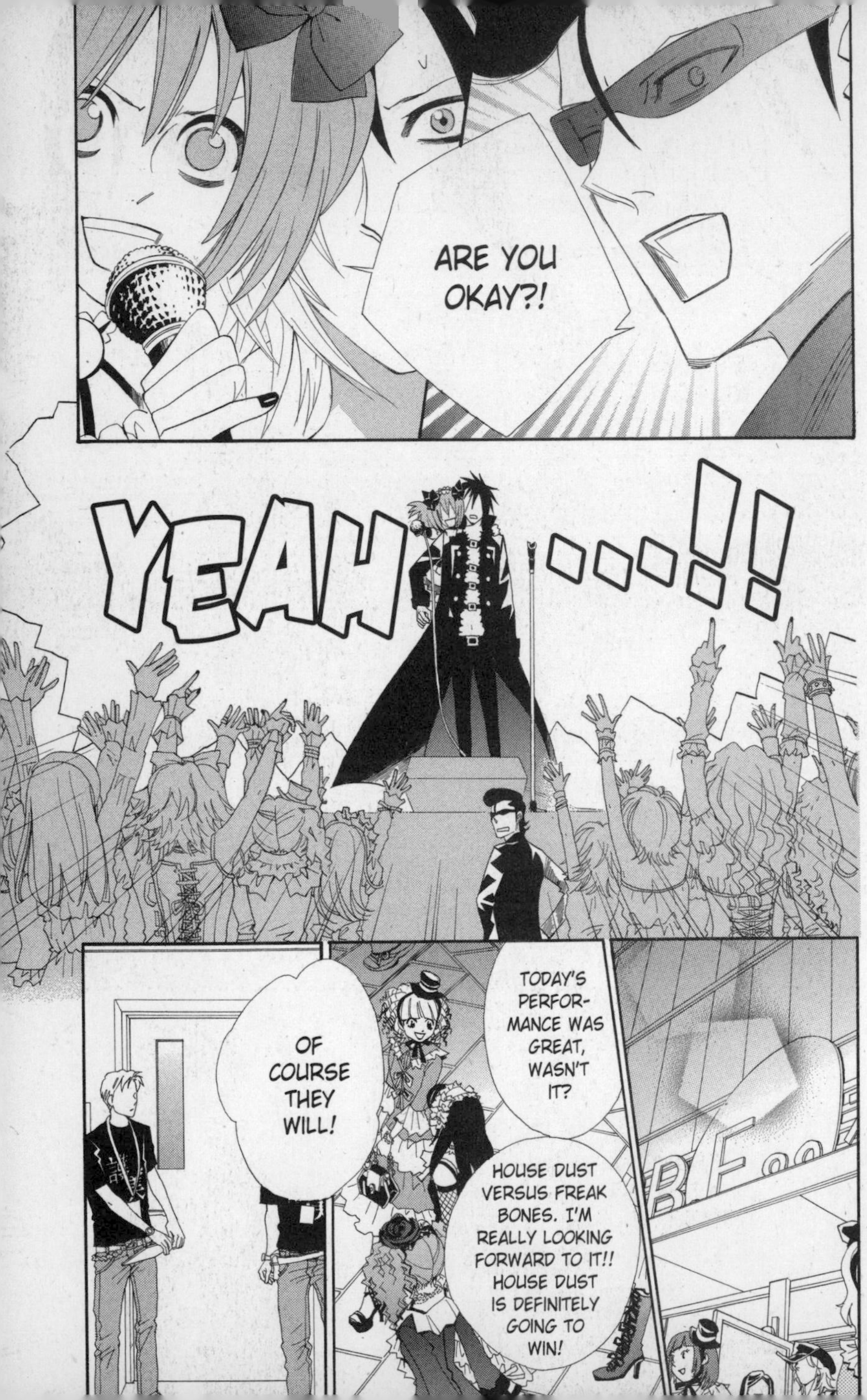
ARE YOU OKAY?!
YEAH...!!
TODAY'S PERFORMANCE WAS GREAT, WASN'T IT?
HOUSE DUST VERSUS FREAK BONES. I'M REALLY LOOKING FORWARD TO IT!! HOUSE DUST IS DEFINITELY GOING TO WIN!
OF COURSE THEY WILL!

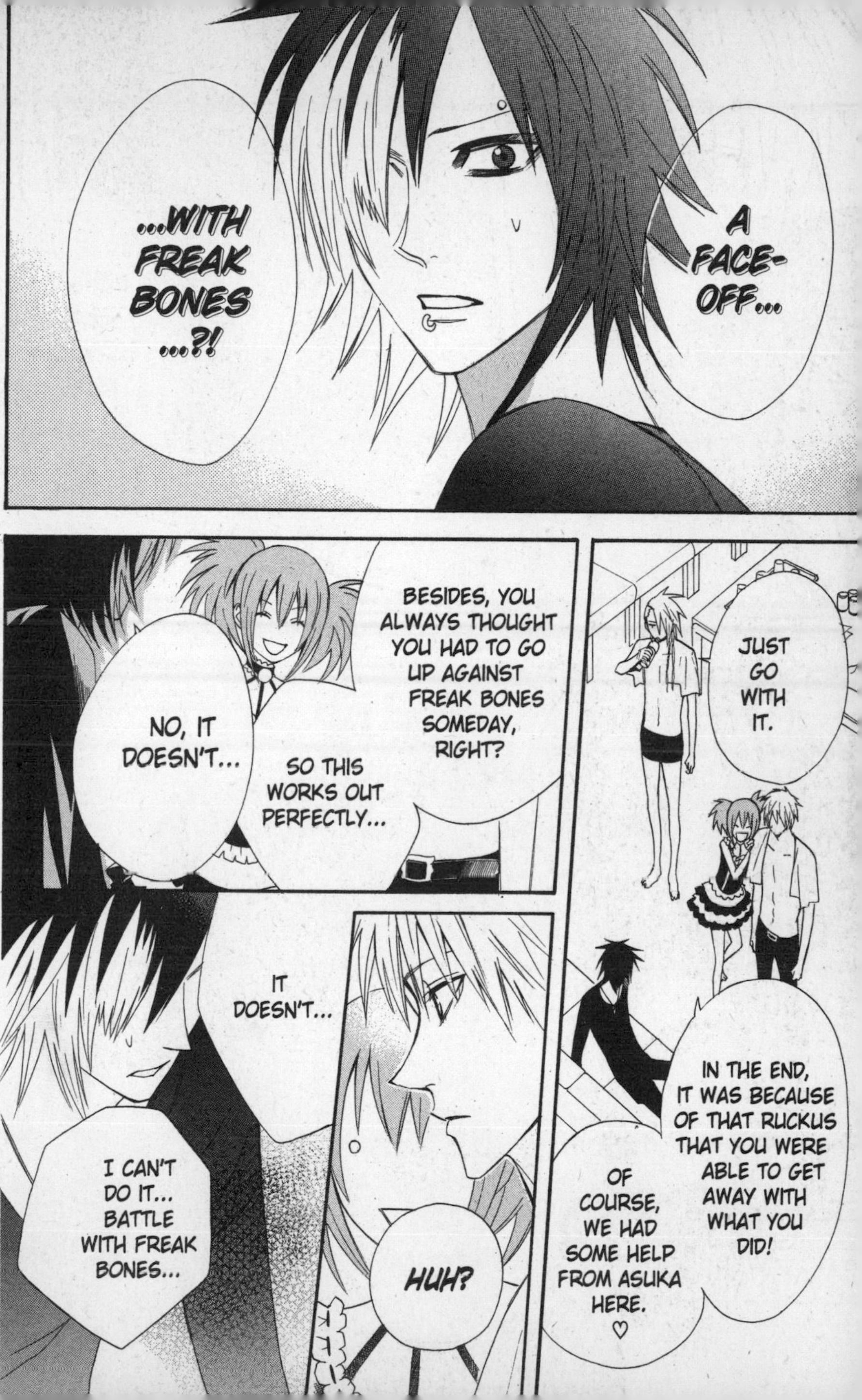
A FACE-OFF...
...WITH FREAK BONES...?!
JUST GO WITH IT.
IN THE END, IT WAS BECAUSE OF THAT RUCKUS THAT YOU WERE ABLE TO GET AWAY WITH WHAT YOU DID!
OF COURSE, WE HAD SOME HELP FROM ASUKA HERE. ♡
BESIDES, YOU ALWAYS THOUGHT YOU HAD TO GO UP AGAINST FREAK BONES SOMEDAY, RIGHT?
SO THIS WORKS OUT PERFECTLY...
NO, IT DOESN'T...
IT DOESN'T...
HUH?
I CAN'T DO IT... BATTLE WITH FREAK BONES...

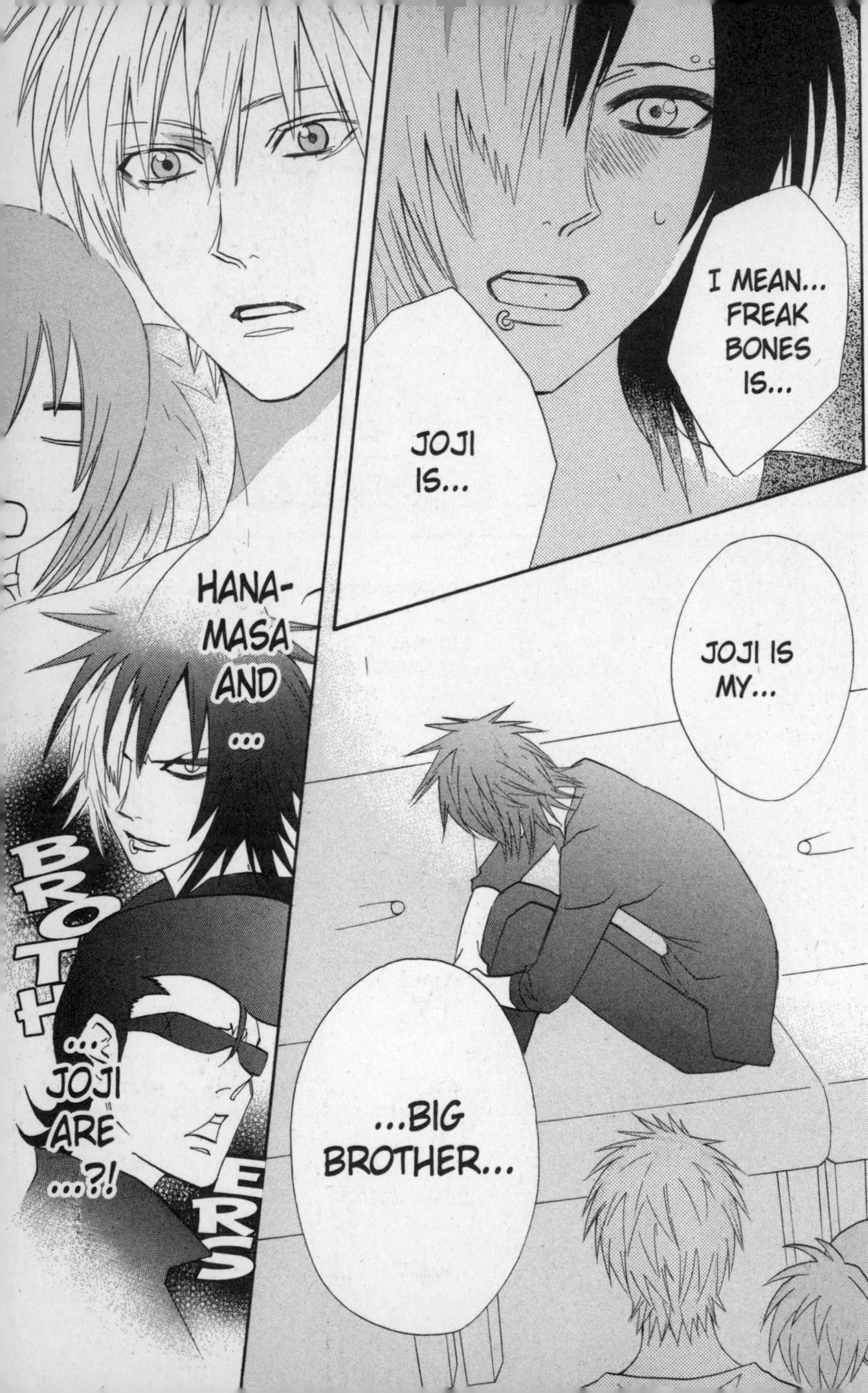
I MEAN... FREAK BONES IS...
JOJI IS...
JOJI IS MY...
...BIG BROTHER...
HANA-MASA AND ...
...JOJI ARE ...?!
BROTHERS

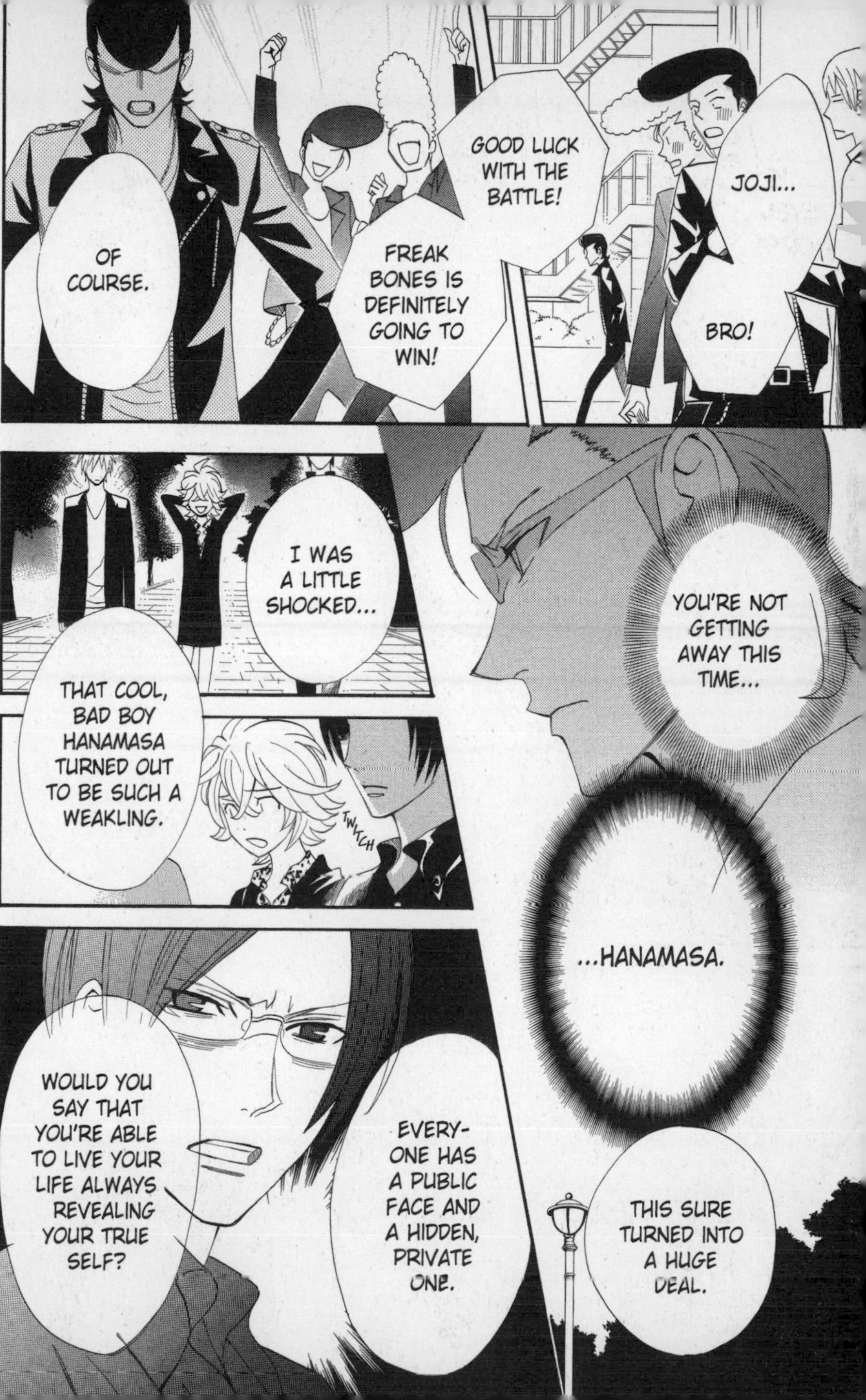
JOJI...
BRO!
GOOD LUCK WITH THE BATTLE!
FREAK BONES IS DEFINITELY GOING TO WIN!
OF COURSE.
YOU'RE NOT GETTING AWAY THIS TIME...
...HANAMASA.
I WAS A LITTLE SHOCKED...
THAT COOL, BAD BOY HANAMASA TURNED OUT TO BE SUCH A WEAKLING.
TWITCH
THIS SURE TURNED INTO A HUGE DEAL.
EVERY-ONE HAS A PUBLIC FACE AND A HIDDEN, PRIVATE ONE.
WOULD YOU SAY THAT YOU'RE ABLE TO LIVE YOUR LIFE ALWAYS REVEALING YOUR TRUE SELF?

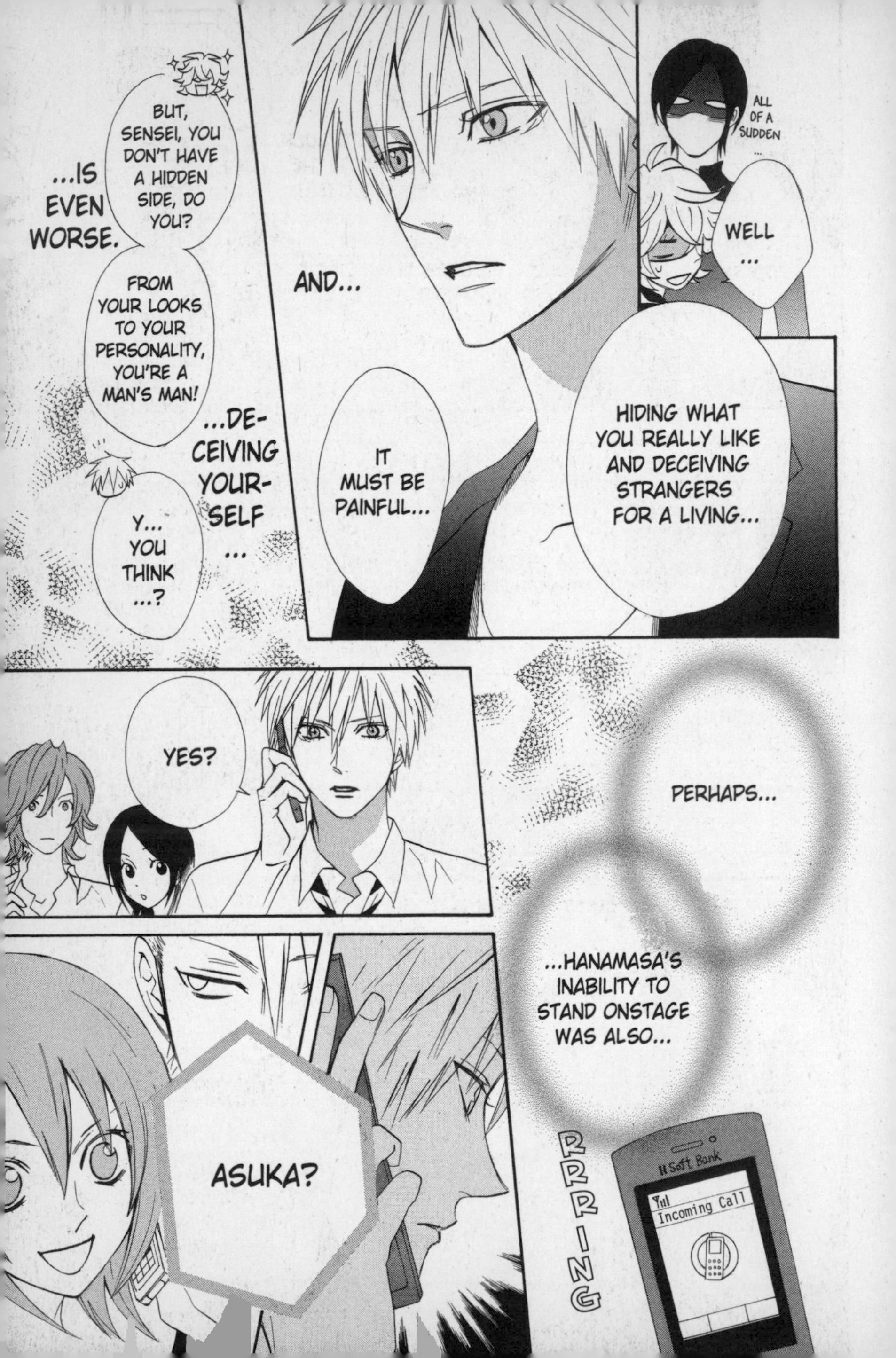
ALL OF A SUDDEN ...
WELL ...
BUT, SENSEI, YOU DON'T HAVE A HIDDEN SIDE, DO YOU?
FROM YOUR LOOKS TO YOUR PERSONALITY, YOU'RE A MAN'S MAN!
Y... YOU THINK ...?
HIDING WHAT YOU REALLY LIKE AND DECEIVING STRANGERS FOR A LIVING...
IT MUST BE PAINFUL...
AND...
...DE-CEIVING YOUR-SELF ...
...IS EVEN WORSE.
PERHAPS...
...HANAMASA'S INABILITY TO STAND ONSTAGE WAS ALSO...
RRRING
Soft Bank
Incoming Call
YES?
ASUKA?

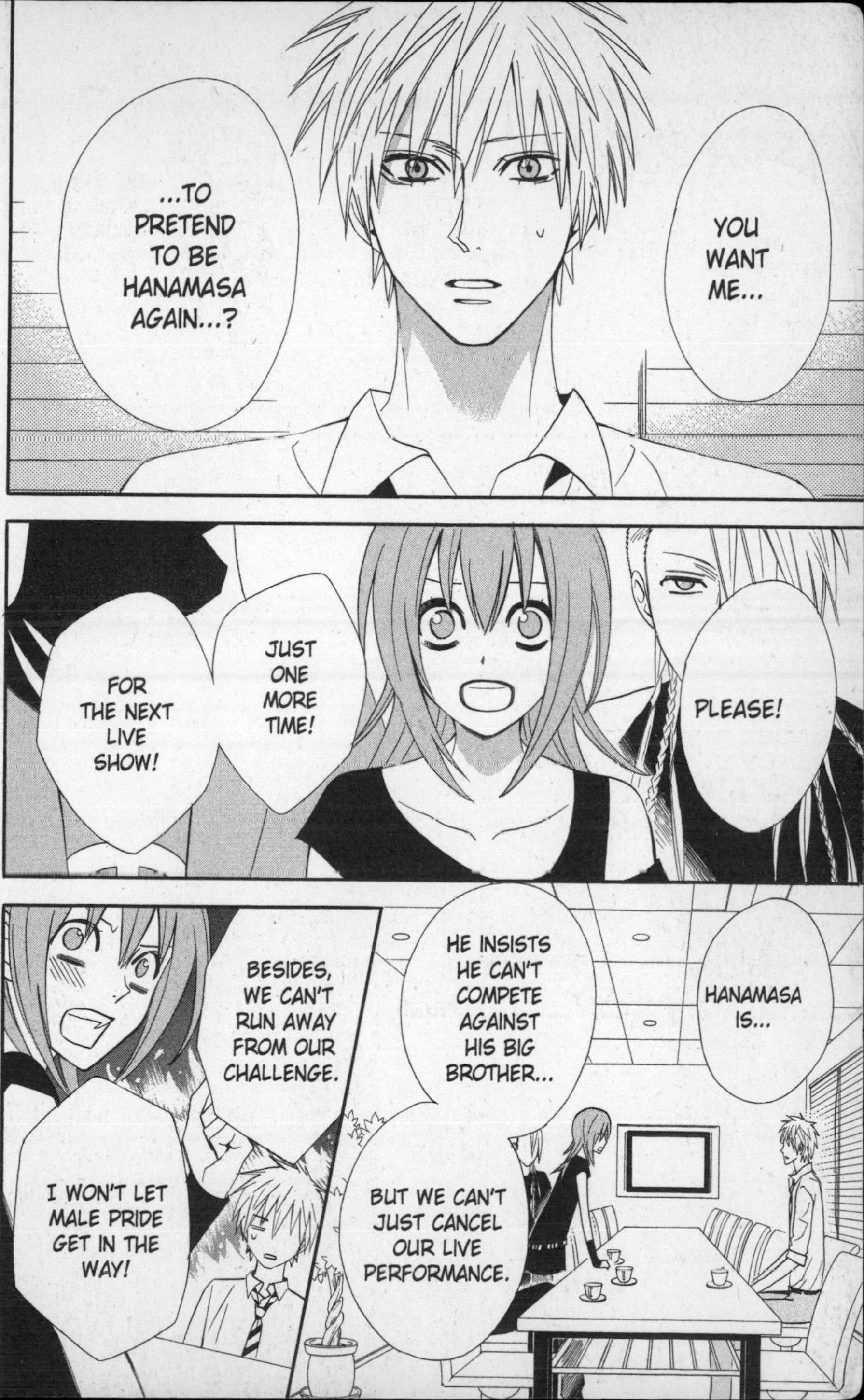
YOU WANT ME...
...TO PRETEND TO BE HANAMASA AGAIN...?
PLEASE!
JUST ONE MORE TIME!
FOR THE NEXT LIVE SHOW!
HANAMASA IS...
HE INSISTS HE CAN'T COMPETE AGAINST HIS BIG BROTHER...
BUT WE CAN'T JUST CANCEL OUR LIVE PERFORMANCE.
BESIDES, WE CAN'T RUN AWAY FROM OUR CHALLENGE.
I WON'T LET MALE PRIDE GET IN THE WAY!

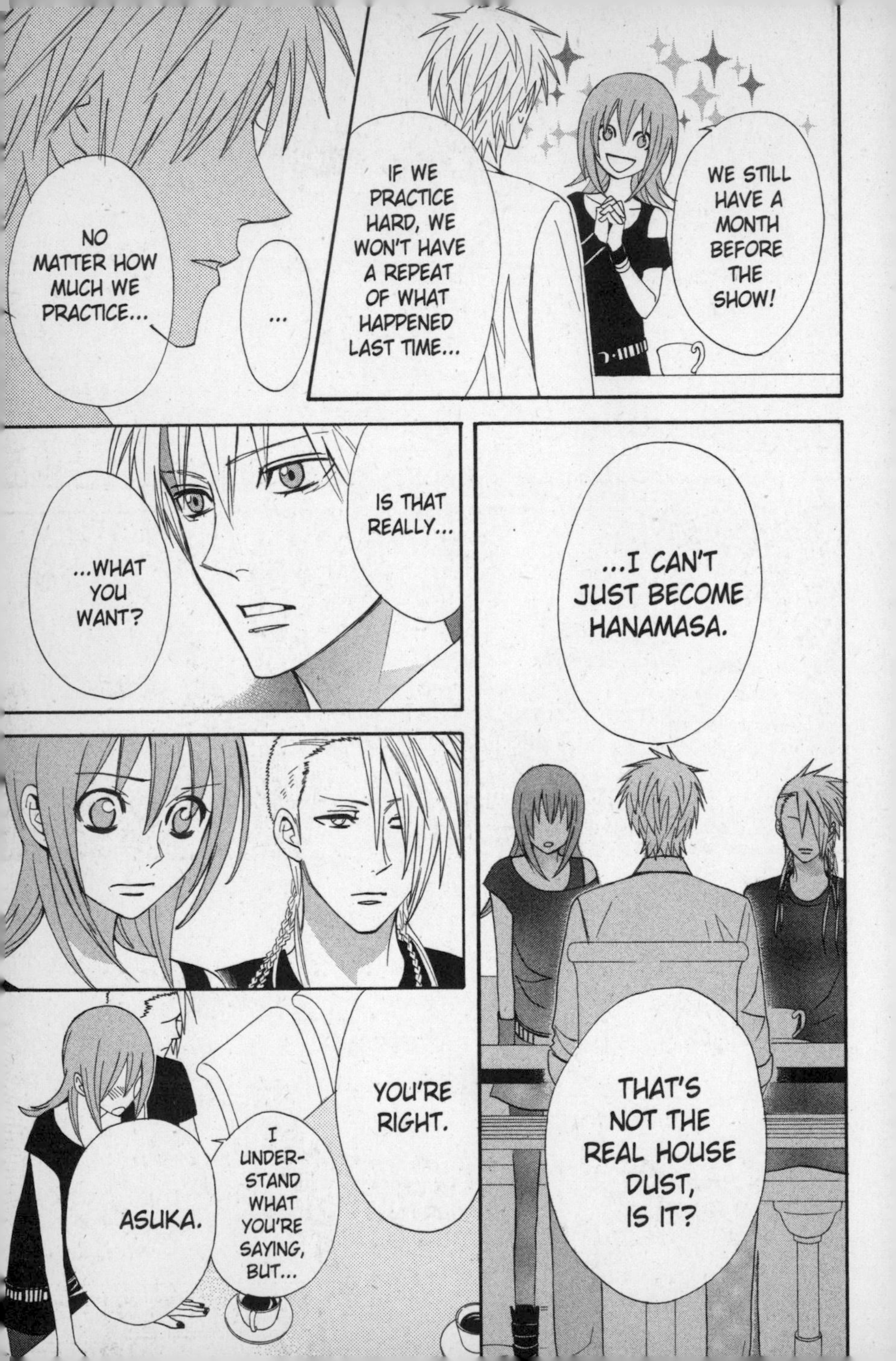
WE STILL HAVE A MONTH BEFORE THE SHOW!
IF WE PRACTICE HARD, WE WON'T HAVE A REPEAT OF WHAT HAPPENED LAST TIME...
...
NO MATTER HOW MUCH WE PRACTICE...
...I CAN'T JUST BECOME HANAMASA.
THAT'S NOT THE REAL HOUSE DUST, IS IT?
IS THAT REALLY...
...WHAT YOU WANT?
YOU'RE RIGHT.
I UNDER-STAND WHAT YOU'RE SAYING, BUT...
ASUKA.

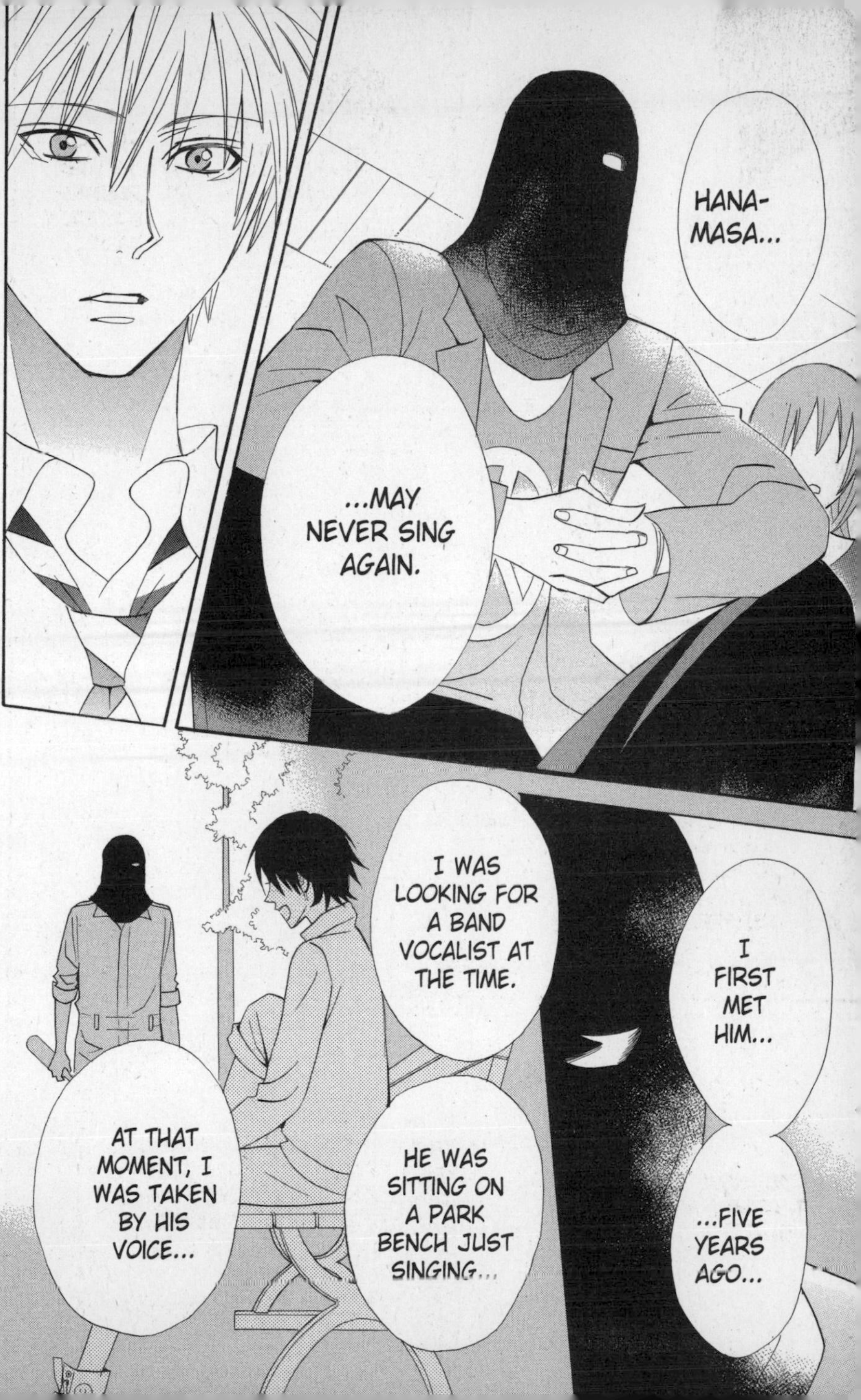
HANA-MASA...
...MAY NEVER SING AGAIN.
I FIRST MET HIM...
...FIVE YEARS AGO...
I WAS LOOKING FOR A BAND VOCALIST AT THE TIME.
HE WAS SITTING ON A PARK BENCH JUST SINGING...
AT THAT MOMENT, I WAS TAKEN BY HIS VOICE...

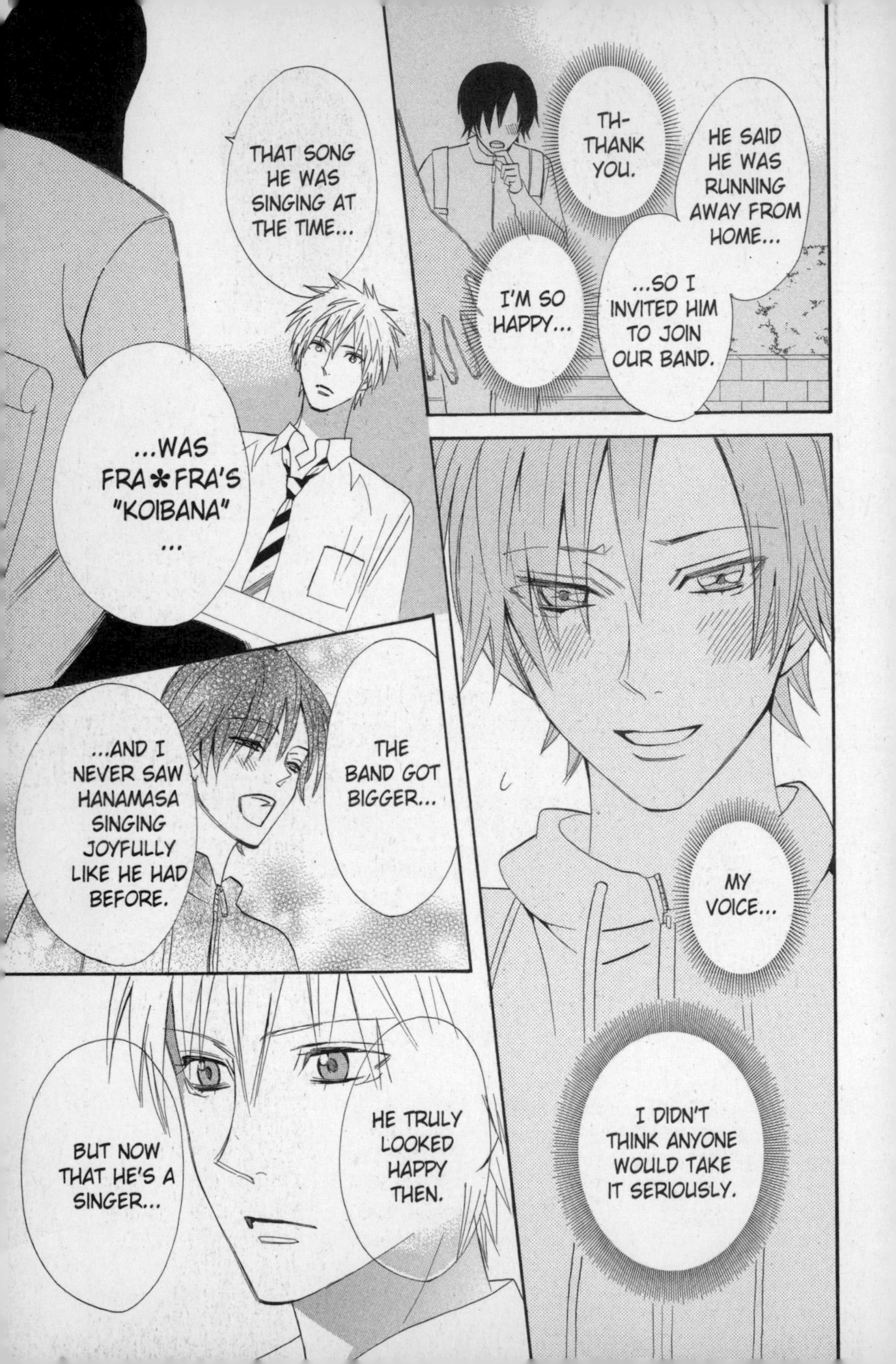
HE SAID HE WAS RUNNING AWAY FROM HOME...
TH-THANK YOU.
...SO I INVITED HIM TO JOIN OUR BAND.
I'M SO HAPPY...
THAT SONG HE WAS SINGING AT THE TIME...
...WAS FRA✻FRA'S "KOIBANA" ...
MY VOICE...
I DIDN'T THINK ANYONE WOULD TAKE IT SERIOUSLY.
THE BAND GOT BIGGER...
...AND I NEVER SAW HANAMASA SINGING JOYFULLY LIKE HE HAD BEFORE.
HE TRULY LOOKED HAPPY THEN.
BUT NOW THAT HE'S A SINGER...

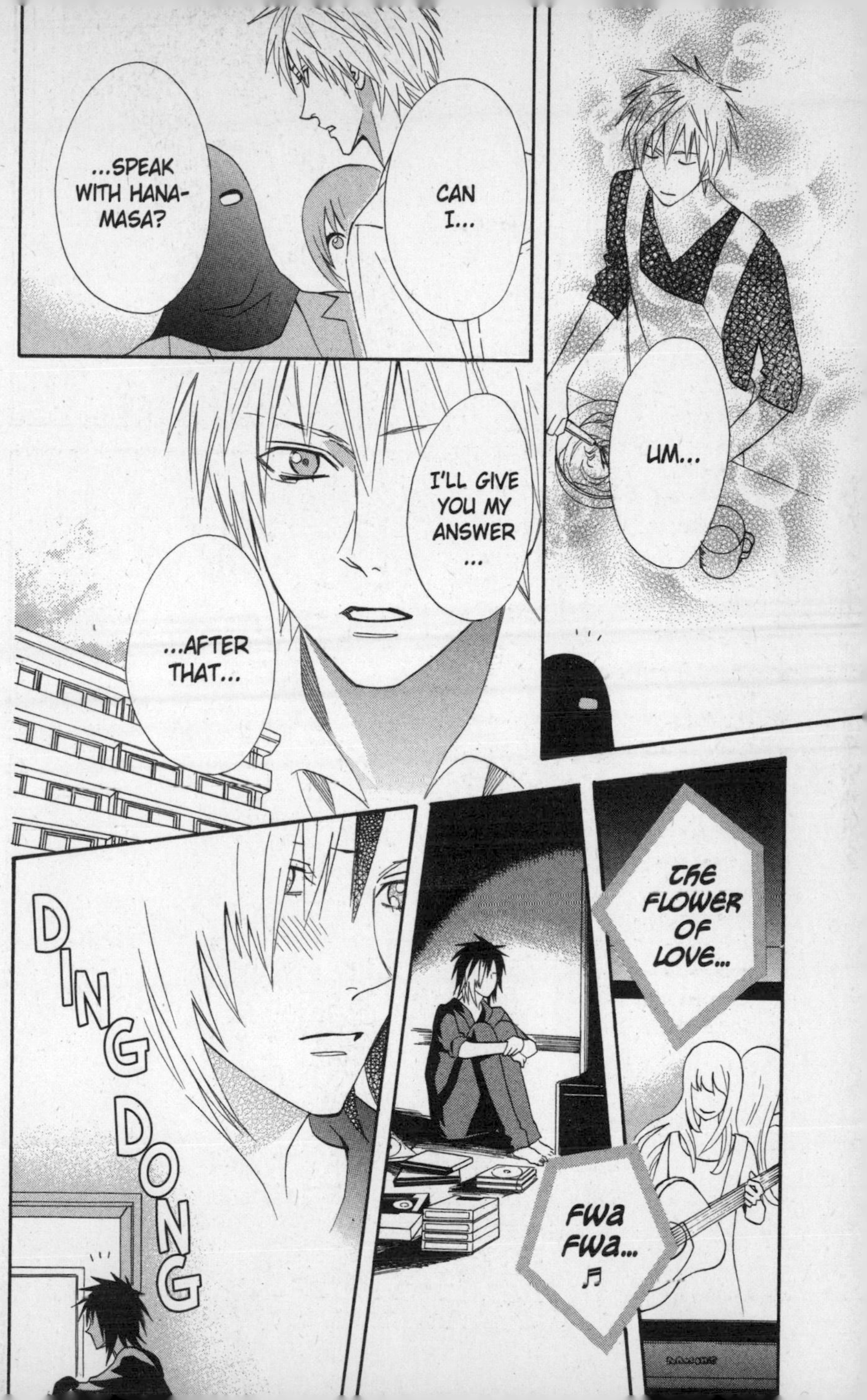
UM...
CAN I...
...SPEAK WITH HANA-MASA?
I'LL GIVE YOU MY ANSWER...
...AFTER THAT...
THE FLOWER OF LOVE...
FWA FWA... ♪
DING DONG

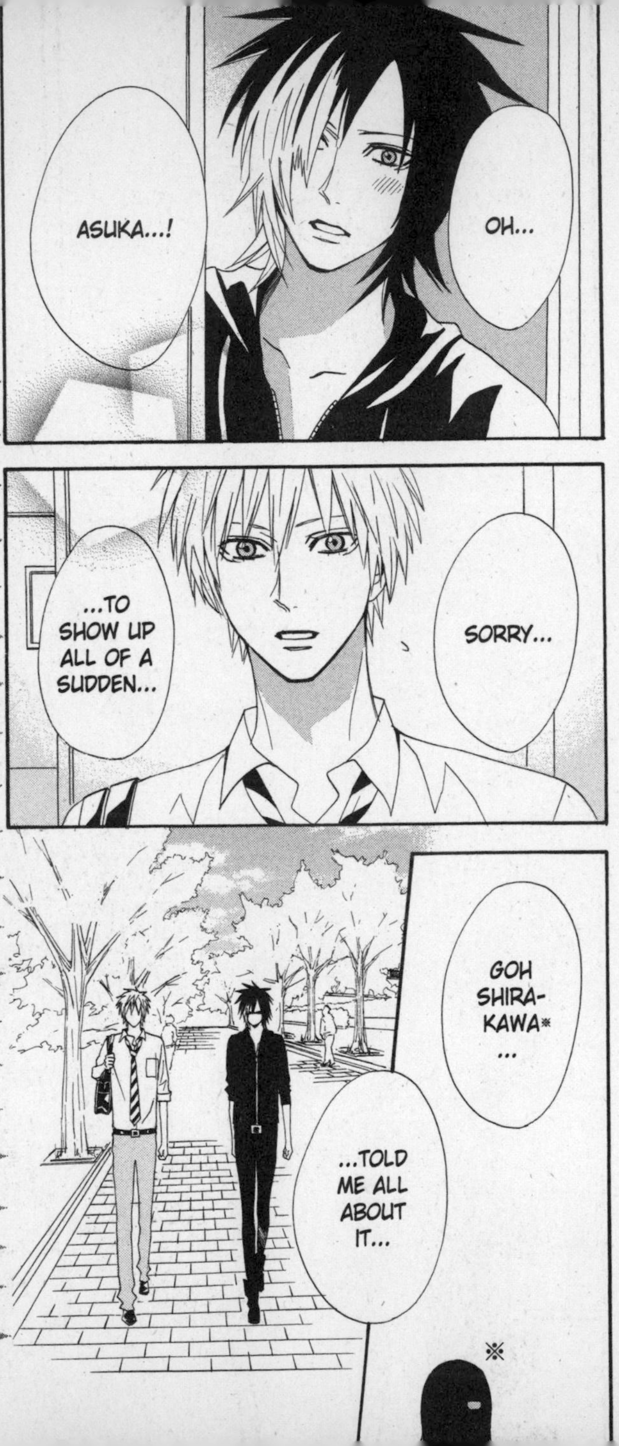
OH...
ASUKA...!
SORRY...
...TO SHOW UP ALL OF A SUDDEN...
GOH SHIRA-KAWA※...
...TOLD ME ALL ABOUT IT...
※

Hello, this is volume 7.

This is the second half of the story about the bands. Drawing the rock bands and the pompadour hairstyle was a lot of fun. Leather jackets, leather pants (showing my age...) and sunglasses... I love them. The brothers are characters I thought of when I first started working on Otomen, so I'm glad I got to include them...
They'll be appearing more and more.

Oh, incidentally, the bassist for House Dust is male. My favorite is Goh Shirakawa.↘

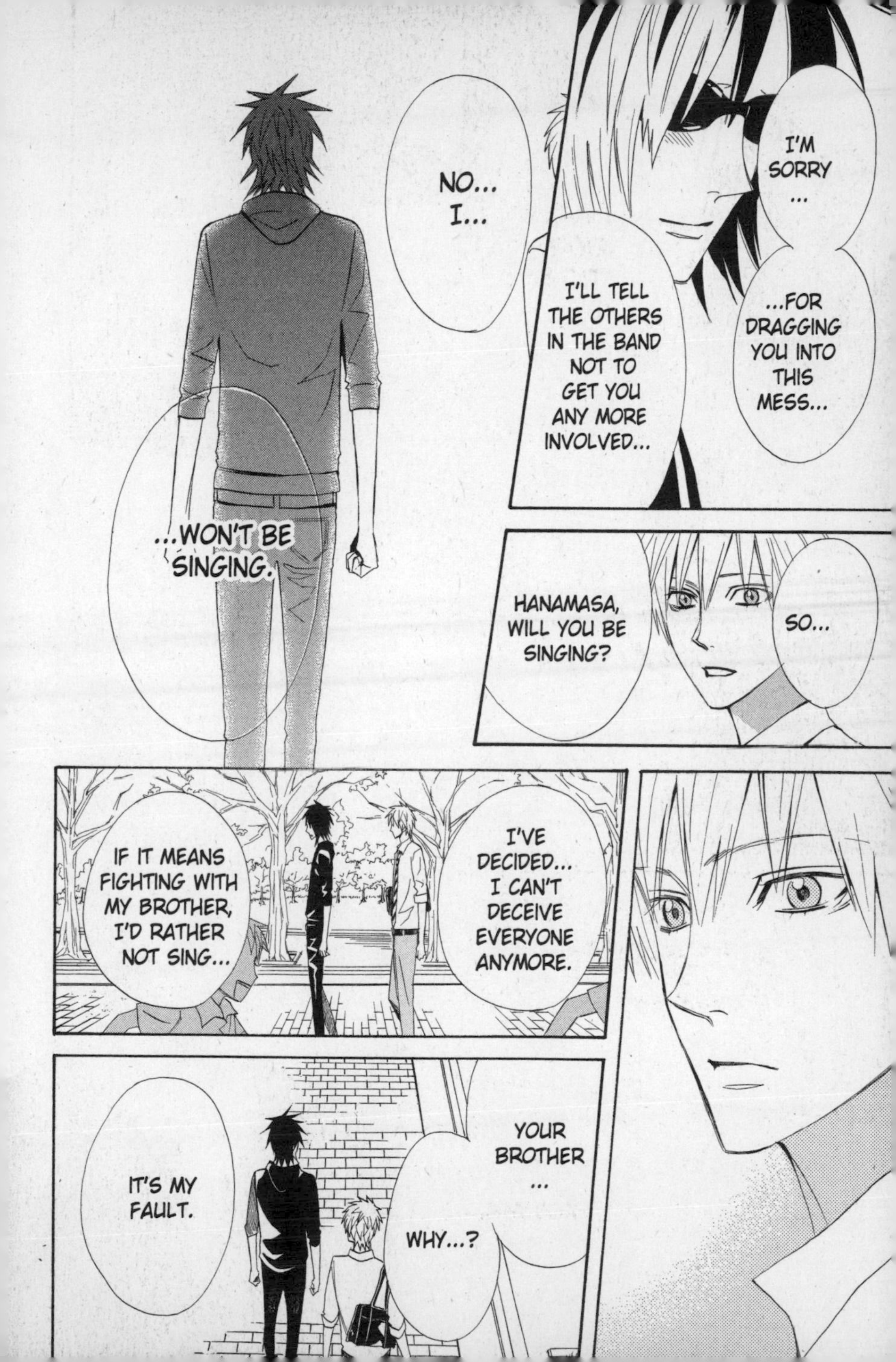
I'M SORRY...
...FOR DRAGGING YOU INTO THIS MESS...
I'LL TELL THE OTHERS IN THE BAND NOT TO GET YOU ANY MORE INVOLVED...
SO...
HANAMASA, WILL YOU BE SINGING?
NO... I...
...WON'T BE SINGING.
I'VE DECIDED... I CAN'T DECEIVE EVERYONE ANYMORE.
IF IT MEANS FIGHTING WITH MY BROTHER, I'D RATHER NOT SING...
YOUR BROTHER...
WHY...?
IT'S MY FAULT.

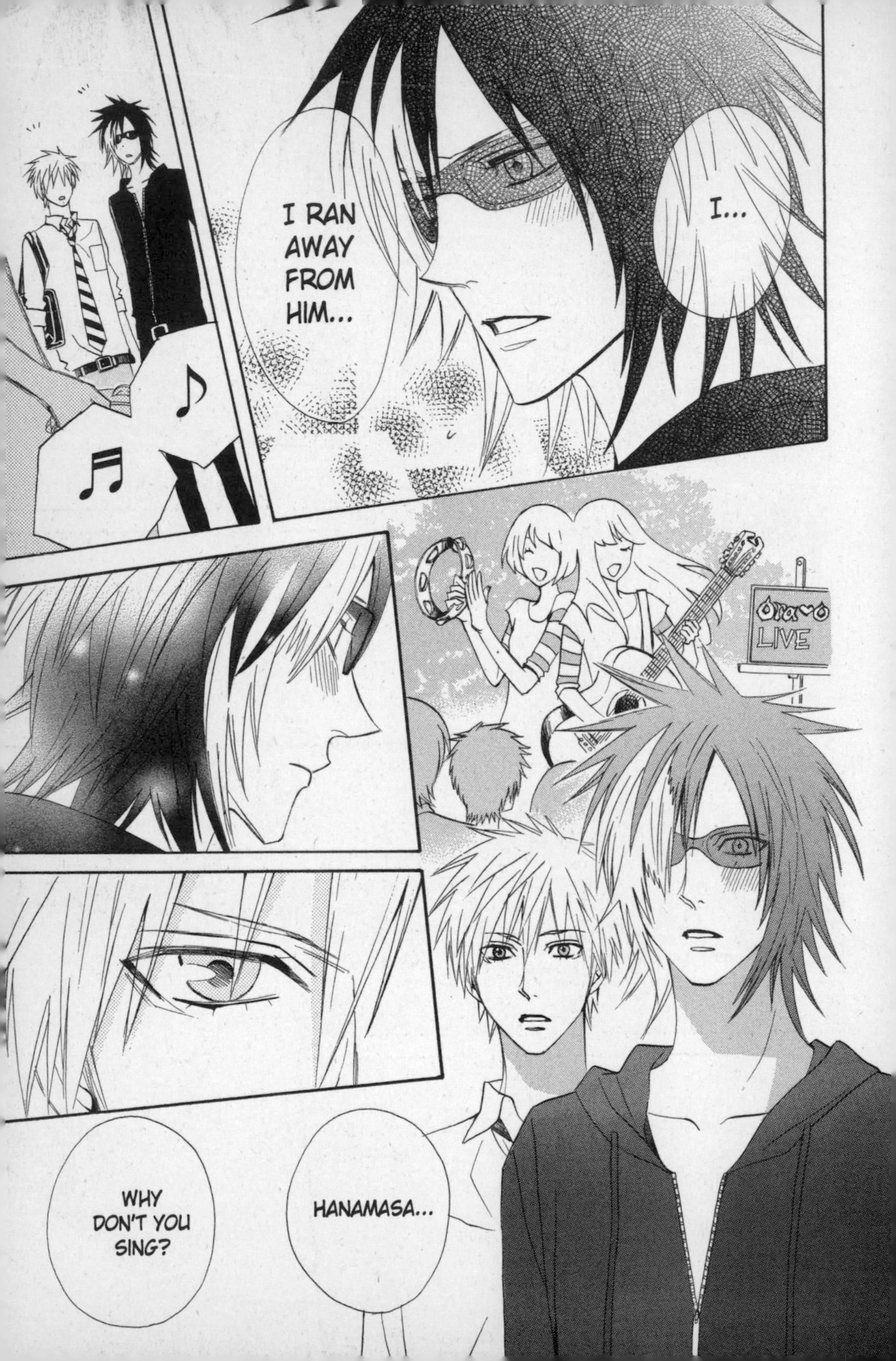
I...
I RAN AWAY FROM HIM...
LIVE
HANAMASA...
WHY DON'T YOU SING?

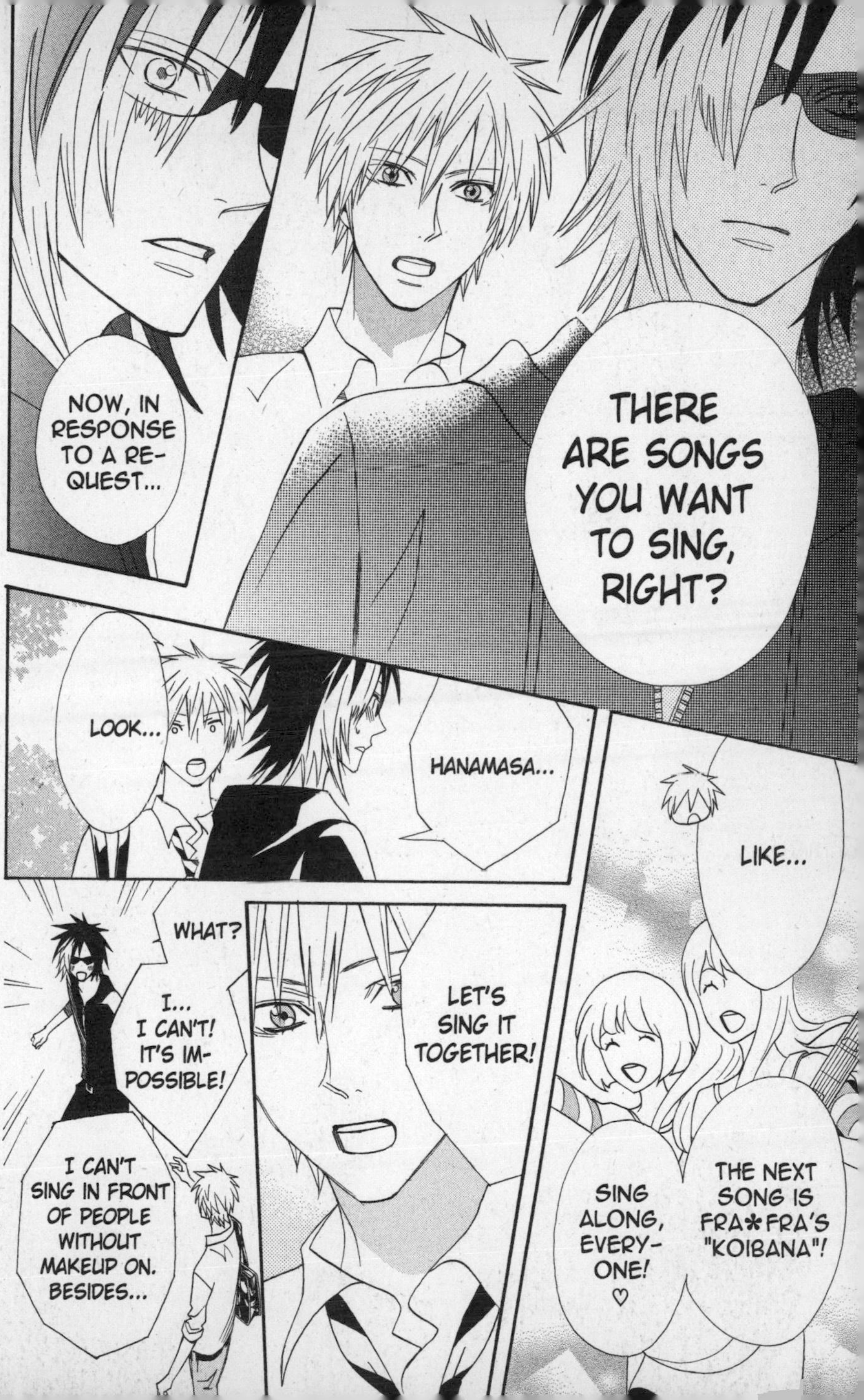
THERE ARE SONGS YOU WANT TO SING, RIGHT?
NOW, IN RESPONSE TO A RE-QUEST...
LIKE...
THE NEXT SONG IS FRA*FRA'S "KOIBANA"!
SING ALONG, EVERY-ONE! ♡
HANAMASA...
LOOK...
LET'S SING IT TOGETHER!
WHAT?
I... I CAN'T! IT'S IM-POSSIBLE!
I CAN'T SING IN FRONT OF PEOPLE WITHOUT MAKEUP ON. BESIDES...

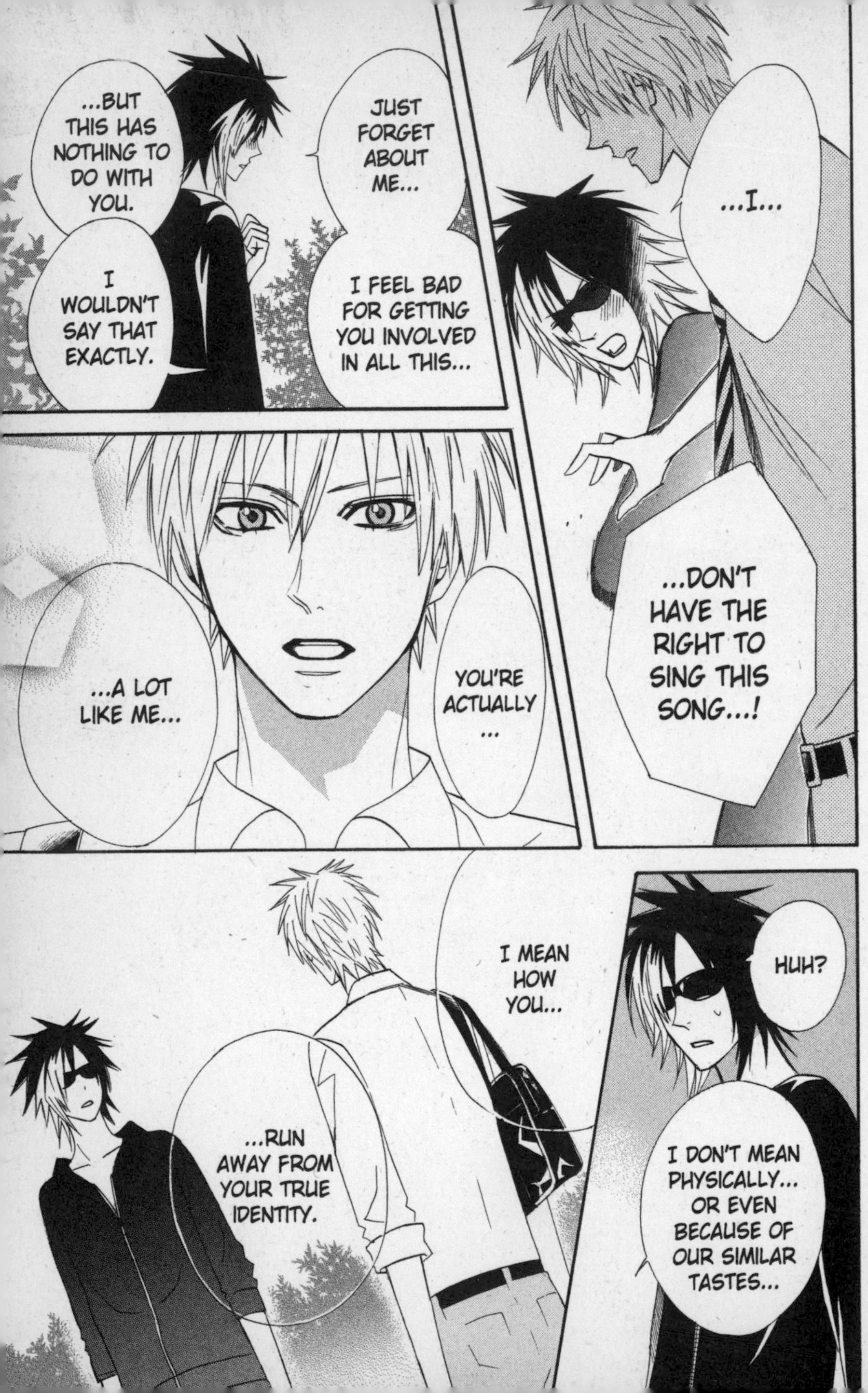
...I...
...DON'T HAVE THE RIGHT TO SING THIS SONG...!
JUST FORGET ABOUT ME...
I FEEL BAD FOR GETTING YOU INVOLVED IN ALL THIS...
...BUT THIS HAS NOTHING TO DO WITH YOU.
I WOULDN'T SAY THAT EXACTLY.
YOU'RE ACTUALLY ...
...A LOT LIKE ME...
HUH?
I DON'T MEAN PHYSICALLY... OR EVEN BECAUSE OF OUR SIMILAR TASTES...
I MEAN HOW YOU...
...RUN AWAY FROM YOUR TRUE IDENTITY.

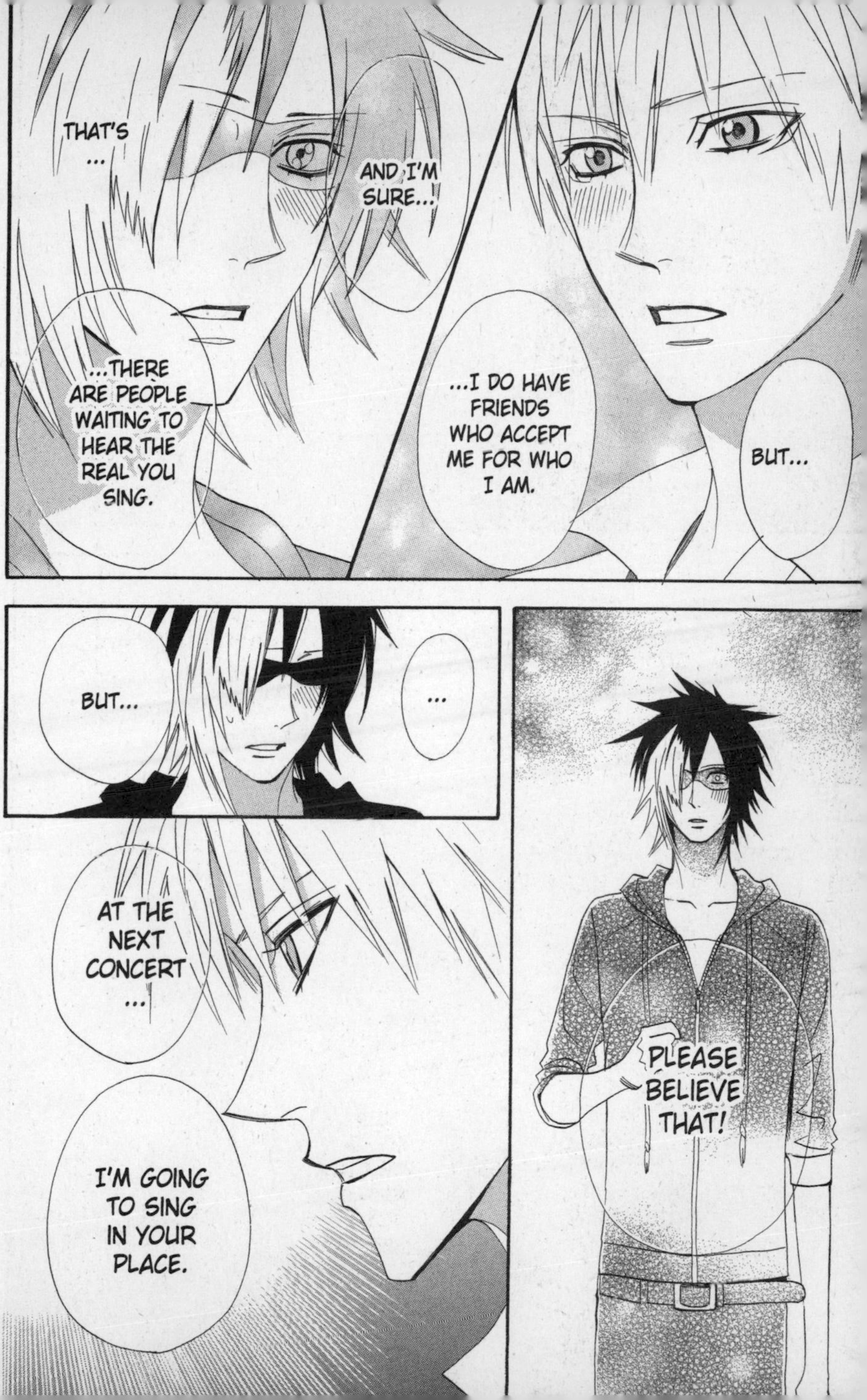
BUT...
...I DO HAVE FRIENDS WHO ACCEPT ME FOR WHO I AM.
THAT'S...
AND I'M SURE...
...THERE ARE PEOPLE WAITING TO HEAR THE REAL YOU SING.
PLEASE BELIEVE THAT!
...
BUT...
AT THE NEXT CONCERT...
I'M GOING TO SING IN YOUR PLACE.

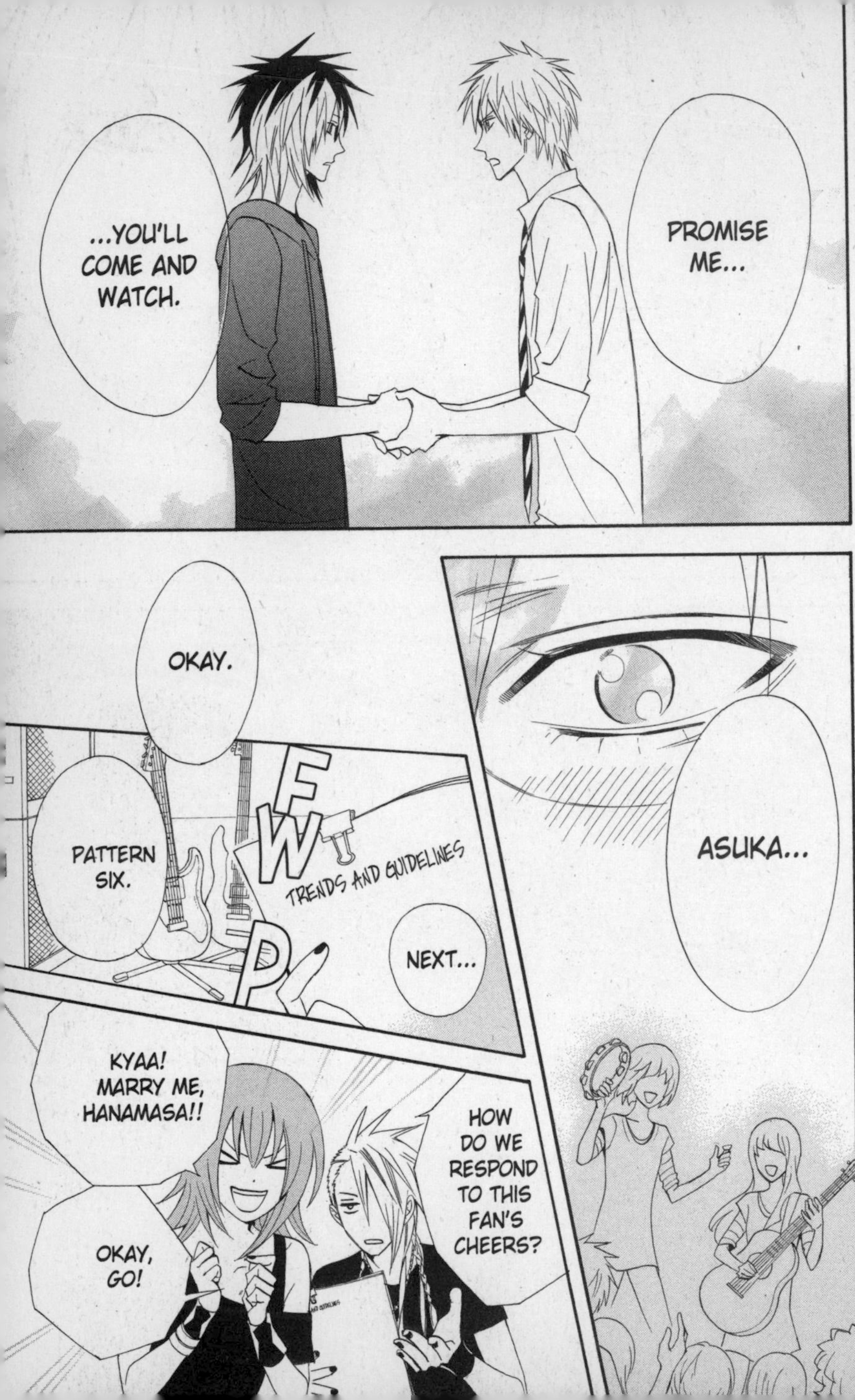
PROMISE ME...
...YOU'LL COME AND WATCH.
OKAY.
ASUKA...
NEXT...
FWP
TRENDS AND GUIDELINES
PATTERN SIX.
HOW DO WE RESPOND TO THIS FAN'S CHEERS?
KYAA! MARRY ME, HANAMASA!!
OKAY, GO!

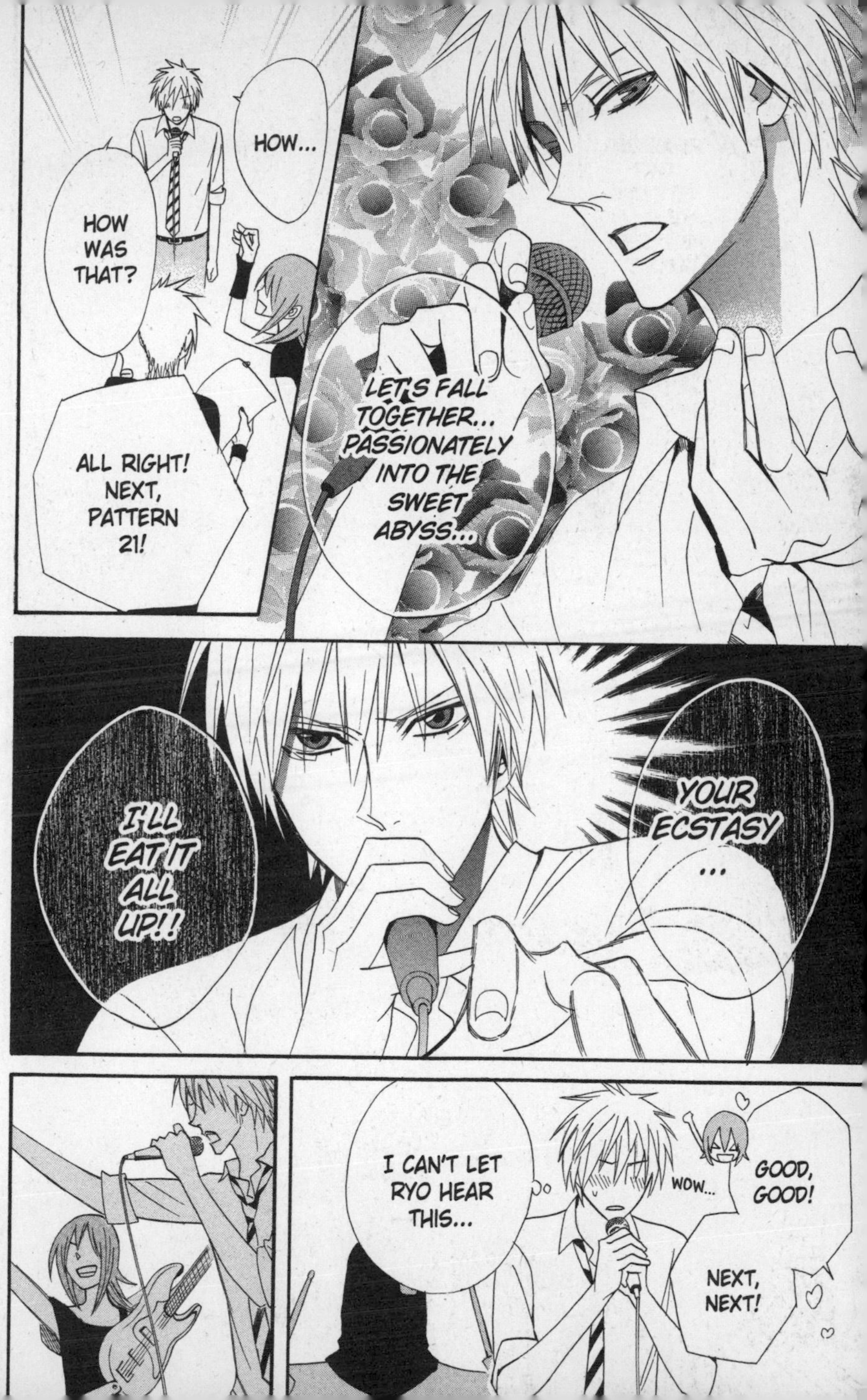
LET'S FALL TOGETHER... PASSIONATELY INTO THE SWEET ABYSS...
HOW...
HOW WAS THAT?
ALL RIGHT! NEXT, PATTERN 21!
YOUR ECSTASY ...
I'LL EAT IT ALL UP!!
GOOD, GOOD!
WOW...
I CAN'T LET RYO HEAR THIS...
NEXT, NEXT!

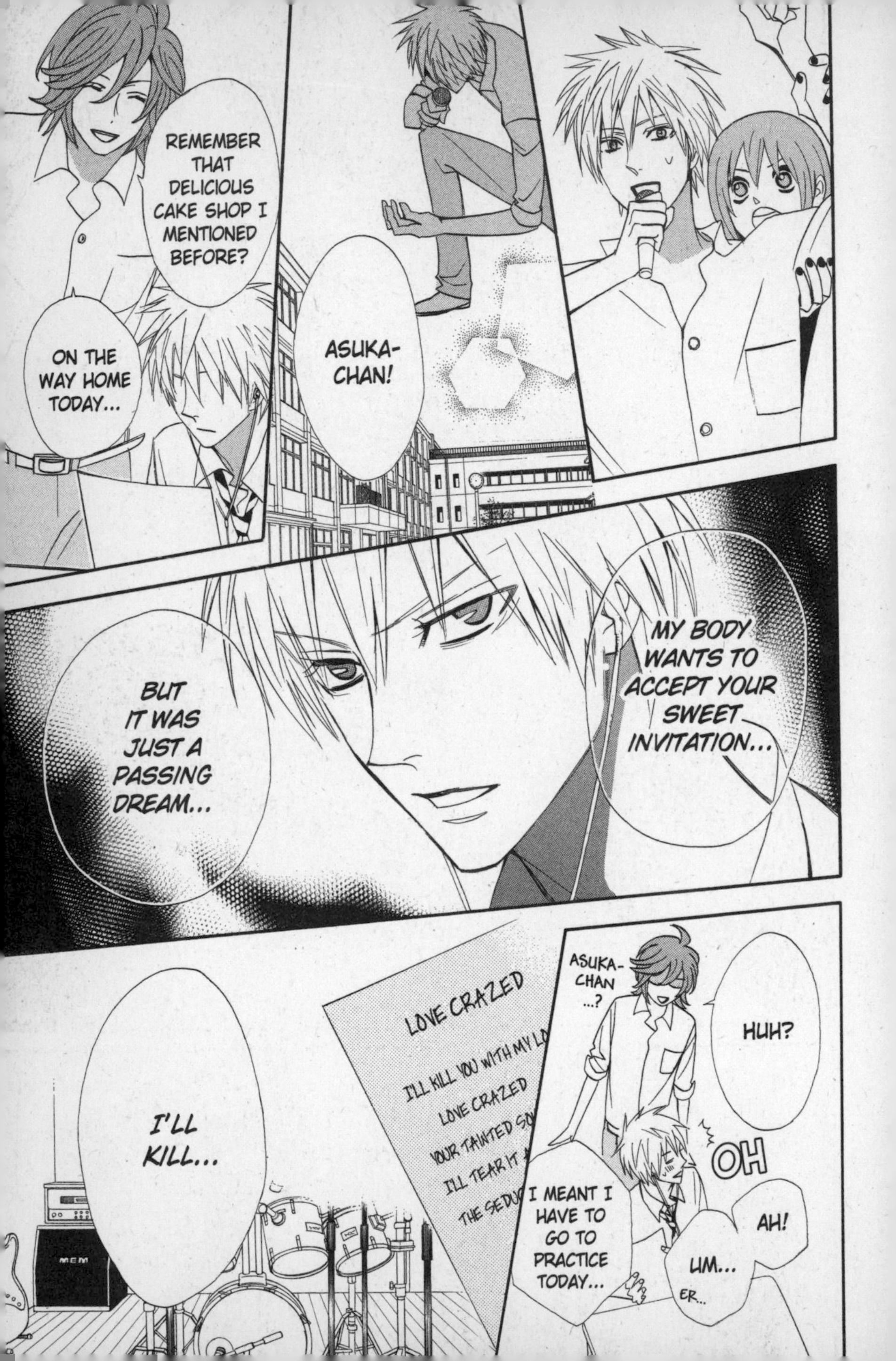
ASUKA-CHAN!
REMEMBER THAT DELICIOUS CAKE SHOP I MENTIONED BEFORE?
ON THE WAY HOME TODAY...
MY BODY WANTS TO ACCEPT YOUR SWEET INVITATION...
BUT IT WAS JUST A PASSING DREAM...
HUH?
ASUKA-CHAN ...?
OH
AH!
UM... ER...
I MEANT I HAVE TO GO TO PRACTICE TODAY...
LOVE CRAZED
I'LL KILL YOU WITH MY
LOVE CRAZED
YOUR TAINTED
I'LL TEAR IT
THE
I'LL KILL...

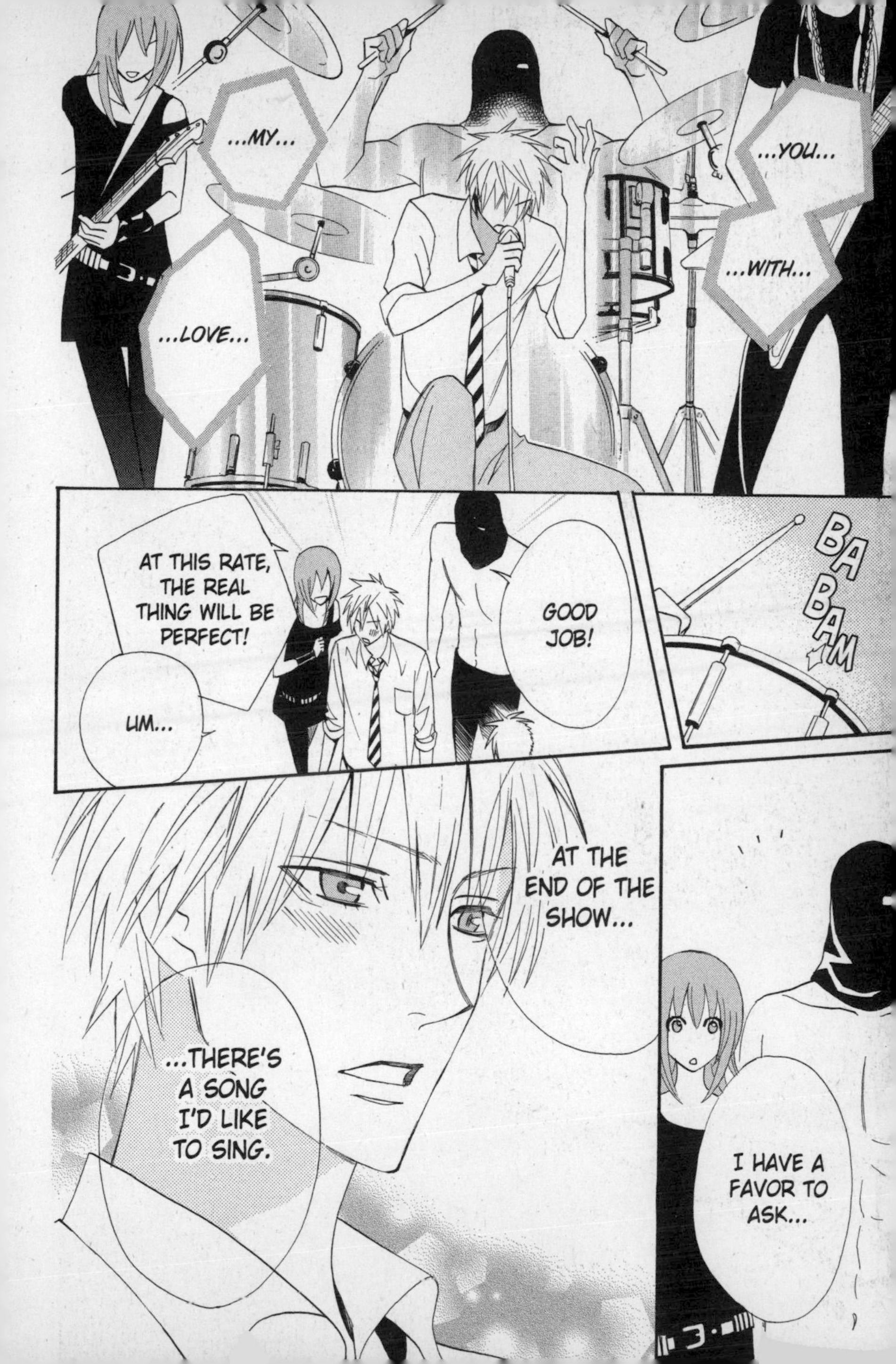
...YOU...
...WITH...
...MY...
...LOVE...
BA BAM
GOOD JOB!
AT THIS RATE, THE REAL THING WILL BE PERFECT!
UM...
I HAVE A FAVOR TO ASK...
AT THE END OF THE SHOW...
...THERE'S A SONG I'D LIKE TO SING.

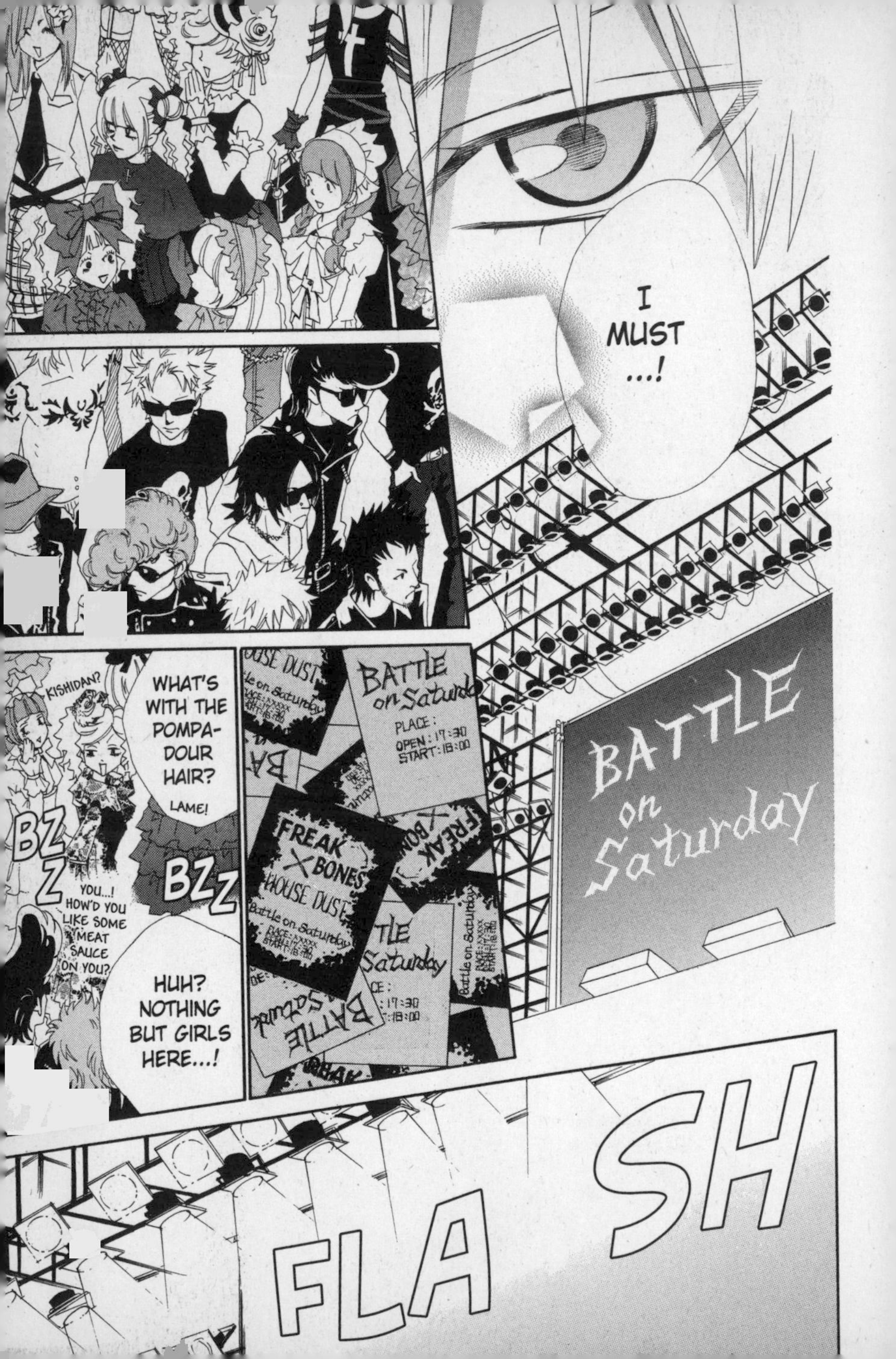
I MUST ...!
BATTLE on Saturday
BATTLE on Saturday
PLACE :
OPEN : 17:30
START : 18:00
FREAK X BONES
HOUSE DUST
Battle on Saturday
WHAT'S WITH THE POMPA-DOUR HAIR?
LAME!
KISHIDAN?
BZZ
BZZ
YOU...! HOW'D YOU LIKE SOME MEAT SAUCE ON YOU?
HUH? NOTHING BUT GIRLS HERE...!
FLASH

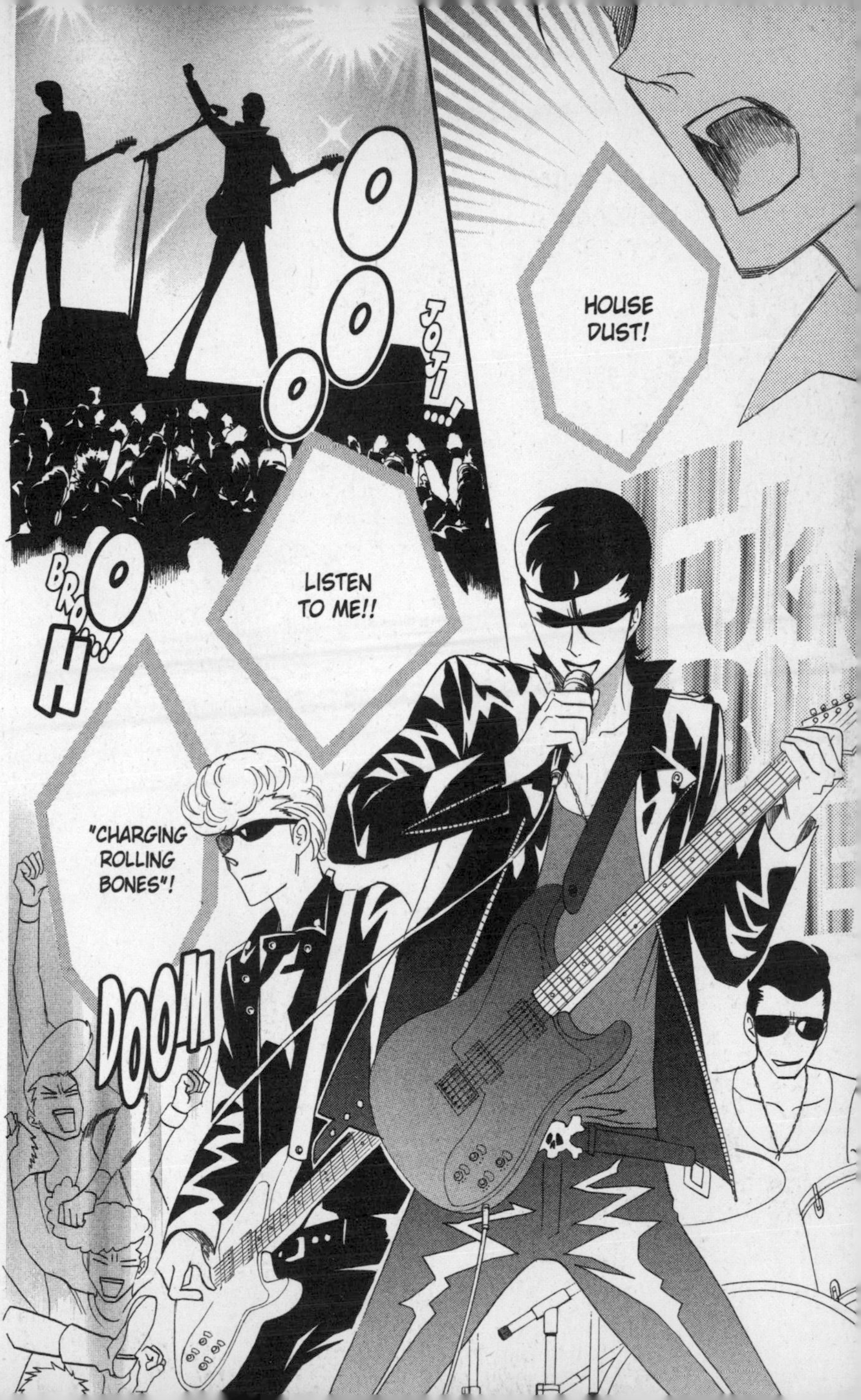
HOUSE DUST!
JOJI...!
OOOOO
LISTEN TO ME!!
"CHARGING ROLLING BONES"!
BROOH...!!
DOOM

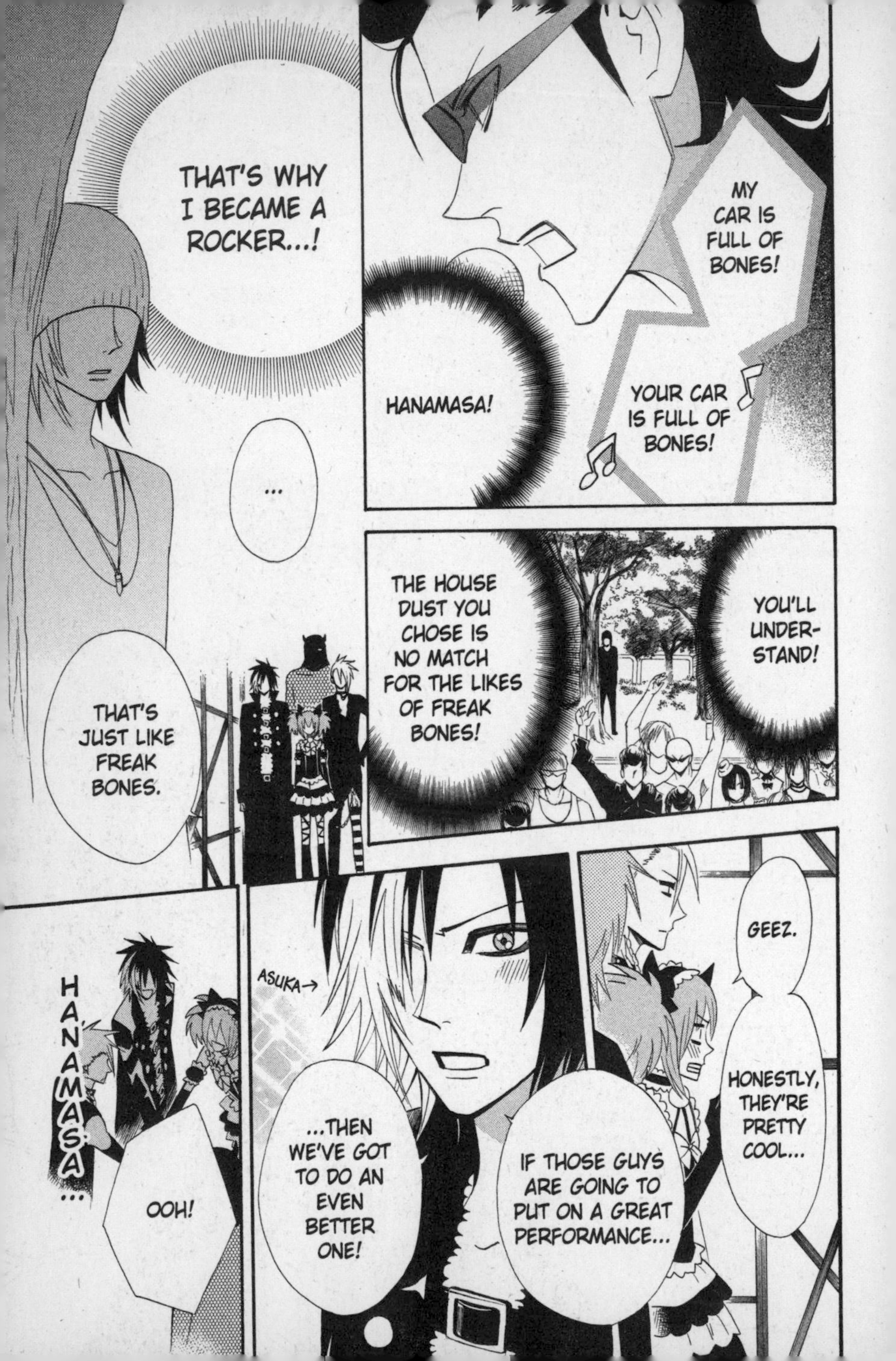
MY CAR IS FULL OF BONES!
YOUR CAR IS FULL OF BONES!
HANAMASA!
YOU'LL UNDER-STAND!
THE HOUSE DUST YOU CHOSE IS NO MATCH FOR THE LIKES OF FREAK BONES!
THAT'S WHY I BECAME A ROCKER...!
...
THAT'S JUST LIKE FREAK BONES.
GEEZ.
HONESTLY, THEY'RE PRETTY COOL...
IF THOSE GUYS ARE GOING TO PUT ON A GREAT PERFORMANCE...
...THEN WE'VE GOT TO DO AN EVEN BETTER ONE!
ASUKA→
HANAMASA...
OOH!

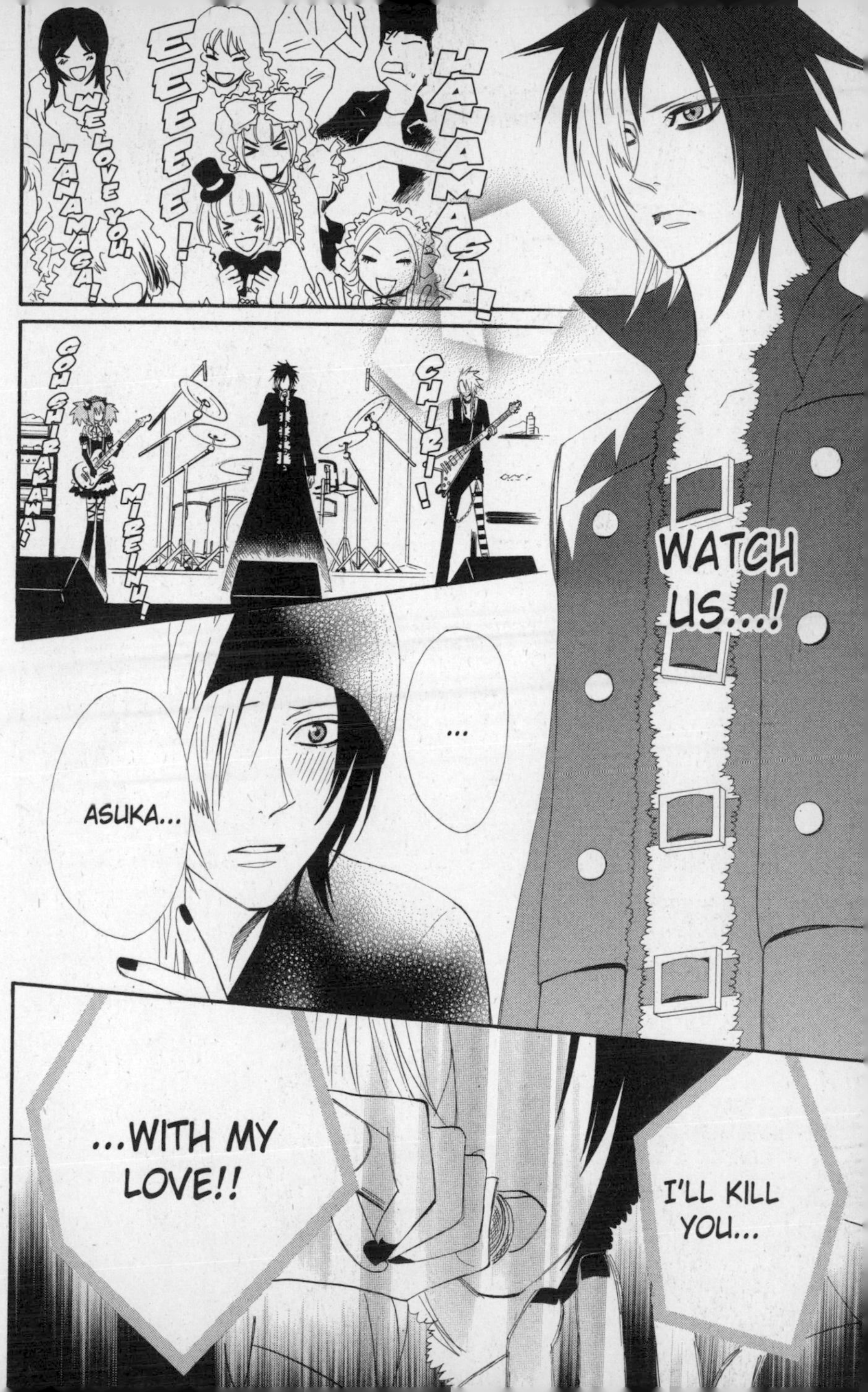
WATCH US...!
HANAMASA!
EEEEE!
WE LOVE YOU,
HANAMASA!
CHIRI!
MIREINU!
GONSHIRAKAWA!
...
ASUKA...
I'LL KILL YOU...
...WITH MY LOVE!!

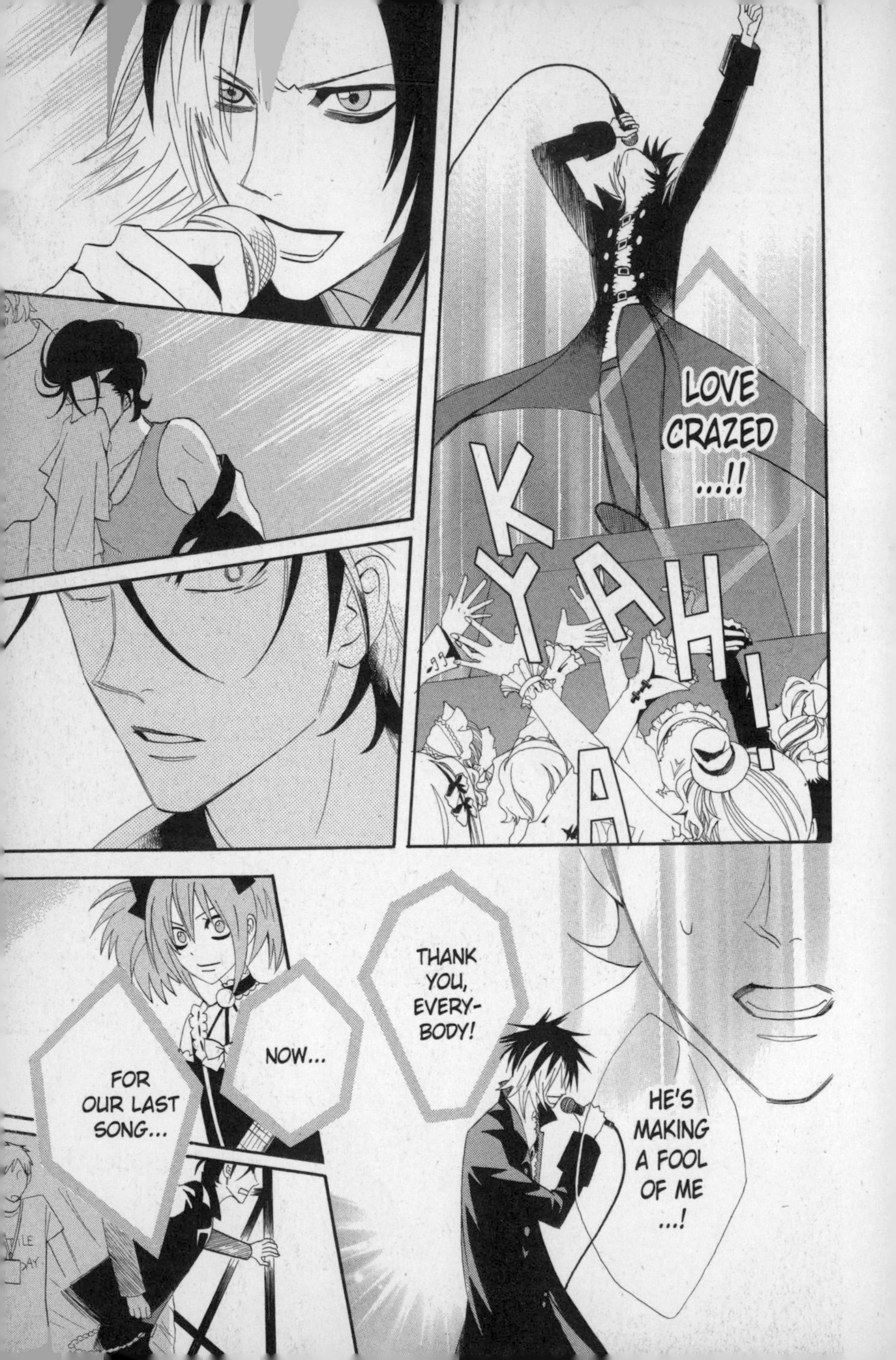
LOVE CRAZED ...!!
KYAAH!!
HE'S MAKING A FOOL OF ME ...!
THANK YOU, EVERY-BODY!
NOW...
FOR OUR LAST SONG...

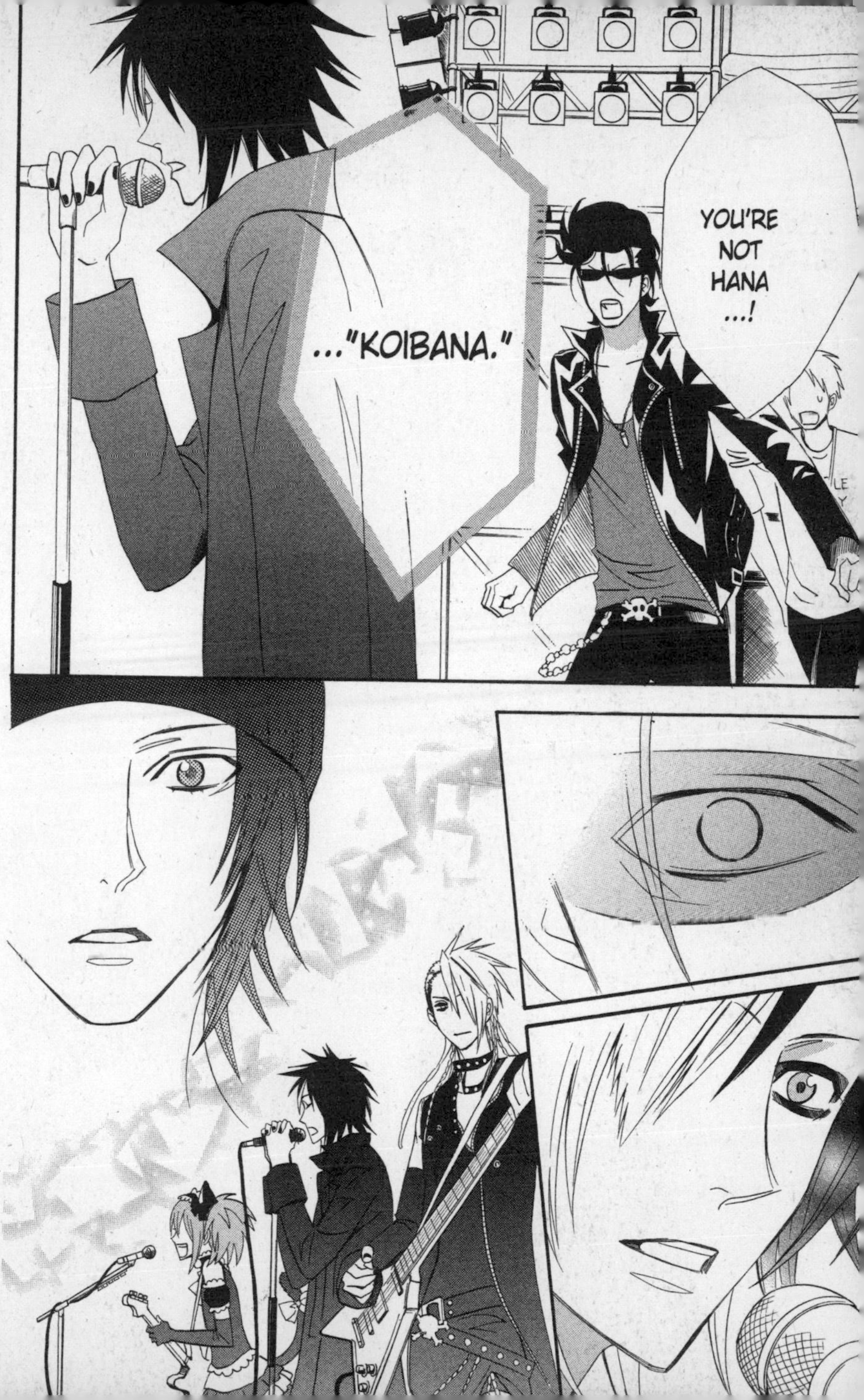
YOU'RE NOT HANA ...!
..."KOIBANA."

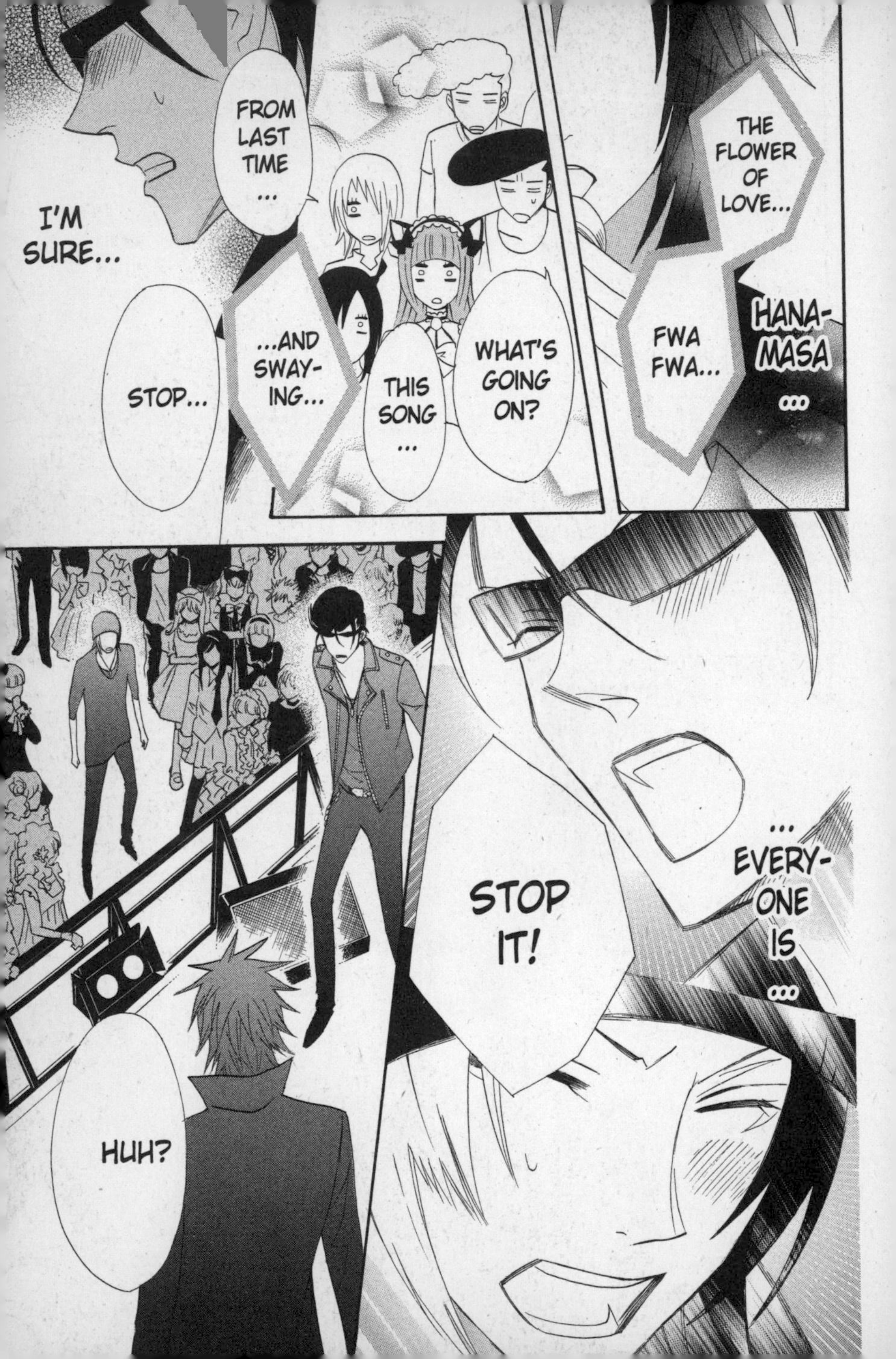
THE FLOWER OF LOVE...
HANA-MASA ...
FWA FWA...
WHAT'S GOING ON?
THIS SONG ...
...AND SWAY-ING...
FROM LAST TIME ...
I'M SURE...
STOP...
... EVERY-ONE IS ...
STOP IT!
HUH?

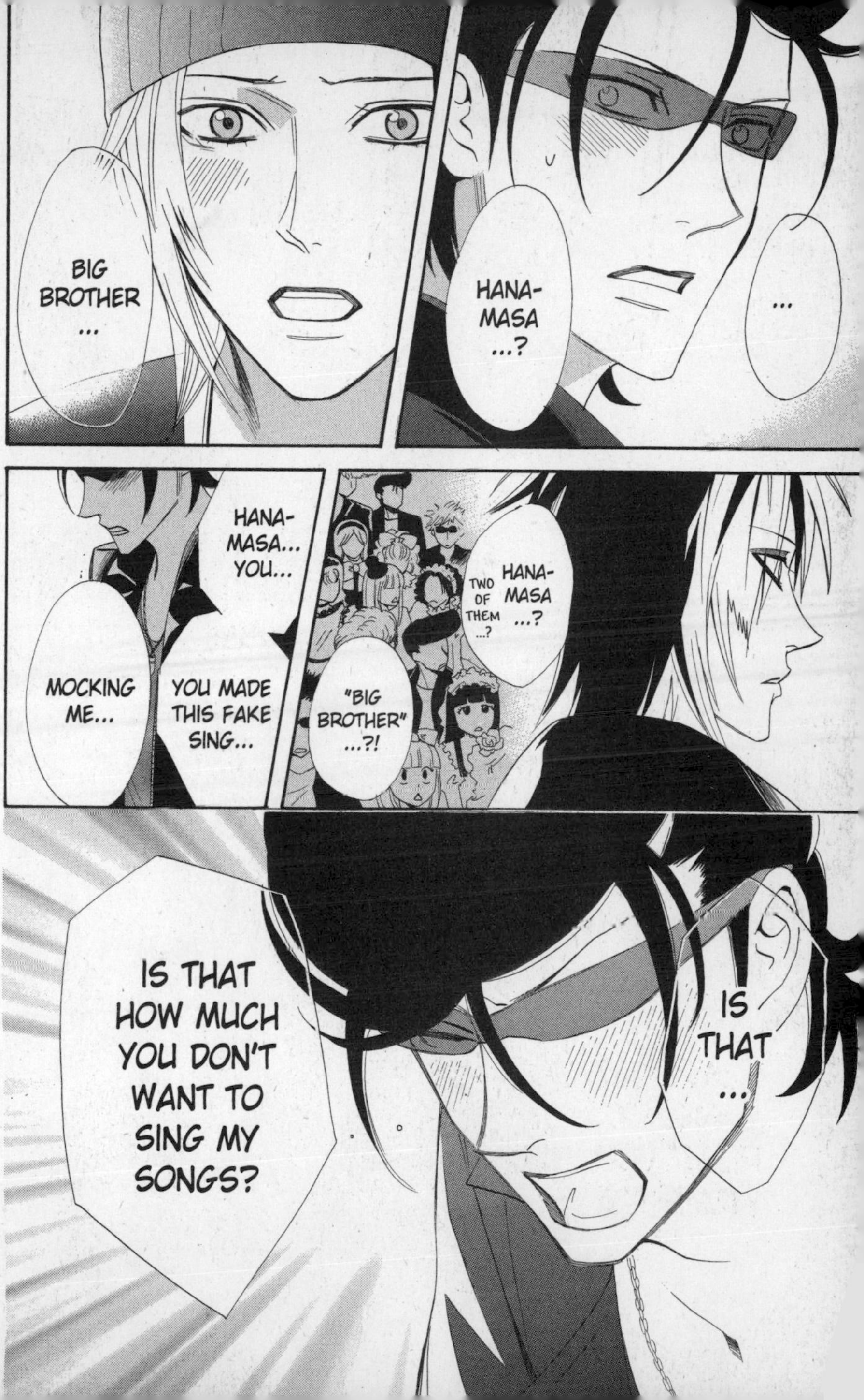
...
HANA-MASA ...?
BIG BROTHER ...
HANA-MASA ...?
TWO OF THEM ...?
"BIG BROTHER" ...?!
HANA-MASA... YOU...
YOU MADE THIS FAKE SING...
MOCKING ME...
IS THAT ...
IS THAT HOW MUCH YOU DON'T WANT TO SING MY SONGS?

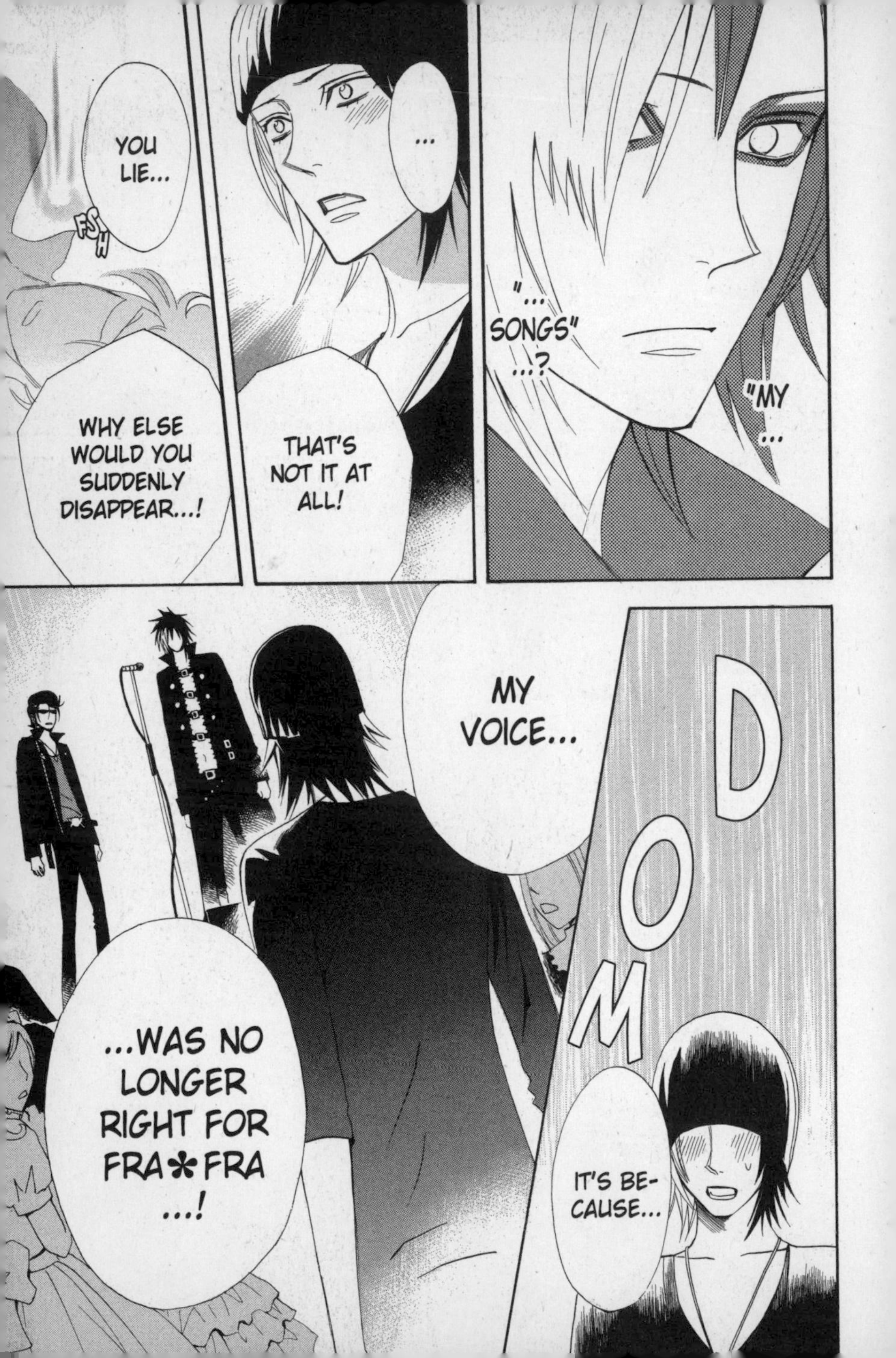

"MY ...
"... SONGS" ...?
...
THAT'S NOT IT AT ALL!
YOU LIE...
FSH
WHY ELSE WOULD YOU SUDDENLY DISAPPEAR...!
DOOM
IT'S BE-CAUSE...
MY VOICE...
...WAS NO LONGER RIGHT FOR FRA✽FRA ...!

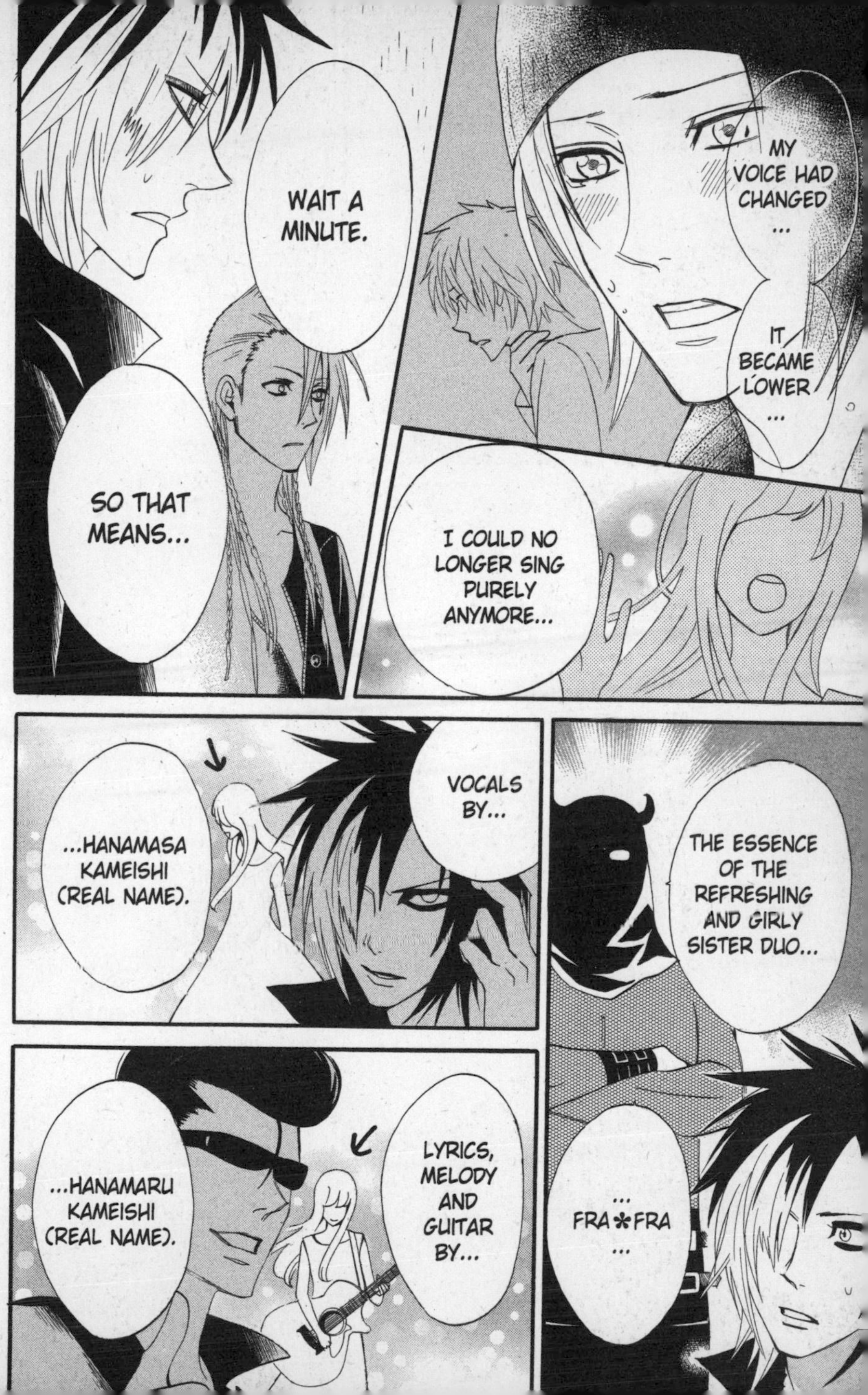
MY VOICE HAD CHANGED ...
IT BECAME LOWER ...
I COULD NO LONGER SING PURELY ANYMORE...
WAIT A MINUTE.
SO THAT MEANS...
THE ESSENCE OF THE REFRESHING AND GIRLY SISTER DUO...
... FRA*FRA ...
VOCALS BY...
...HANAMASA KAMEISHI (REAL NAME).
LYRICS, MELODY AND GUITAR BY...
...HANAMARU KAMEISHI (REAL NAME).

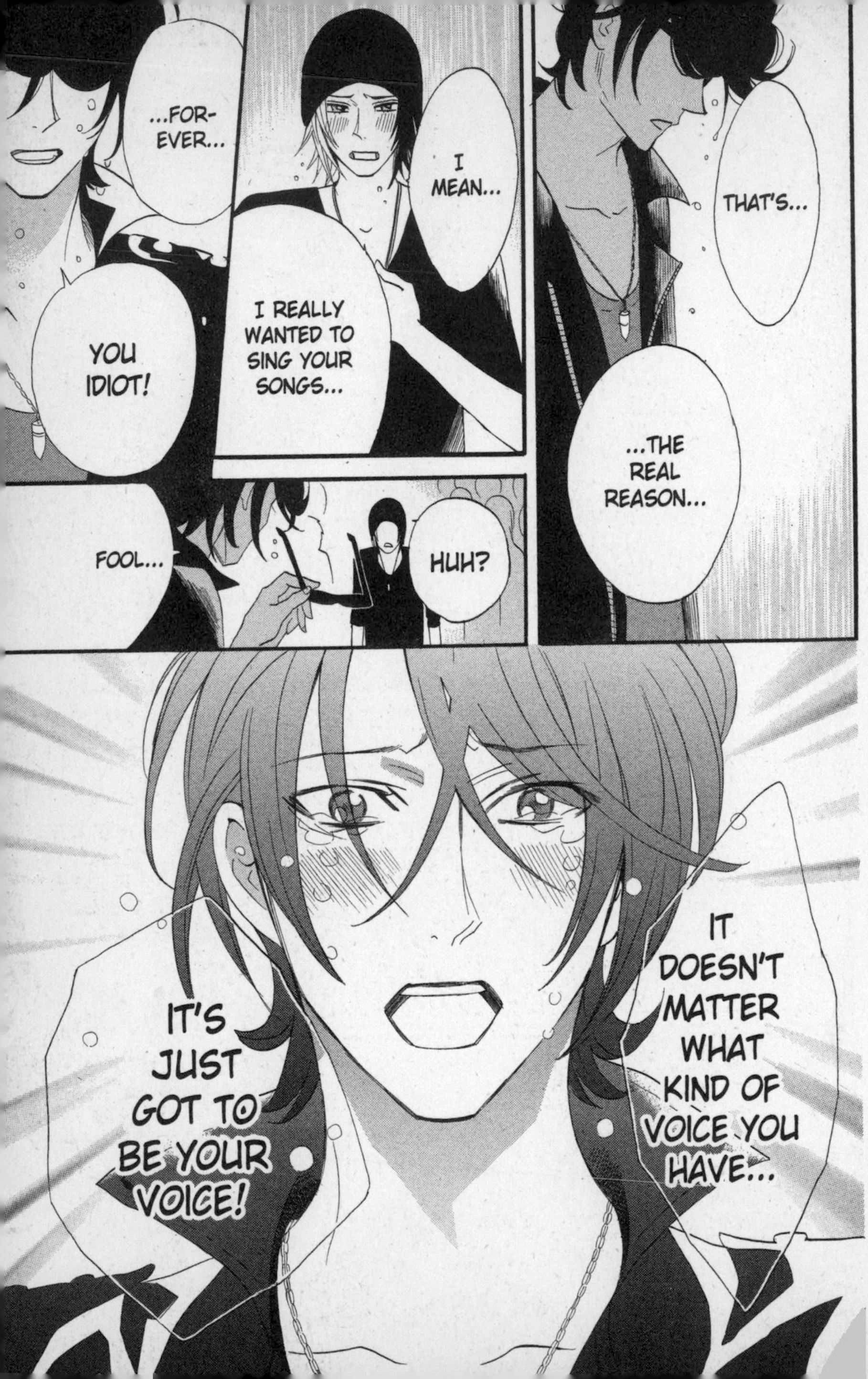
THAT'S...
...THE REAL REASON...
I MEAN...
I REALLY WANTED TO SING YOUR SONGS...
...FOR-EVER...
YOU IDIOT!
HUH?
FOOL...
IT DOESN'T MATTER WHAT KIND OF VOICE YOU HAVE...
IT'S JUST GOT TO BE YOUR VOICE!

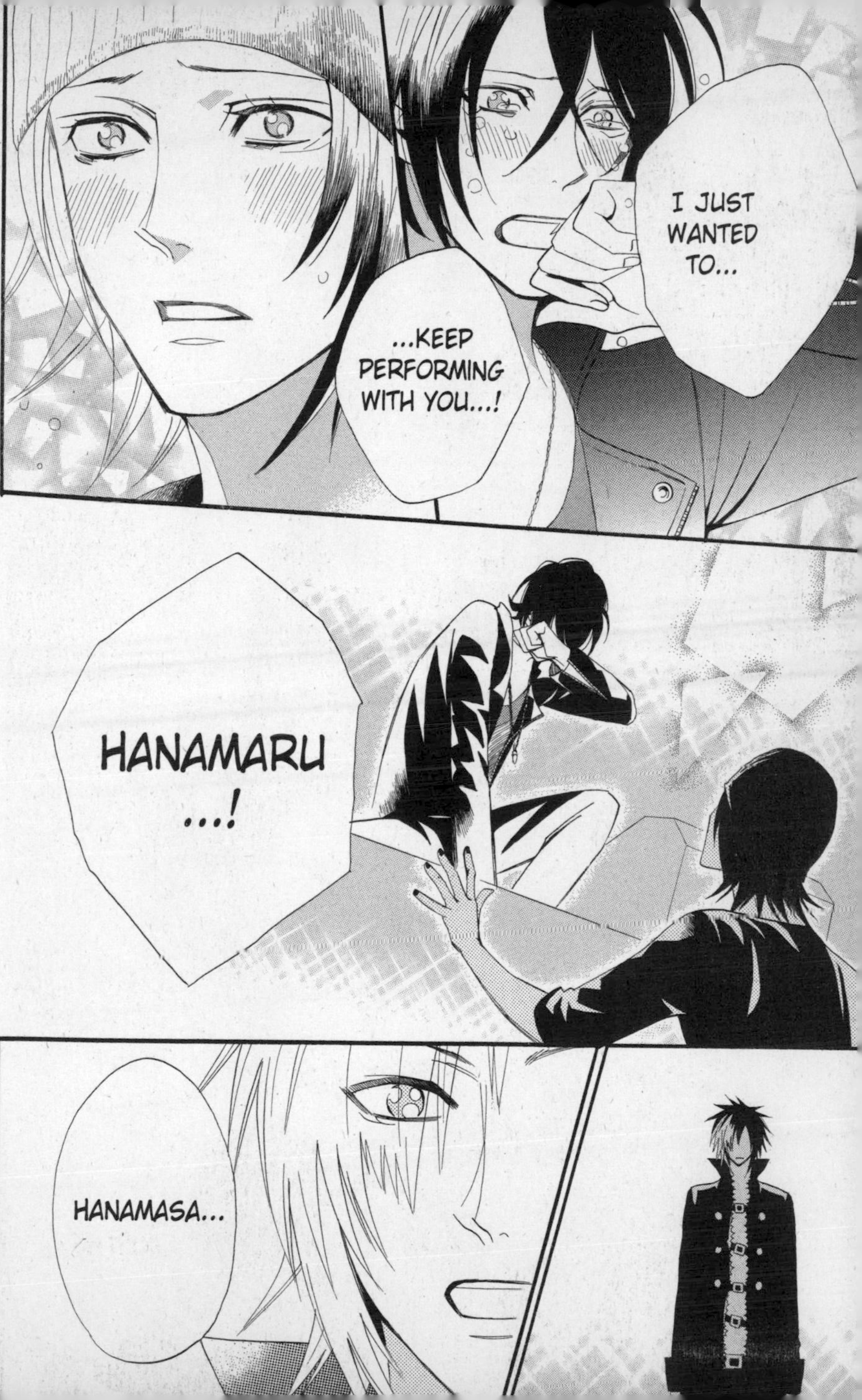
I JUST WANTED TO...
...KEEP PERFORMING WITH YOU...!
HANAMARU ...!
HANAMASA...

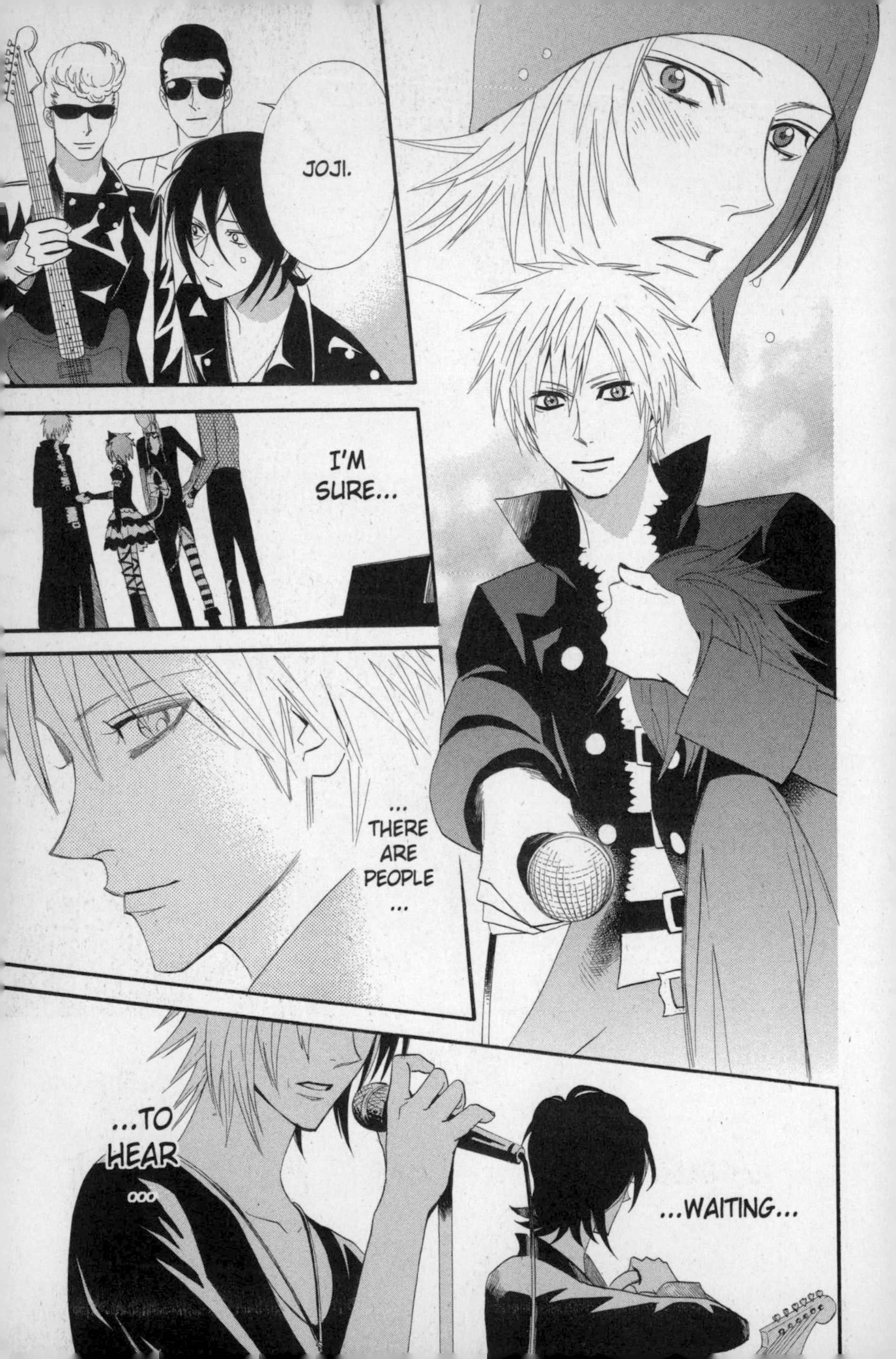
JOJI.
I'M SURE...
...THERE ARE PEOPLE...
...WAITING...
...TO HEAR...

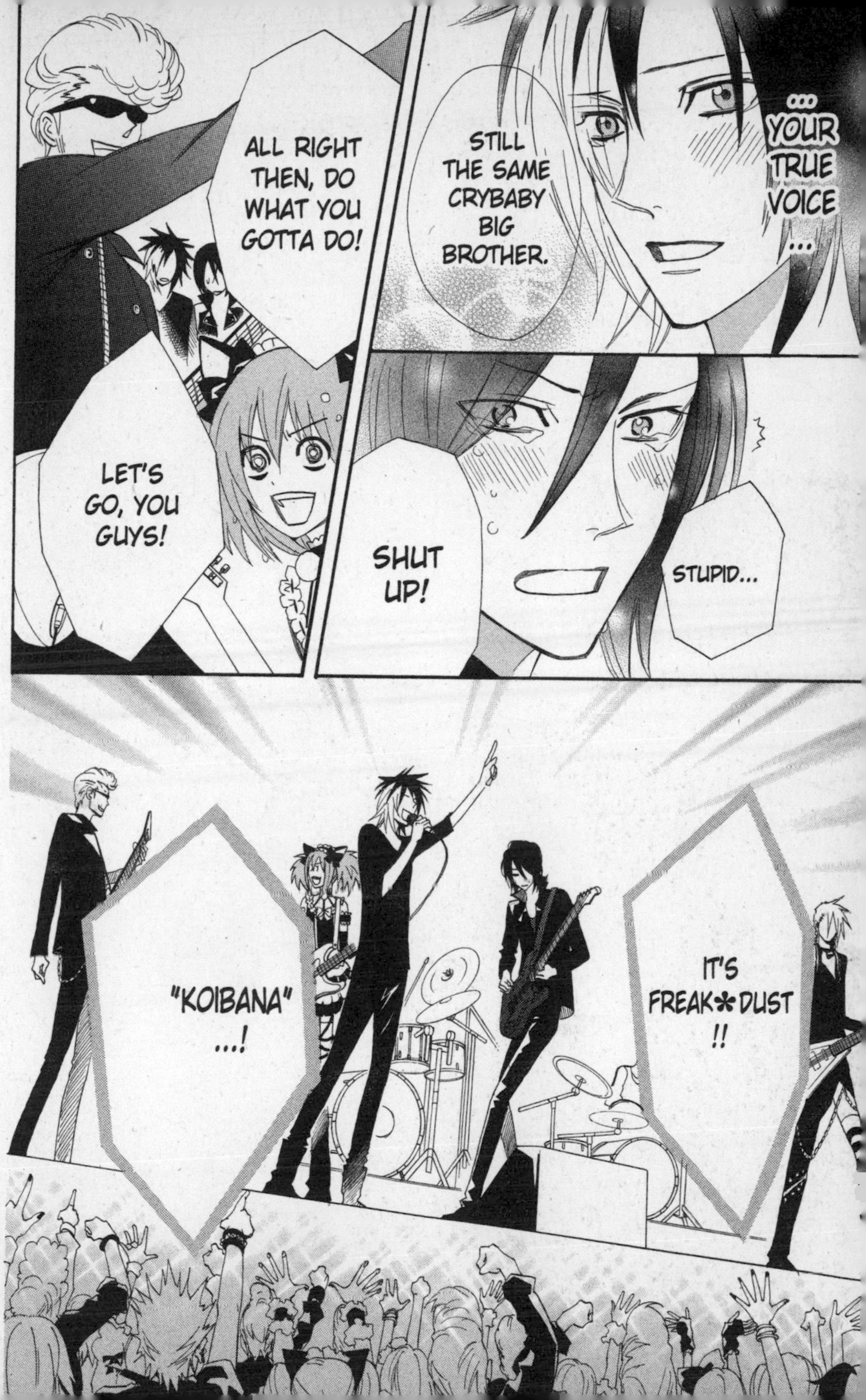
...YOUR TRUE VOICE...
STILL THE SAME CRYBABY BIG BROTHER.
STUPID...
SHUT UP!
ALL RIGHT THEN, DO WHAT YOU GOTTA DO!
LET'S GO, YOU GUYS!
IT'S FREAK✻DUST !!
"KOIBANA" ...!

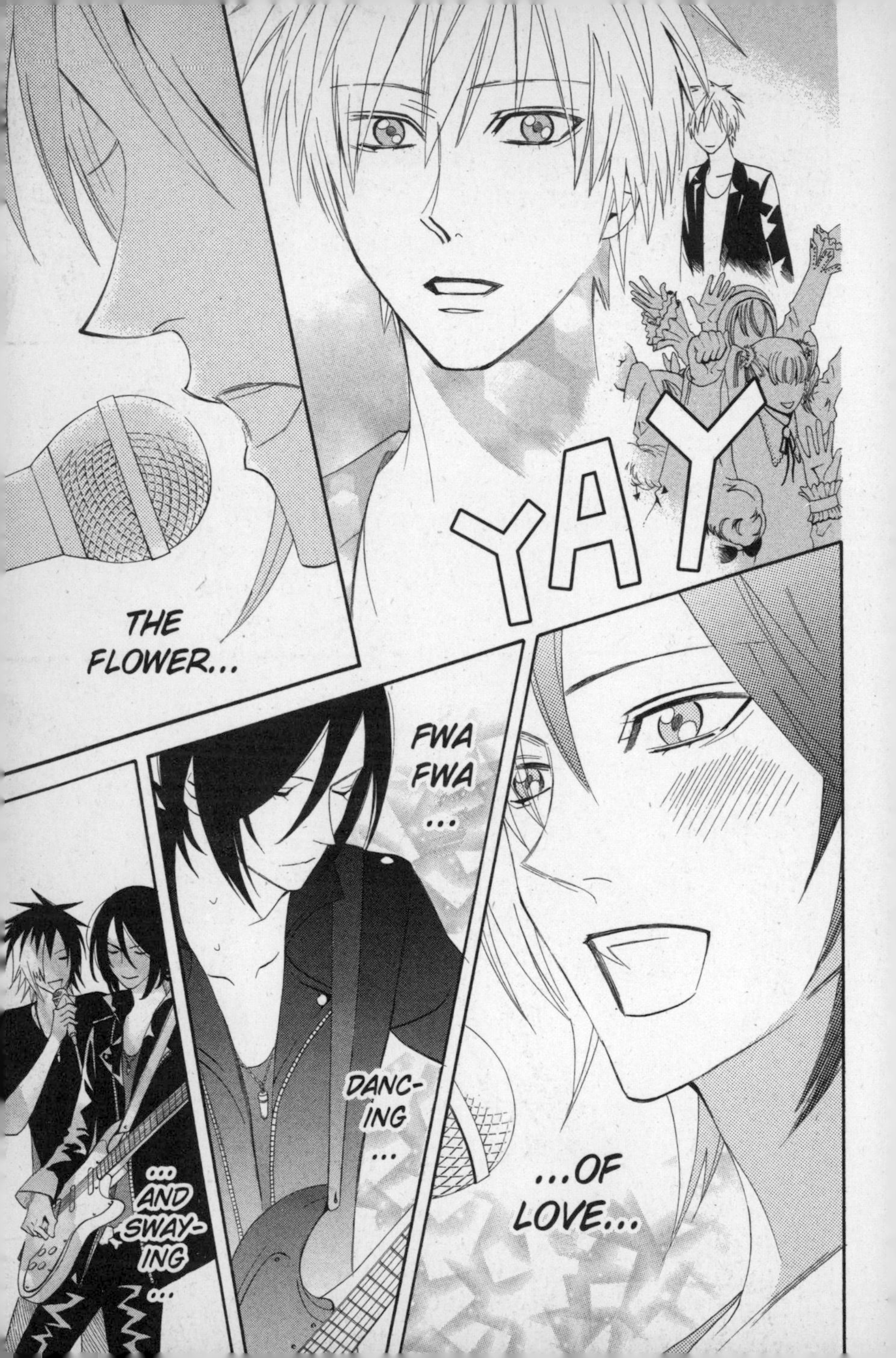
YAY
THE FLOWER...
...OF LOVE...
FWA FWA ...
DANC- ING ...
... AND SWAY- ING ...

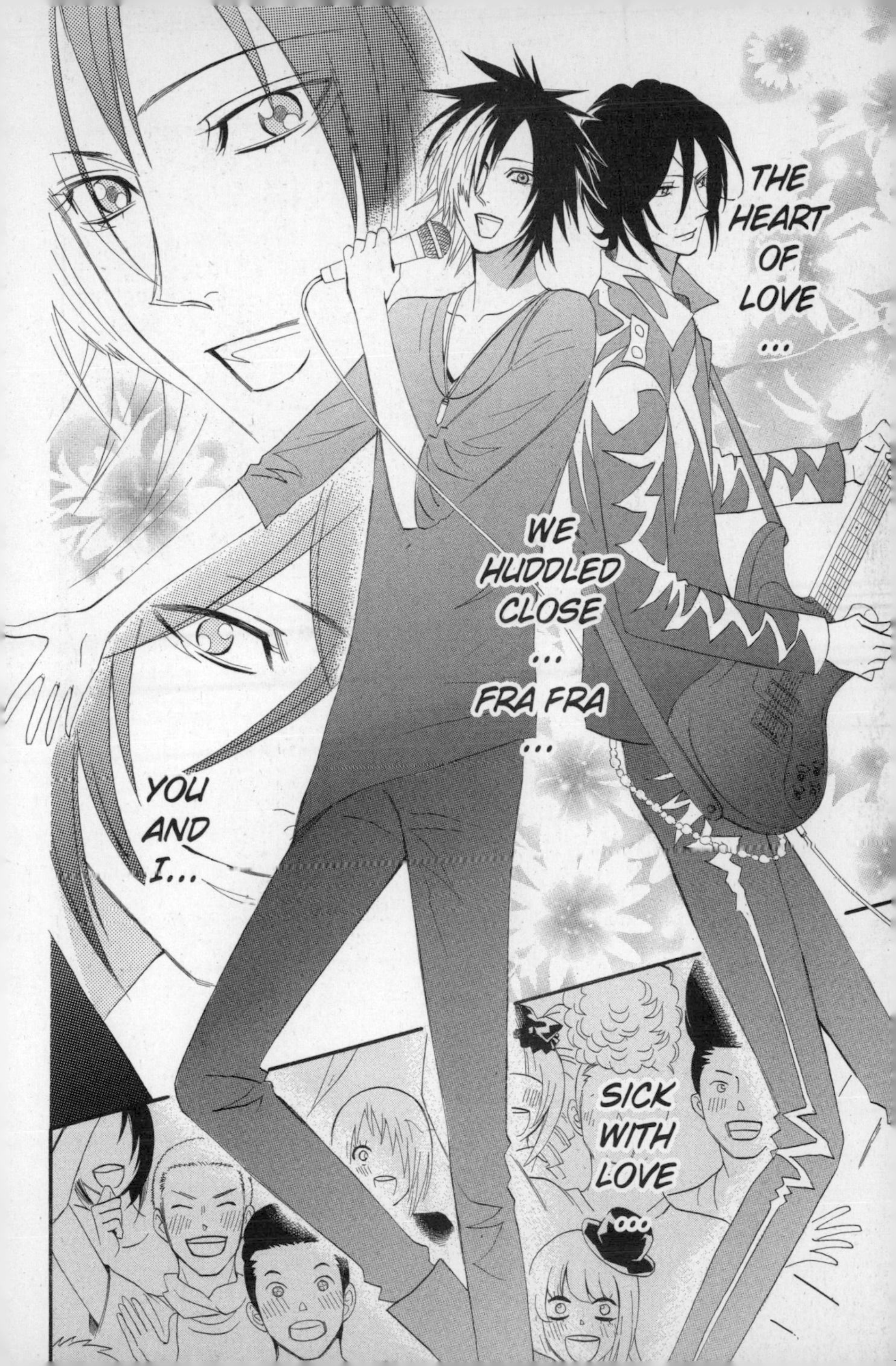
THE HEART OF LOVE ...
WE HUDDLED CLOSE ...
FRA FRA ...
YOU AND I...
SICK WITH LOVE

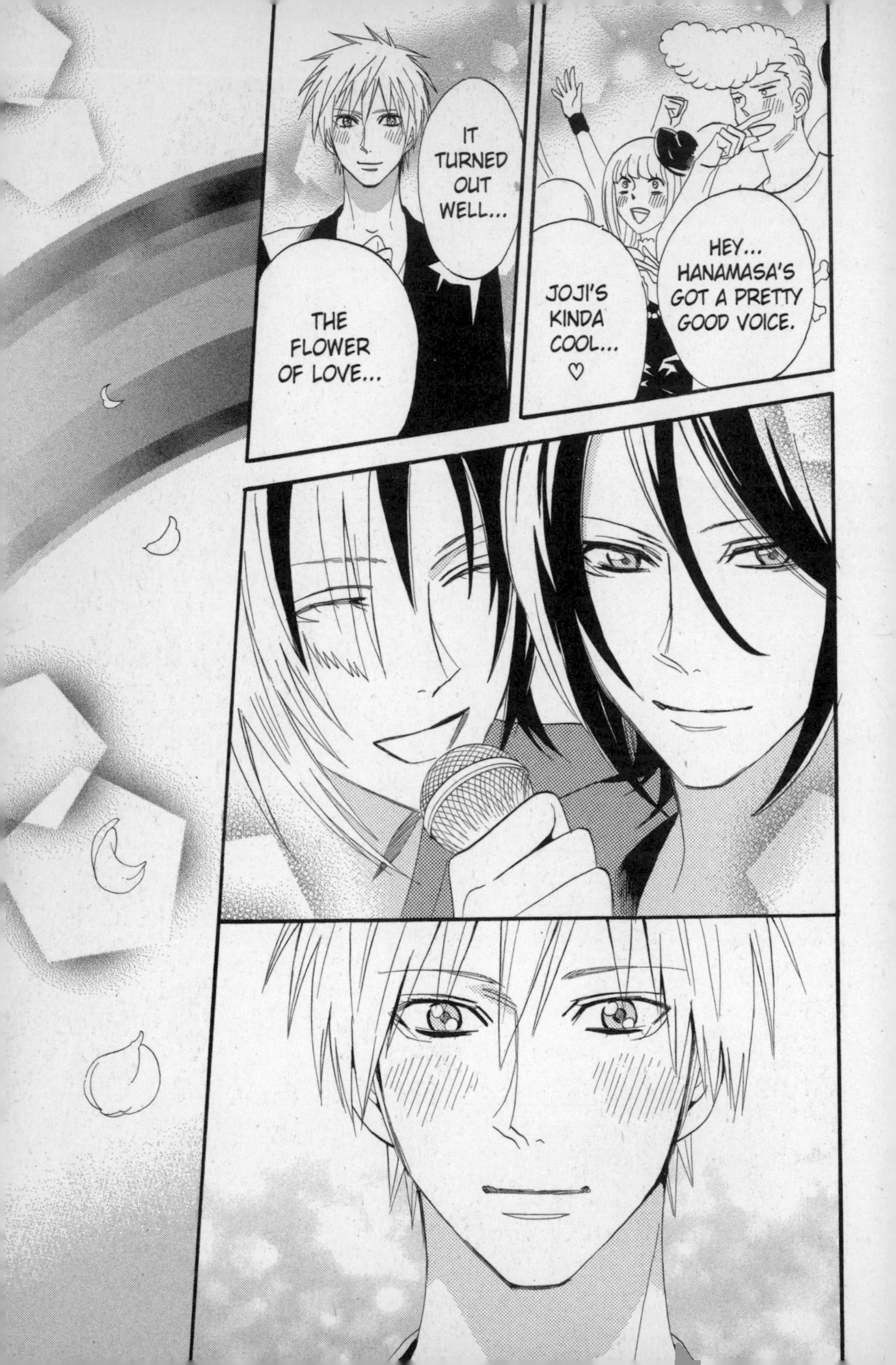
HEY... HANAMASA'S GOT A PRETTY GOOD VOICE.
JOJI'S KINDA COOL... ♡
IT TURNED OUT WELL...
THE FLOWER OF LOVE...

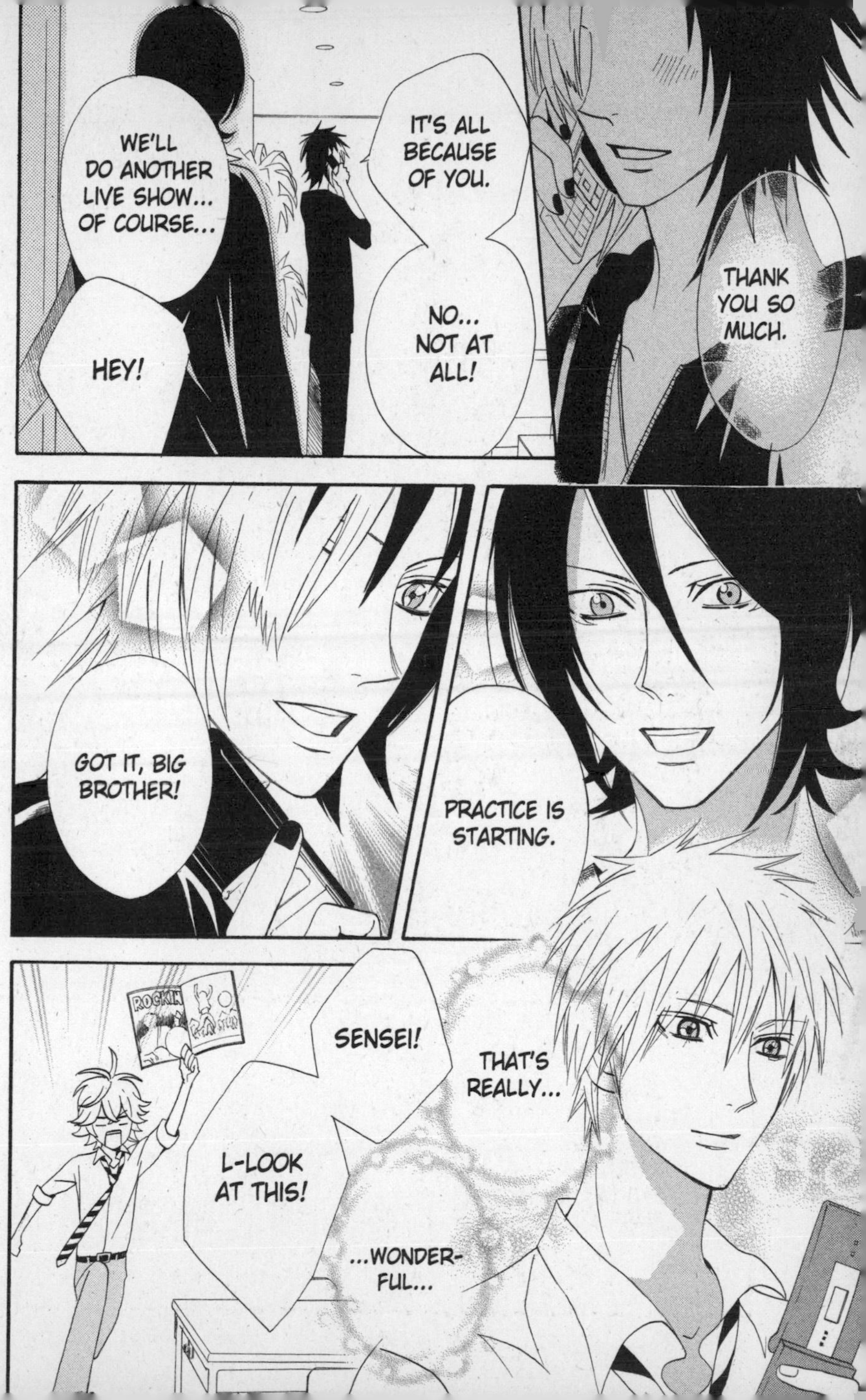
THANK YOU SO MUCH.
IT'S ALL BECAUSE OF YOU.
NO... NOT AT ALL!
WE'LL DO ANOTHER LIVE SHOW... OF COURSE...
HEY!
PRACTICE IS STARTING.
GOT IT, BIG BROTHER!
THAT'S REALLY...
...WONDER-FUL...
SENSEI!
L-LOOK AT THIS!
ROCKIN

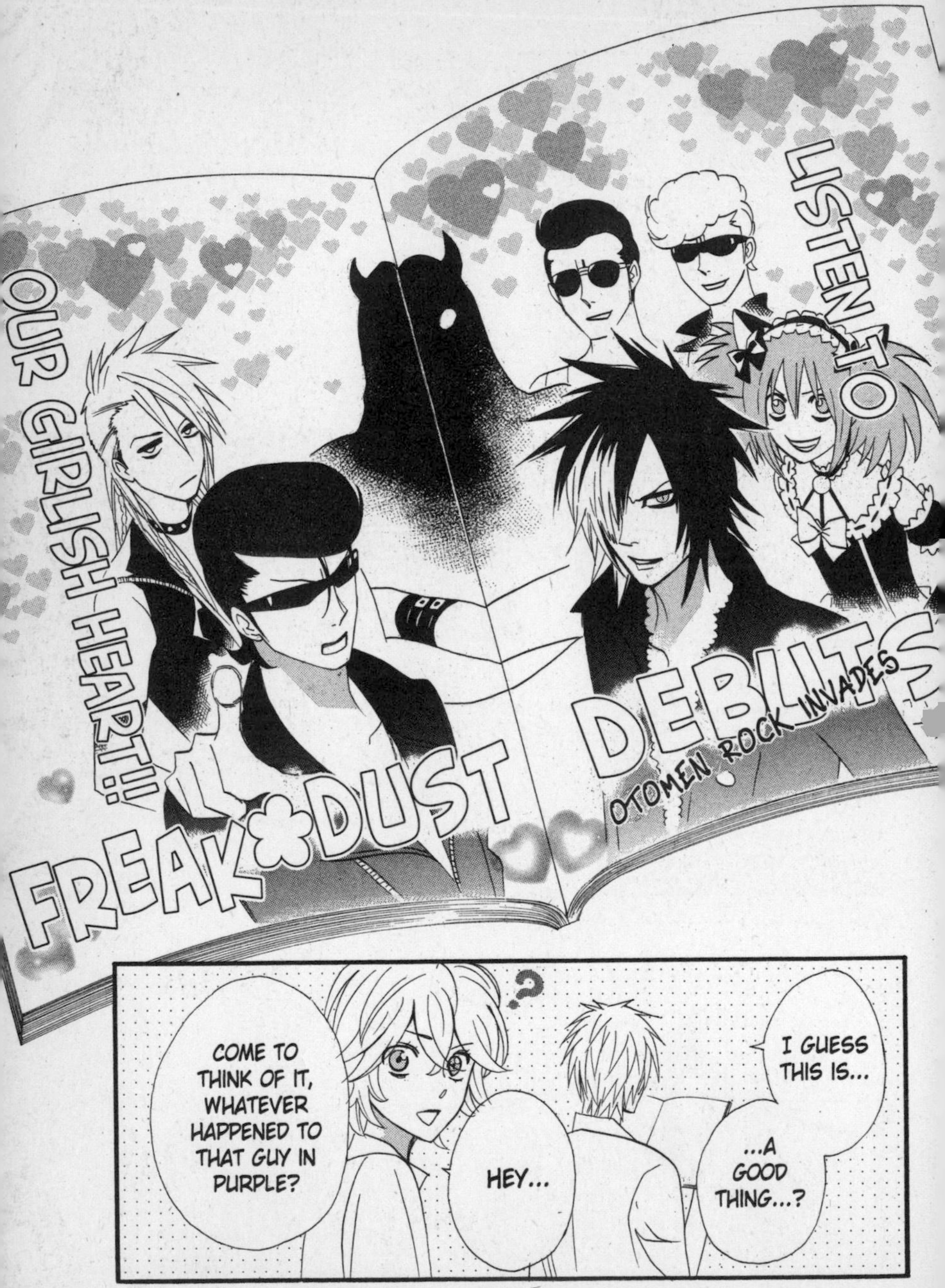
LISTEN TO
OUR GIRLISH HEART!!
OTOMEN ROCK INVADES
FREAK DUST DEBUTS
I GUESS THIS IS...
...A GOOD THING...?
HEY...
COME TO THINK OF IT, WHATEVER HAPPENED TO THAT GUY IN PURPLE?

OTOMEN

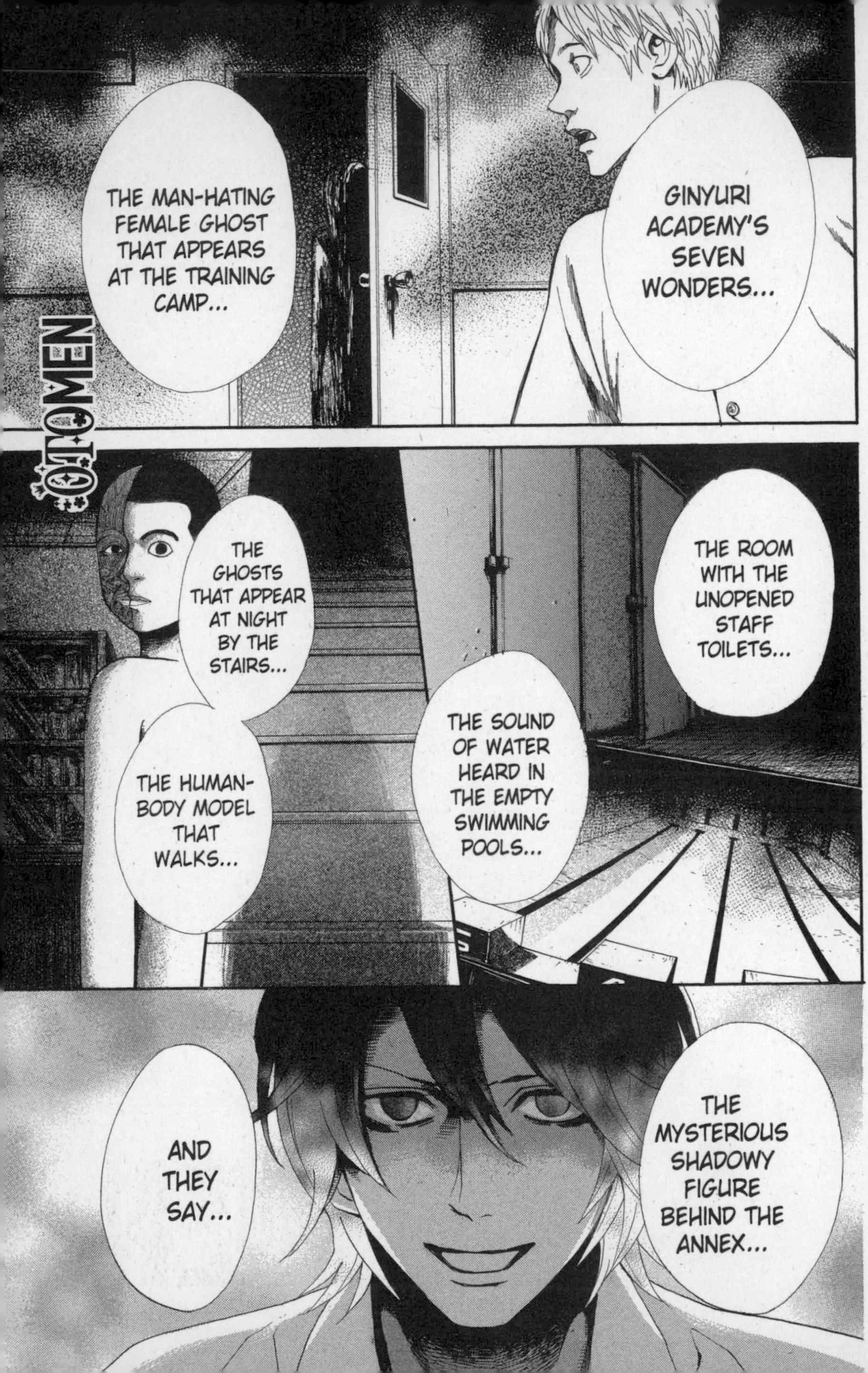
GINYURI ACADEMY'S SEVEN WONDERS...
THE MAN-HATING FEMALE GHOST THAT APPEARS AT THE TRAINING CAMP...
THE ROOM WITH THE UNOPENED STAFF TOILETS...
THE SOUND OF WATER HEARD IN THE EMPTY SWIMMING POOLS...
THE GHOSTS THAT APPEAR AT NIGHT BY THE STAIRS...
THE HUMAN-BODY MODEL THAT WALKS...
THE MYSTERIOUS SHADOWY FIGURE BEHIND THE ANNEX...
AND THEY SAY...

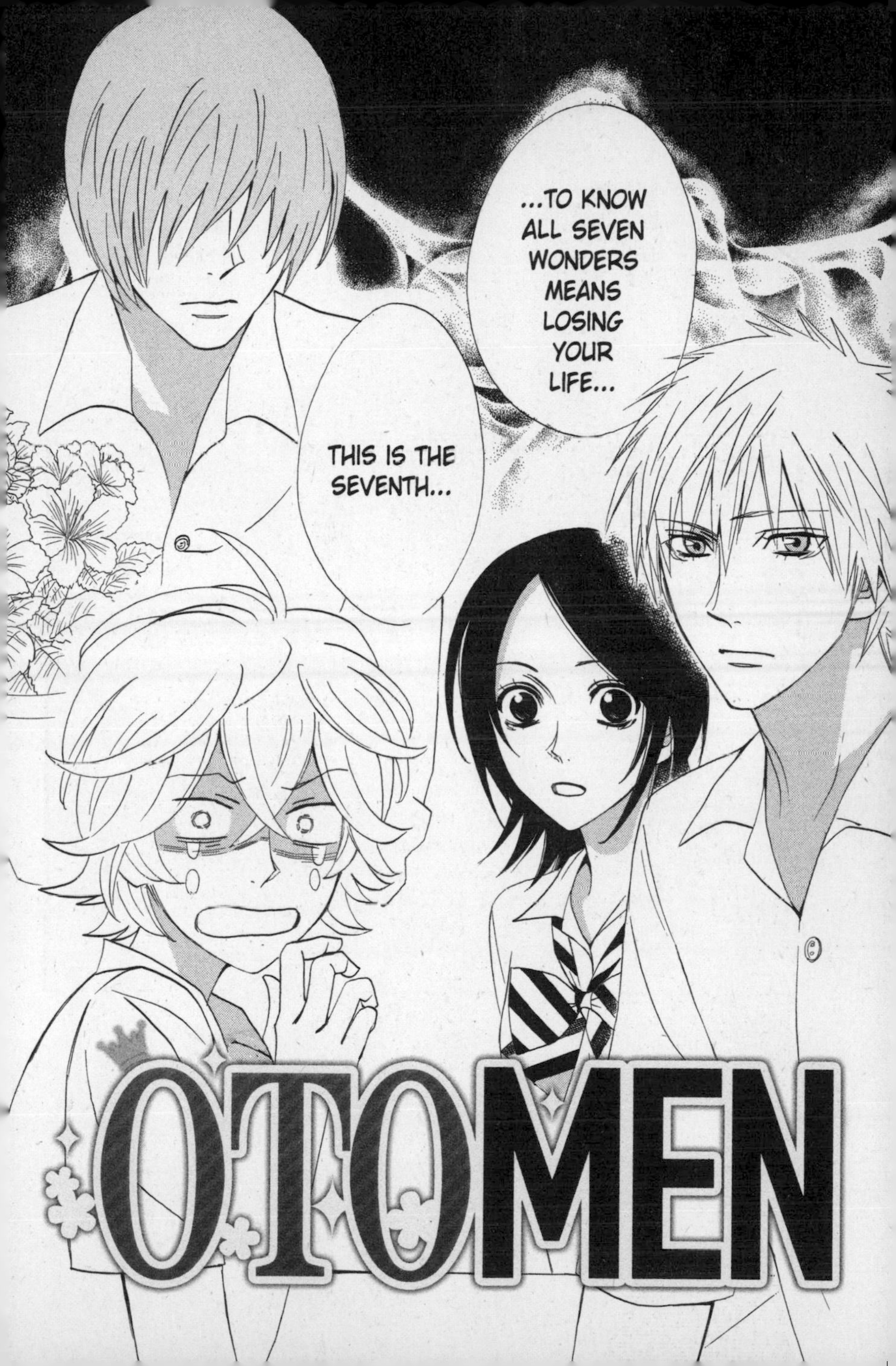
...TO KNOW ALL SEVEN WONDERS MEANS LOSING YOUR LIFE...
THIS IS THE SEVENTH...
OTOMEN

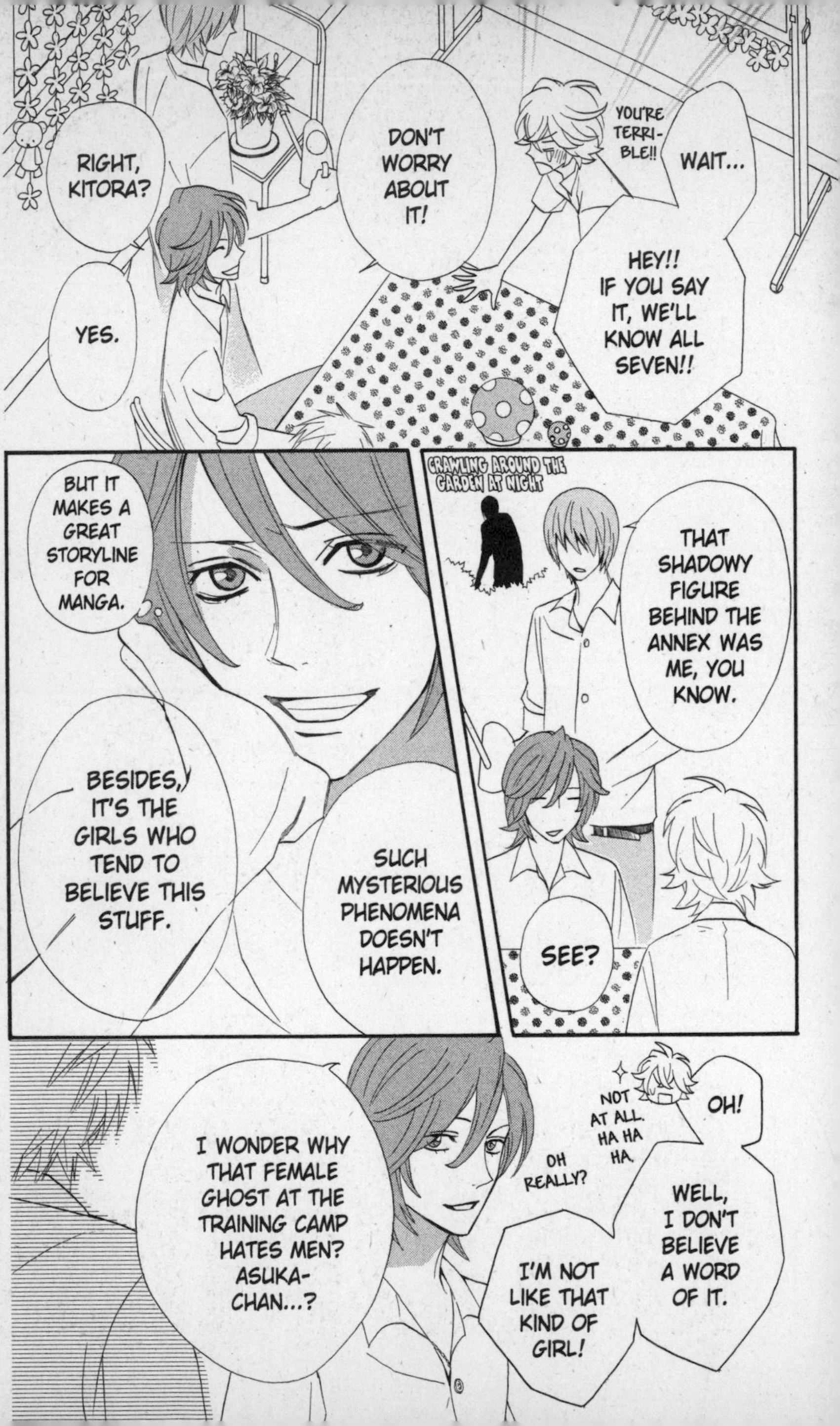
WAIT...
HEY!! IF YOU SAY IT, WE'LL KNOW ALL SEVEN!!
YOU'RE TERRI-BLE!!
DON'T WORRY ABOUT IT!
RIGHT, KITORA?
YES.
CRAWLING AROUND THE GARDEN AT NIGHT
THAT SHADOWY FIGURE BEHIND THE ANNEX WAS ME, YOU KNOW.
SEE?
SUCH MYSTERIOUS PHENOMENA DOESN'T HAPPEN.
BUT IT MAKES A GREAT STORYLINE FOR MANGA.
BESIDES, IT'S THE GIRLS WHO TEND TO BELIEVE THIS STUFF.
OH!
NOT AT ALL. HA HA HA.
OH REALLY?
WELL, I DON'T BELIEVE A WORD OF IT.
I'M NOT LIKE THAT KIND OF GIRL!
I WONDER WHY THAT FEMALE GHOST AT THE TRAINING CAMP HATES MEN? ASUKA-CHAN...?

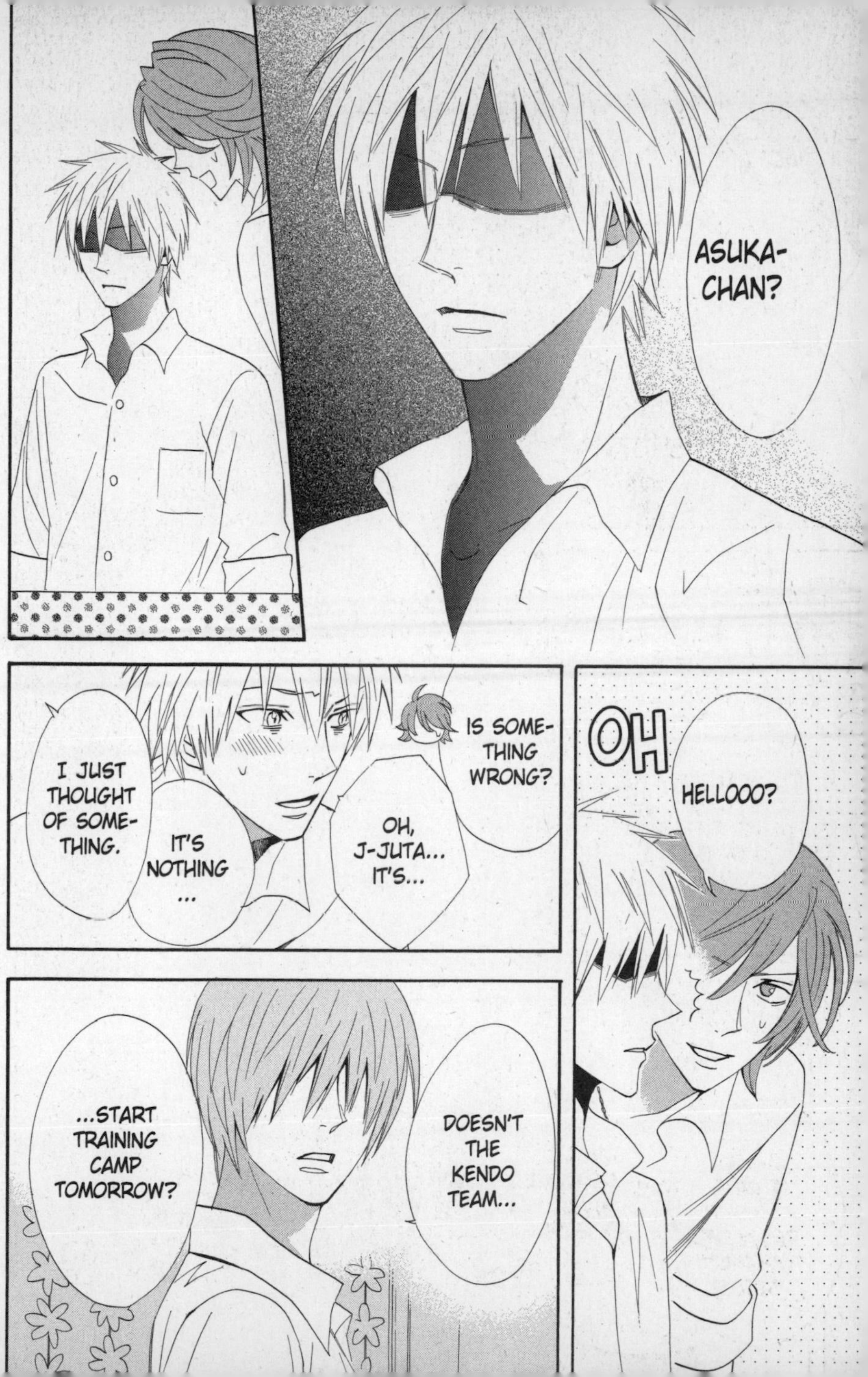
ASUKA-CHAN?
OH
HELLOOO?
IS SOME-THING WRONG?
OH, J-JUTA... IT'S...
IT'S NOTHING ...
I JUST THOUGHT OF SOME-THING.
DOESN'T THE KENDO TEAM...
...START TRAINING CAMP TOMORROW?

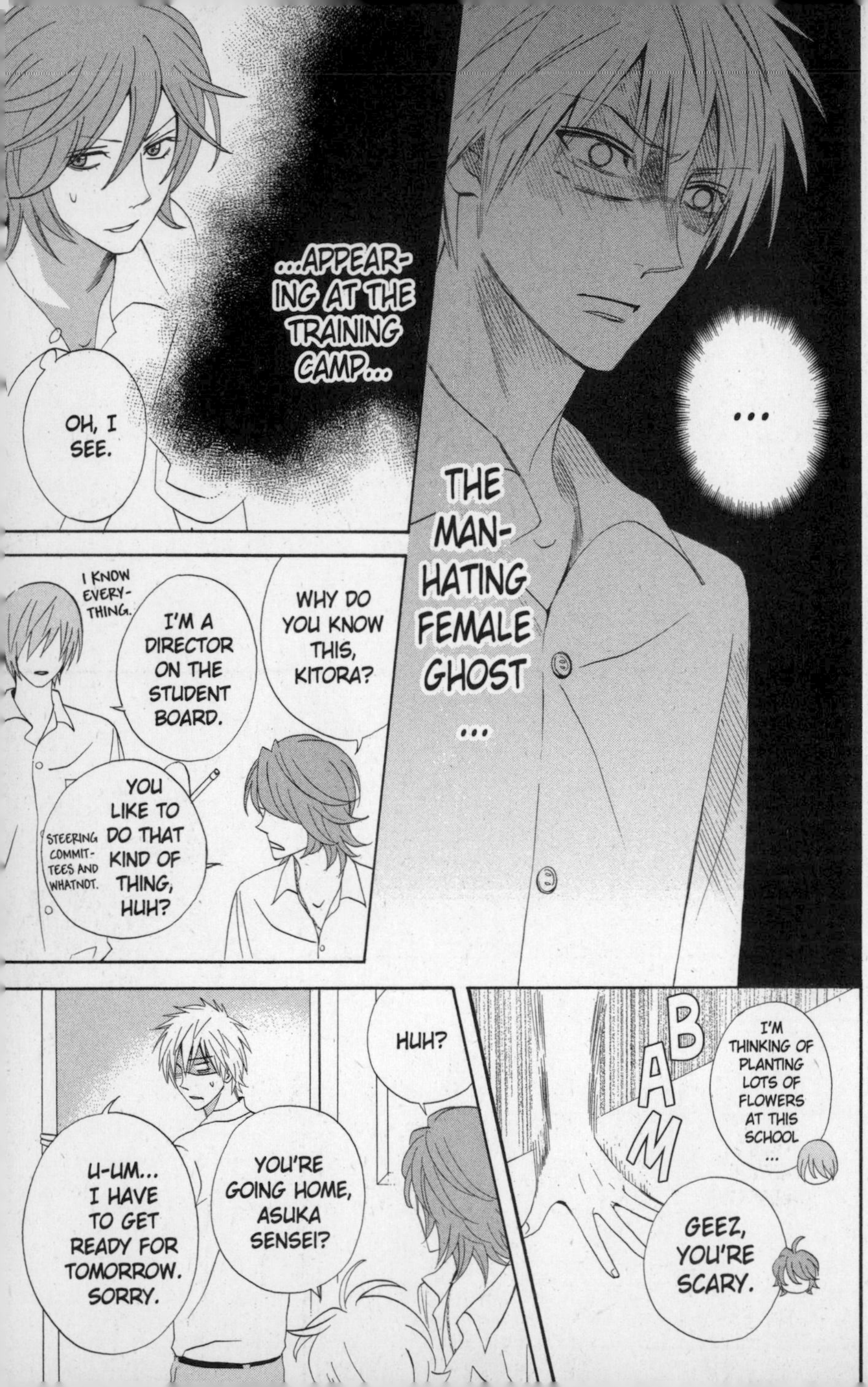
...
THE MAN-HATING FEMALE GHOST ...
...APPEARING AT THE TRAINING CAMP...
OH, I SEE.
WHY DO YOU KNOW THIS, KITORA?
I'M A DIRECTOR ON THE STUDENT BOARD.
I KNOW EVERYTHING.
YOU LIKE TO DO THAT KIND OF THING, HUH?
STEERING COMMITTEES AND WHATNOT.
I'M THINKING OF PLANTING LOTS OF FLOWERS AT THIS SCHOOL ...
BAM
GEEZ, YOU'RE SCARY.
HUH?
YOU'RE GOING HOME, ASUKA SENSEI?
U-UM... I HAVE TO GET READY FOR TOMORROW. SORRY.

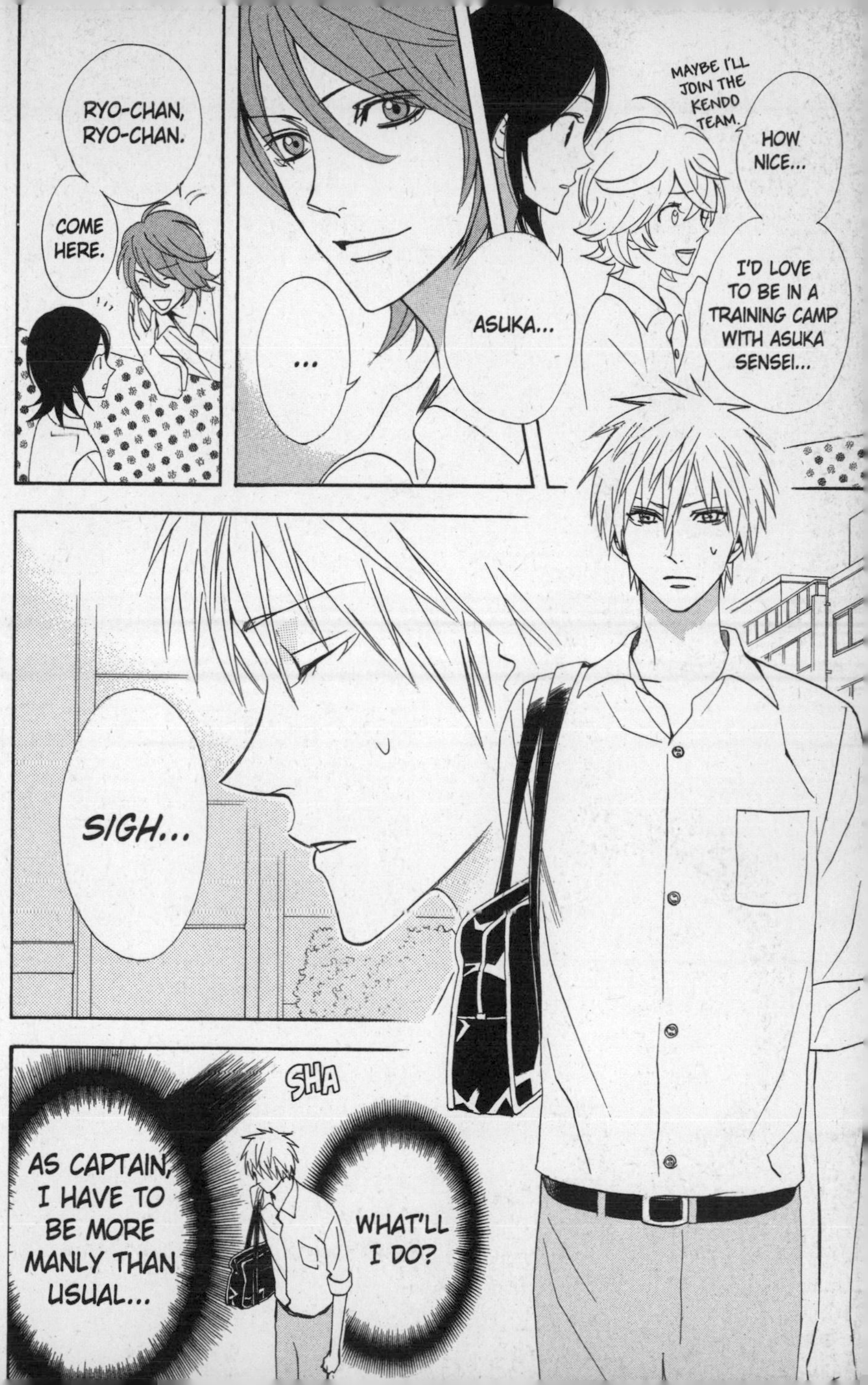

MAYBE I'LL JOIN THE KENDO TEAM.
HOW NICE...
I'D LOVE TO BE IN A TRAINING CAMP WITH ASUKA SENSEI...
ASUKA...
...
RYO-CHAN, RYO-CHAN.
COME HERE.
SIGH...
SHA
WHAT'LL I DO?
AS CAPTAIN, I HAVE TO BE MORE MANLY THAN USUAL...

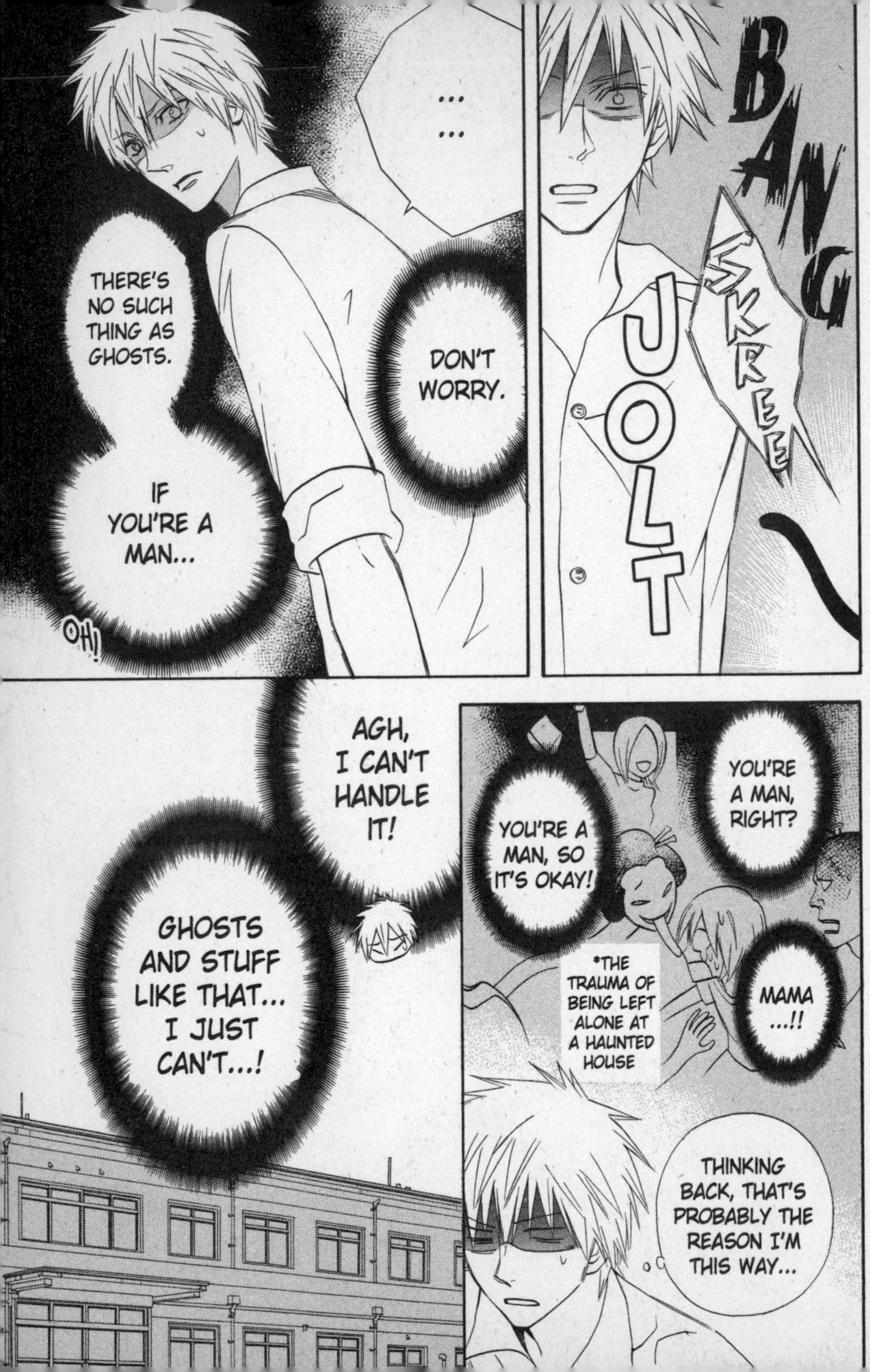
BANG
SKREE
JOLT
...
...
DON'T WORRY.
THERE'S NO SUCH THING AS GHOSTS.
IF YOU'RE A MAN...
OH!
YOU'RE A MAN, RIGHT?
YOU'RE A MAN, SO IT'S OKAY!
MAMA ...!!
*THE TRAUMA OF BEING LEFT ALONE AT A HAUNTED HOUSE
THINKING BACK, THAT'S PROBABLY THE REASON I'M THIS WAY...
AGH, I CAN'T HANDLE IT!
GHOSTS AND STUFF LIKE THAT... I JUST CAN'T...!

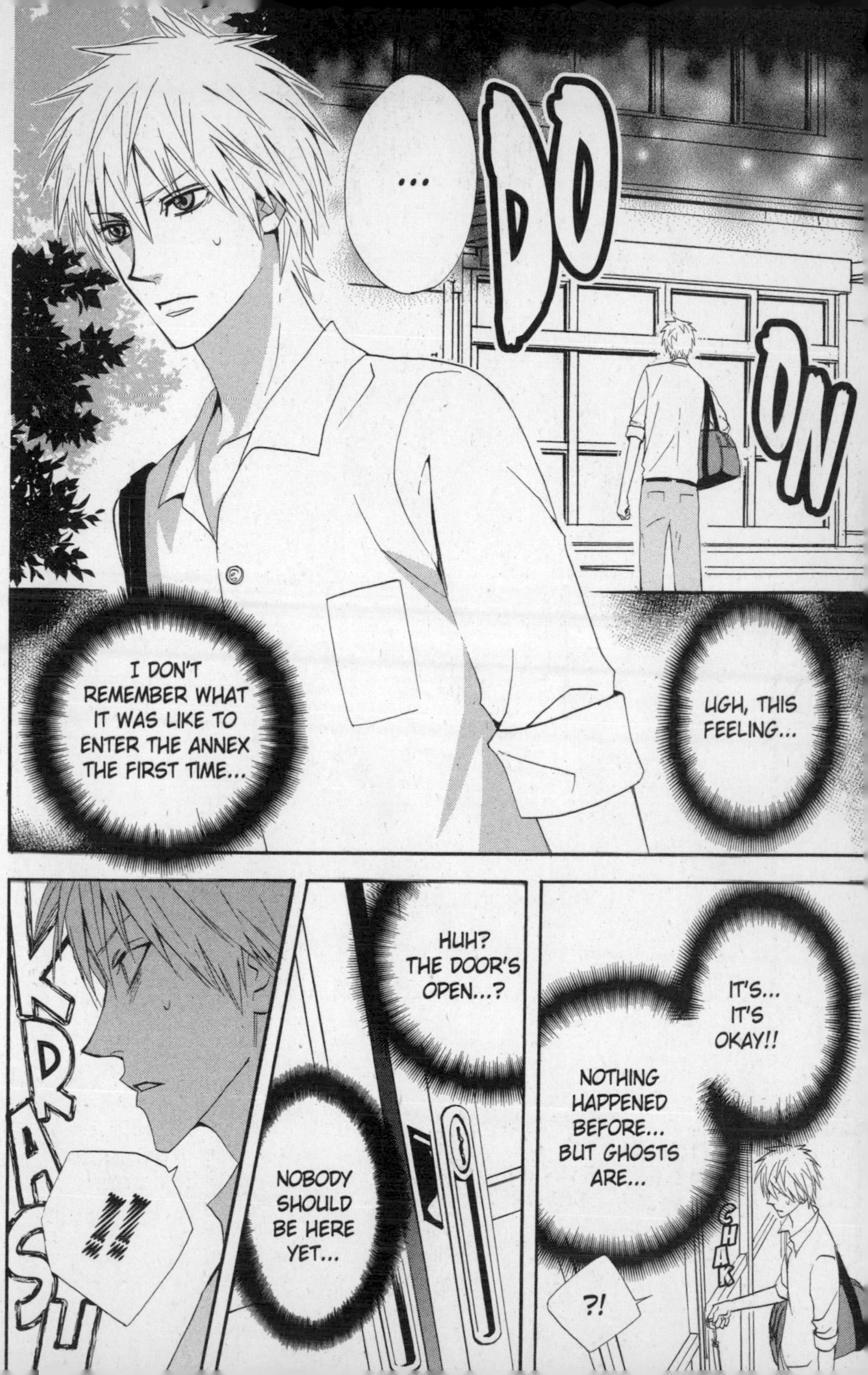
DODON
...
UGH, THIS FEELING...
I DON'T REMEMBER WHAT IT WAS LIKE TO ENTER THE ANNEX THE FIRST TIME...
IT'S... IT'S OKAY!!
NOTHING HAPPENED BEFORE... BUT GHOSTS ARE...
CHAK
?!
HUH? THE DOOR'S OPEN...?
NOBODY SHOULD BE HERE YET...
KRASH
!!

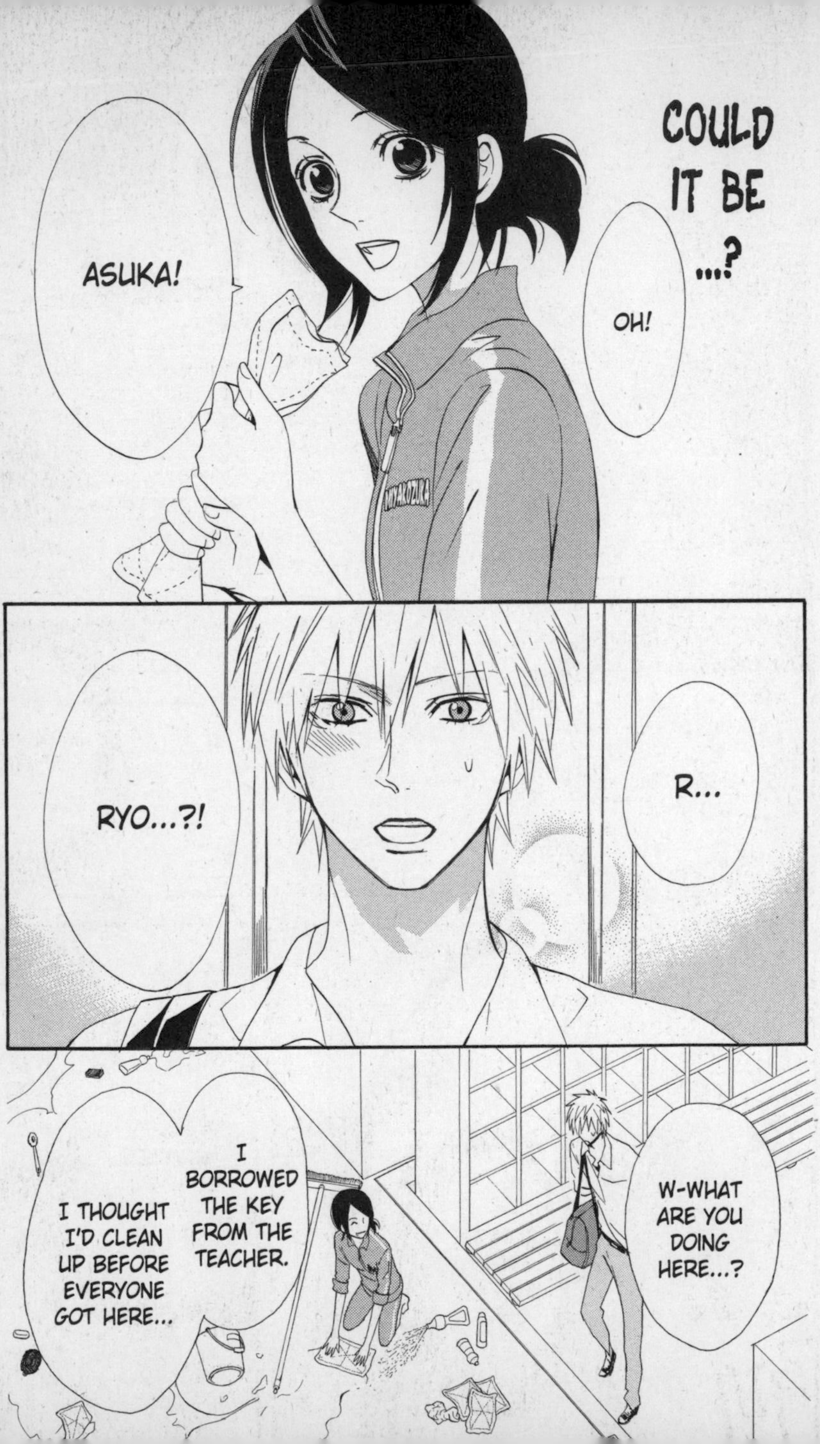
COULD IT BE ...?
OH!
ASUKA!
MIYAKOZUKA
R...
RYO...?!
W-WHAT ARE YOU DOING HERE...?
I BORROWED THE KEY FROM THE TEACHER.
I THOUGHT I'D CLEAN UP BEFORE EVERYONE GOT HERE...

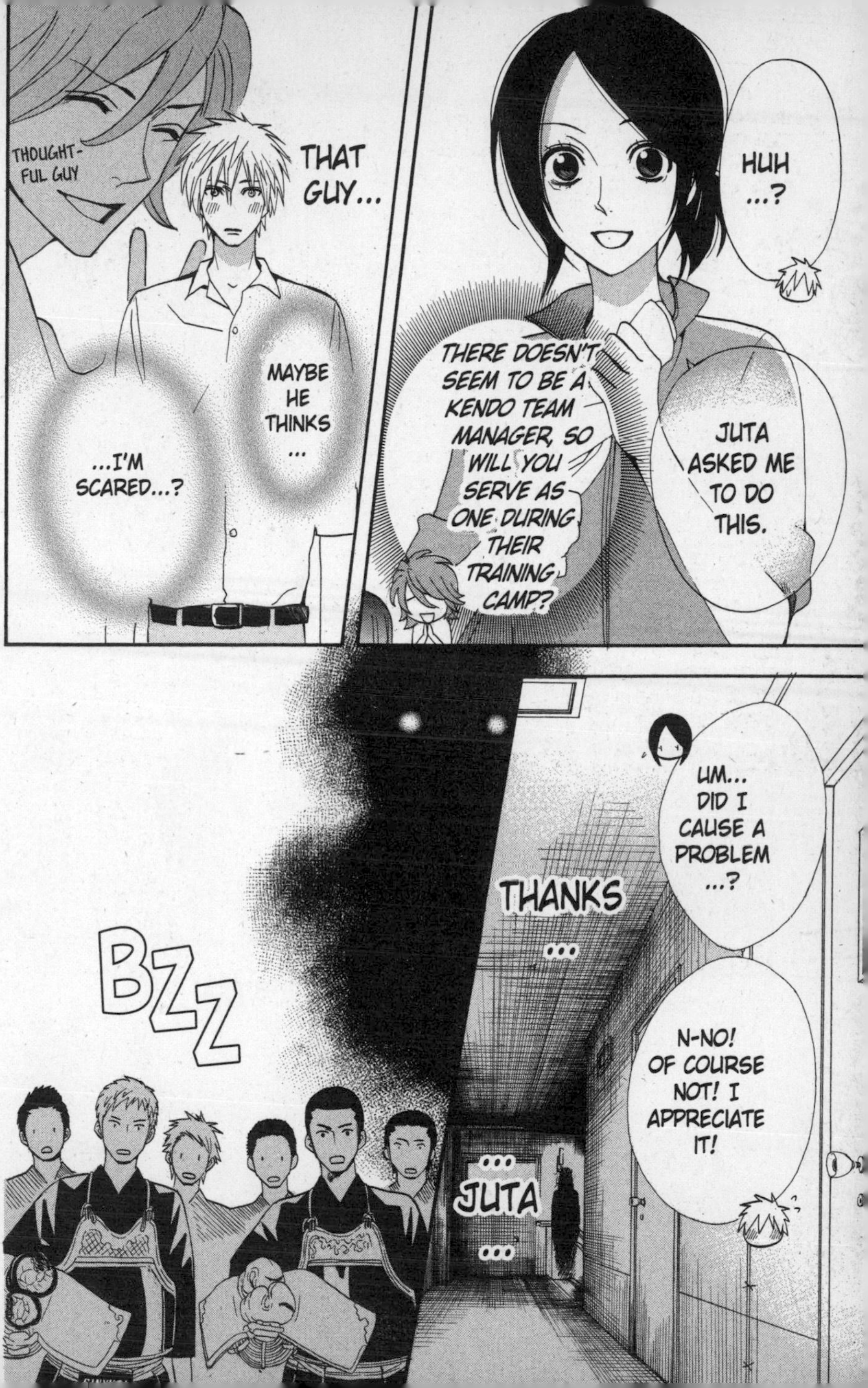
HUH ...?
JUTA ASKED ME TO DO THIS.
THERE DOESN'T SEEM TO BE A KENDO TEAM MANAGER, SO WILL YOU SERVE AS ONE DURING THEIR TRAINING CAMP?
THAT GUY...
THOUGHT-FUL GUY
MAYBE HE THINKS ...
...I'M SCARED...?
UM... DID I CAUSE A PROBLEM ...?
N-NO! OF COURSE NOT! I APPRECIATE IT!
THANKS ...
...JUTA ...
BZZ

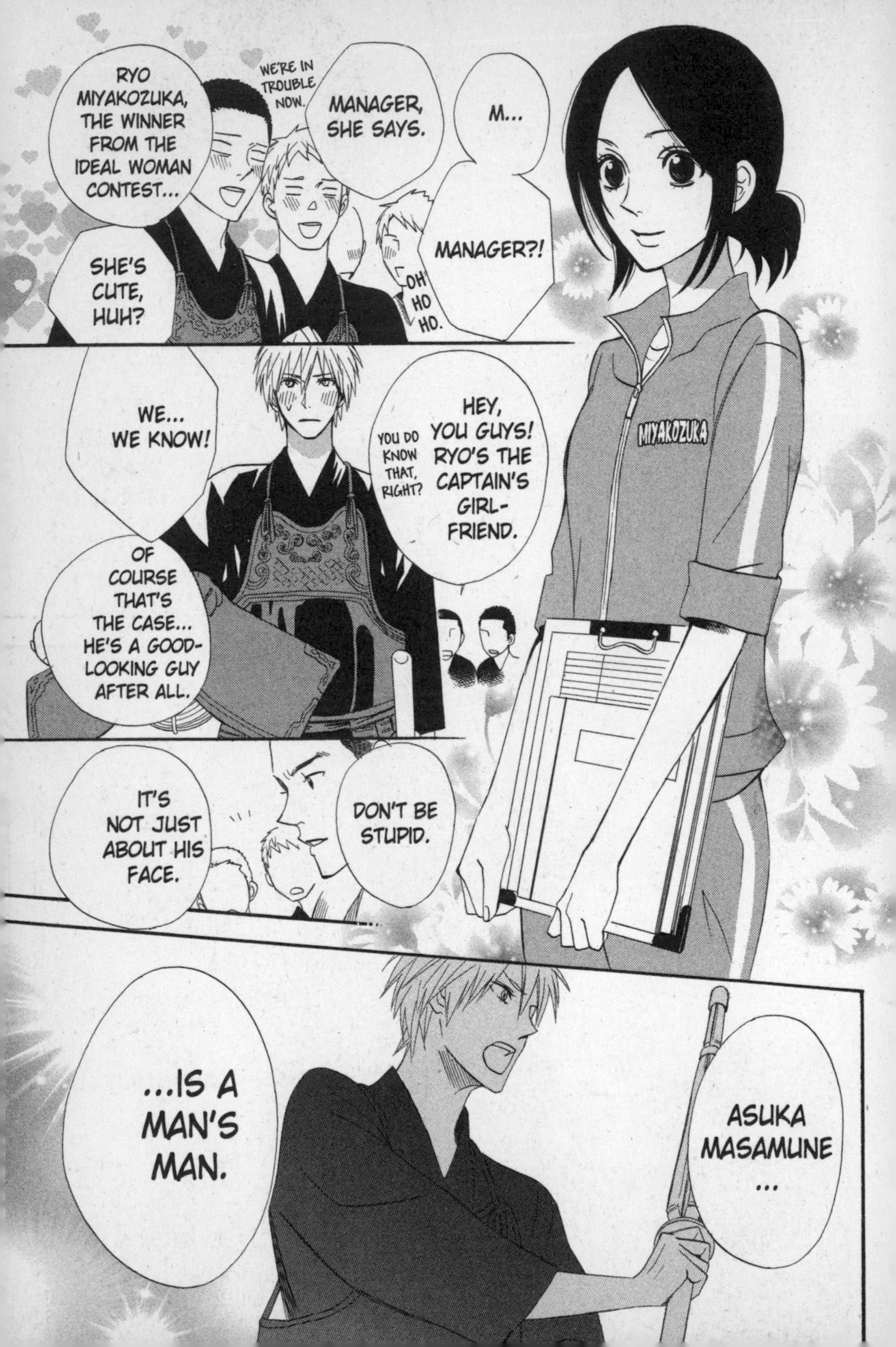
MIYAKOZUKA
M...
MANAGER?!
MANAGER, SHE SAYS.
WE'RE IN TROUBLE NOW.
OH HO HO.
RYO MIYAKOZUKA, THE WINNER FROM THE IDEAL WOMAN CONTEST...
SHE'S CUTE, HUH?
HEY, YOU GUYS! RYO'S THE CAPTAIN'S GIRL-FRIEND.
YOU DO KNOW THAT, RIGHT?
WE... WE KNOW!
OF COURSE THAT'S THE CASE... HE'S A GOOD-LOOKING GUY AFTER ALL.
DON'T BE STUPID.
IT'S NOT JUST ABOUT HIS FACE.
ASUKA MASAMUNE ...
...IS A MAN'S MAN.

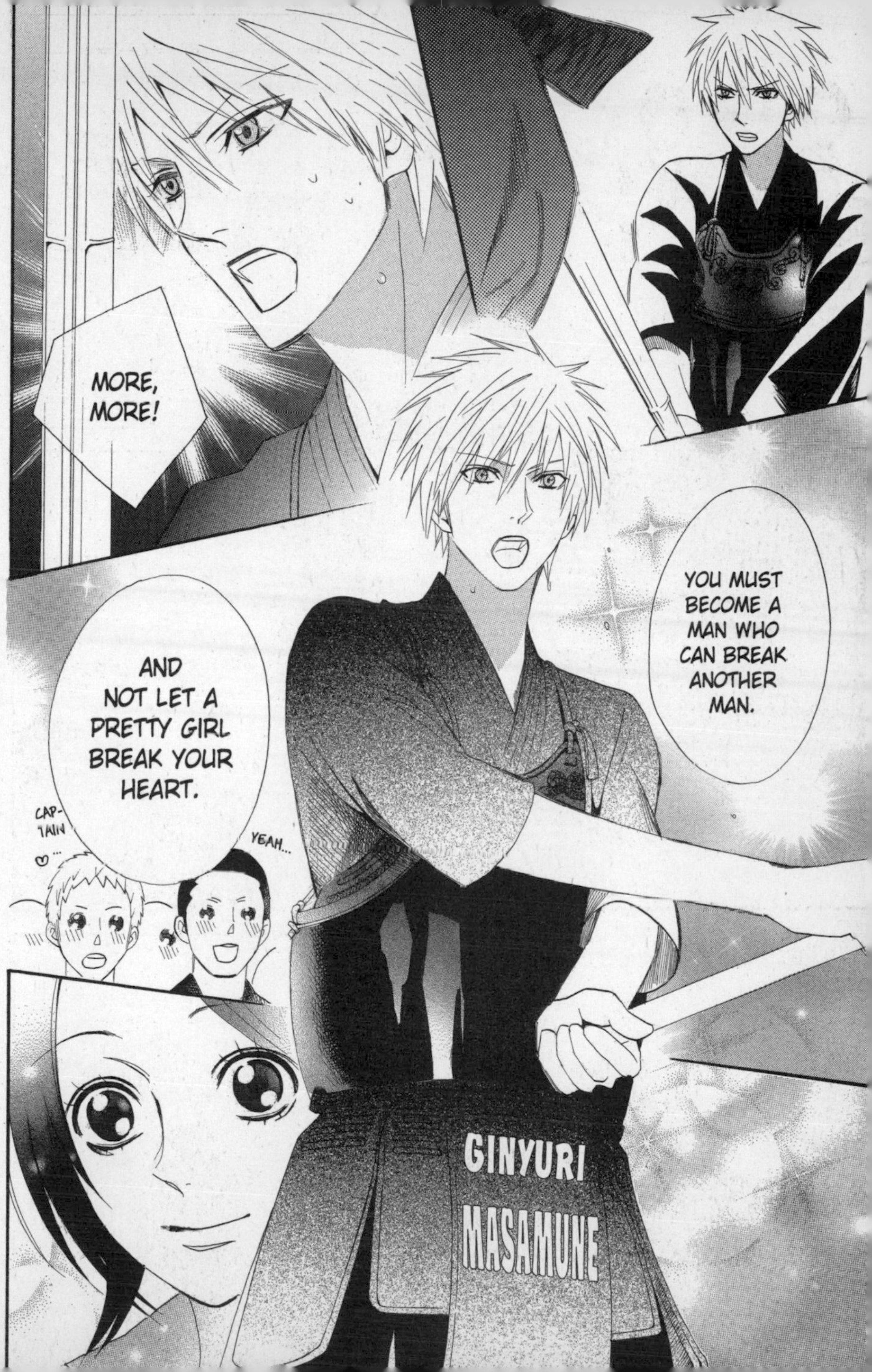
MORE, MORE!
YOU MUST BECOME A MAN WHO CAN BREAK ANOTHER MAN.
AND NOT LET A PRETTY GIRL BREAK YOUR HEART.
CAP-TAIN ♥...
YEAH...
GINYURI MASAMUNE

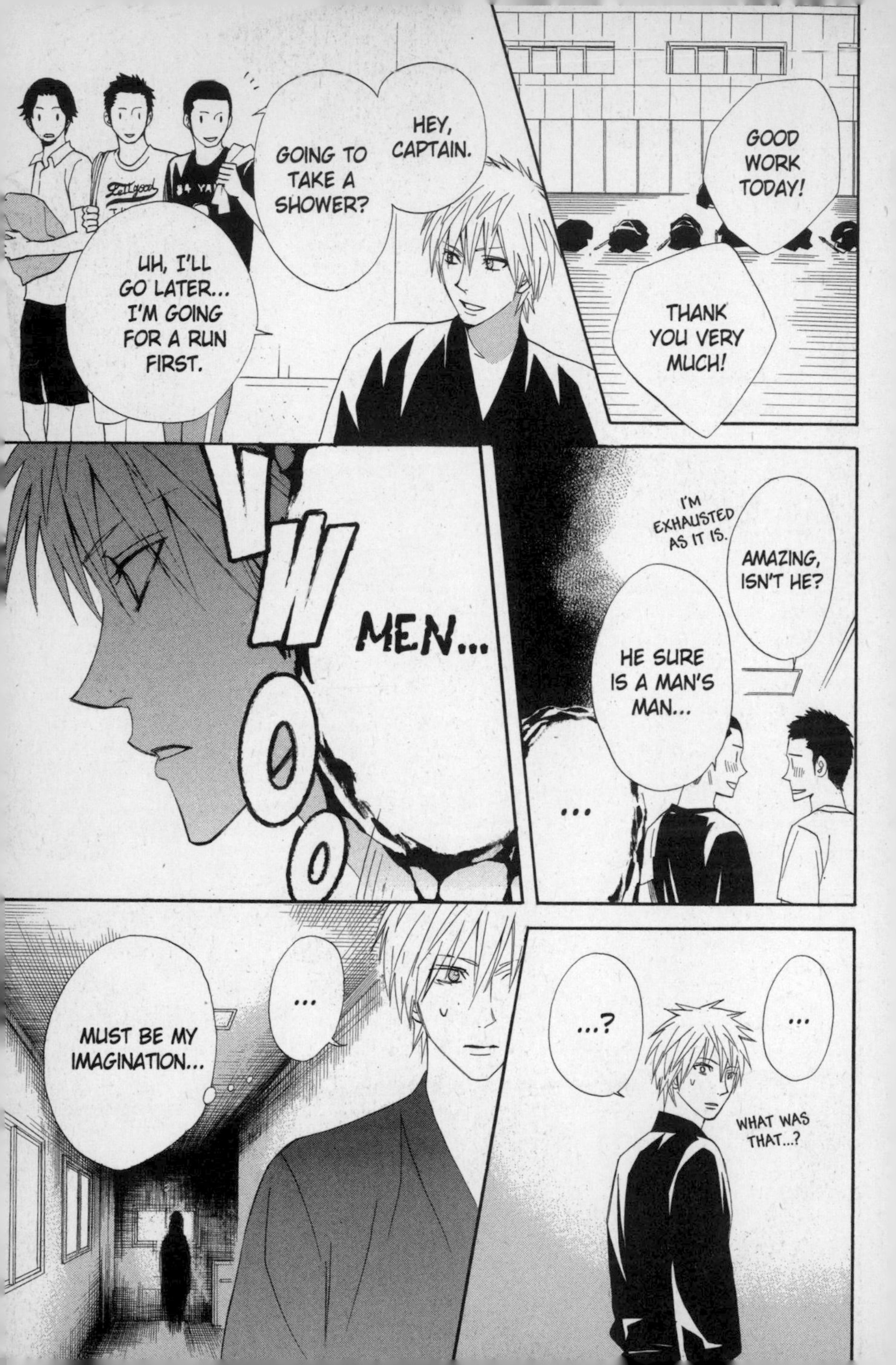
GOOD WORK TODAY!
THANK YOU VERY MUCH!
HEY, CAPTAIN.
GOING TO TAKE A SHOWER?
UH, I'LL GO LATER... I'M GOING FOR A RUN FIRST.
I'M EXHAUSTED AS IT IS.
AMAZING, ISN'T HE?
HE SURE IS A MAN'S MAN...
...
MEN...
...
...?
WHAT WAS THAT...?
...
MUST BE MY IMAGINATION...

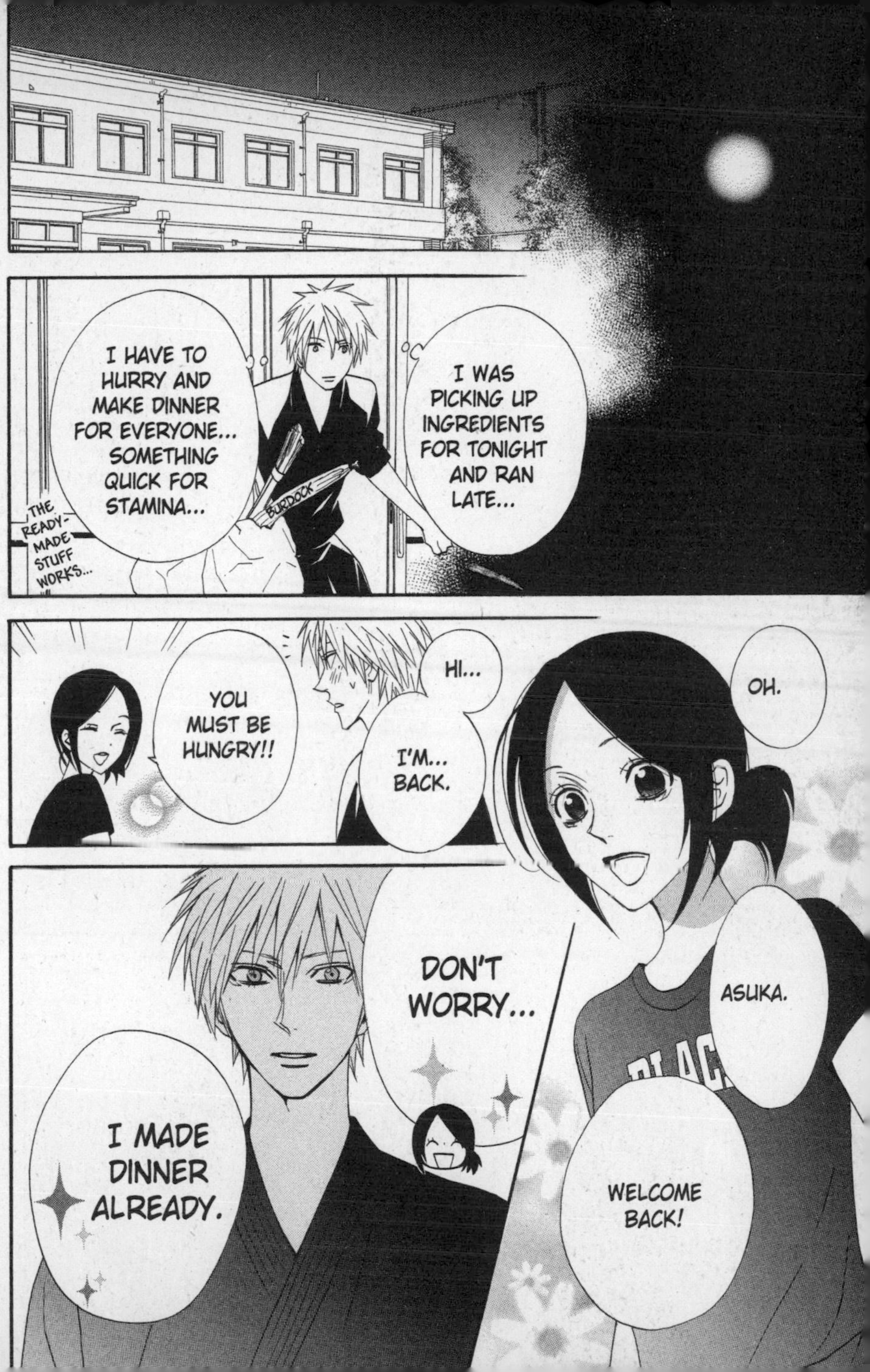
I WAS PICKING UP INGREDIENTS FOR TONIGHT AND RAN LATE...
I HAVE TO HURRY AND MAKE DINNER FOR EVERYONE... SOMETHING QUICK FOR STAMINA...
BURDOCK
THE READY-MADE STUFF WORKS...
OH.
ASUKA.
WELCOME BACK!
HI...
I'M... BACK.
YOU MUST BE HUNGRY!!
DON'T WORRY...
I MADE DINNER ALREADY.

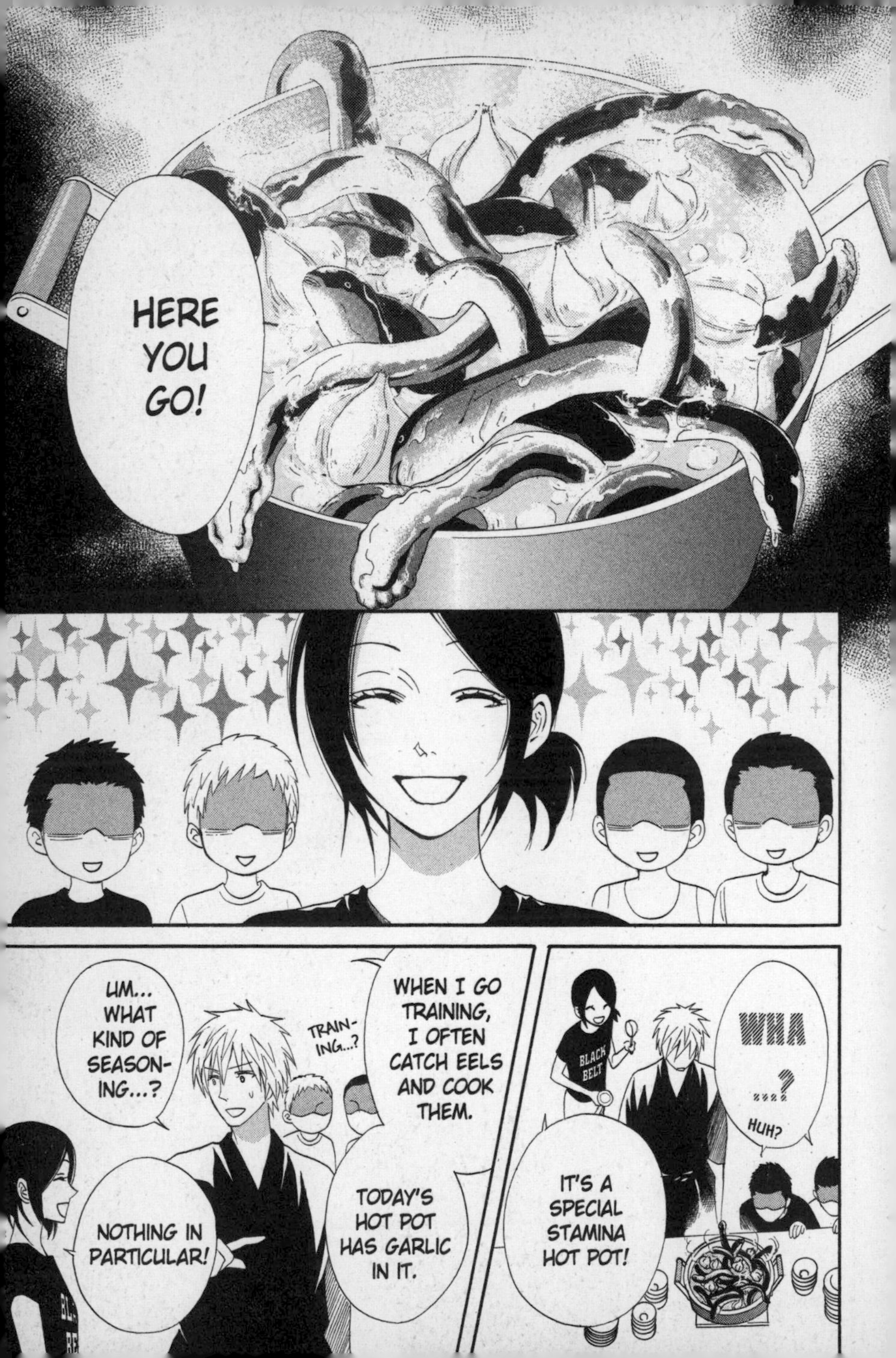
HERE YOU GO!
WHA ...?
HUH?
BLACK BELT
IT'S A SPECIAL STAMINA HOT POT!
WHEN I GO TRAINING, I OFTEN CATCH EELS AND COOK THEM.
TRAIN-ING...?
UM... WHAT KIND OF SEASON-ING...?
TODAY'S HOT POT HAS GARLIC IN IT.
NOTHING IN PARTICULAR!

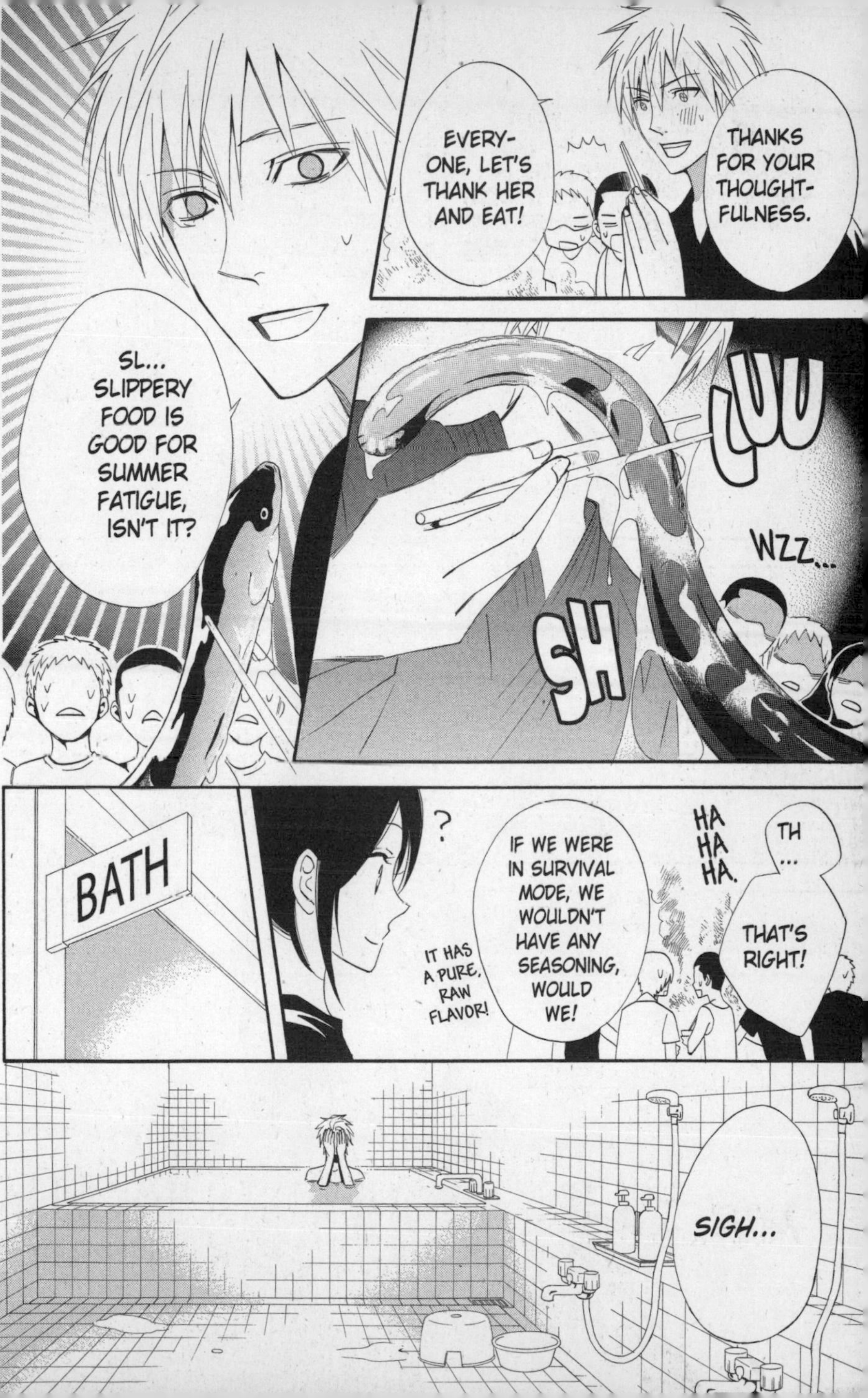
THANKS FOR YOUR THOUGHT-FULNESS.
EVERY-ONE, LET'S THANK HER AND EAT!
LUU
WZZ...
SH
SL... SLIPPERY FOOD IS GOOD FOR SUMMER FATIGUE, ISN'T IT?
TH... THAT'S RIGHT!
HA HA HA.
IF WE WERE IN SURVIVAL MODE, WE WOULDN'T HAVE ANY SEASONING, WOULD WE!
IT HAS A PURE, RAW FLAVOR!
?
BATH
SIGH...

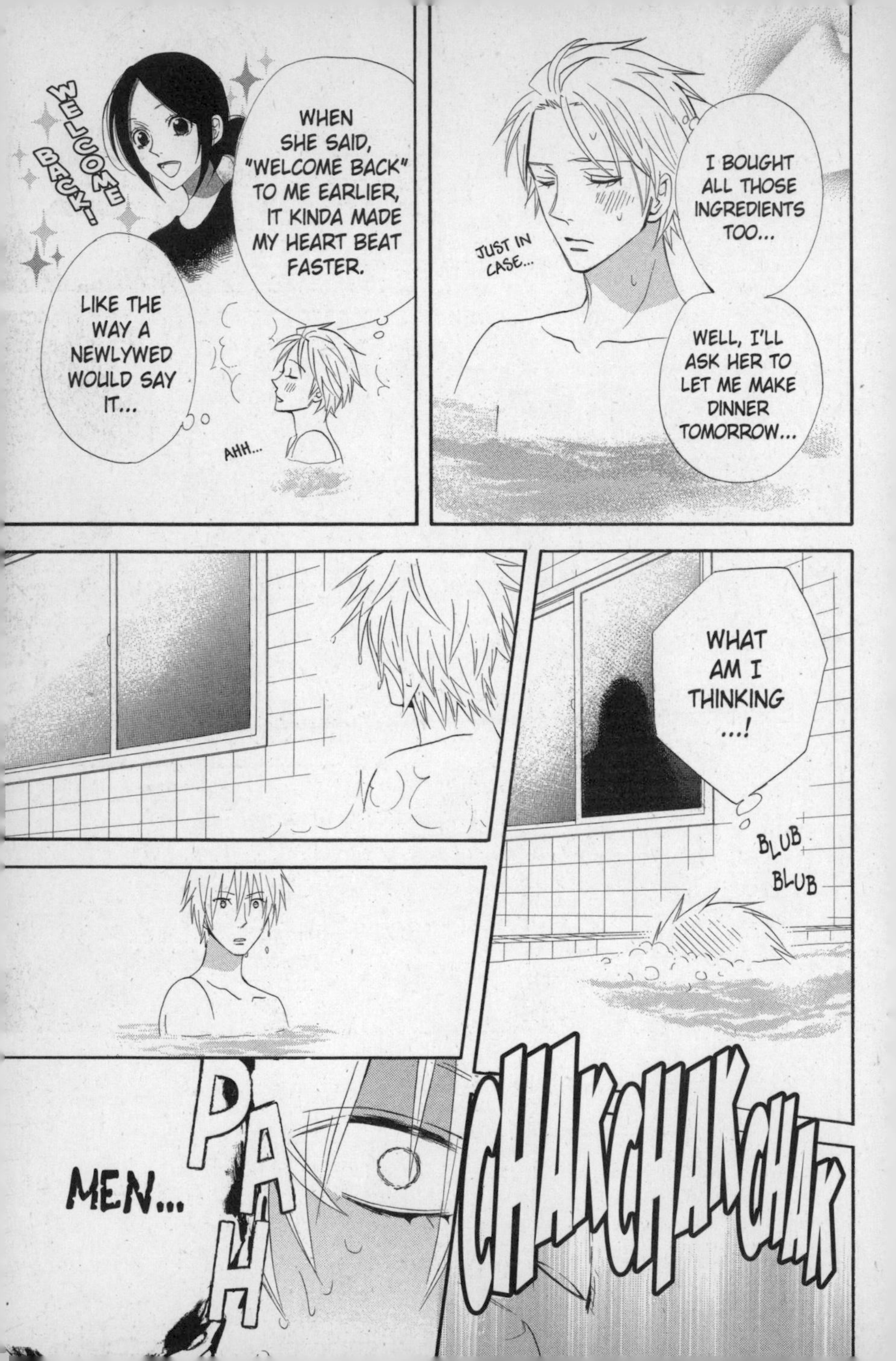
I BOUGHT ALL THOSE INGREDIENTS TOO...
JUST IN CASE...
WELL, I'LL ASK HER TO LET ME MAKE DINNER TOMORROW...
WHEN SHE SAID, "WELCOME BACK" TO ME EARLIER, IT KINDA MADE MY HEART BEAT FASTER.
WELCOME BACK!
LIKE THE WAY A NEWLYWED WOULD SAY IT...
AHH...
WHAT AM I THINKING ...!
BLUB
BLUB
CHAKCHAKCHAKCHAK
PAH
MEN...

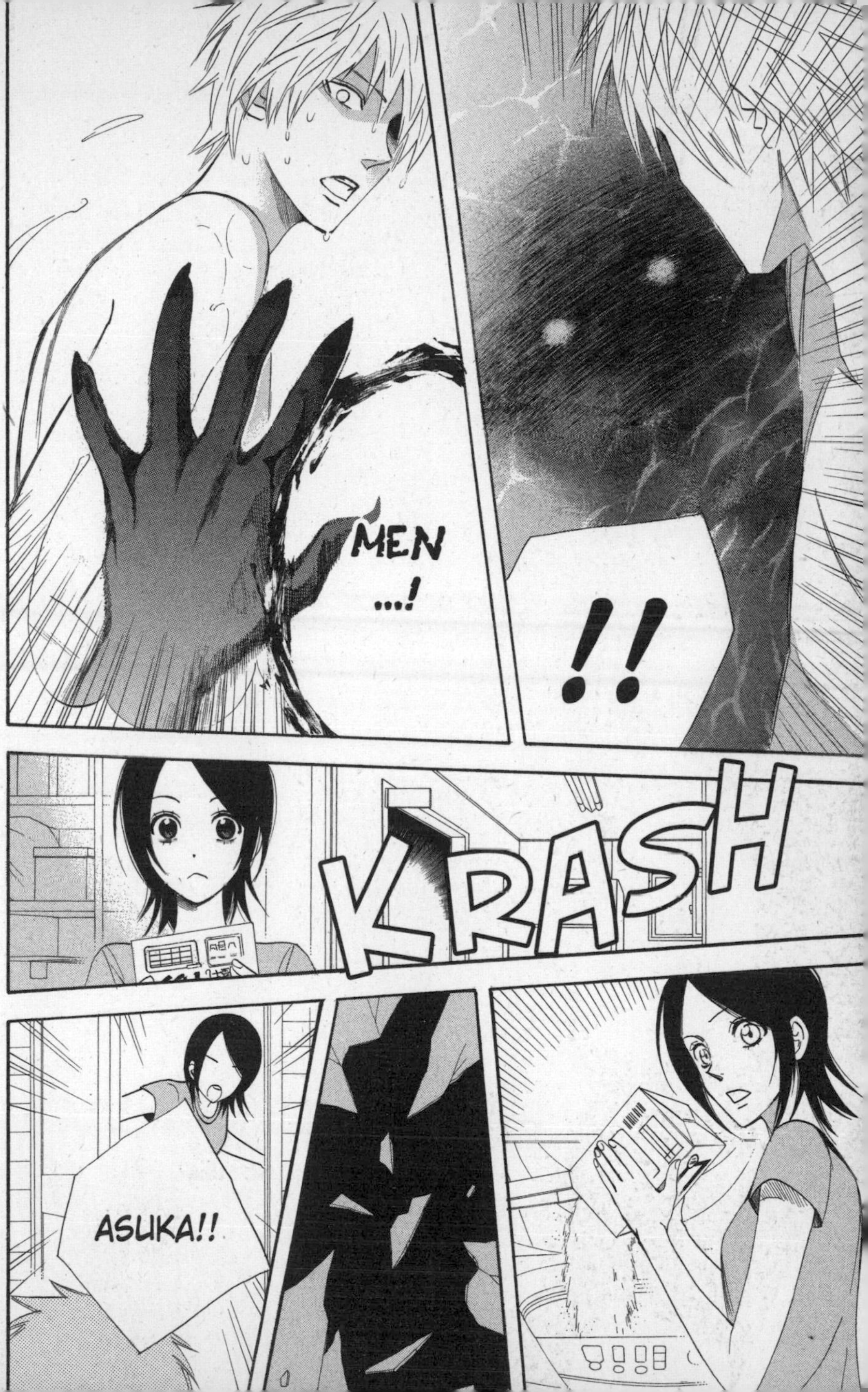
!!
MEN ...!
KRASH
ASUKA!!

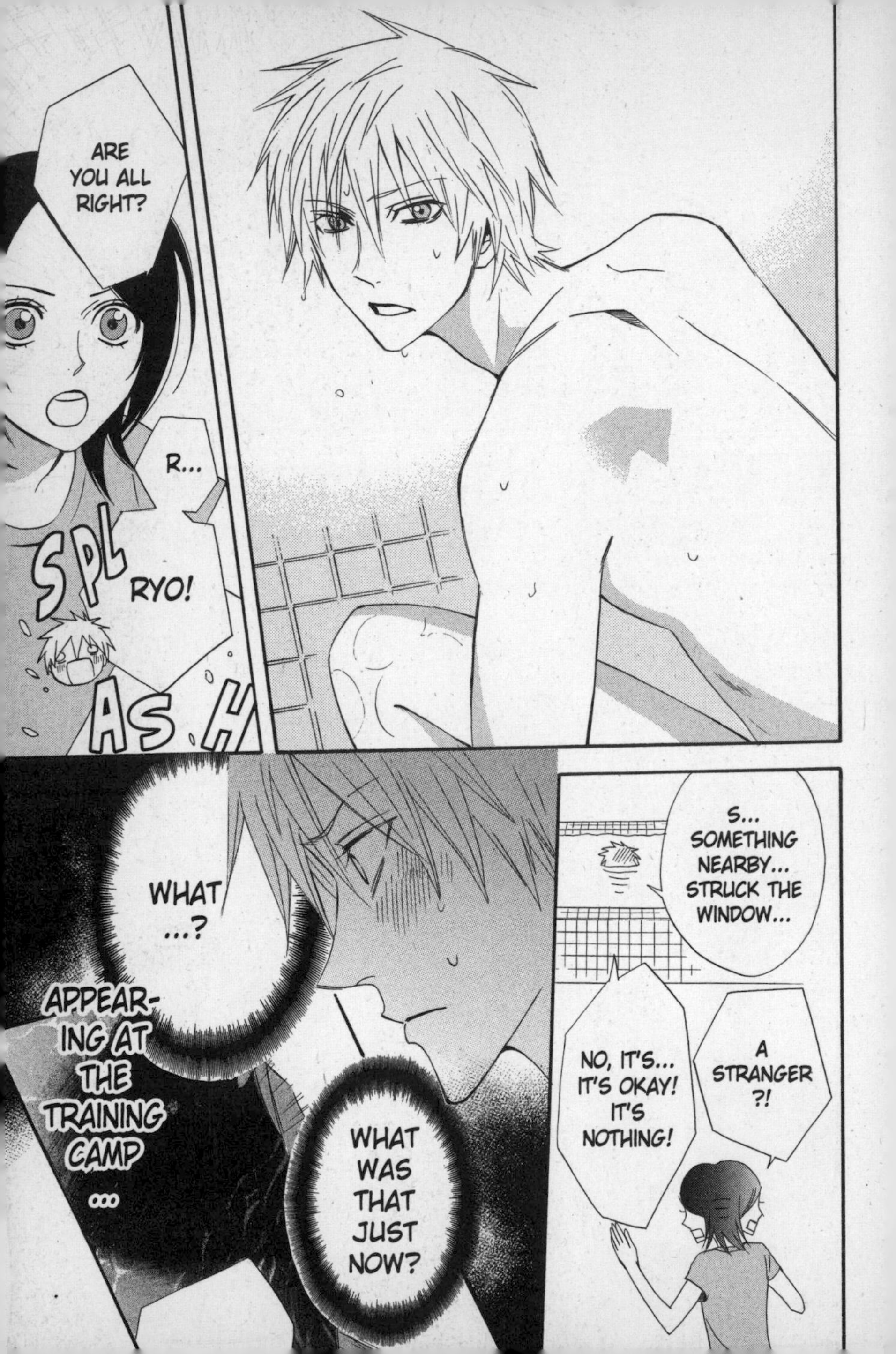
ARE YOU ALL RIGHT?
R...
SPLASH
RYO!
S... SOMETHING NEARBY... STRUCK THE WINDOW...
A STRANGER?!
NO, IT'S... IT'S OKAY! IT'S NOTHING!
WHAT ...?
WHAT WAS THAT JUST NOW?
APPEARING AT THE TRAINING CAMP...

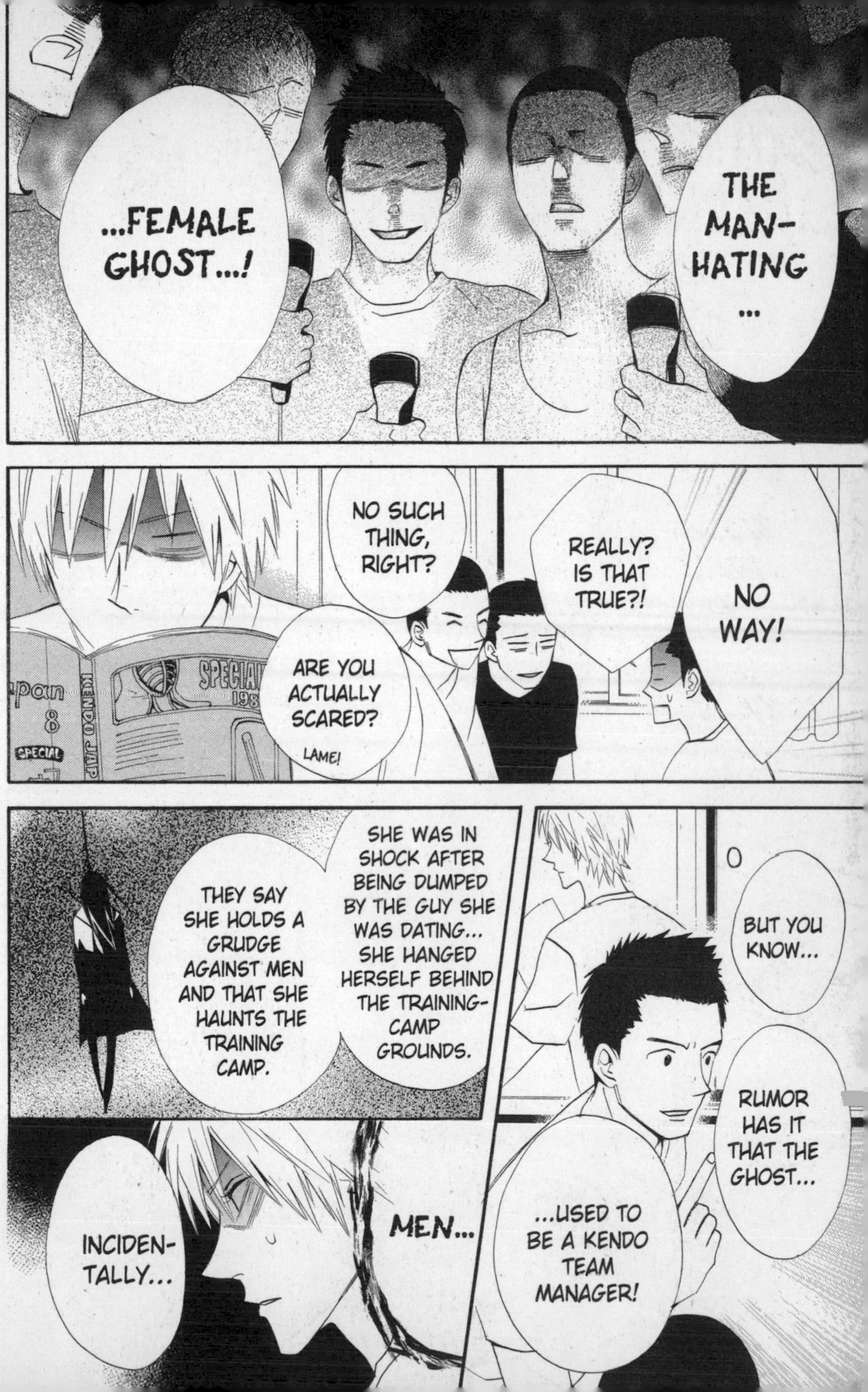
THE MAN-HATING...
...FEMALE GHOST...!
NO WAY!
REALLY? IS THAT TRUE?!
NO SUCH THING, RIGHT?
ARE YOU ACTUALLY SCARED?
LAME!
BUT YOU KNOW...
RUMOR HAS IT THAT THE GHOST...
...USED TO BE A KENDO TEAM MANAGER!
SHE WAS IN SHOCK AFTER BEING DUMPED BY THE GUY SHE WAS DATING... SHE HANGED HERSELF BEHIND THE TRAINING-CAMP GROUNDS.
THEY SAY SHE HOLDS A GRUDGE AGAINST MEN AND THAT SHE HAUNTS THE TRAINING CAMP.
MEN...
INCIDENTALLY...

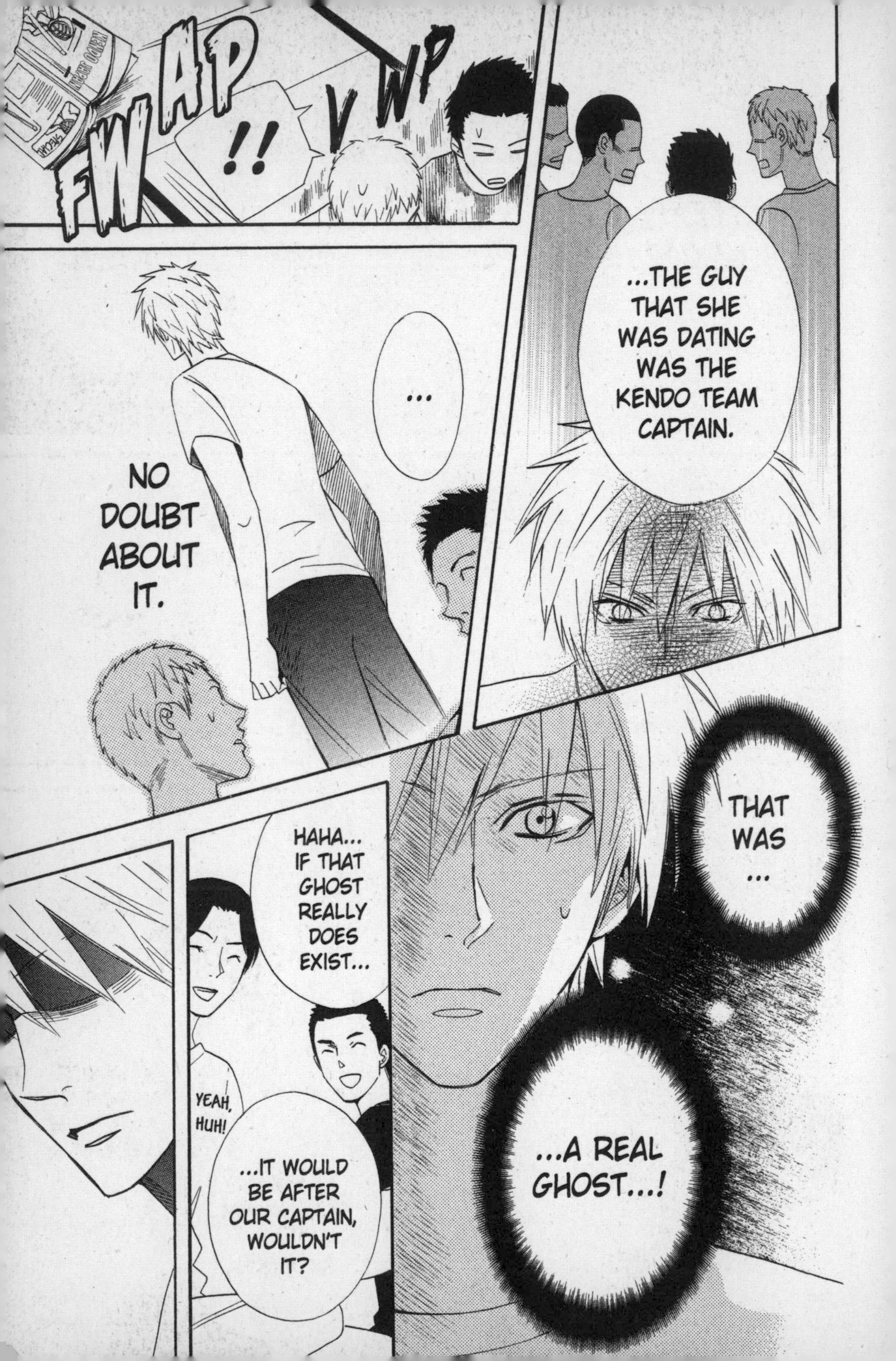
...THE GUY THAT SHE WAS DATING WAS THE KENDO TEAM CAPTAIN.
VWP
FWAP
!!
...
NO DOUBT ABOUT IT.
THAT WAS ...
...A REAL GHOST...!
HAHA... IF THAT GHOST REALLY DOES EXIST...
YEAH, HUH!
...IT WOULD BE AFTER OUR CAPTAIN, WOULDN'T IT?

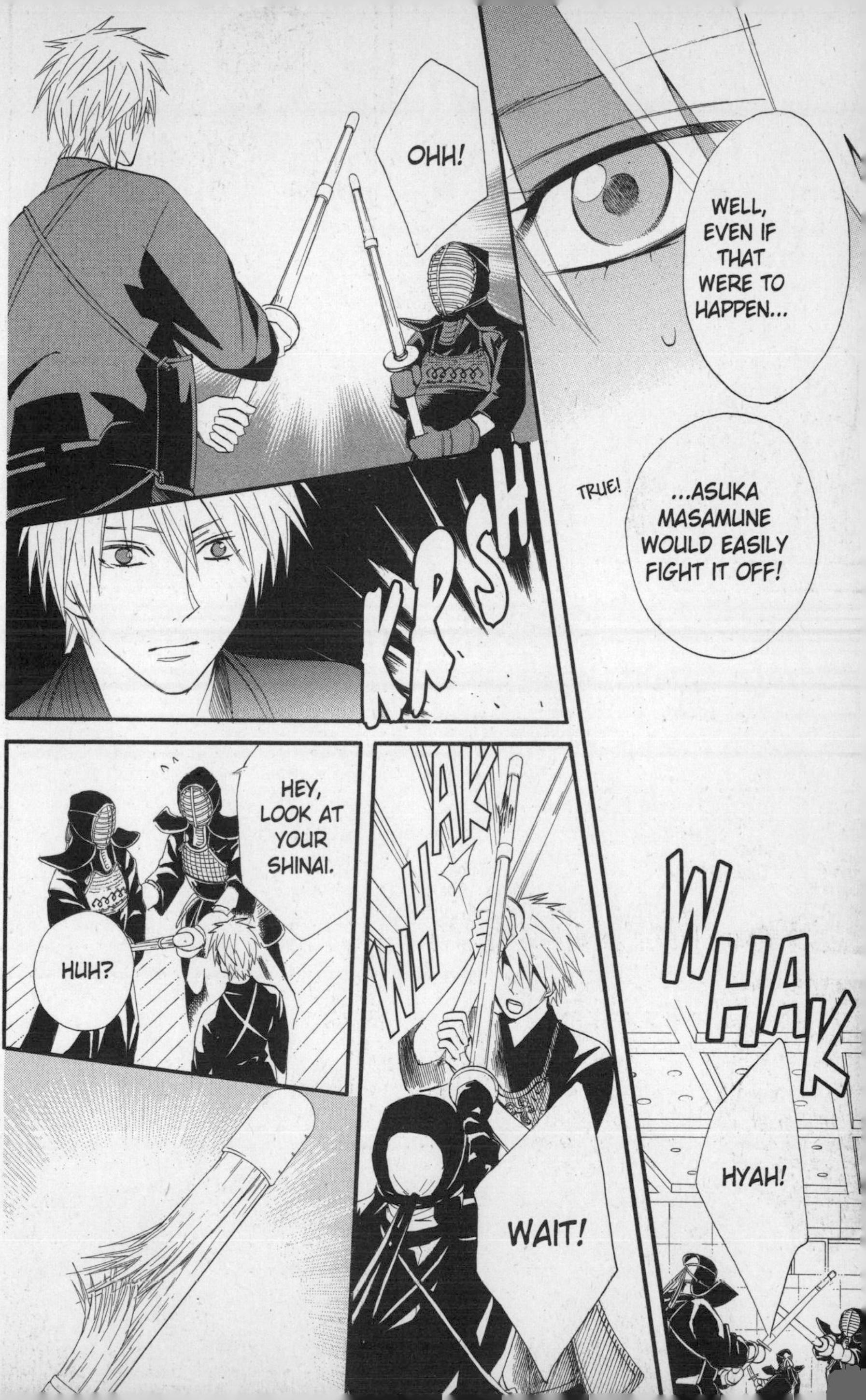
WELL, EVEN IF THAT WERE TO HAPPEN...
...ASUKA MASAMUNE WOULD EASILY FIGHT IT OFF!
TRUE!
OHH!
KRSH
WHAK
HYAH!
WHAK
WAIT!
HEY, LOOK AT YOUR SHINAI.
HUH?

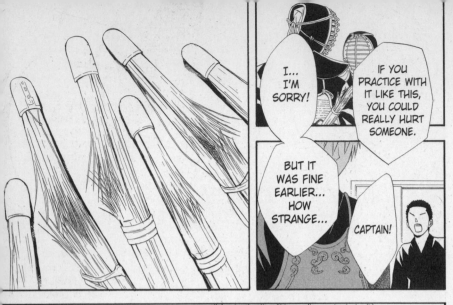

I... I'M SORRY!

IF YOU PRACTICE WITH IT LIKE THIS, YOU COULD REALLY HURT SOMEONE.

BUT IT WAS FINE EARLIER... HOW STRANGE...

CAPTAIN!

THAT'S AWFUL...

EVERY SINGLE ONE OF THEM?

...

THEN HOW...?

NOTHING WAS WRONG WITH THEM BEFORE?

NO ONE CAME IN HERE DURING PRACTICE.

SKREE

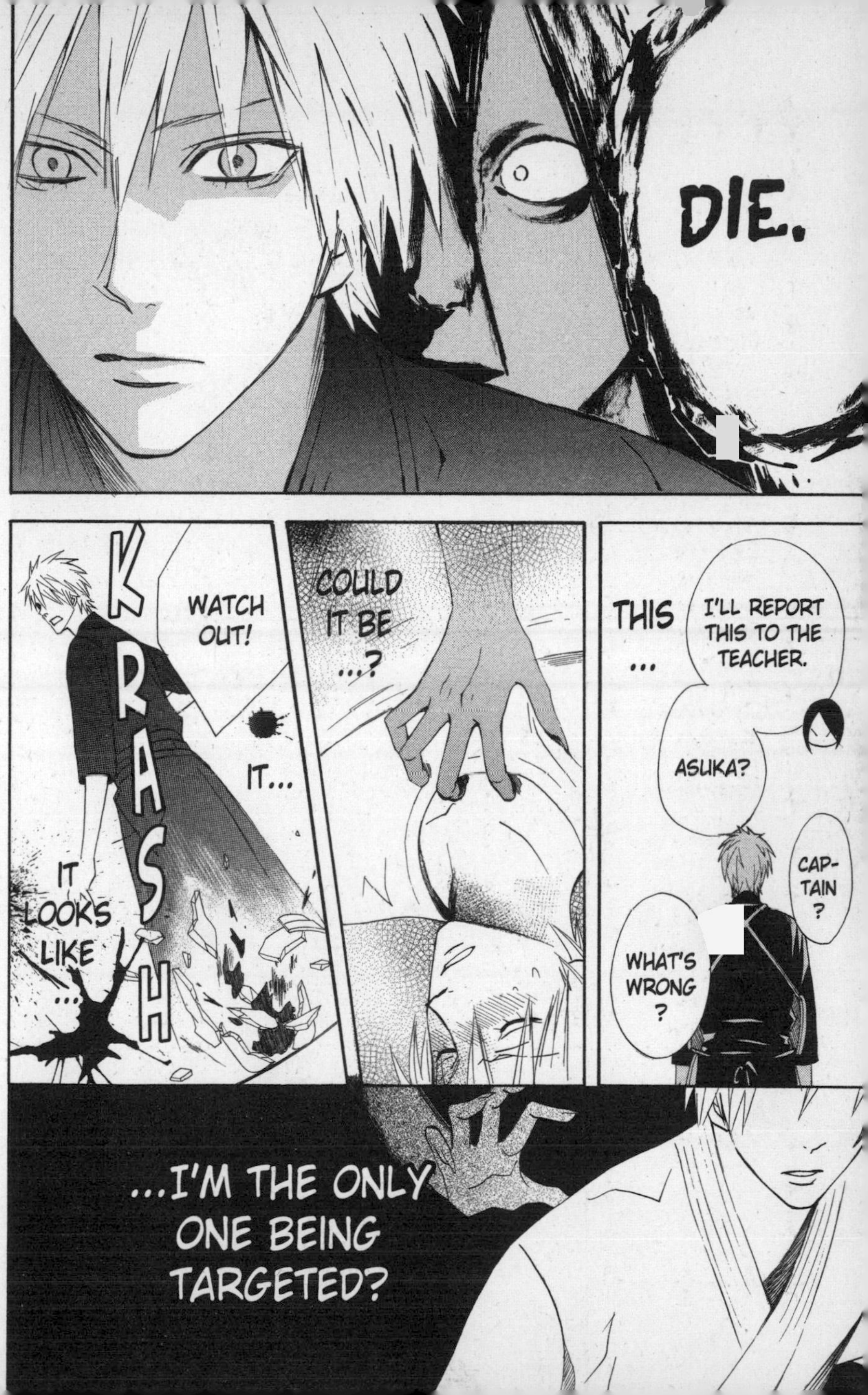
DIE.
I'LL REPORT THIS TO THE TEACHER.
THIS ...
ASUKA?
CAPTAIN?
WHAT'S WRONG?
COULD IT BE ...?
WATCH OUT!
KRASH
IT...
IT LOOKS LIKE ...
...I'M THE ONLY ONE BEING TARGETED?

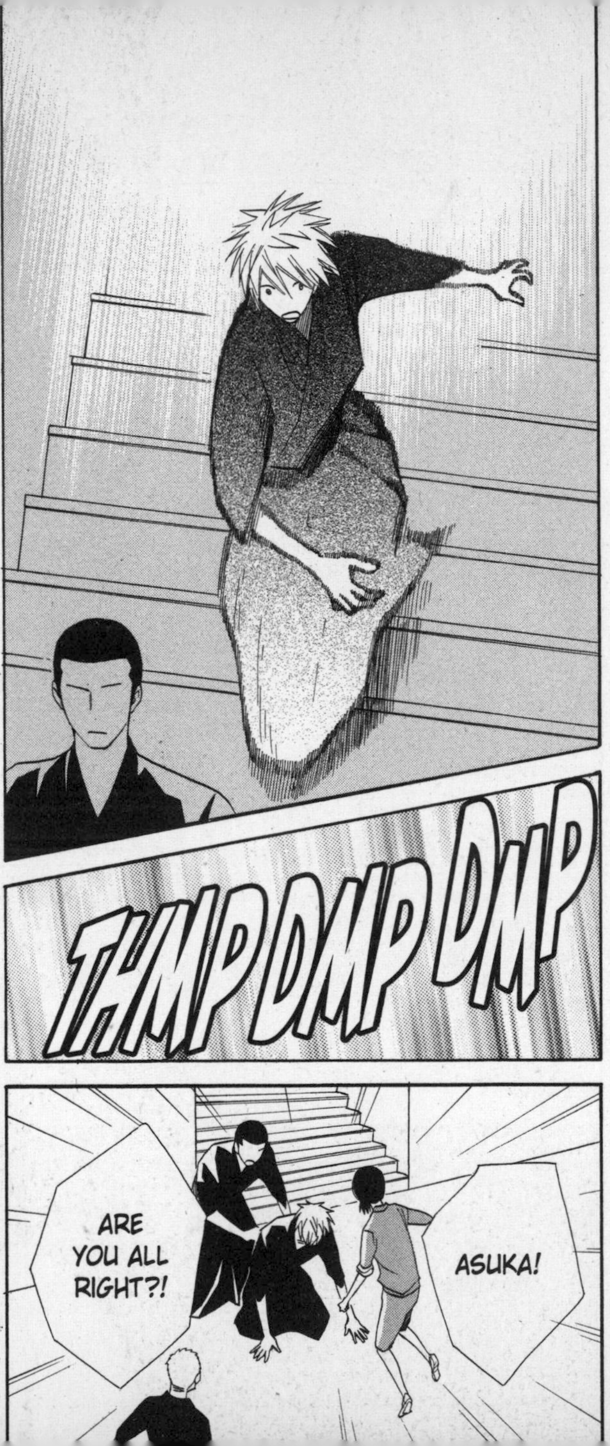
THMP DMP DMP
ASUKA!
ARE YOU ALL RIGHT?!

Oh, horror.
I love scary stories.
I don't completely believe all the numerous stories out there (like photos with ghost images and whatnot), but I like them.
A long time ago, I wanted to draw a horror manga, so I'm enjoying drawing this story.
My apologies to those of you who hate scary stories though.
But this story isn't that scary, is it?
As for those slimy eels that appeared earlier, I think I went a little overboard.
My apologies to those of you who hate slimy things.
But I'm having fun...

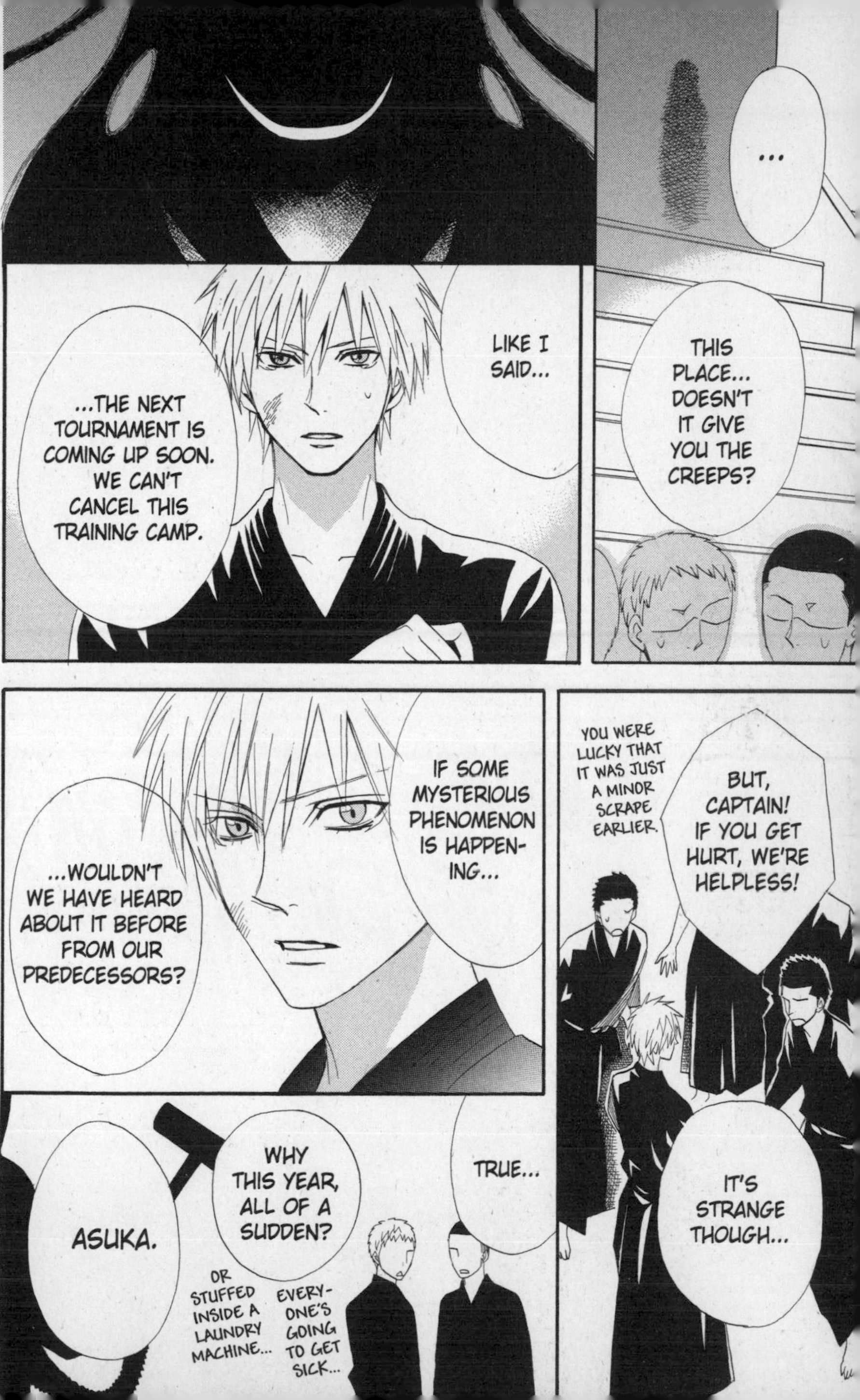
...
THIS PLACE... DOESN'T IT GIVE YOU THE CREEPS?
LIKE I SAID...
...THE NEXT TOURNAMENT IS COMING UP SOON. WE CAN'T CANCEL THIS TRAINING CAMP.
BUT, CAPTAIN! IF YOU GET HURT, WE'RE HELPLESS!
YOU WERE LUCKY THAT IT WAS JUST A MINOR SCRAPE EARLIER.
IT'S STRANGE THOUGH...
IF SOME MYSTERIOUS PHENOMENON IS HAPPEN-ING...
...WOULDN'T WE HAVE HEARD ABOUT IT BEFORE FROM OUR PREDECESSORS?
TRUE...
WHY THIS YEAR, ALL OF A SUDDEN?
EVERY-ONE'S GOING TO GET SICK...
OR STUFFED INSIDE A LAUNDRY MACHINE...
ASUKA.

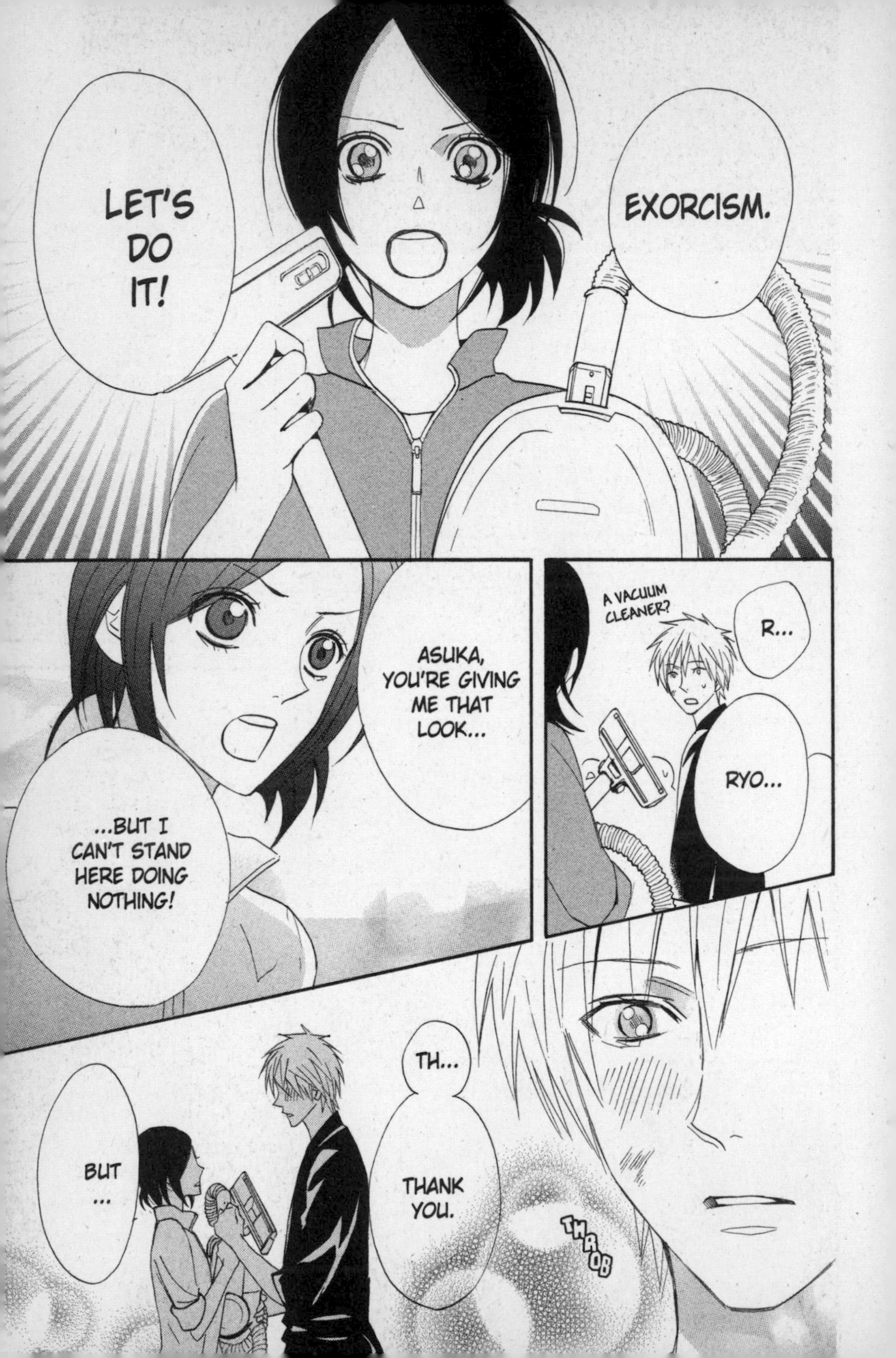
EXORCISM.
LET'S DO IT!
A VACUUM CLEANER?
R...
RYO...
ASUKA, YOU'RE GIVING ME THAT LOOK...
...BUT I CAN'T STAND HERE DOING NOTHING!
THROB
TH...
THANK YOU.
BUT ...

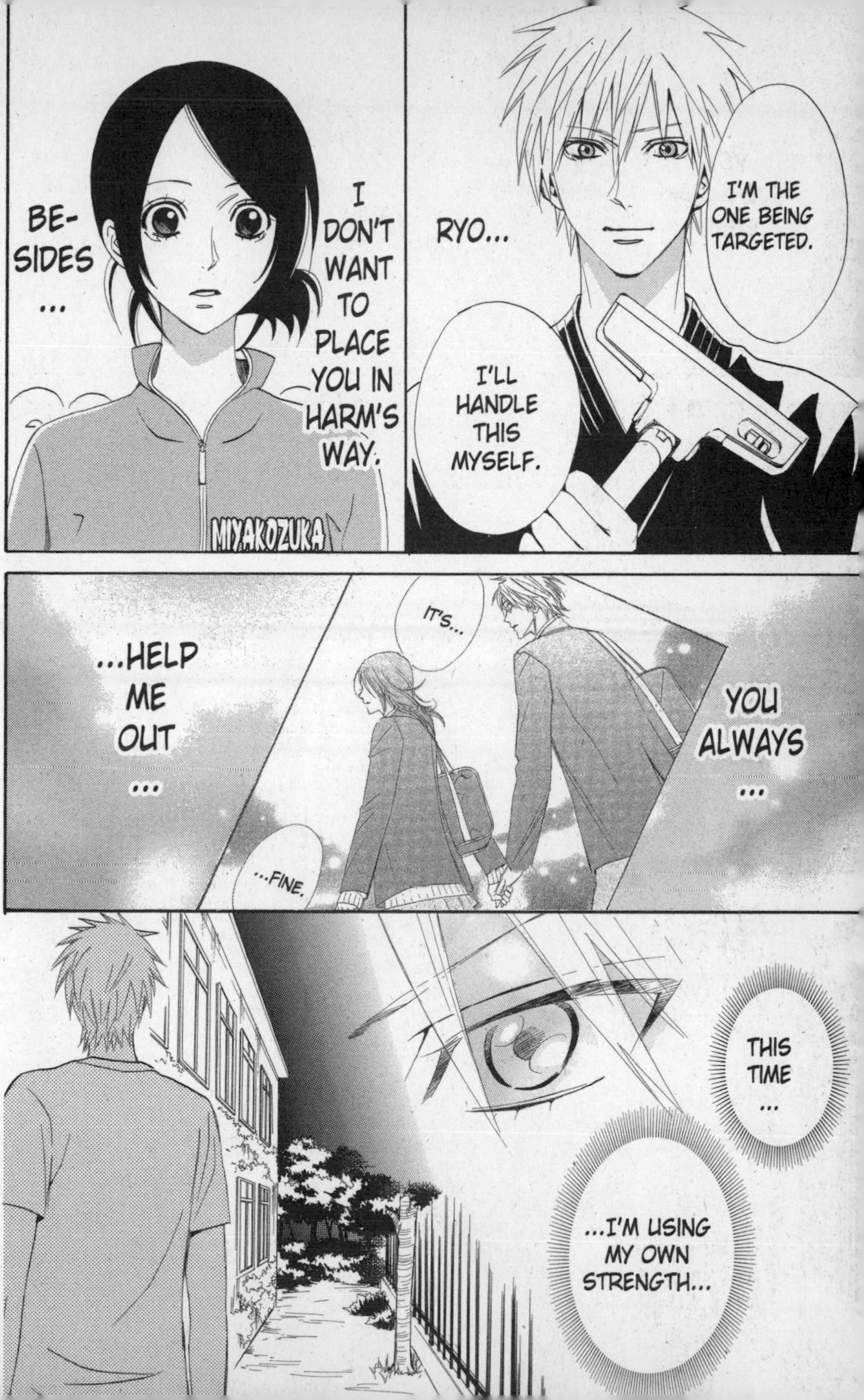
I'M THE ONE BEING TARGETED.
I'LL HANDLE THIS MYSELF.
RYO...
I DON'T WANT TO PLACE YOU IN HARM'S WAY.
BESIDES...
MIYAKOZUKA
YOU ALWAYS...
IT'S...
...FINE.
...HELP ME OUT...
THIS TIME...
...I'M USING MY OWN STRENGTH...

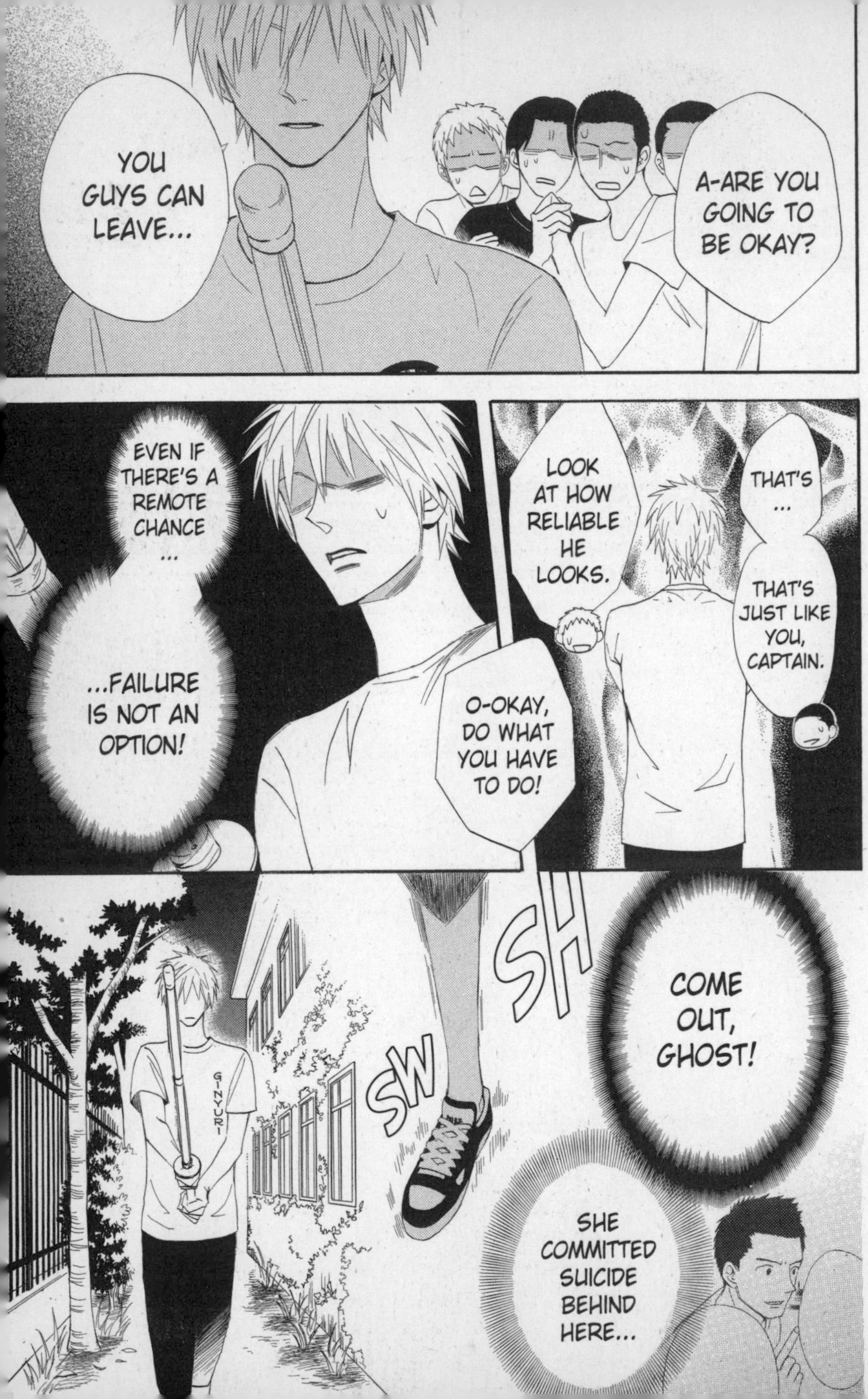
A-ARE YOU GOING TO BE OKAY?
YOU GUYS CAN LEAVE...
LOOK AT HOW RELIABLE HE LOOKS.
THAT'S ...
THAT'S JUST LIKE YOU, CAPTAIN.
O-OKAY, DO WHAT YOU HAVE TO DO!
EVEN IF THERE'S A REMOTE CHANCE ...
...FAILURE IS NOT AN OPTION!
SH
COME OUT, GHOST!
SW
SHE COMMITTED SUICIDE BEHIND HERE...
GINYURI

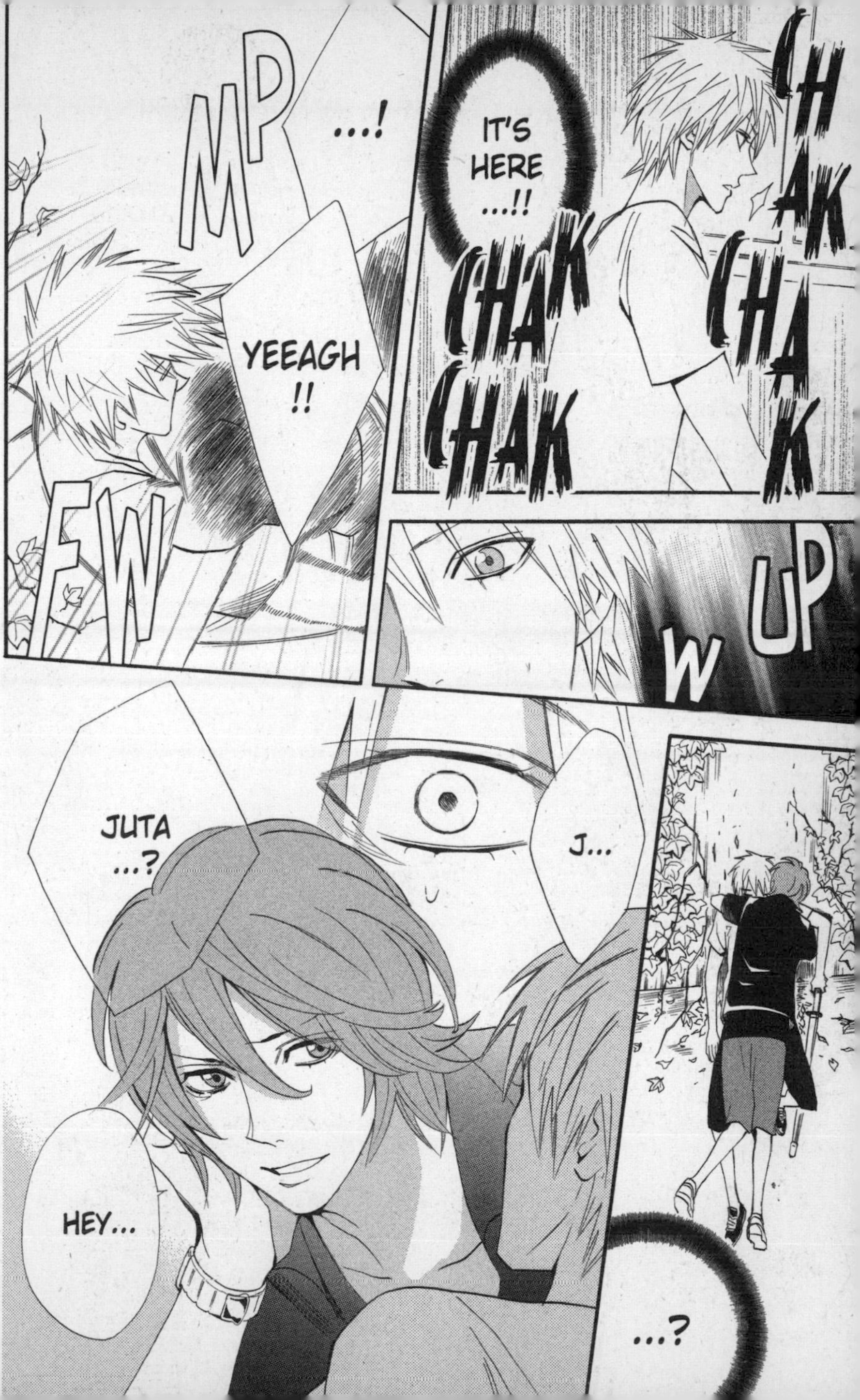
CHAK CHAK
IT'S HERE ...!!
CHAK CHAK
UP
W
...!
MP
YEEAGH !!
FW
...?
J...
JUTA ...?
HEY...

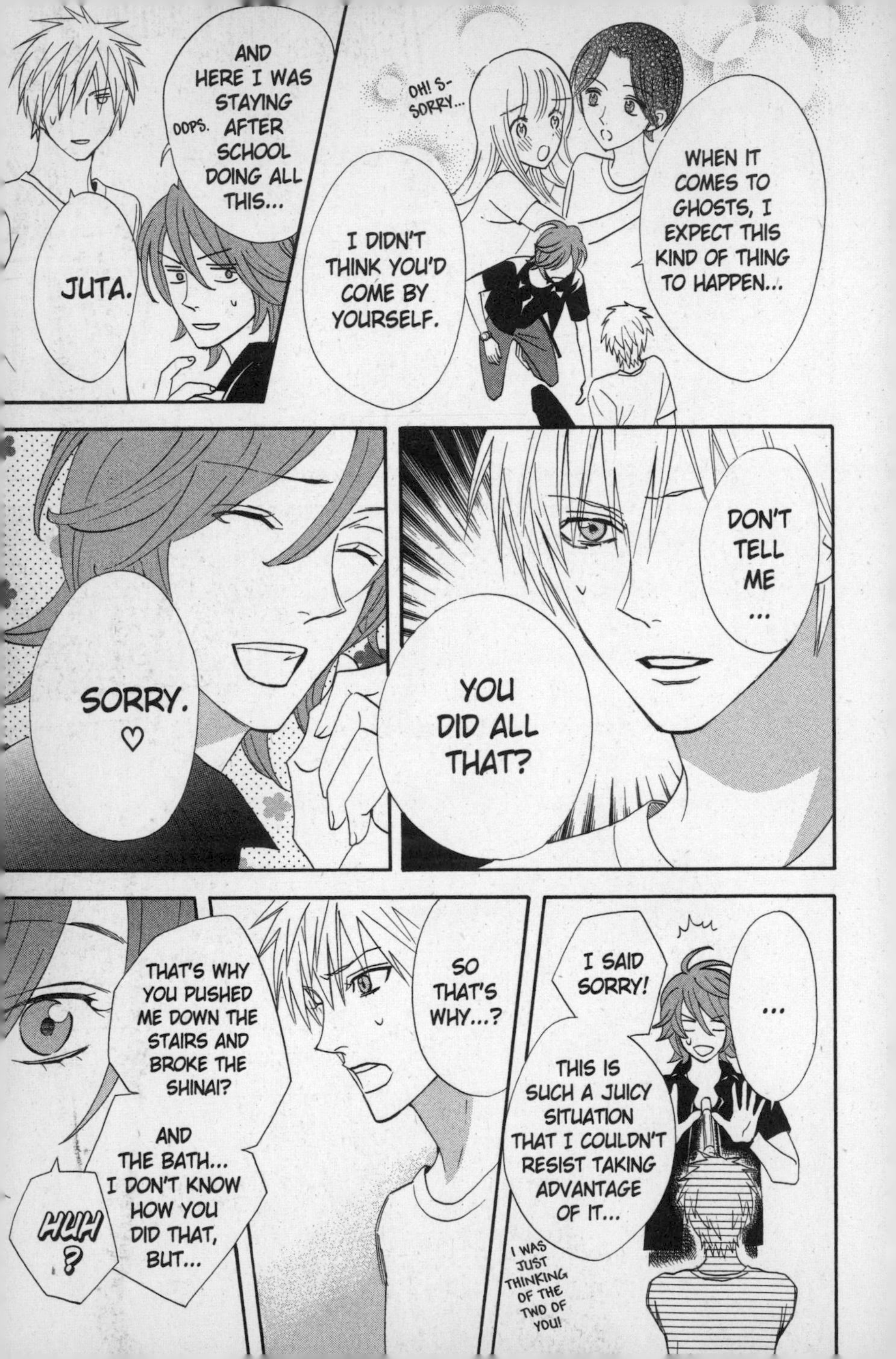
OH! S-SORRY...
WHEN IT COMES TO GHOSTS, I EXPECT THIS KIND OF THING TO HAPPEN...
I DIDN'T THINK YOU'D COME BY YOURSELF.
AND HERE I WAS STAYING AFTER SCHOOL DOING ALL THIS...
OOPS.
JUTA.
DON'T TELL ME ...
YOU DID ALL THAT?
SORRY. ♡
...
I SAID SORRY!
THIS IS SUCH A JUICY SITUATION THAT I COULDN'T RESIST TAKING ADVANTAGE OF IT...
I WAS JUST THINKING OF THE TWO OF YOU!
SO THAT'S WHY...?
THAT'S WHY YOU PUSHED ME DOWN THE STAIRS AND BROKE THE SHINAI?
AND THE BATH... I DON'T KNOW HOW YOU DID THAT, BUT...
HUH ?

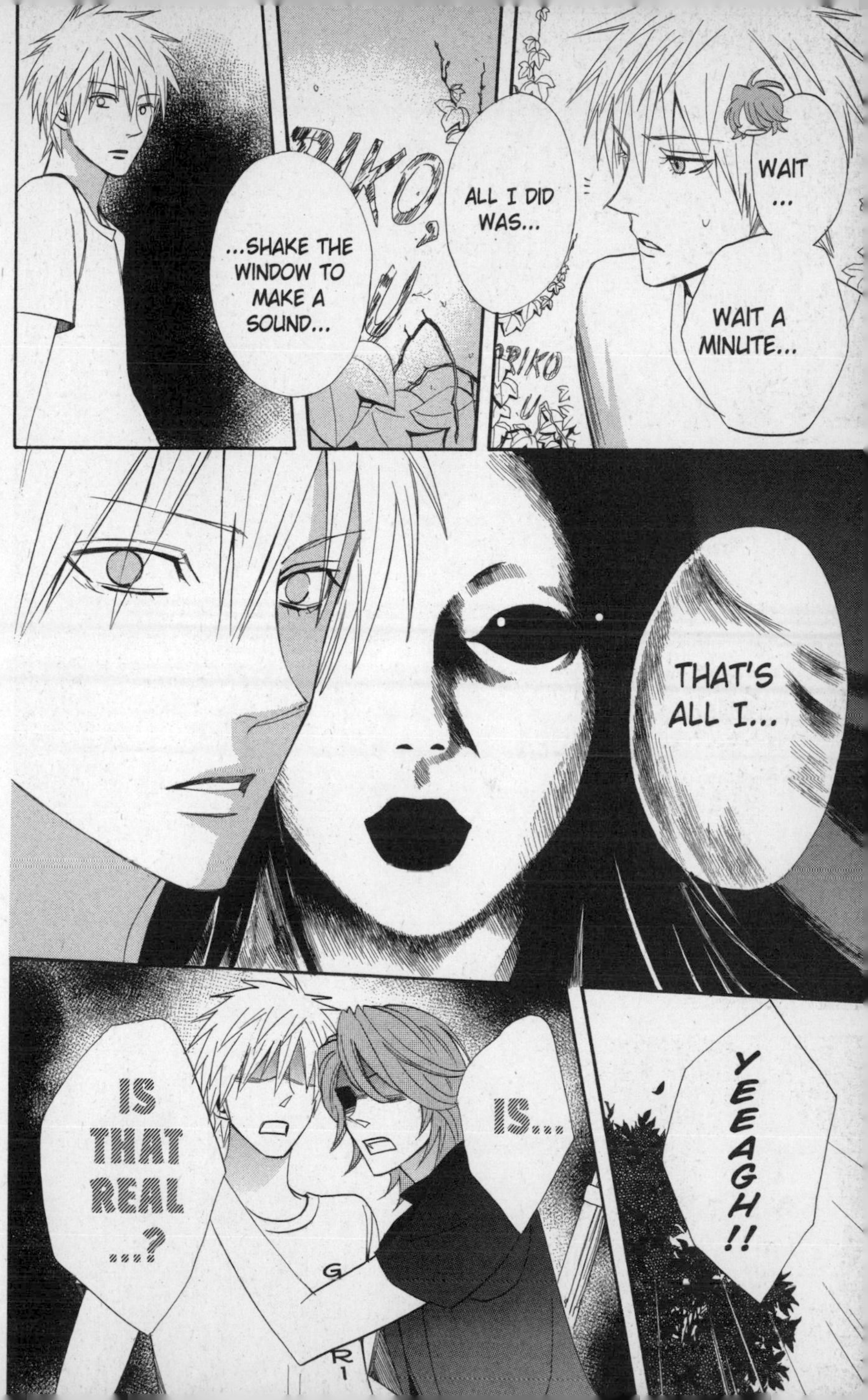
WAIT ...
WAIT A MINUTE...
ALL I DID WAS...
...SHAKE THE WINDOW TO MAKE A SOUND...
THAT'S ALL I...
YEEAGH!!
IS...
IS THAT REAL ...?

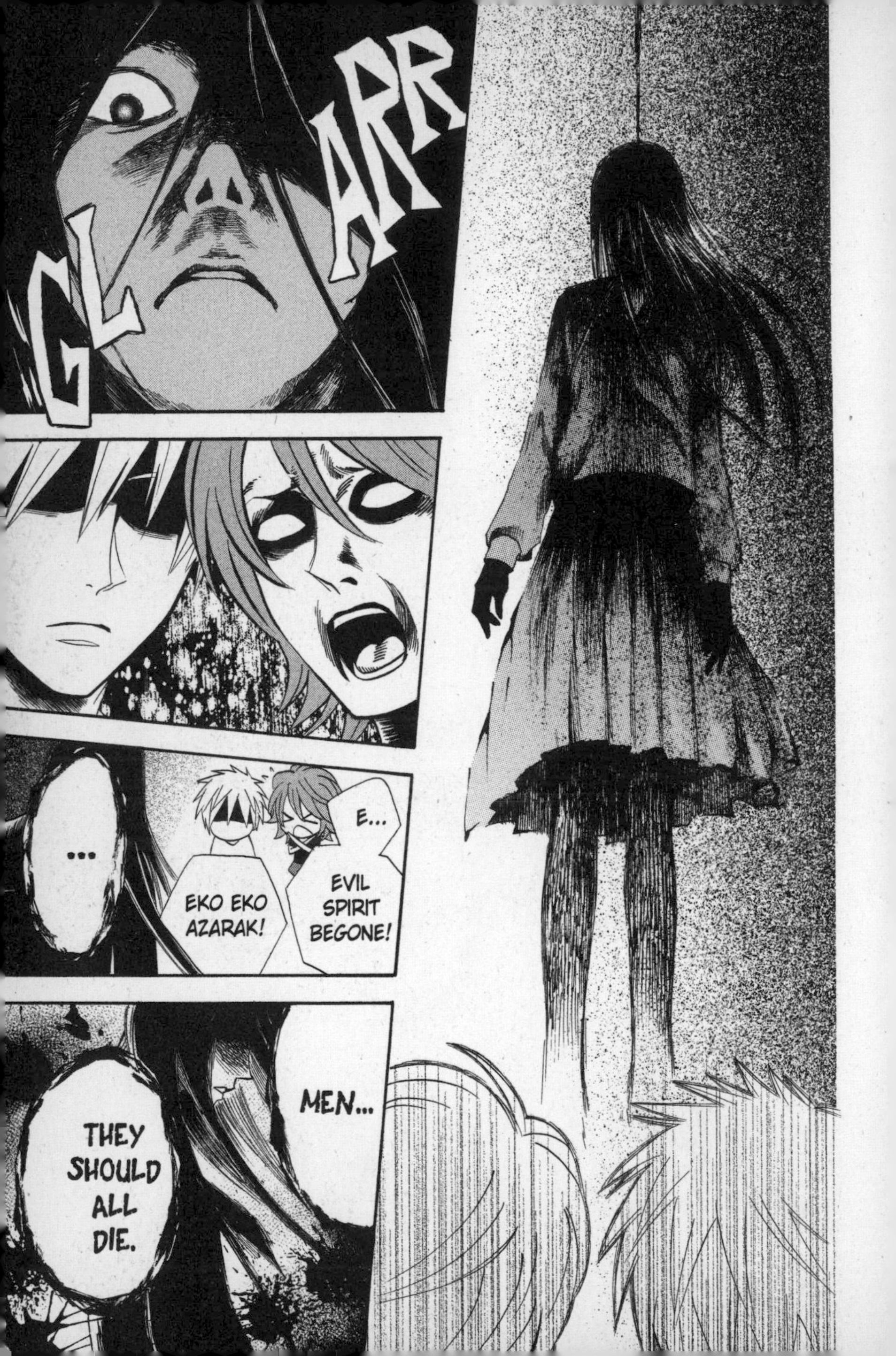
GLARR
E...
EVIL SPIRIT BEGONE!
EKO EKO AZARAK!
...
MEN...
THEY SHOULD ALL DIE.

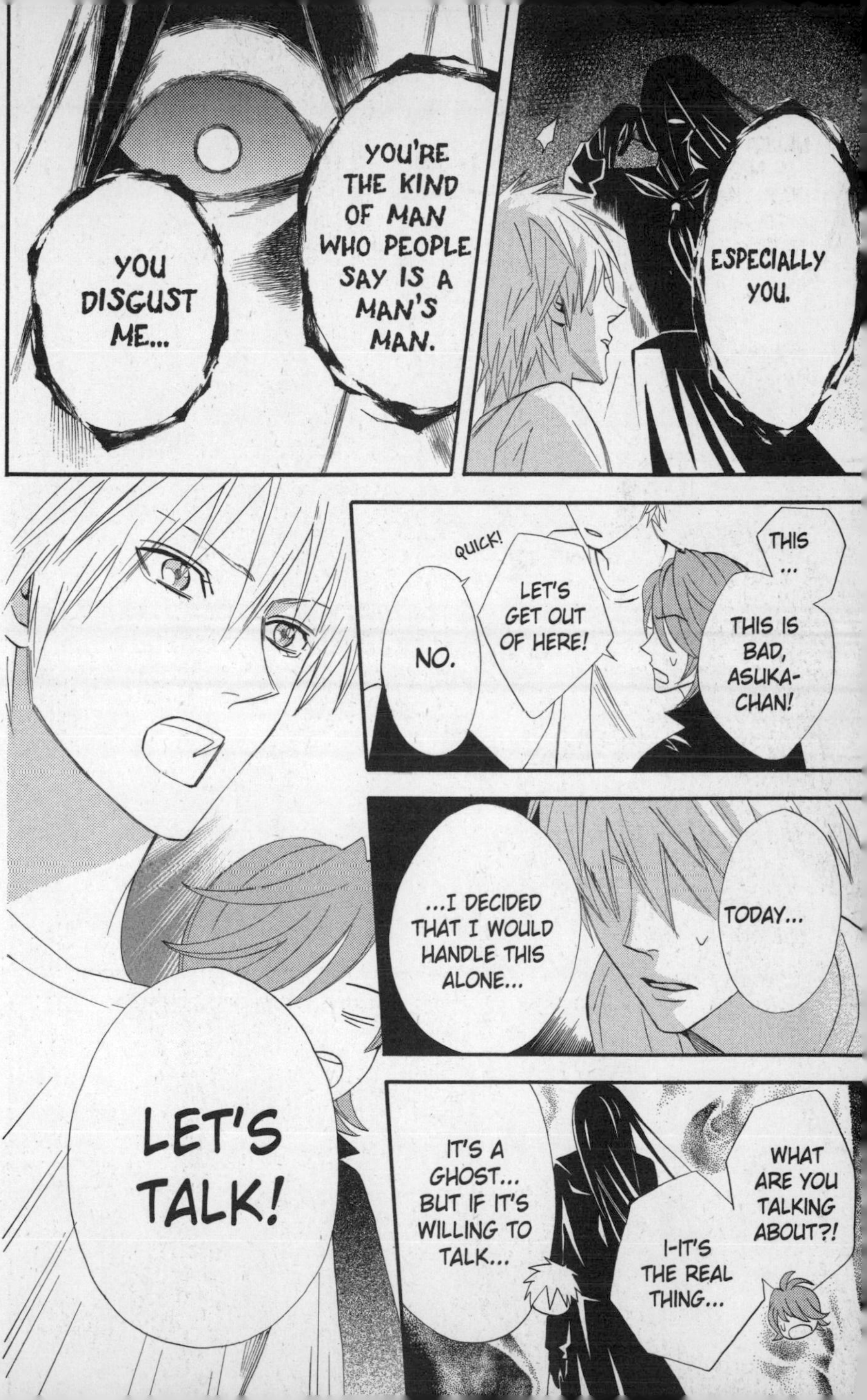
ESPECIALLY YOU.
YOU'RE THE KIND OF MAN WHO PEOPLE SAY IS A MAN'S MAN.
YOU DISGUST ME...
THIS ...
THIS IS BAD, ASUKA-CHAN!
LET'S GET OUT OF HERE!
QUICK!
NO.
TODAY...
...I DECIDED THAT I WOULD HANDLE THIS ALONE...
WHAT ARE YOU TALKING ABOUT?!
I-IT'S THE REAL THING...
IT'S A GHOST... BUT IF IT'S WILLING TO TALK...
LET'S TALK!

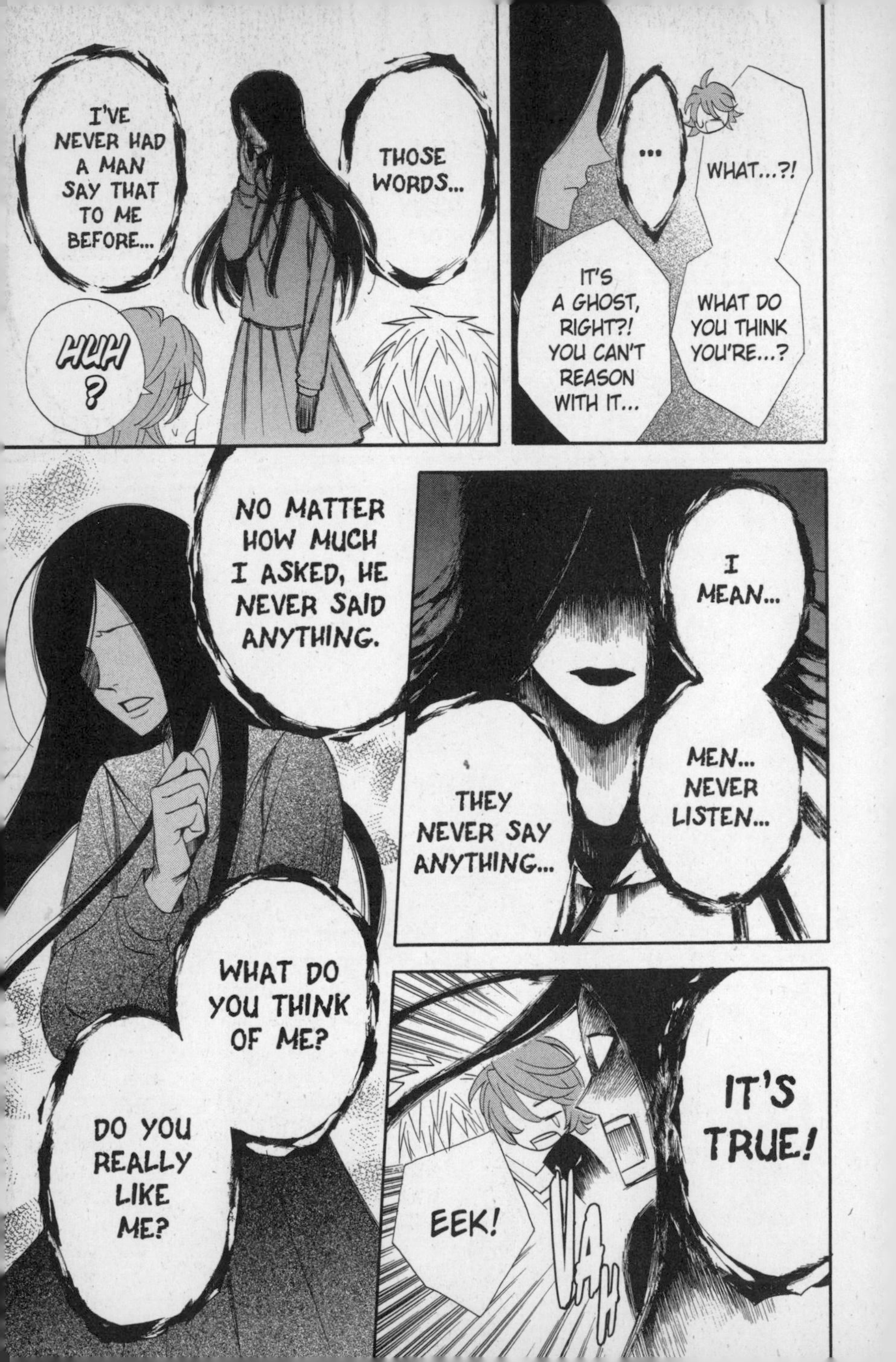
WHAT...?!
...
WHAT DO YOU THINK YOU'RE...?
IT'S A GHOST, RIGHT?! YOU CAN'T REASON WITH IT...
THOSE WORDS...
I'VE NEVER HAD A MAN SAY THAT TO ME BEFORE...
HUH?
I MEAN...
MEN... NEVER LISTEN...
THEY NEVER SAY ANYTHING...
IT'S TRUE!
EEK!
VAH
NO MATTER HOW MUCH I ASKED, HE NEVER SAID ANYTHING.
WHAT DO YOU THINK OF ME?
DO YOU REALLY LIKE ME?

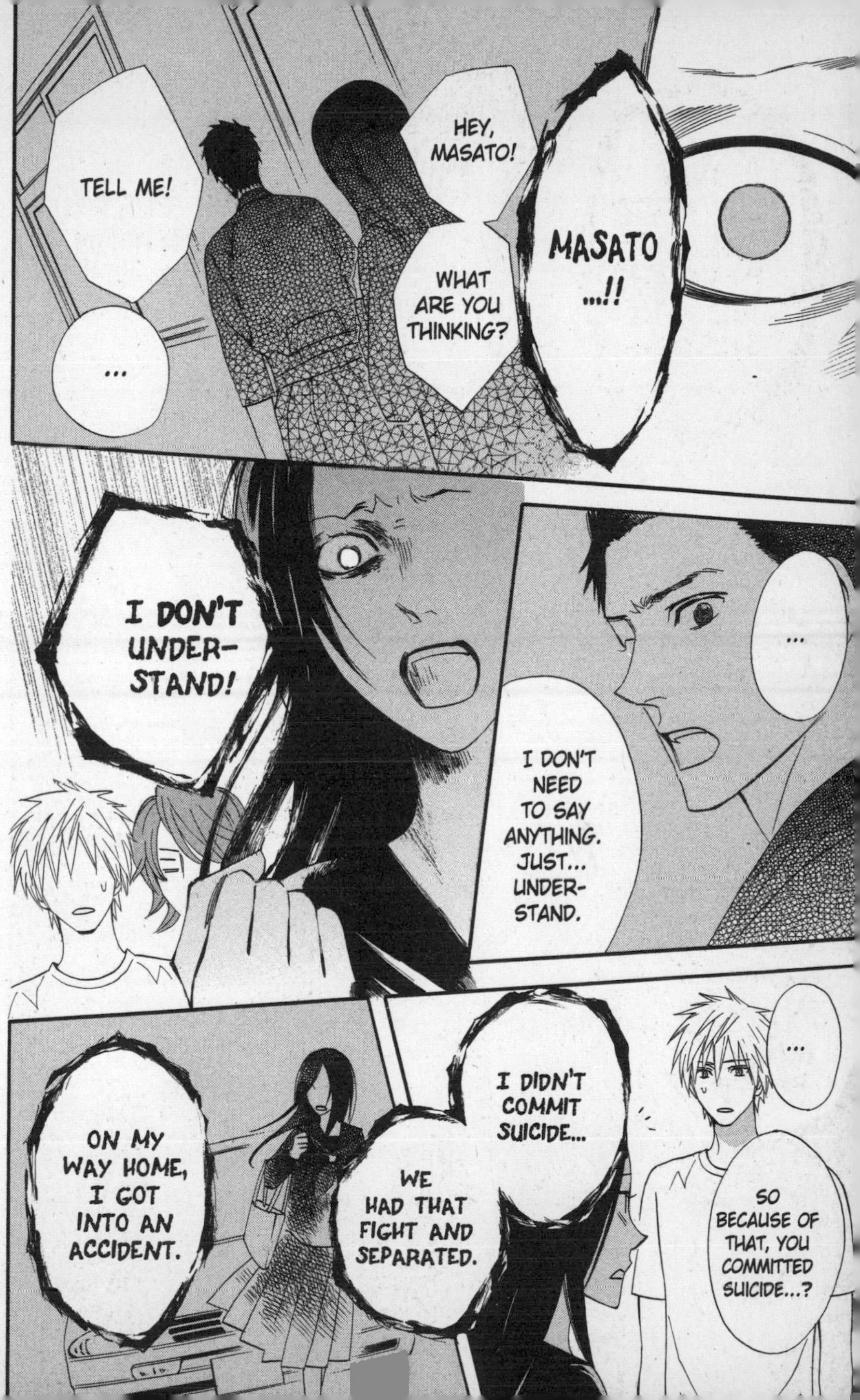
MASATO ...!!
HEY, MASATO!
WHAT ARE YOU THINKING?
TELL ME!
...
...
I DON'T NEED TO SAY ANYTHING. JUST... UNDER-STAND.
I DON'T UNDER-STAND!
...
SO BECAUSE OF THAT, YOU COMMITTED SUICIDE...?
I DIDN'T COMMIT SUICIDE...
WE HAD THAT FIGHT AND SEPARATED.
ON MY WAY HOME, I GOT INTO AN ACCIDENT.

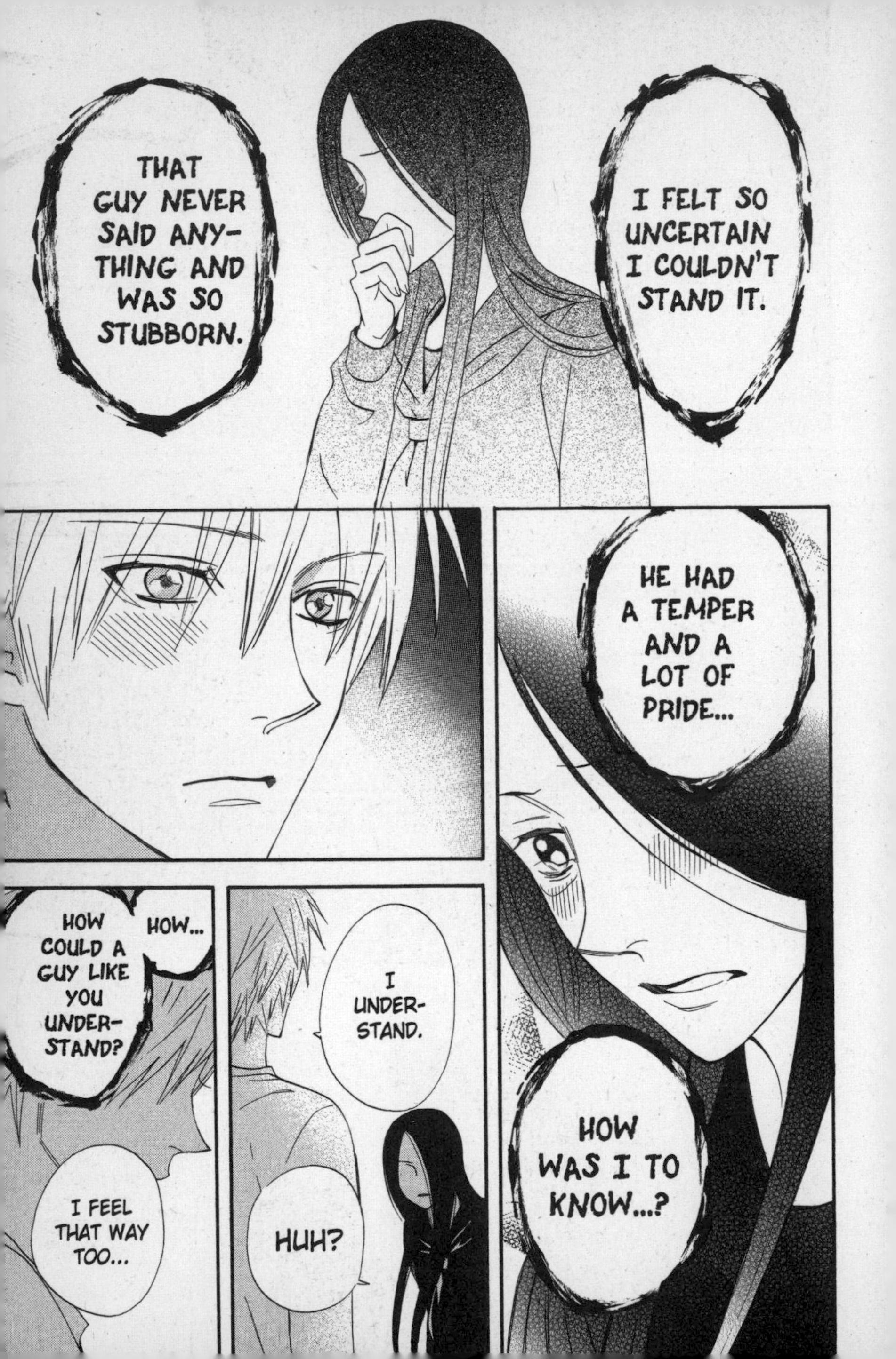
I FELT SO UNCERTAIN I COULDN'T STAND IT.
THAT GUY NEVER SAID ANY-THING AND WAS SO STUBBORN.
HE HAD A TEMPER AND A LOT OF PRIDE...
HOW WAS I TO KNOW...?
I UNDER-STAND.
HUH?
HOW...
HOW COULD A GUY LIKE YOU UNDER-STAND?
I FEEL THAT WAY TOO...

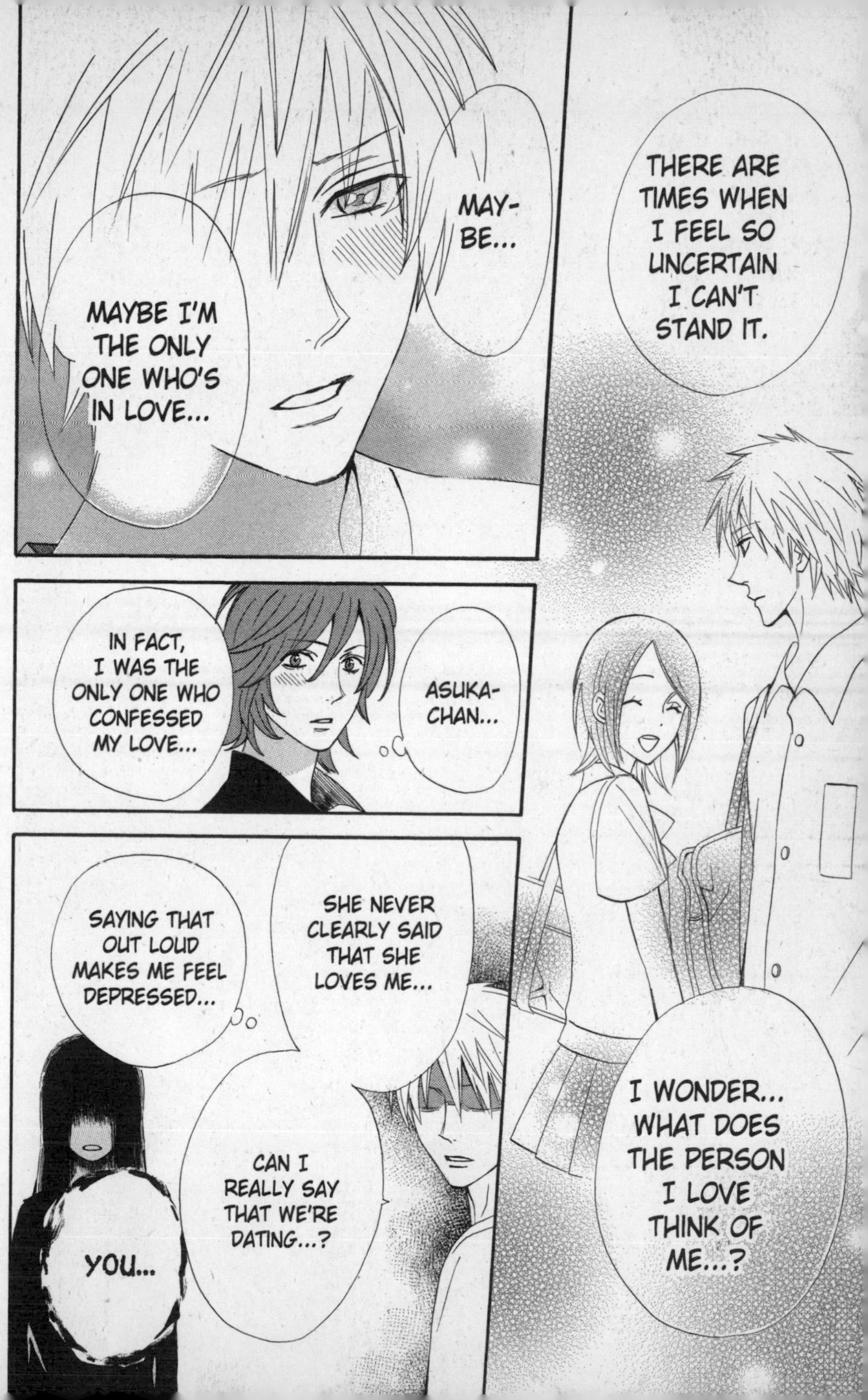
THERE ARE TIMES WHEN I FEEL SO UNCERTAIN I CAN'T STAND IT.
I WONDER... WHAT DOES THE PERSON I LOVE THINK OF ME...?
MAY-BE...
MAYBE I'M THE ONLY ONE WHO'S IN LOVE...
ASUKA-CHAN...
IN FACT, I WAS THE ONLY ONE WHO CONFESSED MY LOVE...
SHE NEVER CLEARLY SAID THAT SHE LOVES ME...
SAYING THAT OUT LOUD MAKES ME FEEL DEPRESSED...
CAN I REALLY SAY THAT WE'RE DATING...?
YOU...

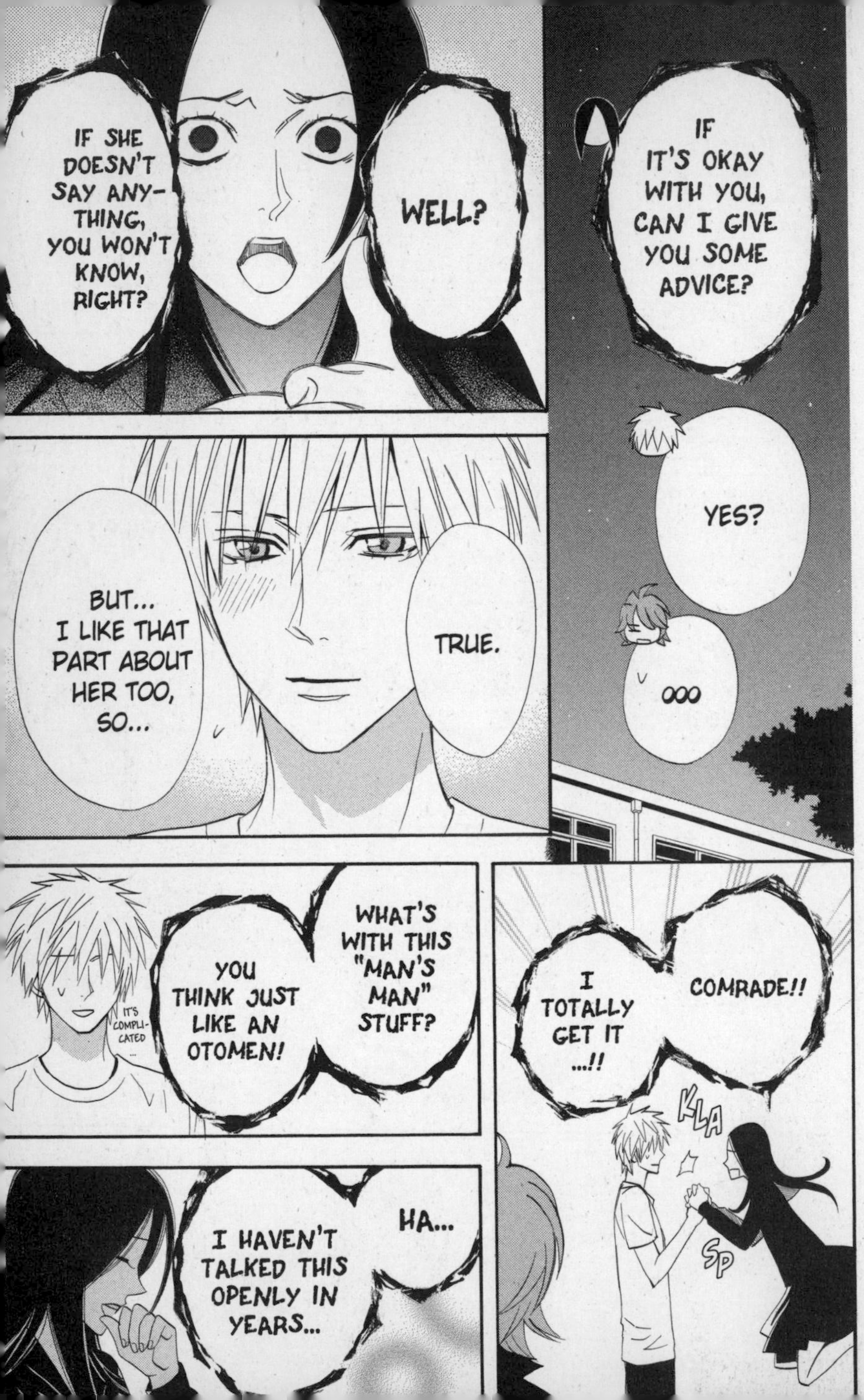
IF IT'S OKAY WITH YOU, CAN I GIVE YOU SOME ADVICE?
YES?
OOO
WELL?
IF SHE DOESN'T SAY ANY-THING, YOU WON'T KNOW, RIGHT?
TRUE.
BUT... I LIKE THAT PART ABOUT HER TOO, SO...
COMRADE!!
I TOTALLY GET IT ...!!
KLA
SP
WHAT'S WITH THIS "MAN'S MAN" STUFF?
YOU THINK JUST LIKE AN OTOMEN!
IT'S COMPLICATED ...
HA...
I HAVEN'T TALKED THIS OPENLY IN YEARS...

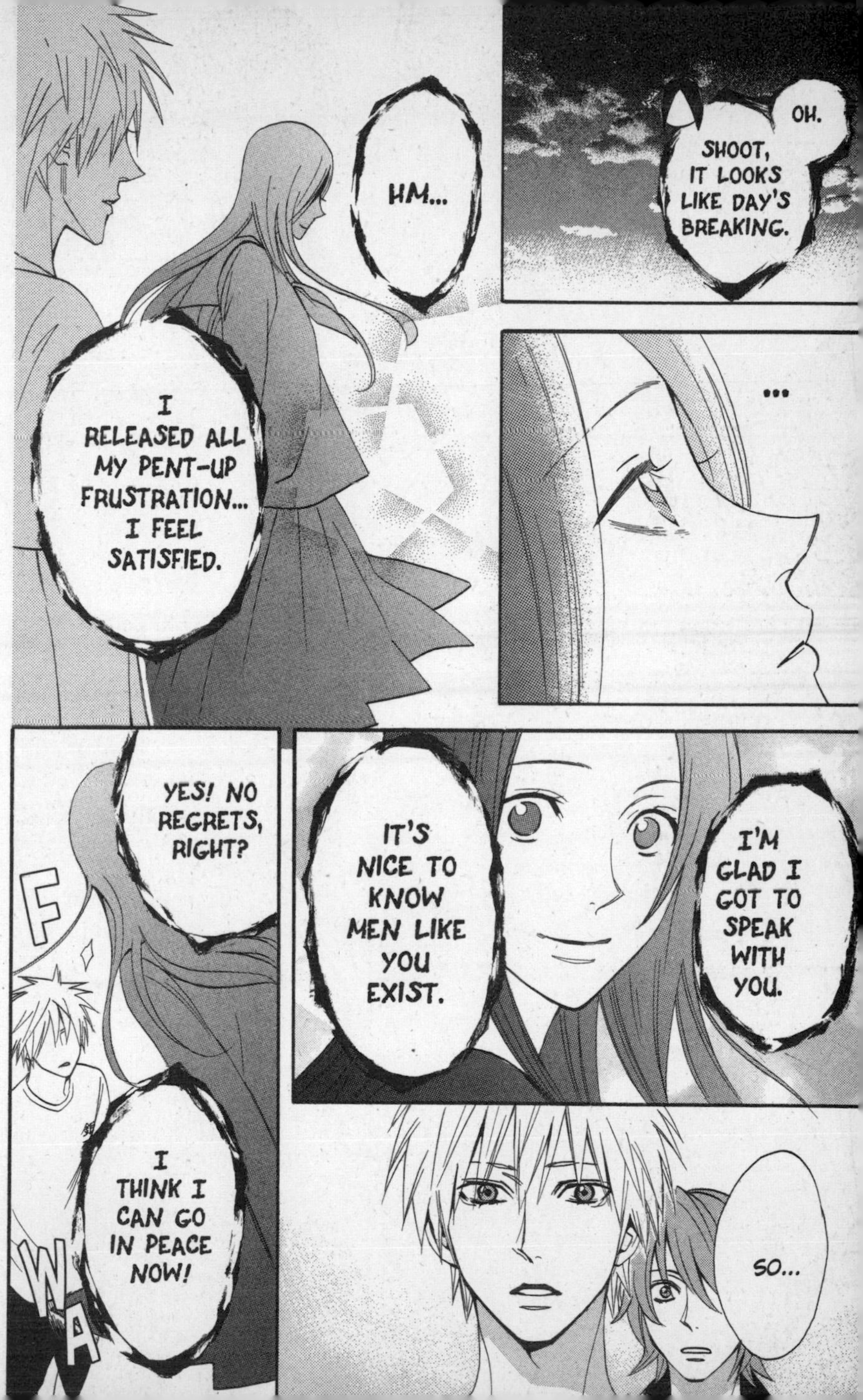
OH.
SHOOT, IT LOOKS LIKE DAY'S BREAKING.
...
HM...
I RELEASED ALL MY PENT-UP FRUSTRATION... I FEEL SATISFIED.
I'M GLAD I GOT TO SPEAK WITH YOU.
IT'S NICE TO KNOW MEN LIKE YOU EXIST.
SO...
YES! NO REGRETS, RIGHT?
F
I THINK I CAN GO IN PEACE NOW!
WAA

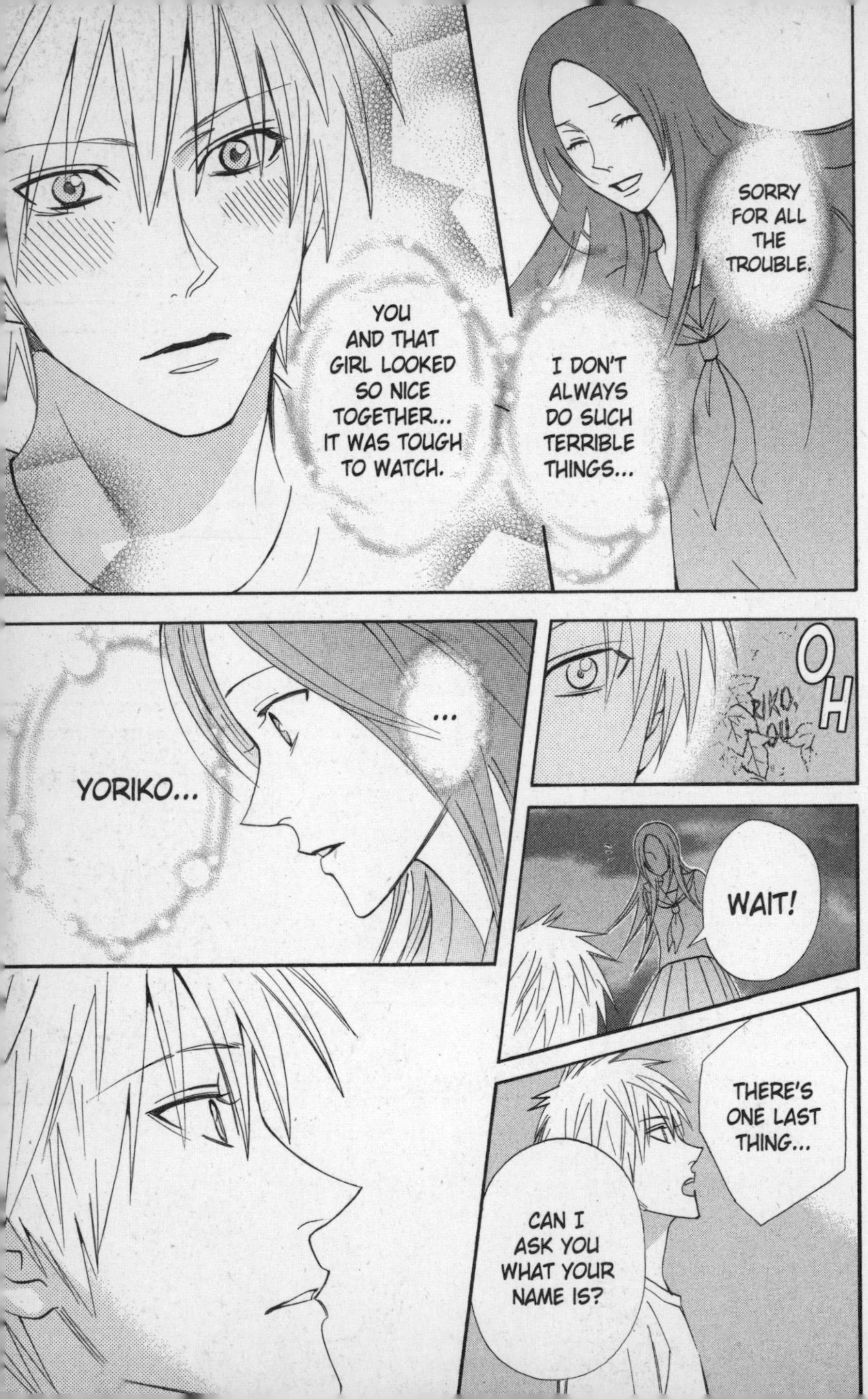
SORRY FOR ALL THE TROUBLE.
I DON'T ALWAYS DO SUCH TERRIBLE THINGS...
YOU AND THAT GIRL LOOKED SO NICE TOGETHER... IT WAS TOUGH TO WATCH.
OH
...
YORIKO...
WAIT!
THERE'S ONE LAST THING...
CAN I ASK YOU WHAT YOUR NAME IS?

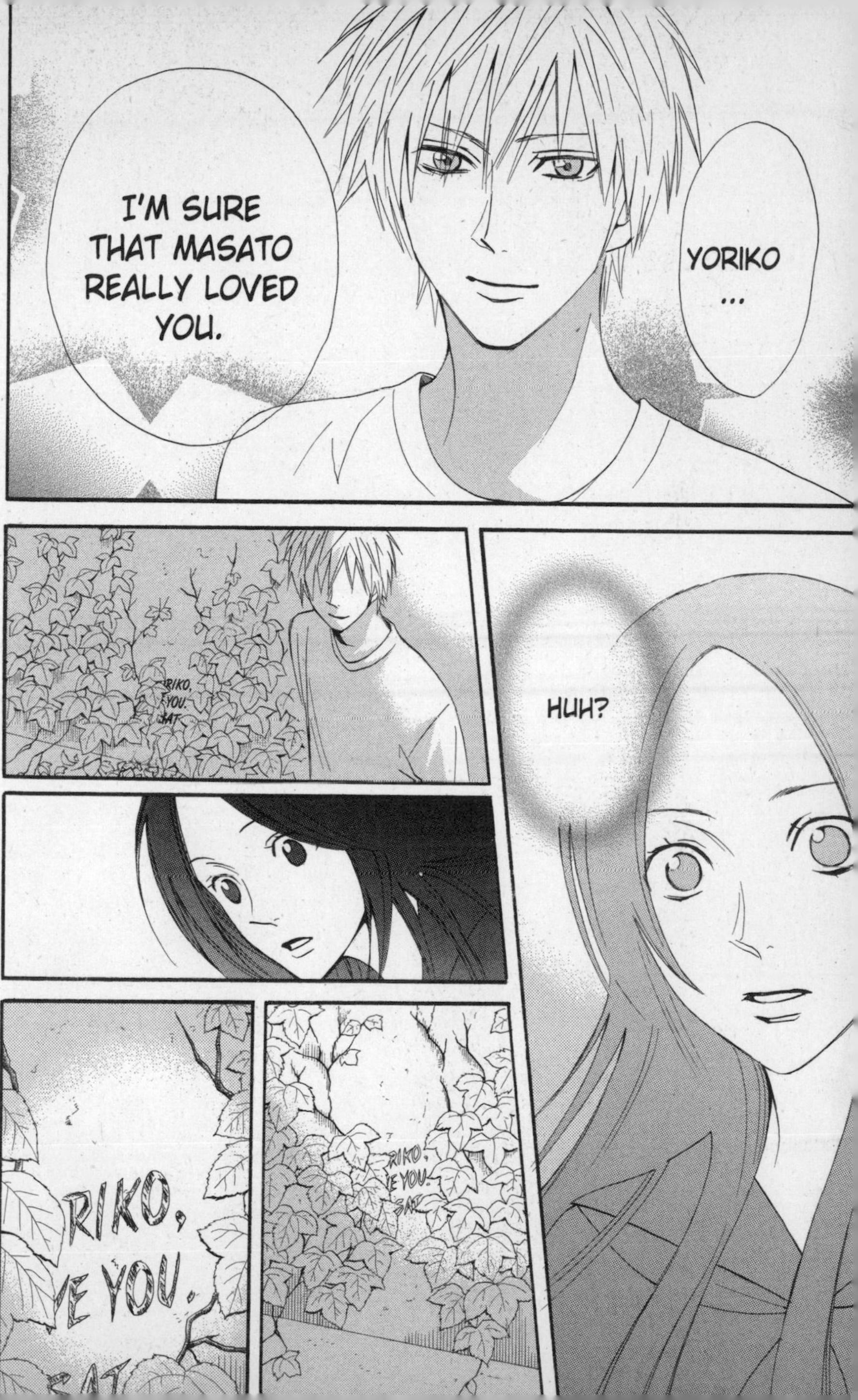
YORIKO ...
I'M SURE THAT MASATO REALLY LOVED YOU.
HUH?
RIKO,
E YOU.

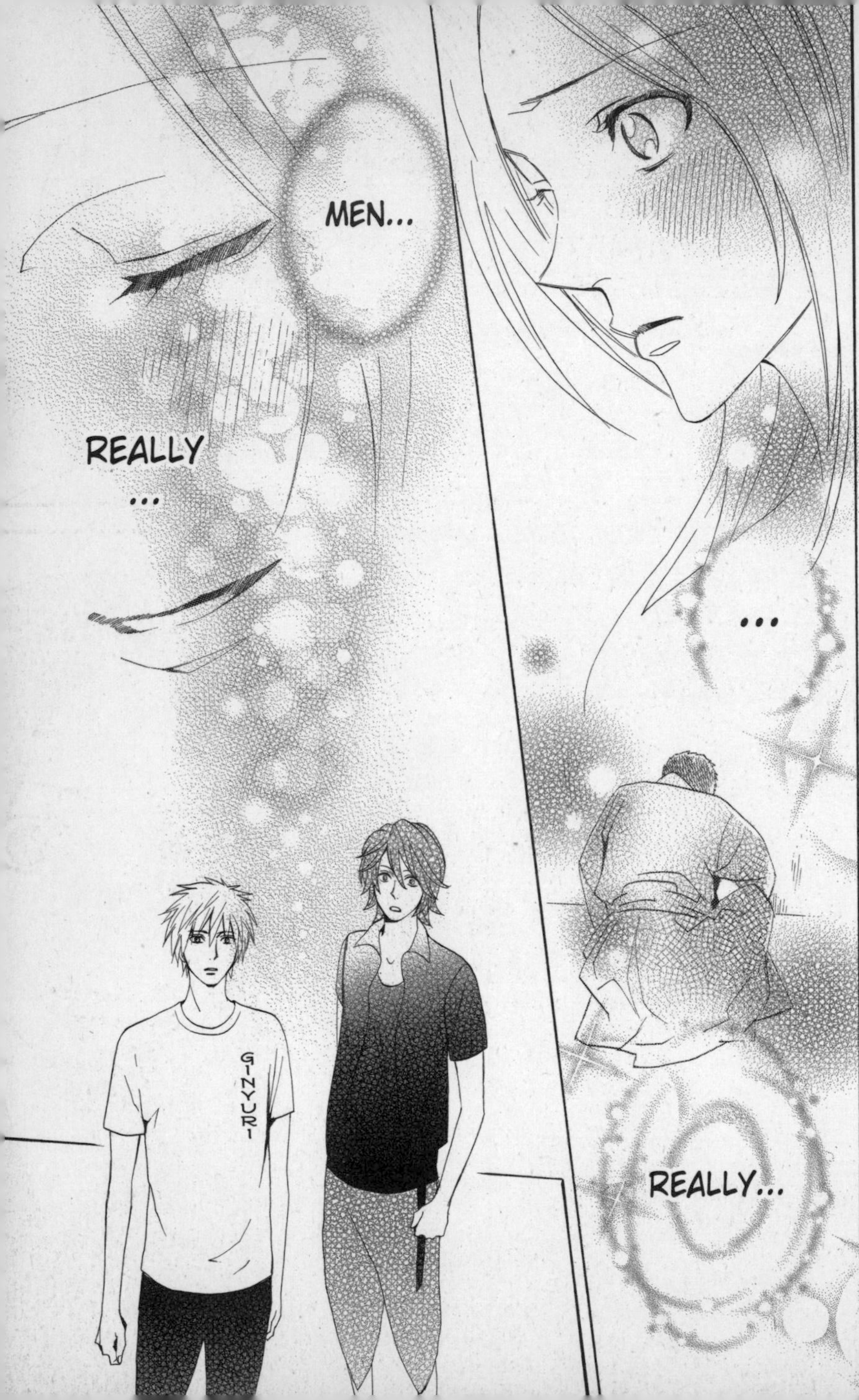
...
REALLY...
MEN...
REALLY ...
GINYURI

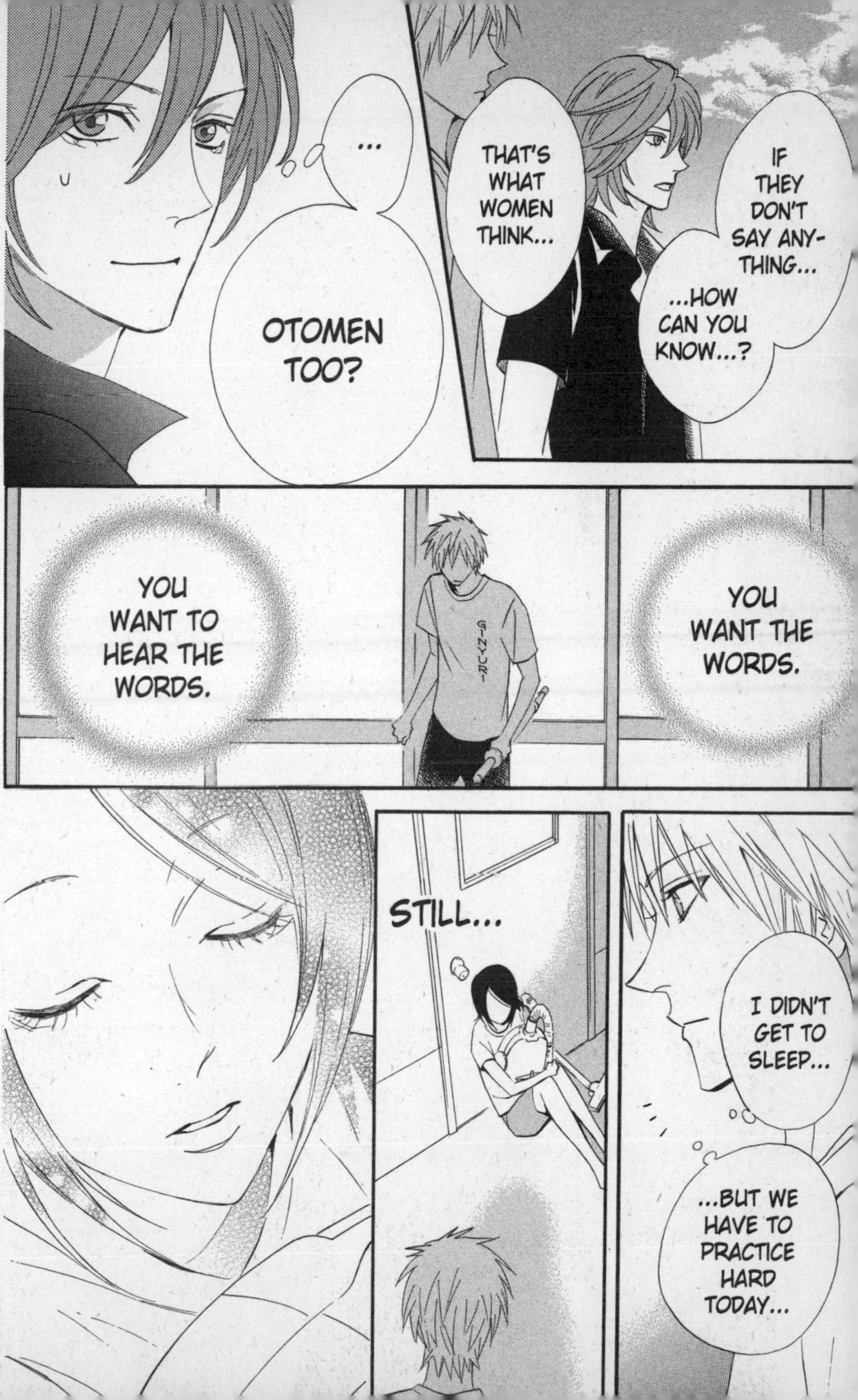
IF THEY DON'T SAY ANYTHING...
...HOW CAN YOU KNOW...?
THAT'S WHAT WOMEN THINK...
...
OTOMEN TOO?
YOU WANT THE WORDS.
GINYURI
YOU WANT TO HEAR THE WORDS.
I DIDN'T GET TO SLEEP...
...BUT WE HAVE TO PRACTICE HARD TODAY...
STILL...

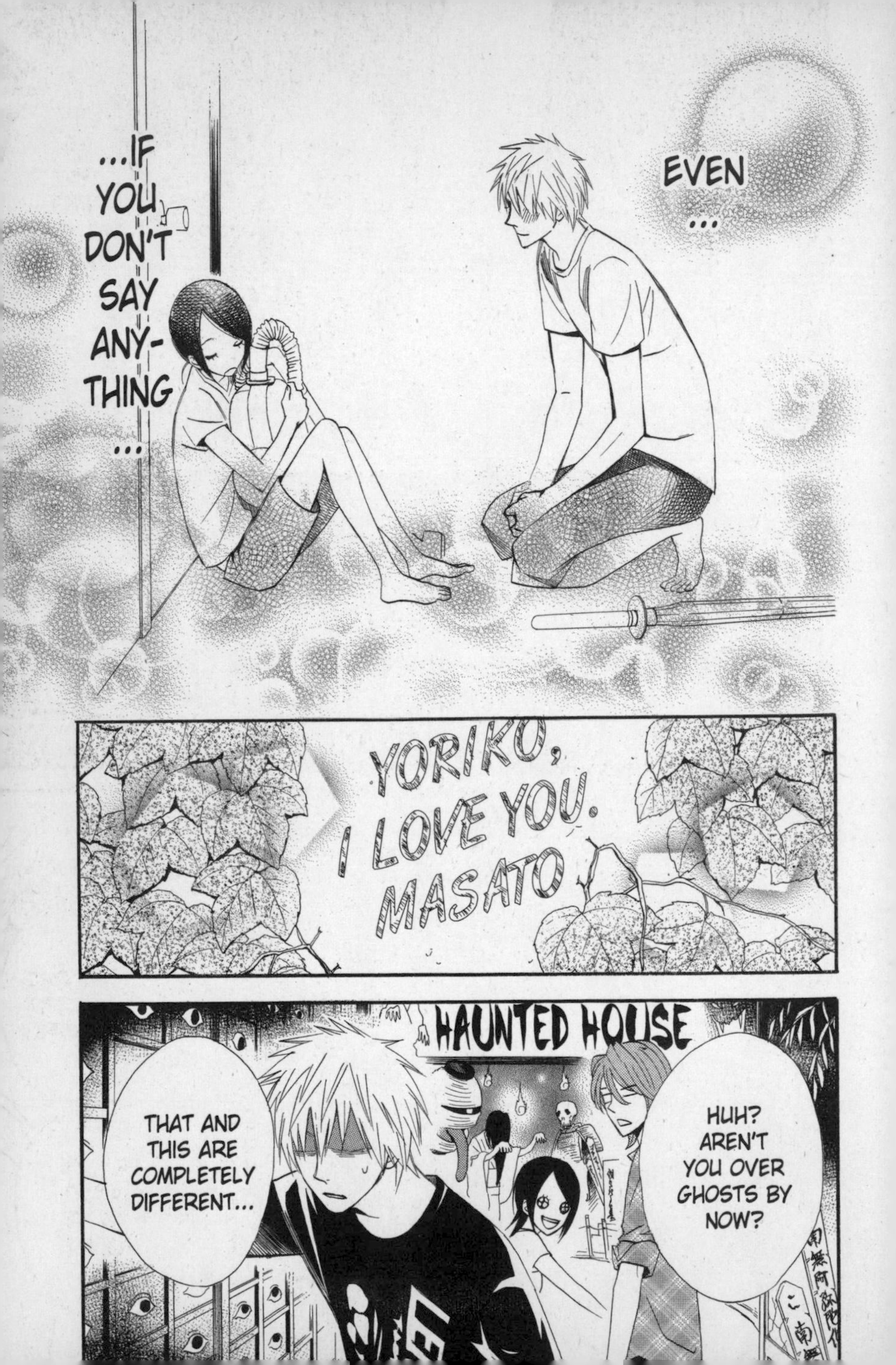
EVEN ...
...IF YOU DON'T SAY ANYTHING ...
YORIKO, I LOVE YOU. MASATO
HAUNTED HOUSE
HUH? AREN'T YOU OVER GHOSTS BY NOW?
THAT AND THIS ARE COMPLETELY DIFFERENT...

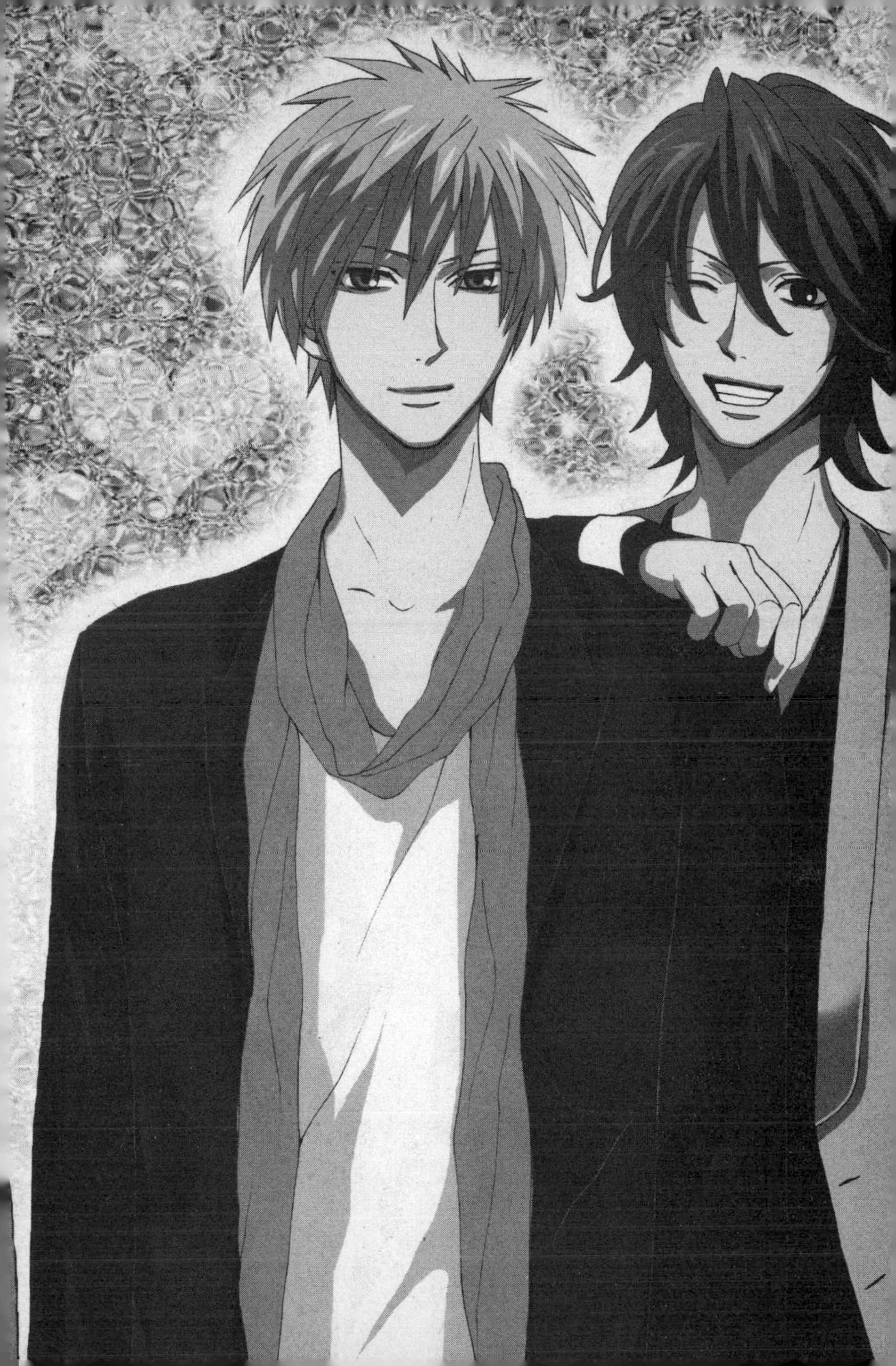

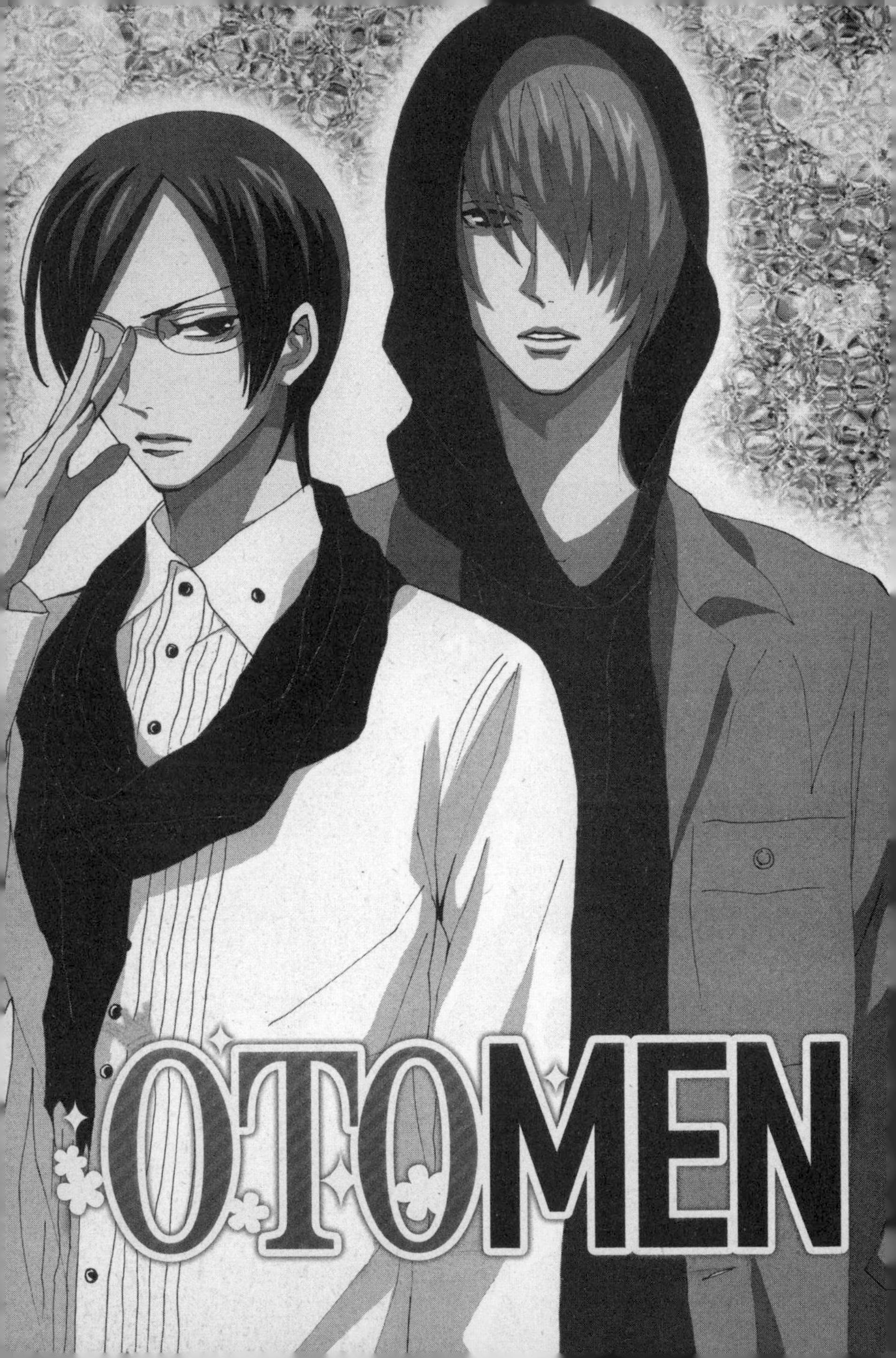
OTOMEN

OTOMEN

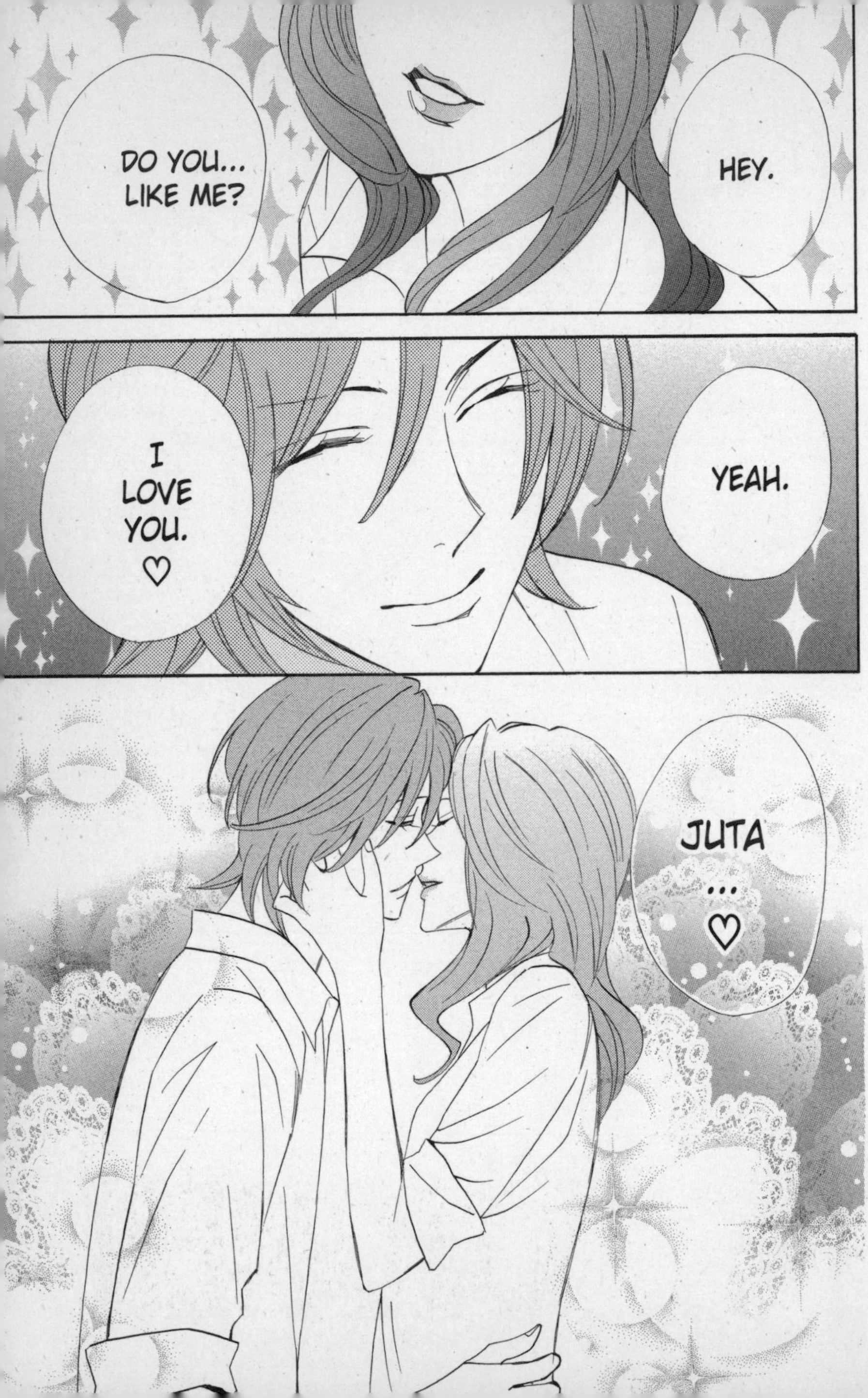
HEY.
DO YOU... LIKE ME?
YEAH.
I LOVE YOU. ♡
JUTA ... ♡

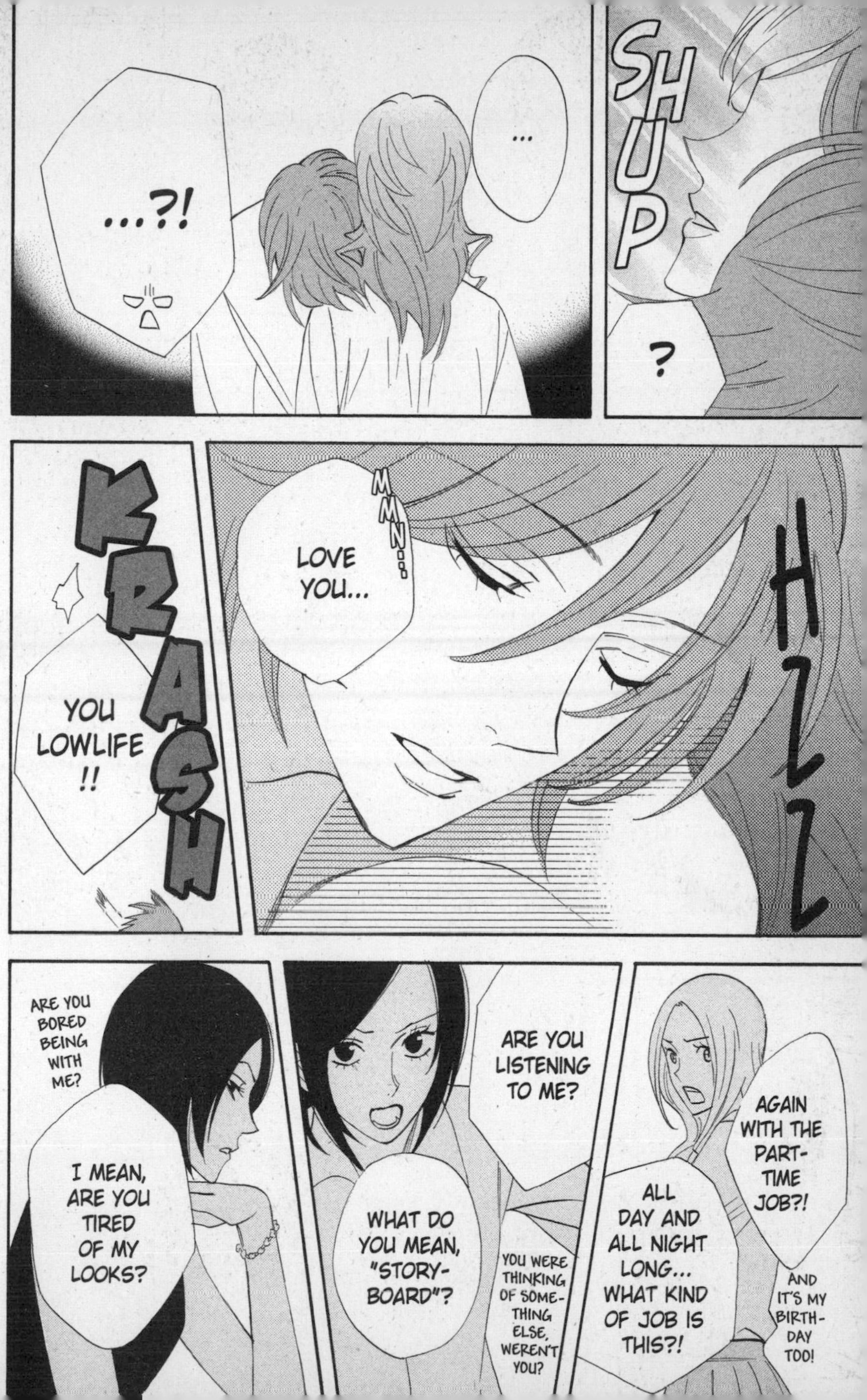
SHUP
?
...
...?!
HZZZ
MMN...
LOVE YOU...
KRASH
YOU LOWLIFE!!
AGAIN WITH THE PART-TIME JOB?!
AND IT'S MY BIRTHDAY TOO!
ALL DAY AND ALL NIGHT LONG... WHAT KIND OF JOB IS THIS?!
ARE YOU LISTENING TO ME?
YOU WERE THINKING OF SOMETHING ELSE, WEREN'T YOU?
WHAT DO YOU MEAN, "STORYBOARD"?
ARE YOU BORED BEING WITH ME?
I MEAN, ARE YOU TIRED OF MY LOOKS?

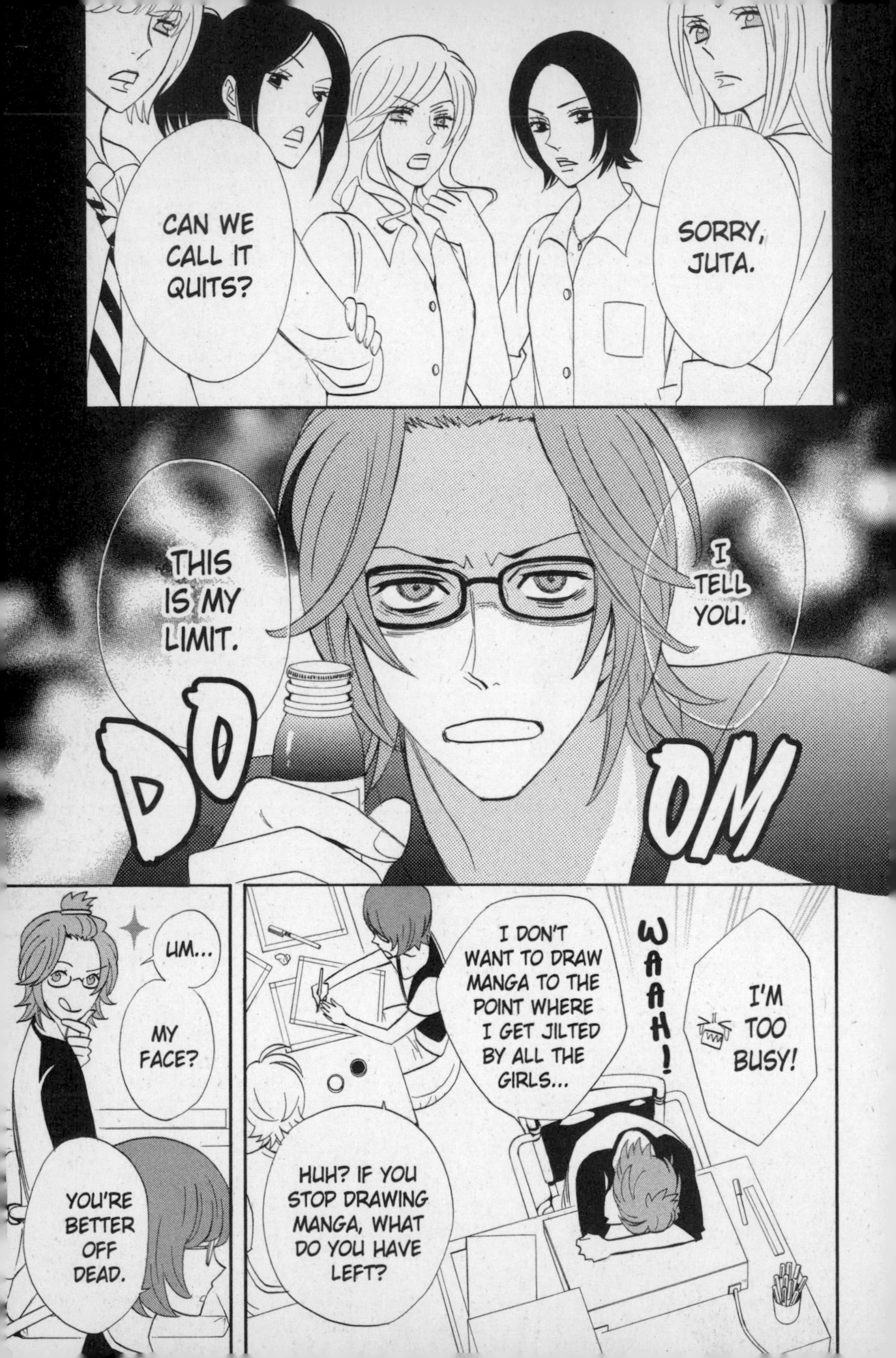
SORRY, JUTA.
CAN WE CALL IT QUITS?
I TELL YOU.
THIS IS MY LIMIT.
DOOM
I'M TOO BUSY!
WAAH!
I DON'T WANT TO DRAW MANGA TO THE POINT WHERE I GET JILTED BY ALL THE GIRLS...
HUH? IF YOU STOP DRAWING MANGA, WHAT DO YOU HAVE LEFT?
UM...
MY FACE?
YOU'RE BETTER OFF DEAD.

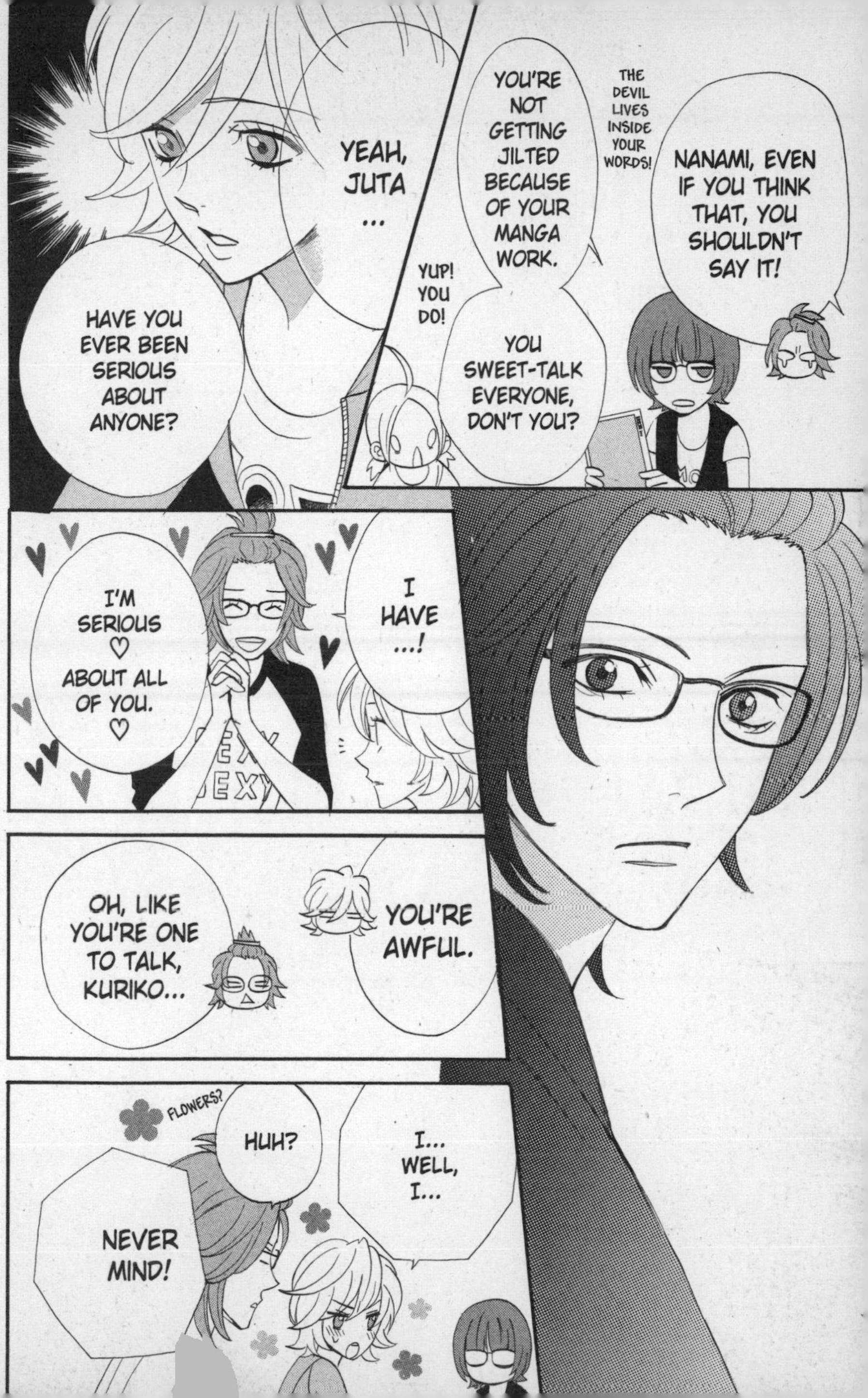
NANAMI, EVEN IF YOU THINK THAT, YOU SHOULDN'T SAY IT!
THE DEVIL LIVES INSIDE YOUR WORDS!
YOU'RE NOT GETTING JILTED BECAUSE OF YOUR MANGA WORK.
YOU SWEET-TALK EVERYONE, DON'T YOU?
YUP! YOU DO!
YEAH, JUTA ...
HAVE YOU EVER BEEN SERIOUS ABOUT ANYONE?
I HAVE ...!
I'M SERIOUS ♡ ABOUT ALL OF YOU. ♡
YOU'RE AWFUL.
OH, LIKE YOU'RE ONE TO TALK, KURIKO...
I... WELL, I...
HUH?
FLOWERS?
NEVER MIND!

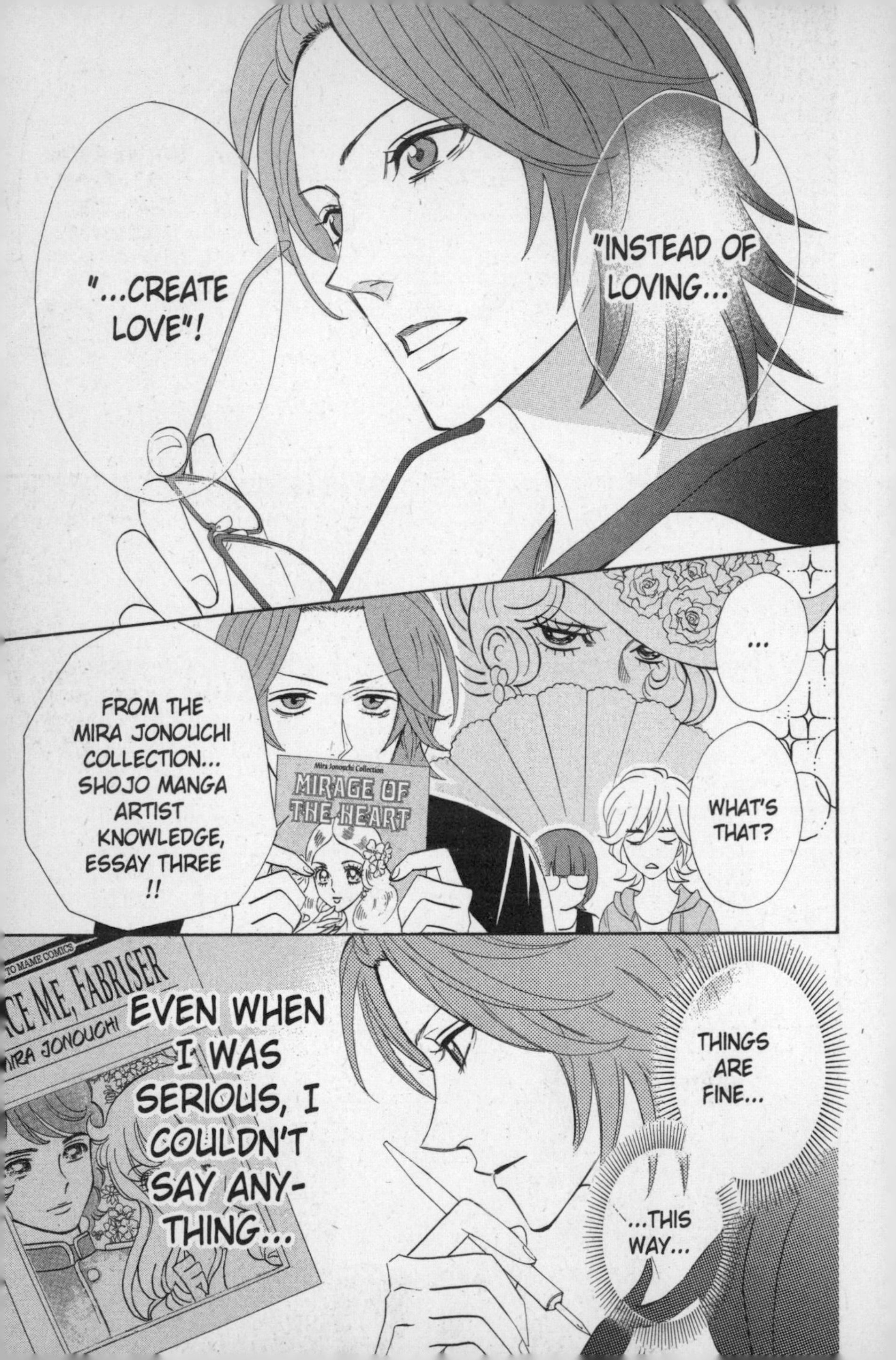
"INSTEAD OF LOVING...
"...CREATE LOVE"!
...
WHAT'S THAT?
FROM THE MIRA JONOUCHI COLLECTION... SHOJO MANGA ARTIST KNOWLEDGE, ESSAY THREE !!
Mira Jonouchi Collection
MIRAGE OF THE HEART
THINGS ARE FINE...
...THIS WAY...
EVEN WHEN I WAS SERIOUS, I COULDN'T SAY ANY-THING...

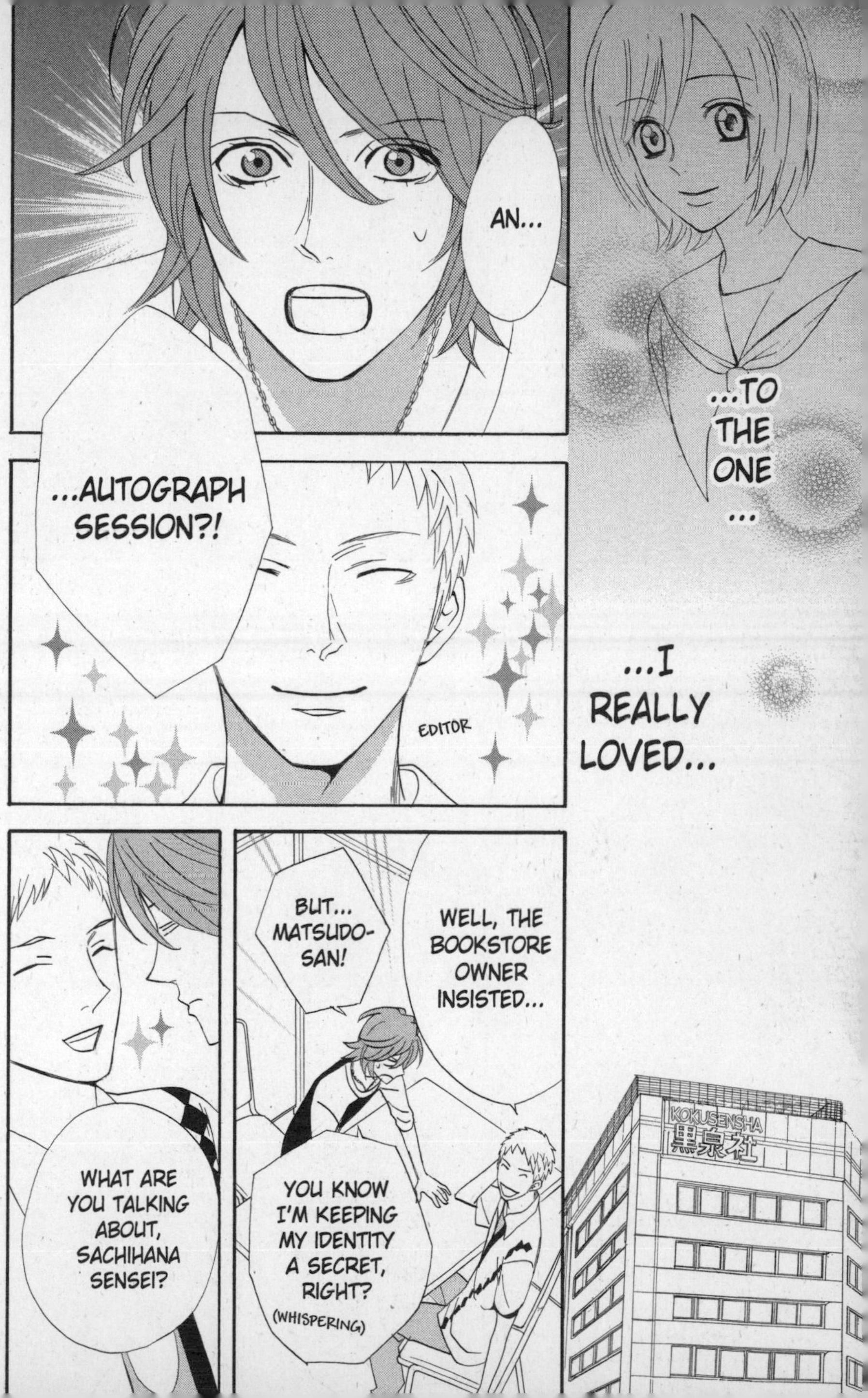
...TO THE ONE ...
...I REALLY LOVED...
AN...
...AUTOGRAPH SESSION?!
EDITOR
KOKUSENSHA 黒泉社
WELL, THE BOOKSTORE OWNER INSISTED...
BUT... MATSUDO-SAN!
YOU KNOW I'M KEEPING MY IDENTITY A SECRET, RIGHT?
(WHISPERING)
WHAT ARE YOU TALKING ABOUT, SACHIHANA SENSEI?

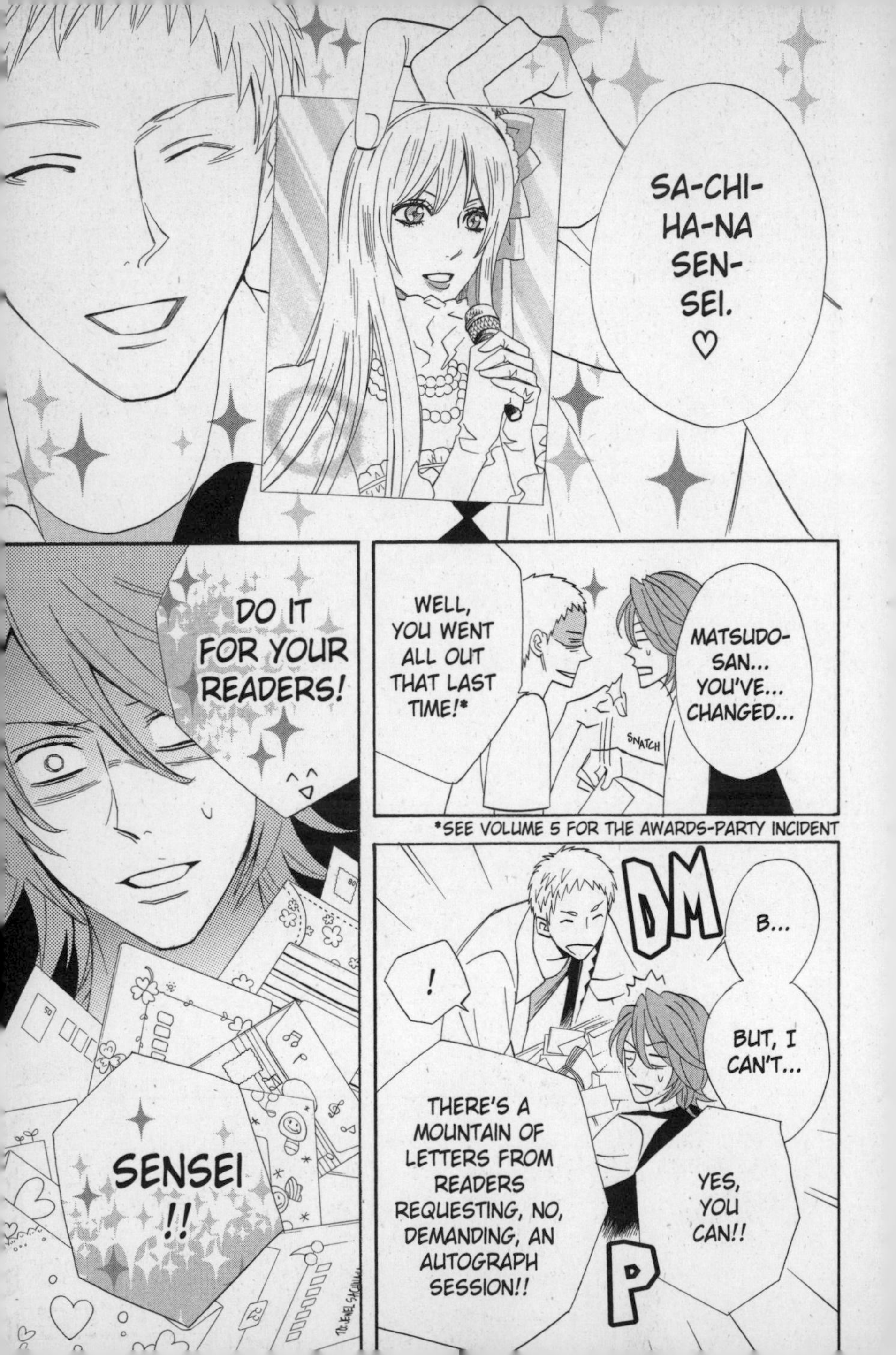
SA-CHI-HA-NA SEN-SEI. ♡
MATSUDO-SAN... YOU'VE... CHANGED...
WELL, YOU WENT ALL OUT THAT LAST TIME!*
SNATCH
*SEE VOLUME 5 FOR THE AWARDS-PARTY INCIDENT
B...
DM
BUT, I CAN'T...
!
YES, YOU CAN!!
THERE'S A MOUNTAIN OF LETTERS FROM READERS REQUESTING, NO, DEMANDING, AN AUTOGRAPH SESSION!!
P
DO IT FOR YOUR READERS!
SENSEI!!

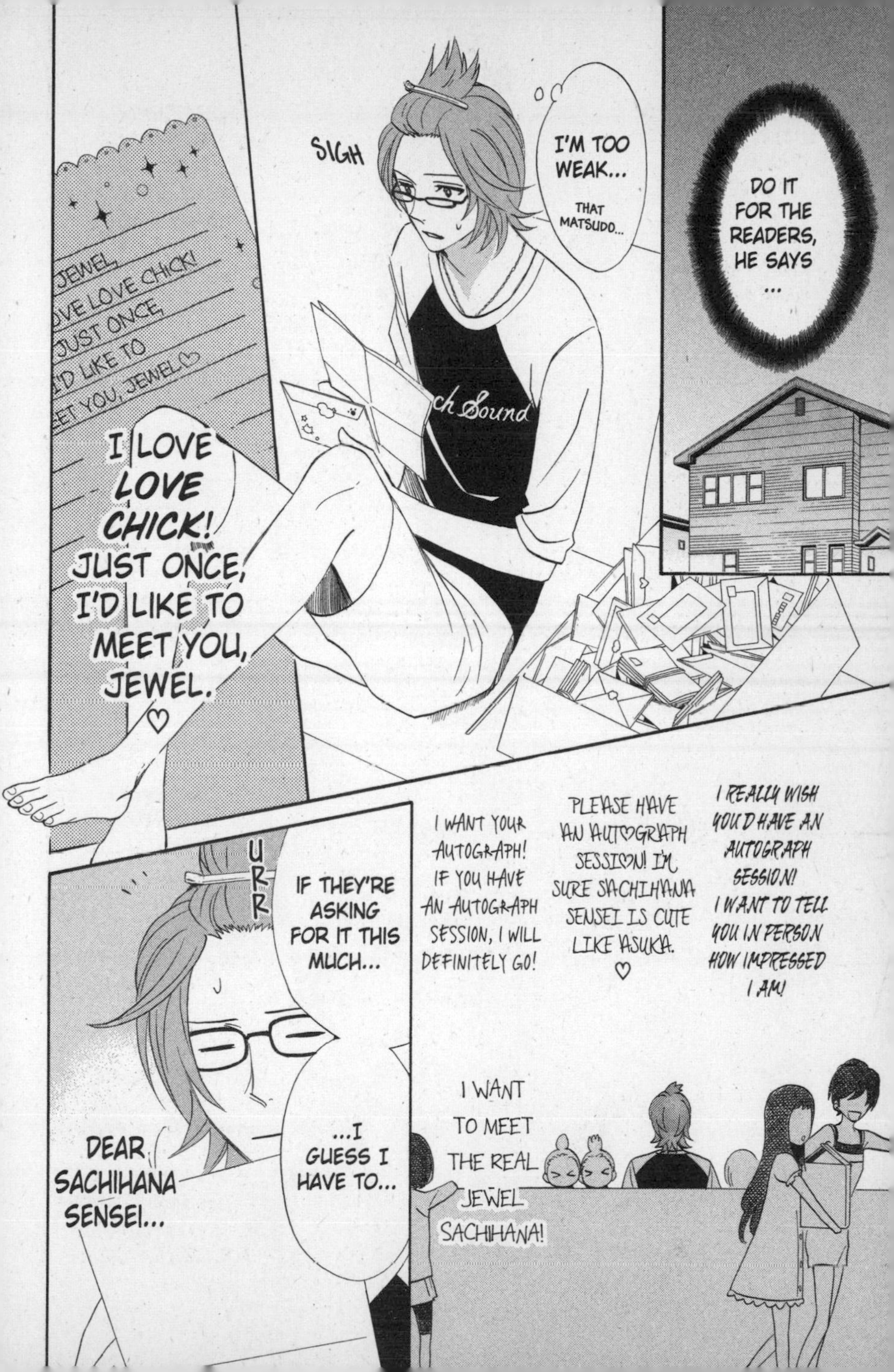
DO IT FOR THE READERS, HE SAYS ...
I'M TOO WEAK...
THAT MATSUDO...
SIGH
I LOVE LOVE CHICK! JUST ONCE, I'D LIKE TO MEET YOU, JEWEL. ♡
I REALLY WISH YOU'D HAVE AN AUTOGRAPH SESSION! I WANT TO TELL YOU IN PERSON HOW IMPRESSED I AM!
PLEASE HAVE AN AUTOGRAPH SESSION! I'M SURE SACHIHANA SENSEI IS CUTE LIKE ASUKA. ♡
I WANT YOUR AUTOGRAPH! IF YOU HAVE AN AUTOGRAPH SESSION, I WILL DEFINITELY GO!
I WANT TO MEET THE REAL JEWEL SACHIHANA!
URR
IF THEY'RE ASKING FOR IT THIS MUCH...
...I GUESS I HAVE TO...
DEAR SACHIHANA SENSEI...

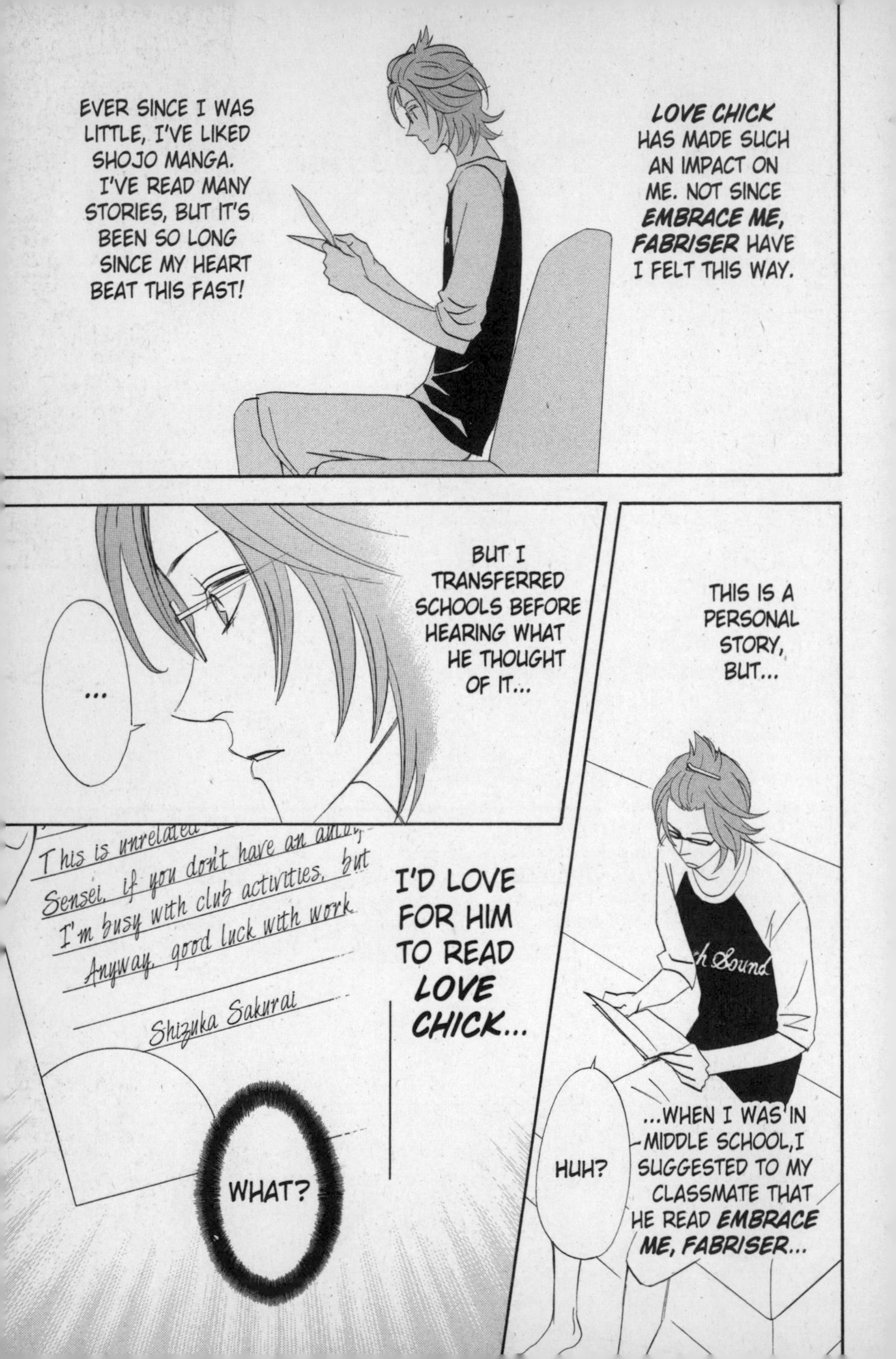
LOVE CHICK HAS MADE SUCH AN IMPACT ON ME. NOT SINCE EMBRACE ME, FABRISER HAVE I FELT THIS WAY.
EVER SINCE I WAS LITTLE, I'VE LIKED SHOJO MANGA. I'VE READ MANY STORIES, BUT IT'S BEEN SO LONG SINCE MY HEART BEAT THIS FAST!
THIS IS A PERSONAL STORY, BUT...
...WHEN I WAS IN MIDDLE SCHOOL, I SUGGESTED TO MY CLASSMATE THAT HE READ EMBRACE ME, FABRISER...
HUH?
BUT I TRANSFERRED SCHOOLS BEFORE HEARING WHAT HE THOUGHT OF IT...
...
I'D LOVE FOR HIM TO READ LOVE CHICK...
This is unrelated
Sensei, if you don't have an
I'm busy with club activities, but
Anyway, good luck with work.
Shizuka Sakurai
WHAT?

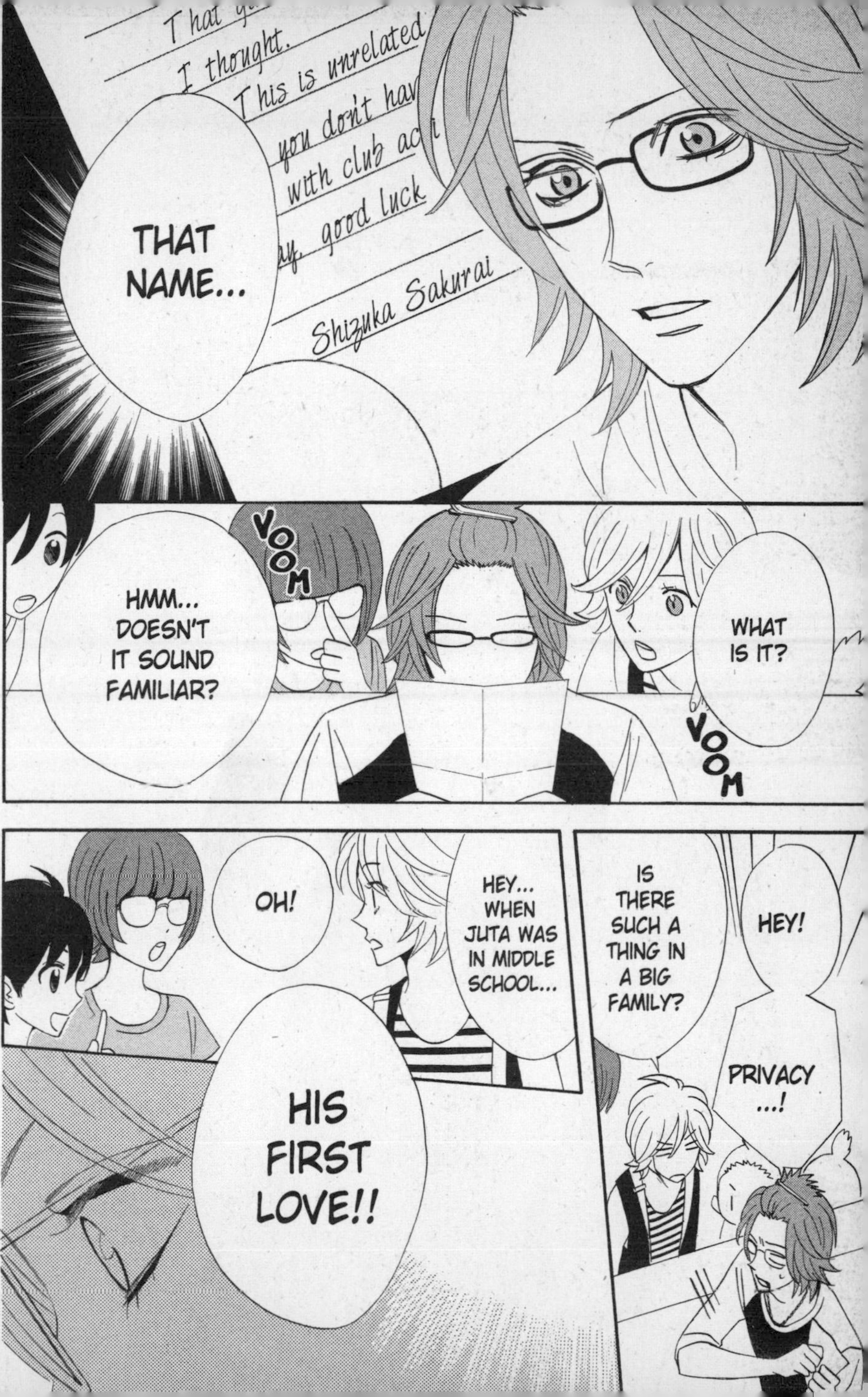
That y
I thought.
This is unrelated
you don't hav
with club ac
y, good luck
Shizuka Sakurai
THAT NAME...
WHAT IS IT?
VOOM
VOOM
HMM... DOESN'T IT SOUND FAMILIAR?
HEY!
PRIVACY ...!
IS THERE SUCH A THING IN A BIG FAMILY?
HEY... WHEN JUTA WAS IN MIDDLE SCHOOL...
OH!
HIS FIRST LOVE!!

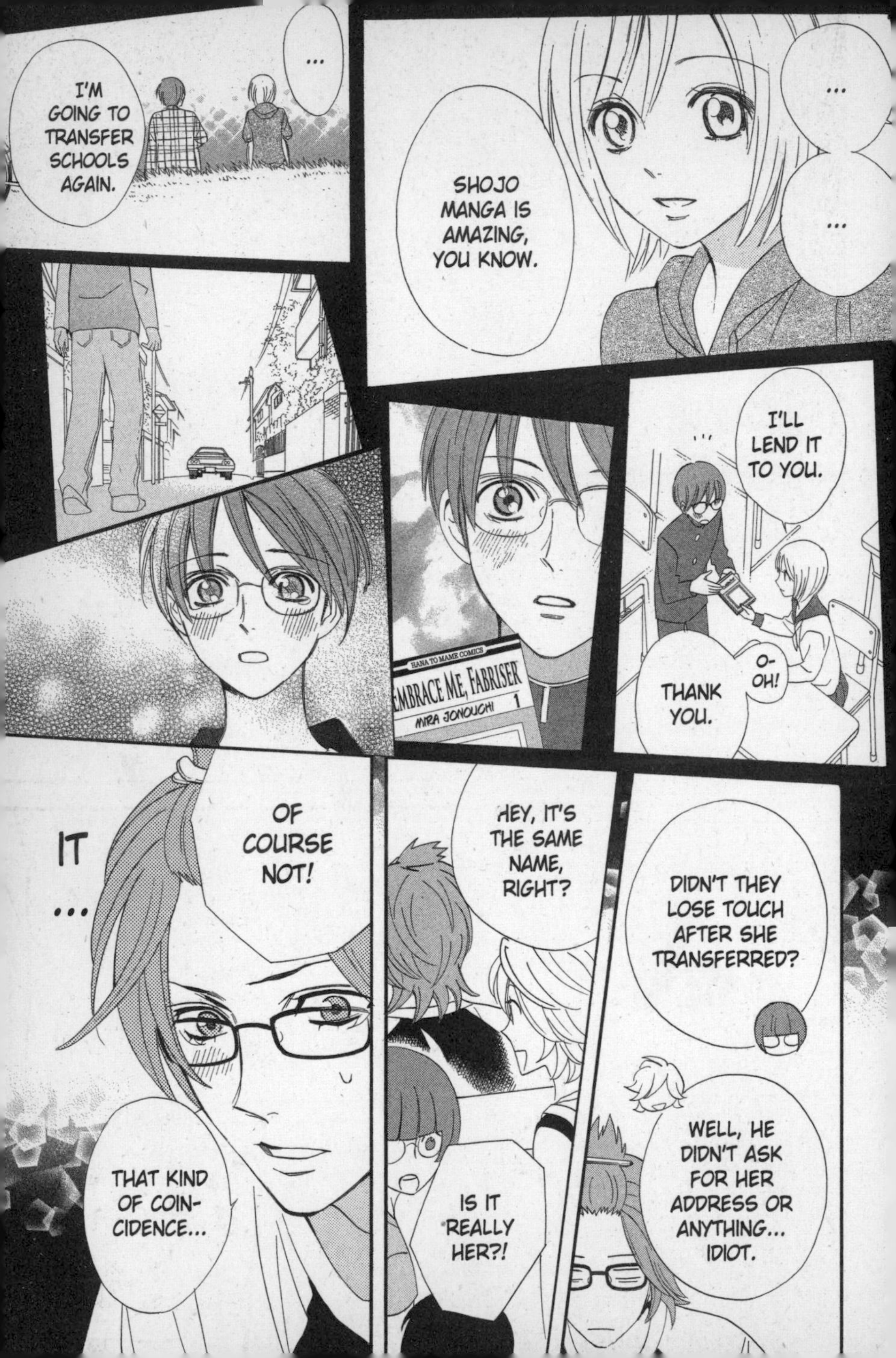
...
...
SHOJO MANGA IS AMAZING, YOU KNOW.
...
I'M GOING TO TRANSFER SCHOOLS AGAIN.
I'LL LEND IT TO YOU.
O-OH!
THANK YOU.
HANA TO MAME COMICS
EMBRACE ME, FABRISER 1
MIRA JONOUCHI
DIDN'T THEY LOSE TOUCH AFTER SHE TRANSFERRED?
WELL, HE DIDN'T ASK FOR HER ADDRESS OR ANYTHING... IDIOT.
HEY, IT'S THE SAME NAME, RIGHT?
IS IT REALLY HER?!
OF COURSE NOT!
IT...
THAT KIND OF COIN-CIDENCE...

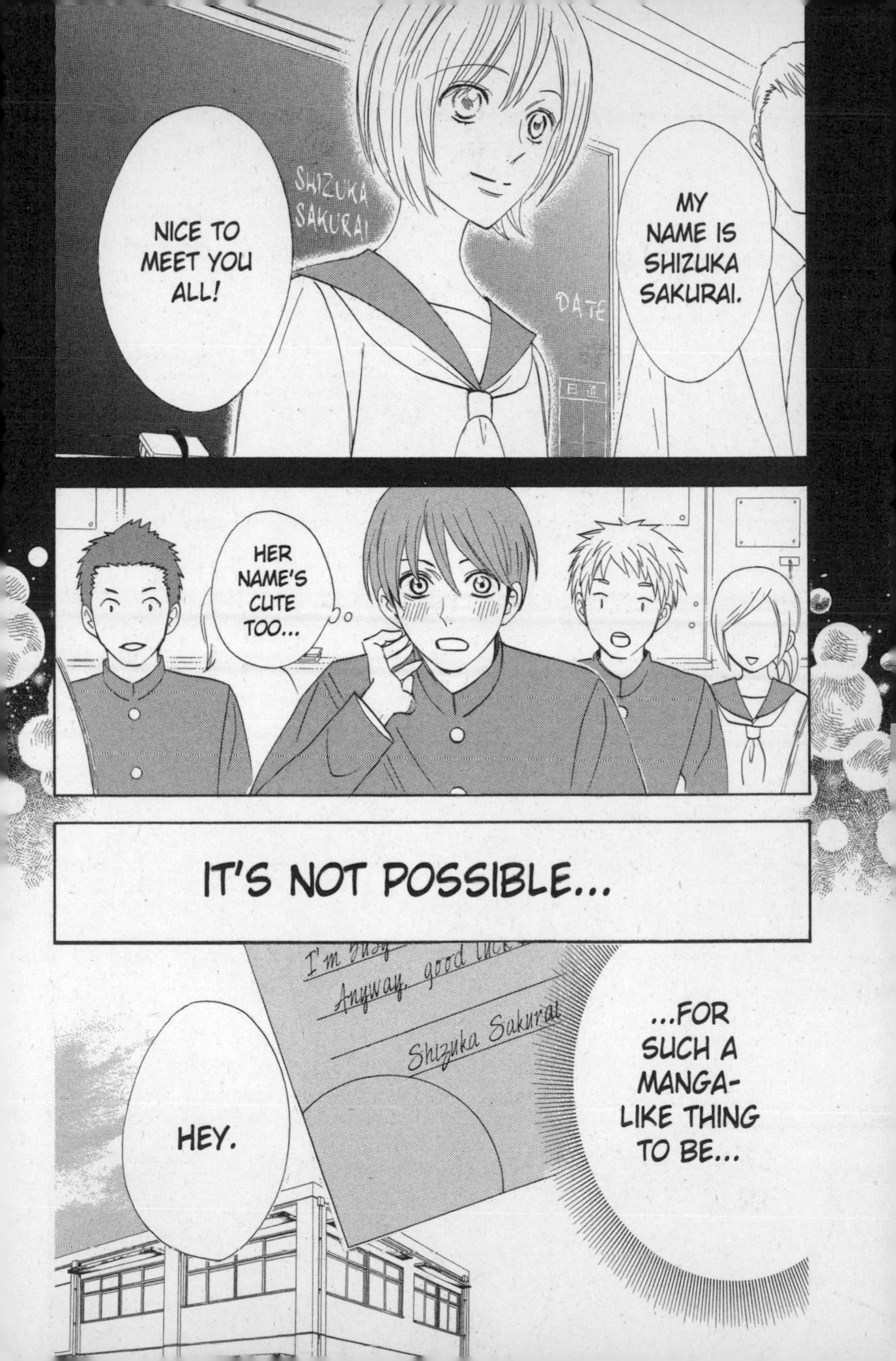
SHIZUKA SAKURAI
DATE
MY NAME IS SHIZUKA SAKURAI.
NICE TO MEET YOU ALL!
HER NAME'S CUTE TOO...
IT'S NOT POSSIBLE...
...FOR SUCH A MANGA-LIKE THING TO BE...
Shizuka Sakurai
HEY.

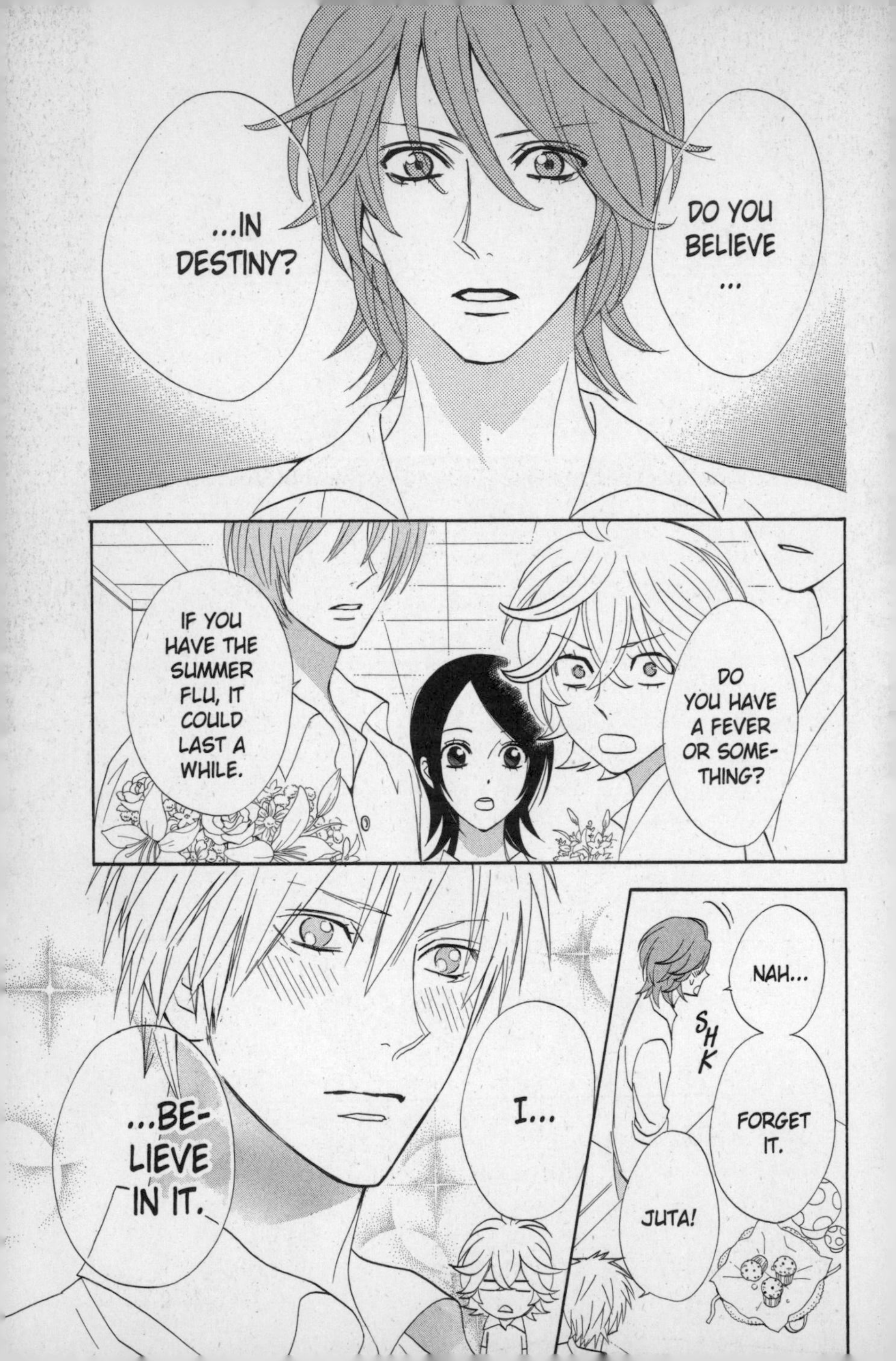

DO YOU BELIEVE ...
...IN DESTINY?
DO YOU HAVE A FEVER OR SOME-THING?
IF YOU HAVE THE SUMMER FLU, IT COULD LAST A WHILE.
NAH...
SHK
FORGET IT.
JUTA!
I...
...BE-LIEVE IN IT.

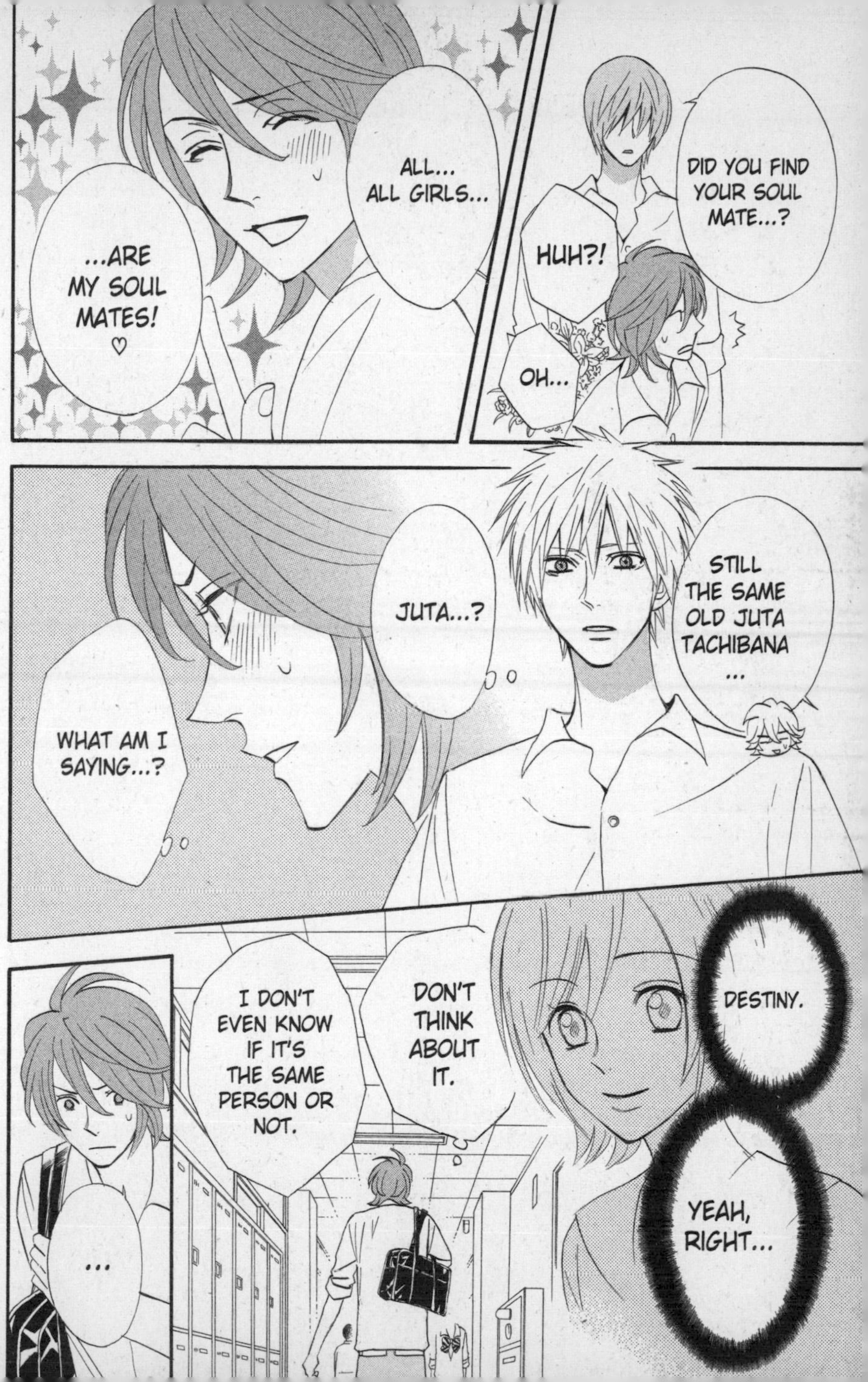
DID YOU FIND YOUR SOUL MATE...?
HUH?!
OH...
ALL... ALL GIRLS...
...ARE MY SOUL MATES! ♡
STILL THE SAME OLD JUTA TACHIBANA ...
JUTA...?
WHAT AM I SAYING...?
DESTINY.
YEAH, RIGHT...
DON'T THINK ABOUT IT.
I DON'T EVEN KNOW IF IT'S THE SAME PERSON OR NOT.
...

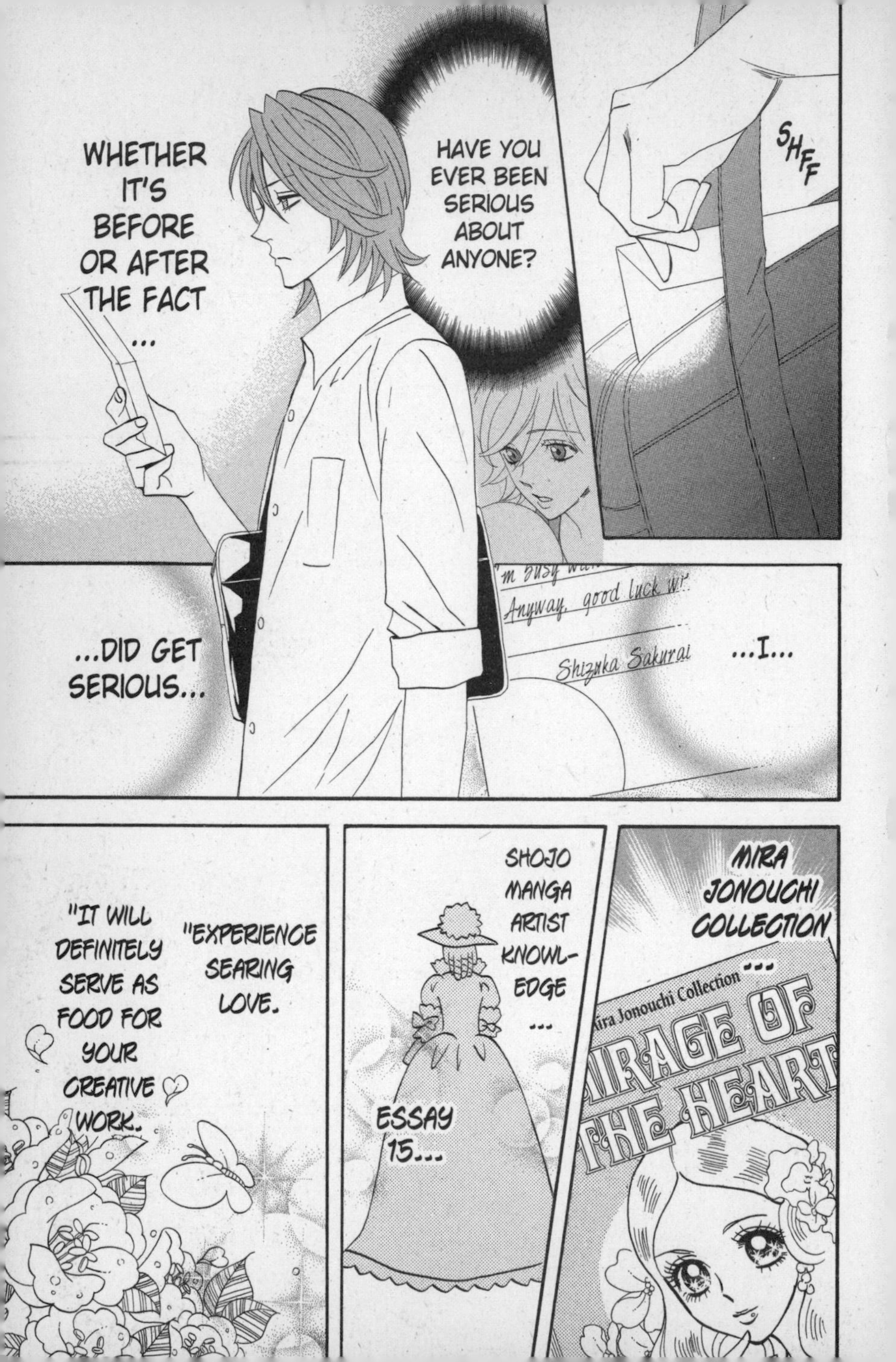
SHFF
HAVE YOU EVER BEEN SERIOUS ABOUT ANYONE?
WHETHER IT'S BEFORE OR AFTER THE FACT ...
...I...
Anyway, good luck
Shizuka Sakurai
...DID GET SERIOUS...
MIRA JONOUCHI COLLECTION ...
Mira Jonouchi Collection
IRAGE OF THE HEART
SHOJO MANGA ARTIST KNOWL-EDGE ...
ESSAY 15...
"EXPERIENCE SEARING LOVE.
"IT WILL DEFINITELY SERVE AS FOOD FOR YOUR CREATIVE WORK.

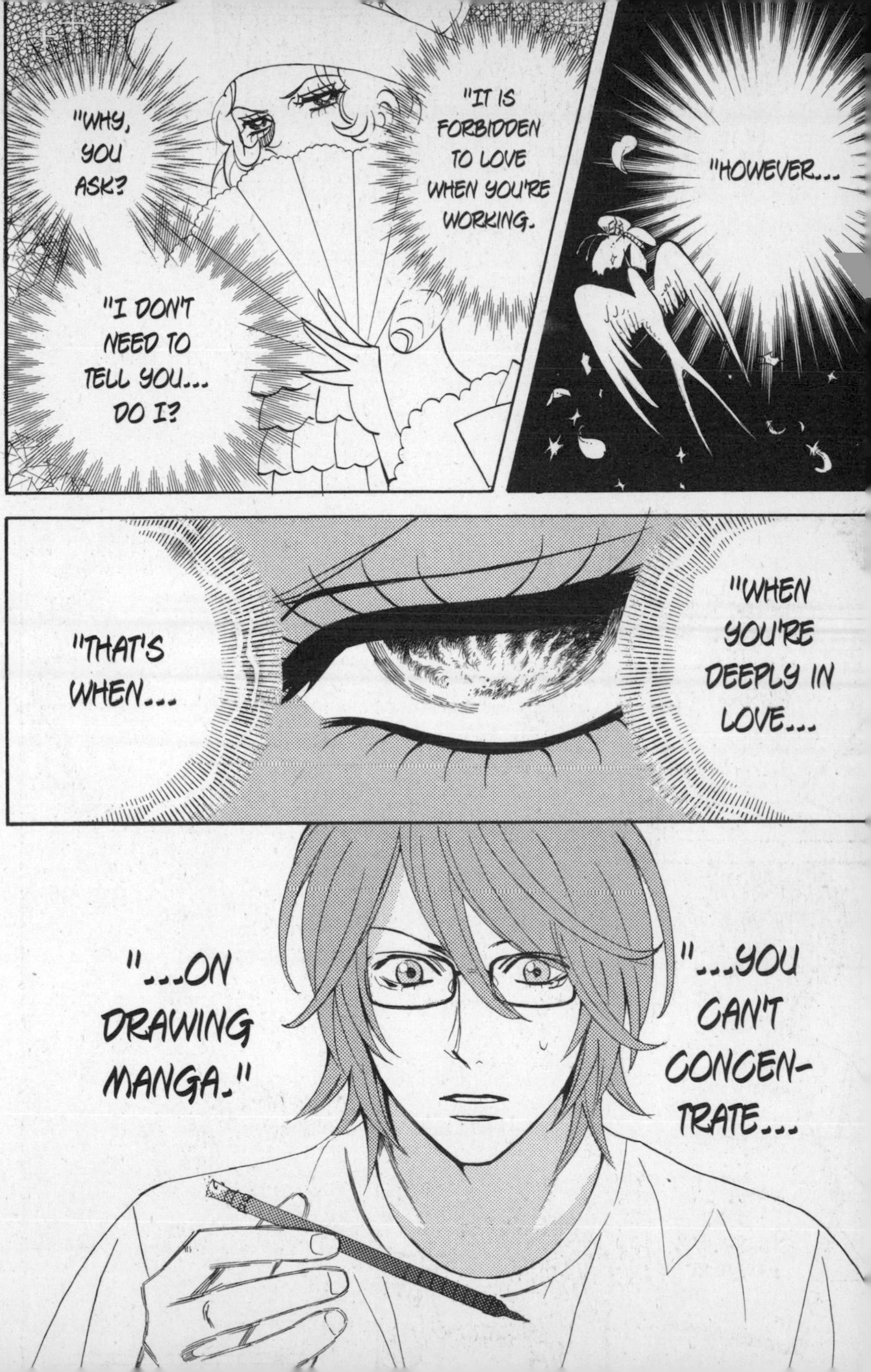
"HOWEVER...
"IT IS FORBIDDEN TO LOVE WHEN YOU'RE WORKING.
"WHY, YOU ASK?
"I DON'T NEED TO TELL YOU... DO I?
"WHEN YOU'RE DEEPLY IN LOVE...
"THAT'S WHEN...
"...YOU CAN'T CONCEN-TRATE...
"...ON DRAWING MANGA."

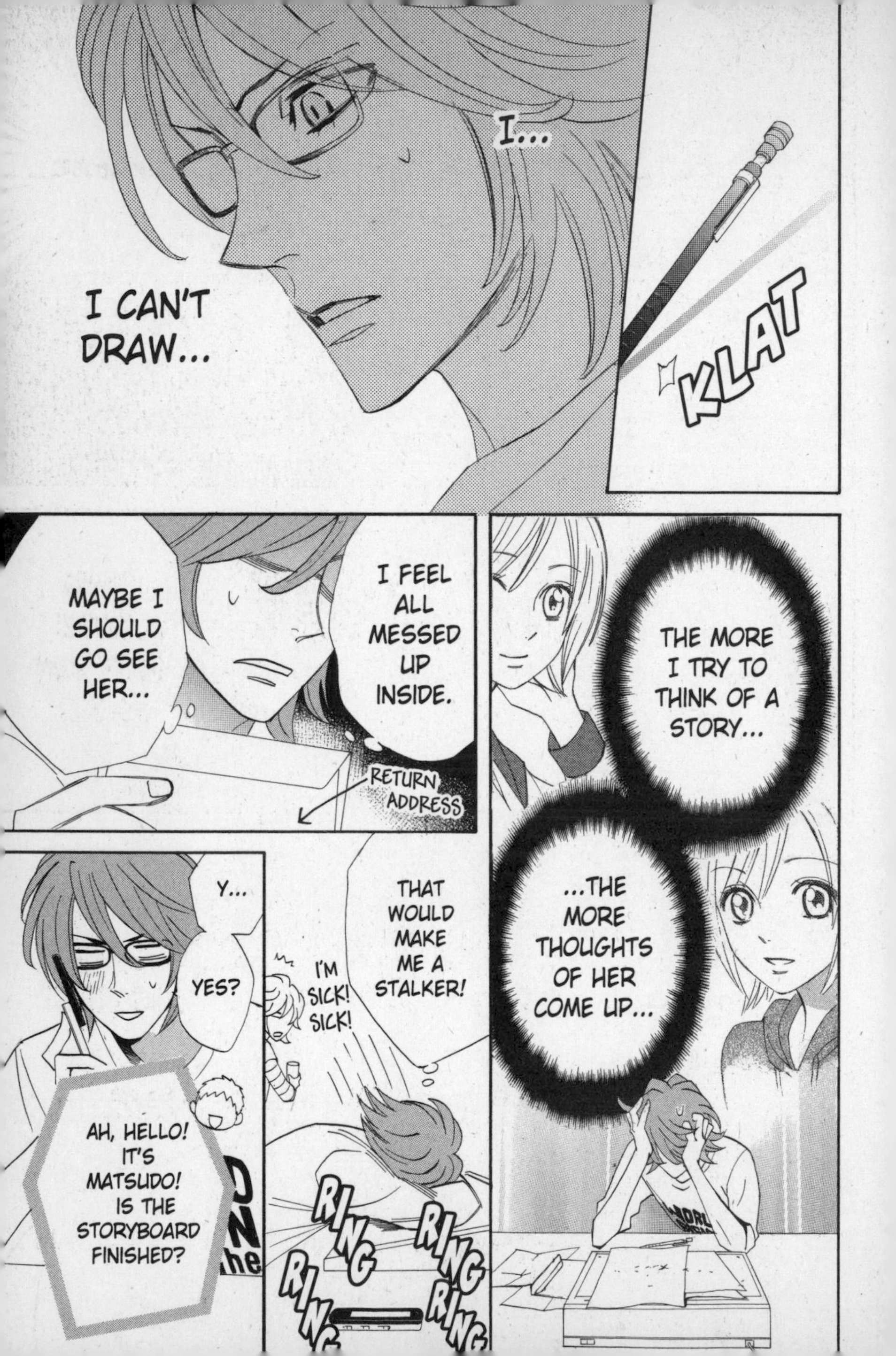
I...
KLAT
I CAN'T DRAW...
THE MORE I TRY TO THINK OF A STORY...
...THE MORE THOUGHTS OF HER COME UP...
I FEEL ALL MESSED UP INSIDE.
RETURN ADDRESS
MAYBE I SHOULD GO SEE HER...
THAT WOULD MAKE ME A STALKER!
I'M SICK! SICK!
RING RING
RING RING
Y...
YES?
AH, HELLO! IT'S MATSUDO! IS THE STORYBOARD FINISHED?

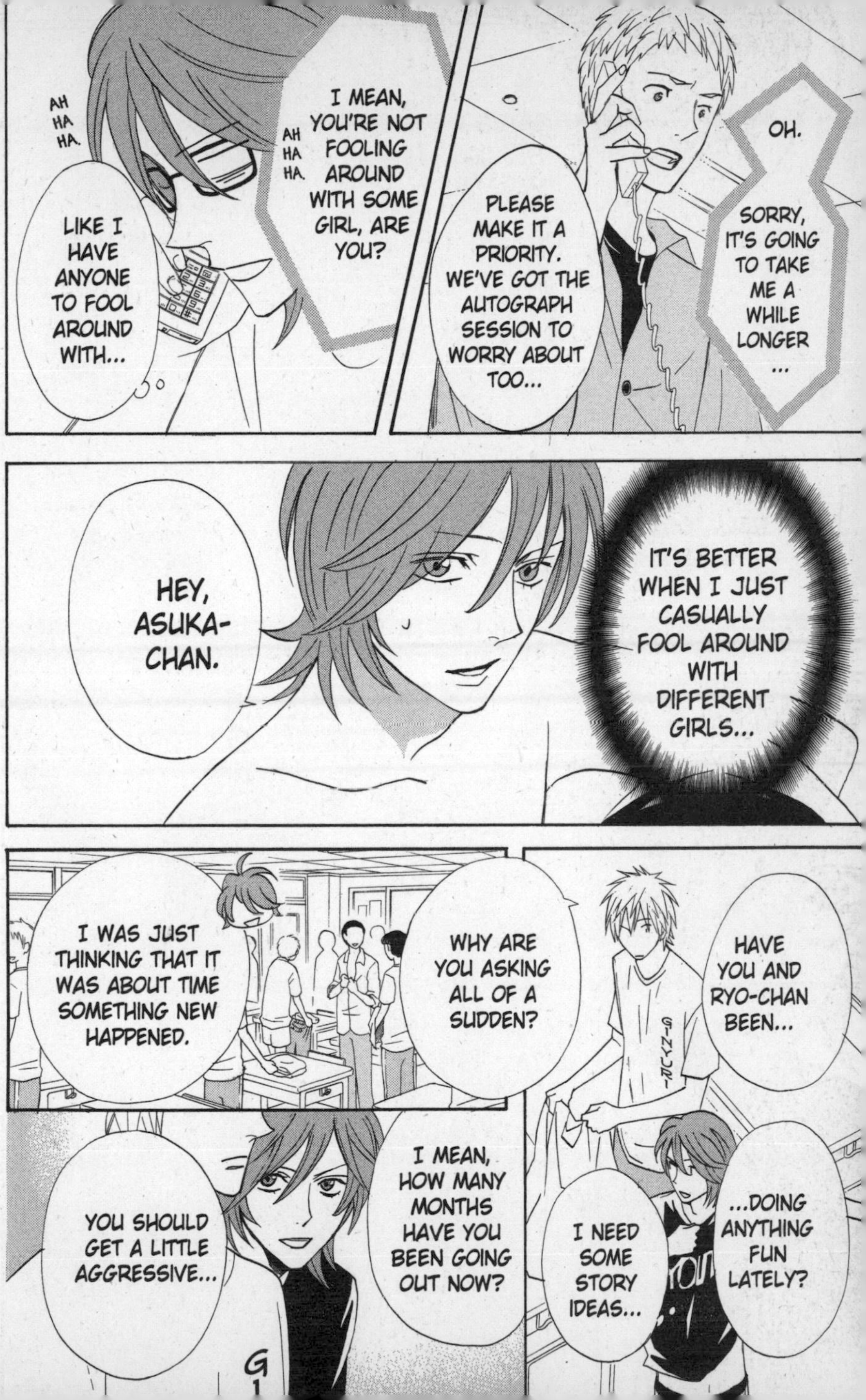
OH.
SORRY, IT'S GOING TO TAKE ME A WHILE LONGER ...
PLEASE MAKE IT A PRIORITY. WE'VE GOT THE AUTOGRAPH SESSION TO WORRY ABOUT TOO...
I MEAN, YOU'RE NOT FOOLING AROUND WITH SOME GIRL, ARE YOU?
AH HA HA.
AH HA HA.
LIKE I HAVE ANYONE TO FOOL AROUND WITH...
IT'S BETTER WHEN I JUST CASUALLY FOOL AROUND WITH DIFFERENT GIRLS...
HEY, ASUKA-CHAN.
HAVE YOU AND RYO-CHAN BEEN...
GINYURI
...DOING ANYTHING FUN LATELY?
I NEED SOME STORY IDEAS...
WHY ARE YOU ASKING ALL OF A SUDDEN?
I WAS JUST THINKING THAT IT WAS ABOUT TIME SOMETHING NEW HAPPENED.
I MEAN, HOW MANY MONTHS HAVE YOU BEEN GOING OUT NOW?
YOU SHOULD GET A LITTLE AGGRESSIVE...

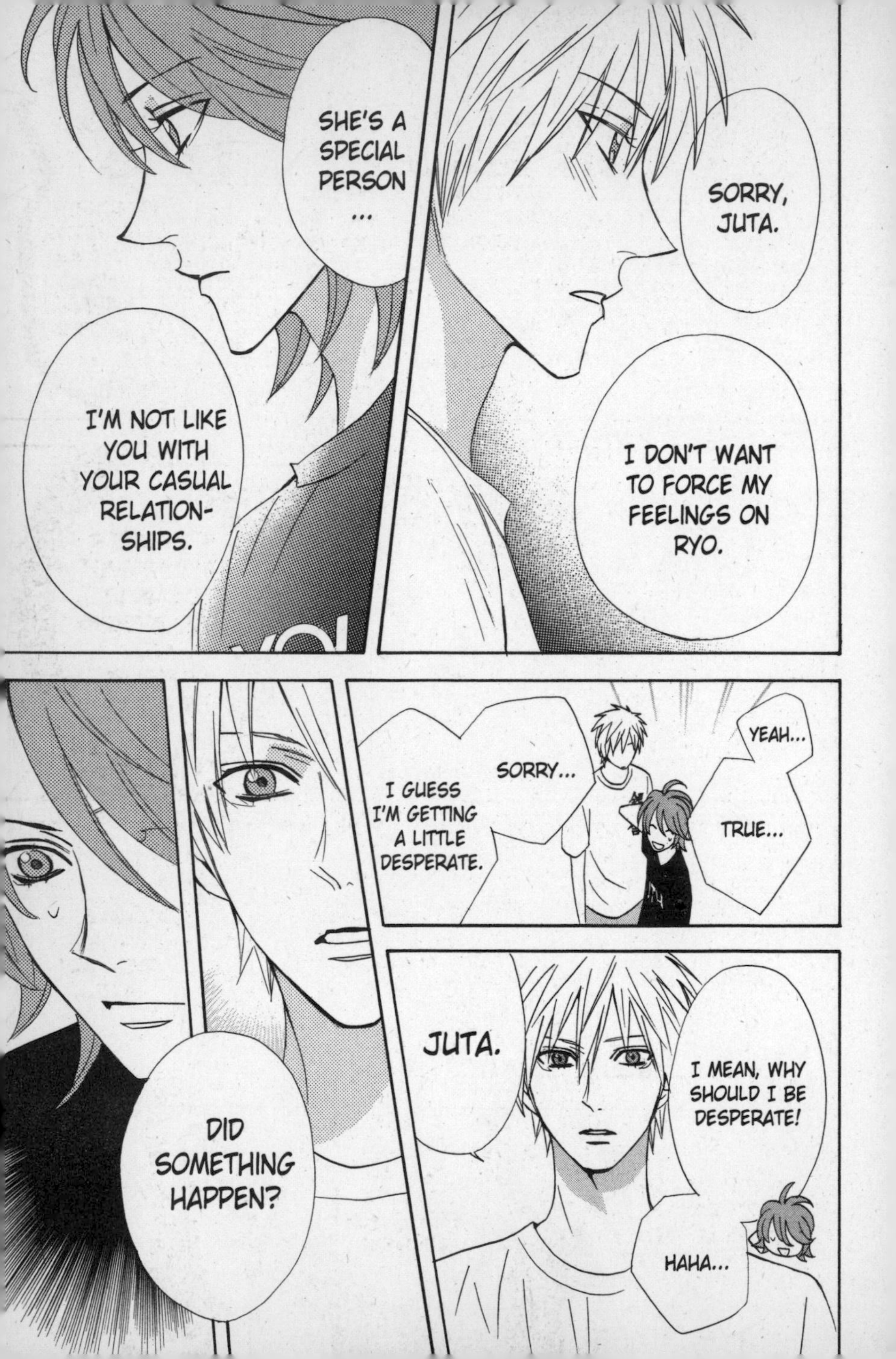
SORRY, JUTA.
I DON'T WANT TO FORCE MY FEELINGS ON RYO.
SHE'S A SPECIAL PERSON ...
I'M NOT LIKE YOU WITH YOUR CASUAL RELATION-SHIPS.
YEAH...
TRUE...
SORRY...
I GUESS I'M GETTING A LITTLE DESPERATE.
I MEAN, WHY SHOULD I BE DESPERATE!
HAHA...
JUTA.
DID SOMETHING HAPPEN?

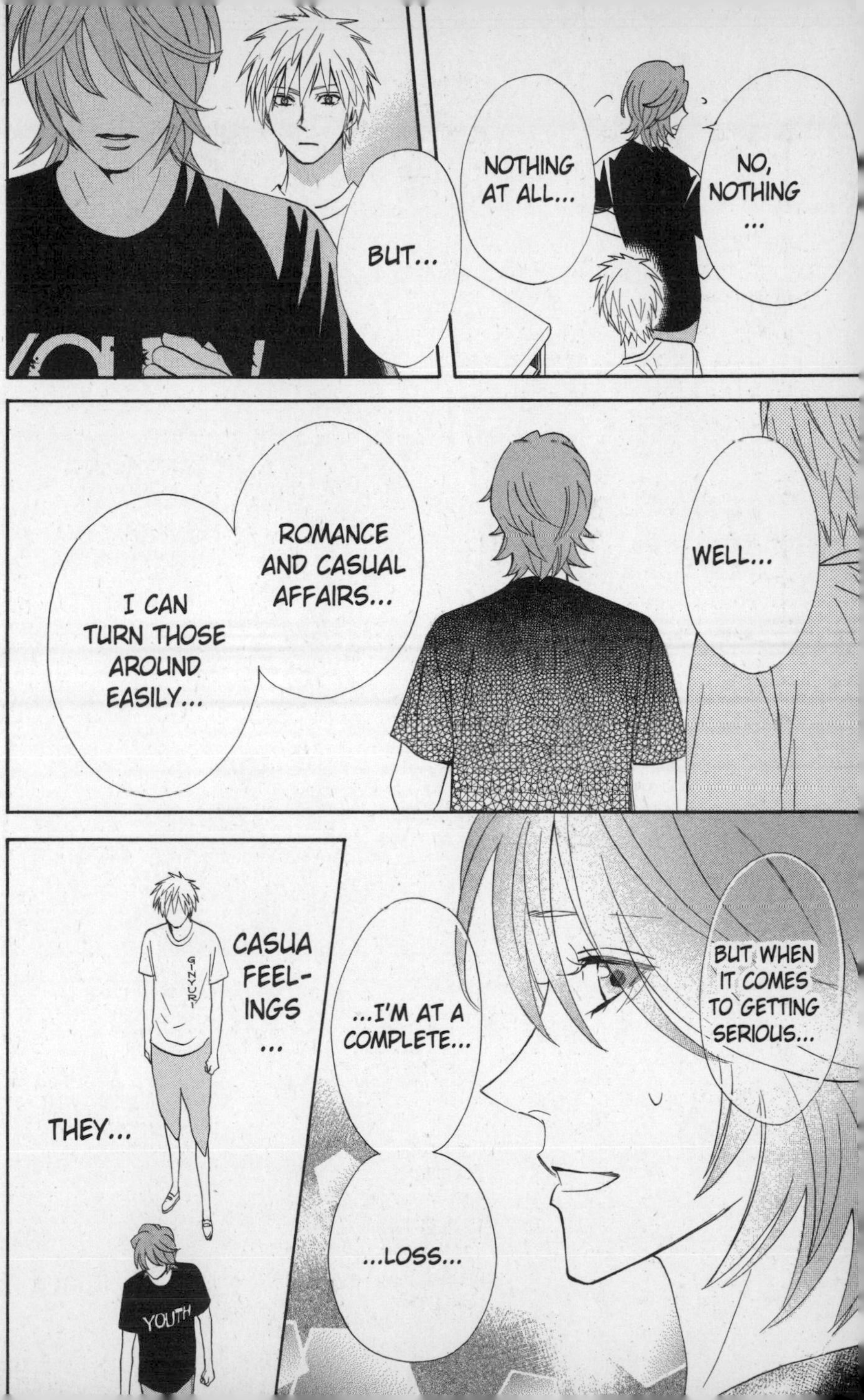
NO, NOTHING ...
NOTHING AT ALL...
BUT...
WELL...
ROMANCE AND CASUAL AFFAIRS...
I CAN TURN THOSE AROUND EASILY...
BUT WHEN IT COMES TO GETTING SERIOUS...
...I'M AT A COMPLETE...
...LOSS...
CASUA FEEL- INGS ...
GINYURI
THEY...
YOUTH

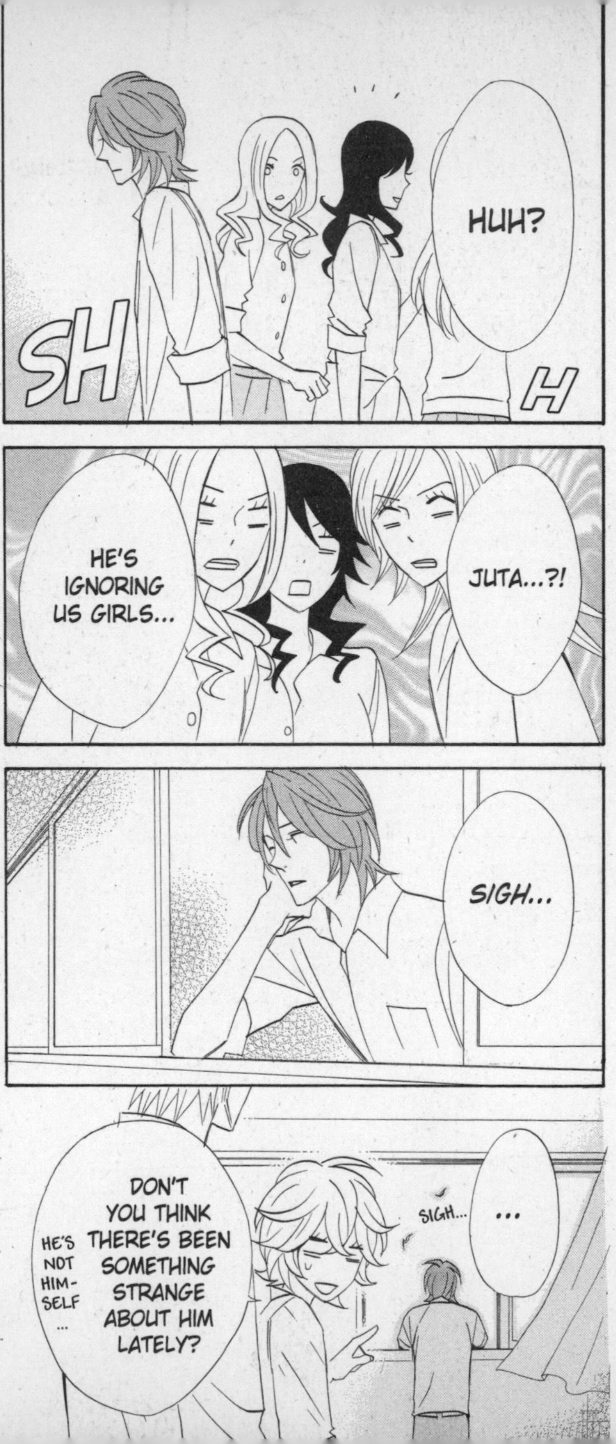
HUH?
SH
H
JUTA...?!
HE'S IGNORING US GIRLS...
SIGH...
...
SIGH...
DON'T YOU THINK THERE'S BEEN SOMETHING STRANGE ABOUT HIM LATELY?
HE'S NOT HIM-SELF ...

This is Juta. It's been a while since he was the main character. Soon after I drew this story, I went to Taiwan for an autograph session. I was very happy to be able to meet and speak directly with the fans there. To everyone in Taiwan, thank you very much. You have a wonderful country. As I was drawing this, I was going through my own love story (which only occurs once every two years), so I put my other stories on hold and drew this instead. It's over now, so it'll be another two years...

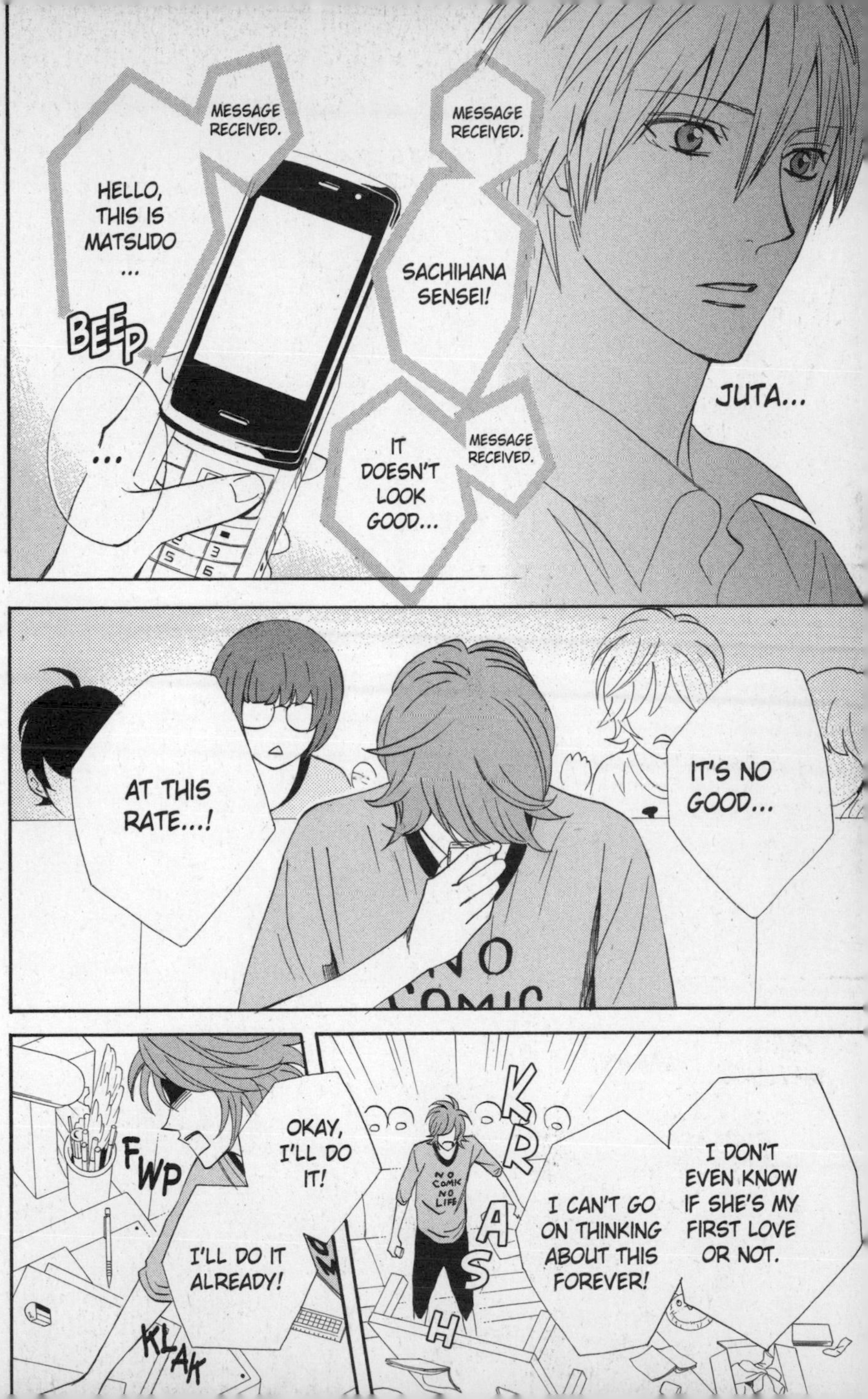
MESSAGE RECEIVED.
SACHIHANA SENSEI!
JUTA...
MESSAGE RECEIVED.
IT DOESN'T LOOK GOOD...
MESSAGE RECEIVED.
HELLO, THIS IS MATSUDO ...
BEEP
...
IT'S NO GOOD...
AT THIS RATE...!
I DON'T EVEN KNOW IF SHE'S MY FIRST LOVE OR NOT.
I CAN'T GO ON THINKING ABOUT THIS FOREVER!
KRASH
NO COMIC NO LIFE
OKAY, I'LL DO IT!
I'LL DO IT ALREADY!
FWP
KLAK

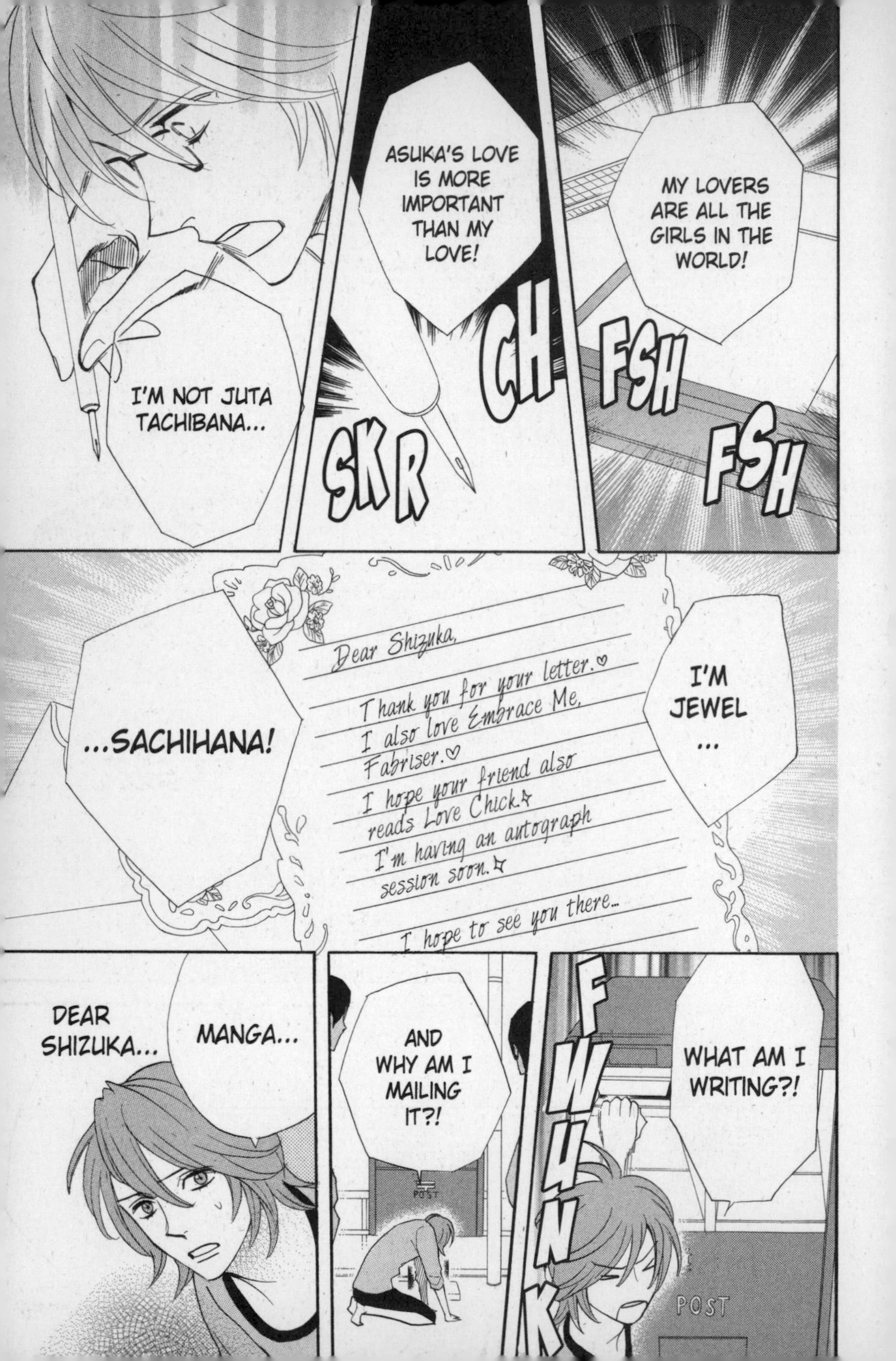
MY LOVERS ARE ALL THE GIRLS IN THE WORLD!
FSH
FSH
ASUKA'S LOVE IS MORE IMPORTANT THAN MY LOVE!
CH
SKR
I'M NOT JUTA TACHIBANA...
I'M JEWEL...
Dear Shizuka,
Thank you for your letter.♡
I also love Embrace Me, Fabriser.♡
I hope your friend also reads Love Chick.☆
I'm having an autograph session soon.☆
I hope to see you there...
...SACHIHANA!
WHAT AM I WRITING?!
FWUNK
POST
AND WHY AM I MAILING IT?!
POST
MANGA...
DEAR SHIZUKA...

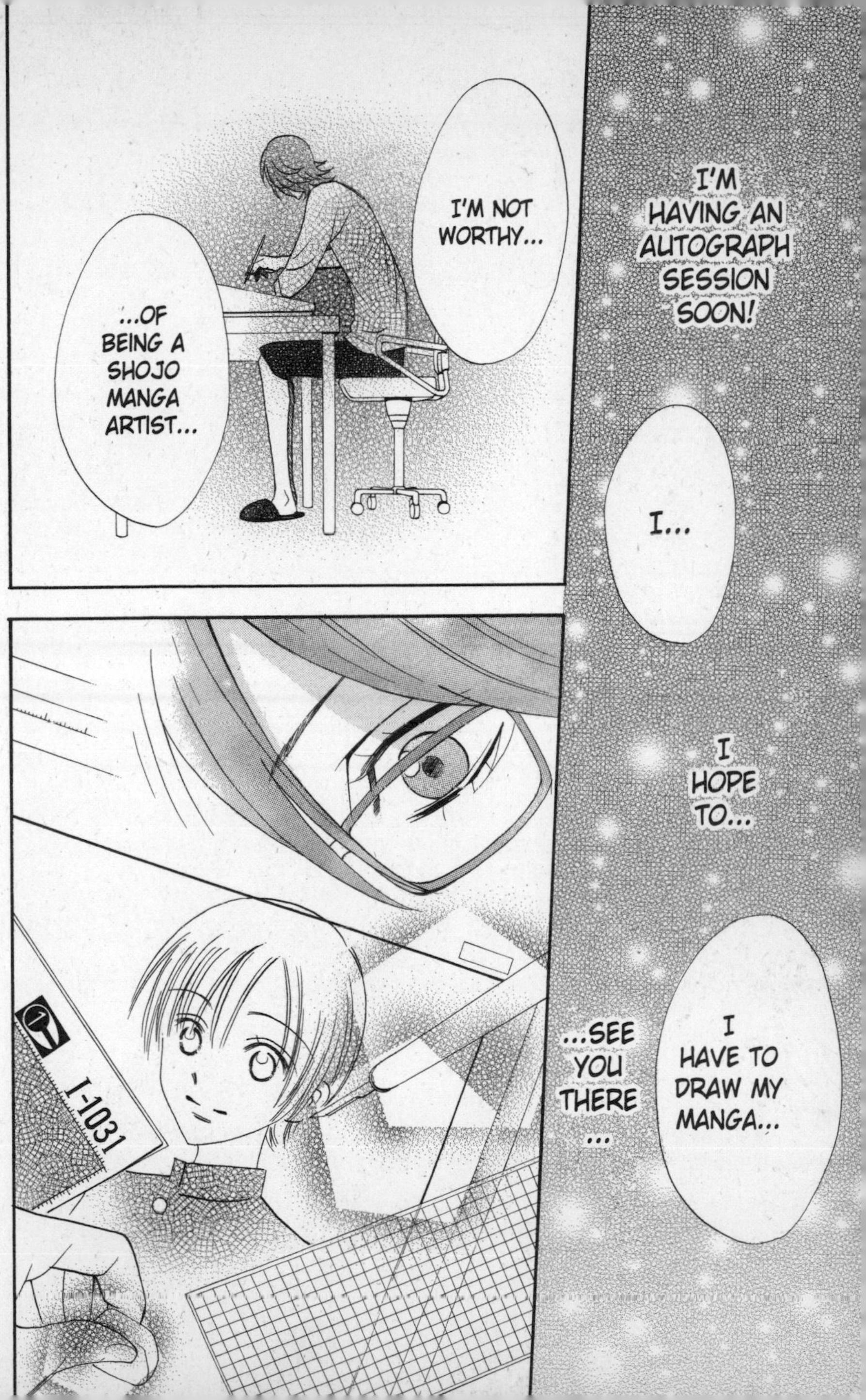
I'M HAVING AN AUTOGRAPH SESSION SOON!
I...
I HOPE TO...
I HAVE TO DRAW MY MANGA...
...SEE YOU THERE ...
I'M NOT WORTHY...
...OF BEING A SHOJO MANGA ARTIST...
I-1031

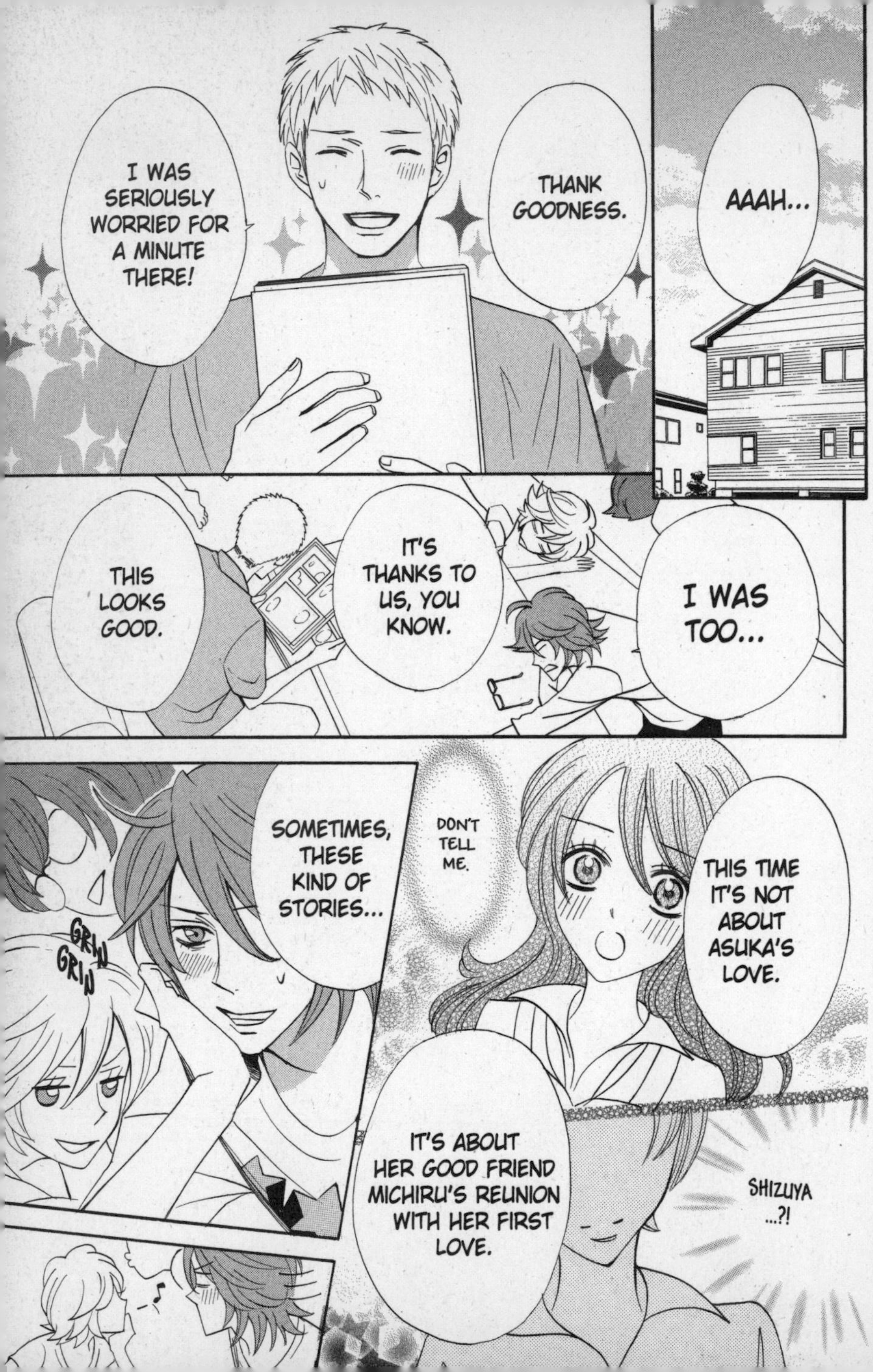
AAAH...
THANK GOODNESS.
I WAS SERIOUSLY WORRIED FOR A MINUTE THERE!
I WAS TOO...
IT'S THANKS TO US, YOU KNOW.
THIS LOOKS GOOD.
THIS TIME IT'S NOT ABOUT ASUKA'S LOVE.
DON'T TELL ME.
SOMETIMES, THESE KIND OF STORIES...
GRIN GRIN
IT'S ABOUT HER GOOD FRIEND MICHIRU'S REUNION WITH HER FIRST LOVE.
SHIZUYA ...?!

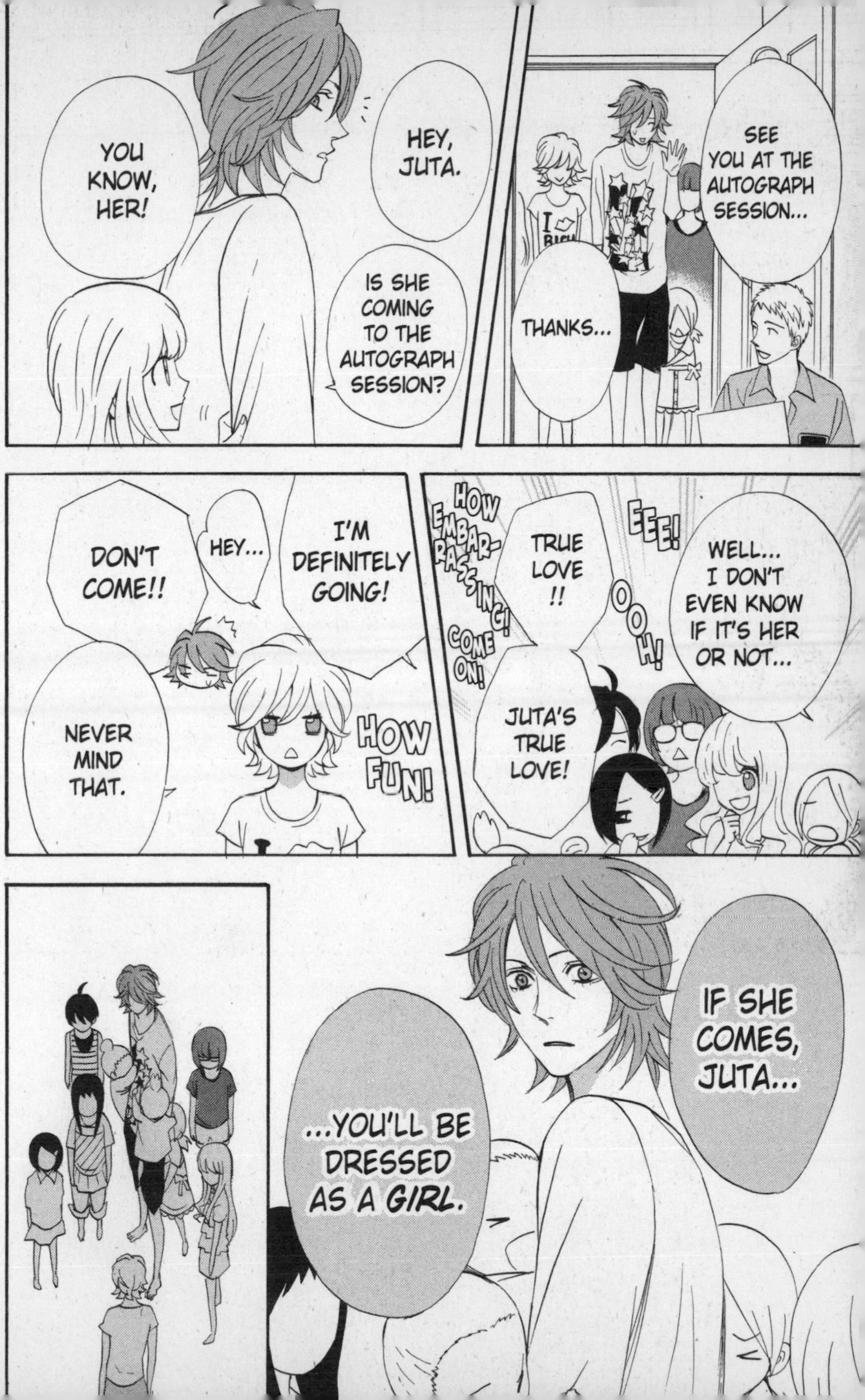
SEE YOU AT THE AUTOGRAPH SESSION...
THANKS...
HEY, JUTA.
YOU KNOW, HER!
IS SHE COMING TO THE AUTOGRAPH SESSION?
WELL... I DON'T EVEN KNOW IF IT'S HER OR NOT...
EEE!
OOOH!
TRUE LOVE!!
HOW EMBARRASSING!
COME ON!
JUTA'S TRUE LOVE!
I'M DEFINITELY GOING!
HEY...
DON'T COME!!
HOW FUN!
NEVER MIND THAT.
IF SHE COMES, JUTA...
...YOU'LL BE DRESSED AS A GIRL.

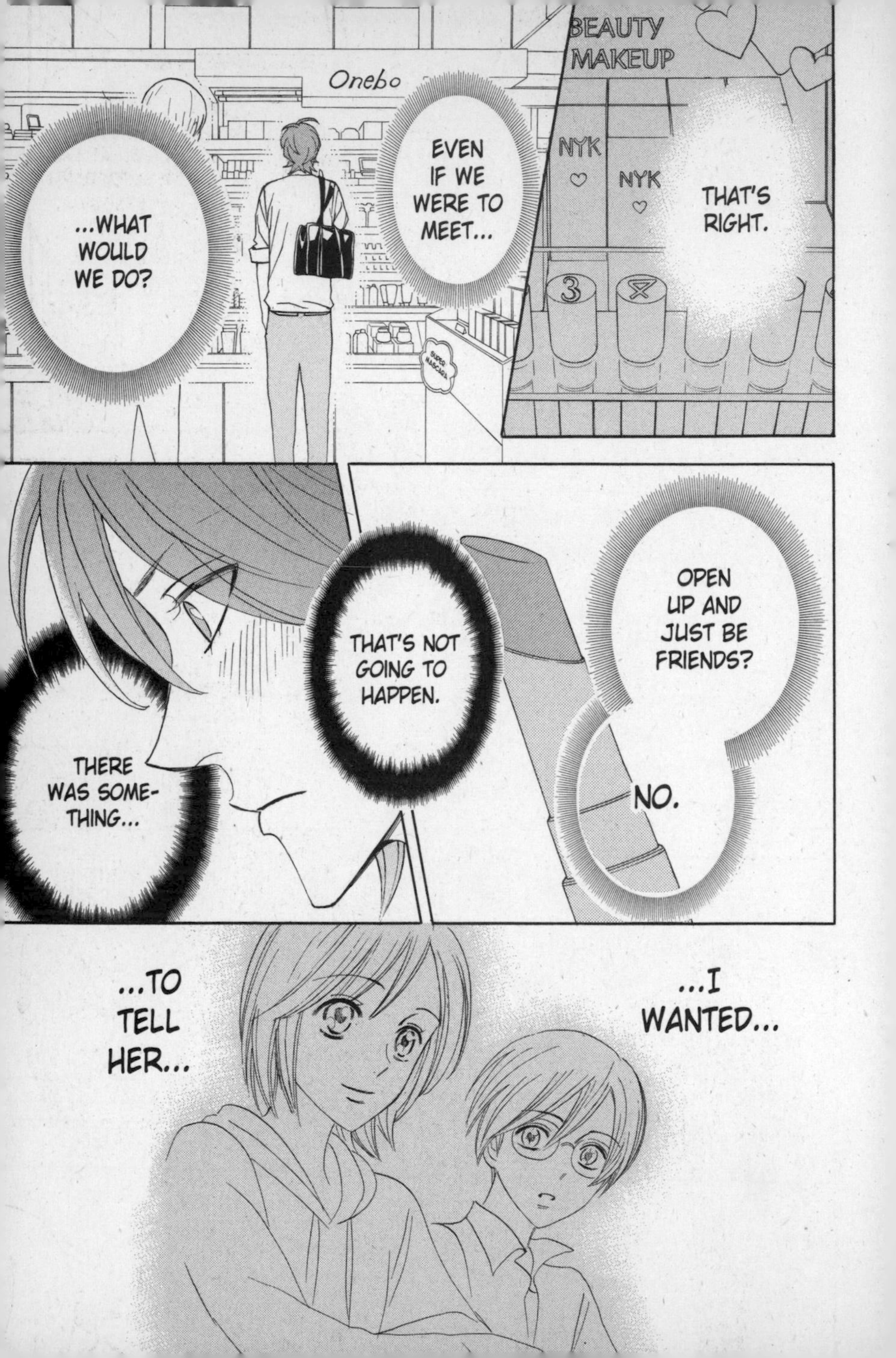
BEAUTY MAKEUP
NYK
NYK
THAT'S RIGHT.
Onebo
EVEN IF WE WERE TO MEET...
...WHAT WOULD WE DO?
SUPER MASCARA
OPEN UP AND JUST BE FRIENDS?
NO.
THAT'S NOT GOING TO HAPPEN.
THERE WAS SOME-THING...
...I WANTED...
...TO TELL HER...

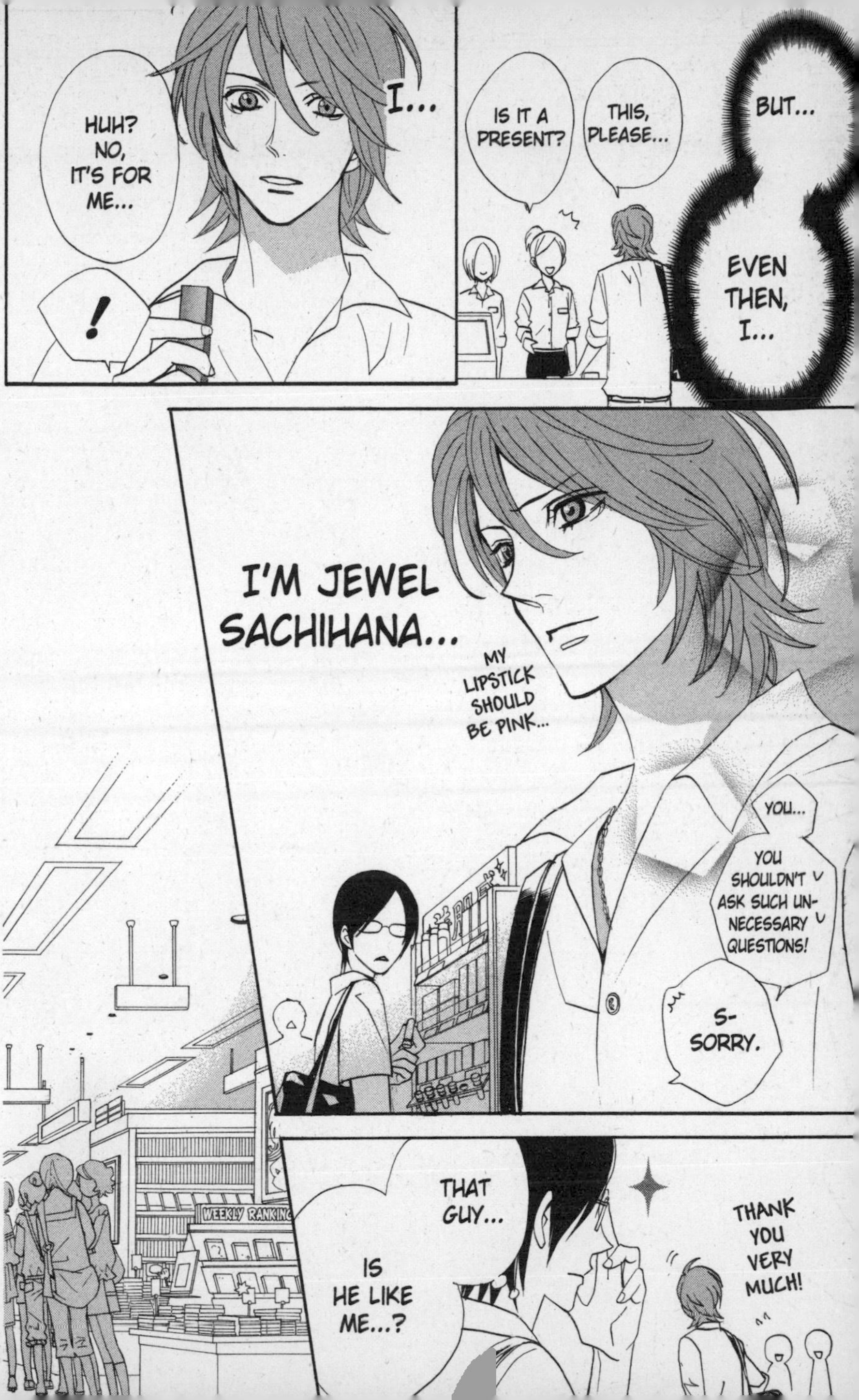
BUT...
EVEN THEN, I...
THIS, PLEASE...
IS IT A PRESENT?
I...
HUH? NO, IT'S FOR ME...
!
I'M JEWEL SACHIHANA...
MY LIPSTICK SHOULD BE PINK...
YOU...
YOU SHOULDN'T ASK SUCH UN-NECESSARY QUESTIONS!
S-SORRY.
THANK YOU VERY MUCH!
THAT GUY...
IS HE LIKE ME...?
WEEKLY RANKING

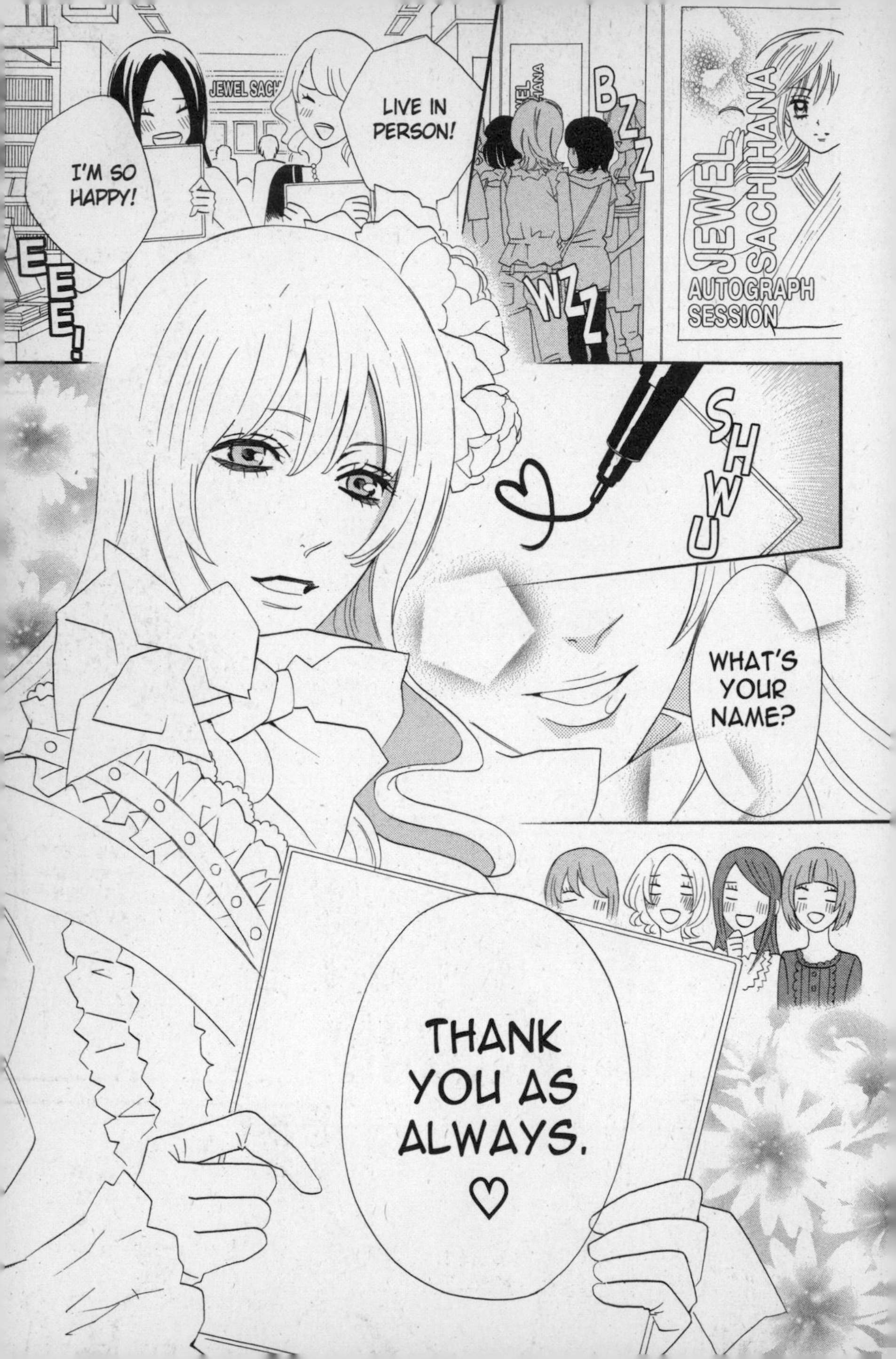
JEWEL SACHIHANA
AUTOGRAPH SESSION
BZZ
WZZ
LIVE IN PERSON!
JEWEL SACH
I'M SO HAPPY!
EEE!
SHWU
WHAT'S YOUR NAME?
THANK YOU AS ALWAYS. ♡

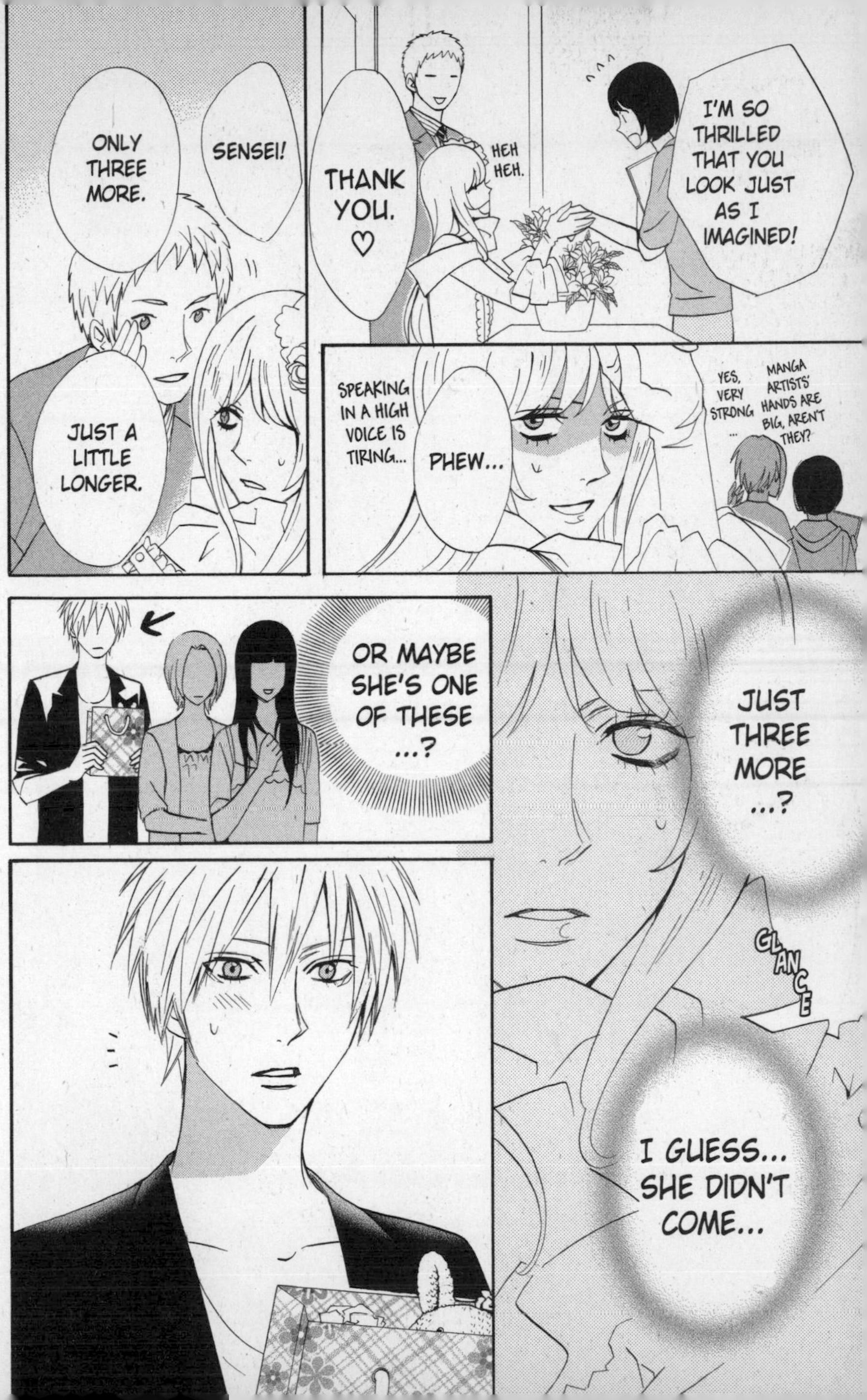
I'M SO THRILLED THAT YOU LOOK JUST AS I IMAGINED!
HEH HEH.
THANK YOU. ♡
MANGA ARTISTS' HANDS ARE BIG, AREN'T THEY?
YES, VERY STRONG ...
PHEW...
SPEAKING IN A HIGH VOICE IS TIRING...
SENSEI!
ONLY THREE MORE.
JUST A LITTLE LONGER.
JUST THREE MORE ...?
GLANCE
I GUESS... SHE DIDN'T COME...
OR MAYBE SHE'S ONE OF THESE ...?

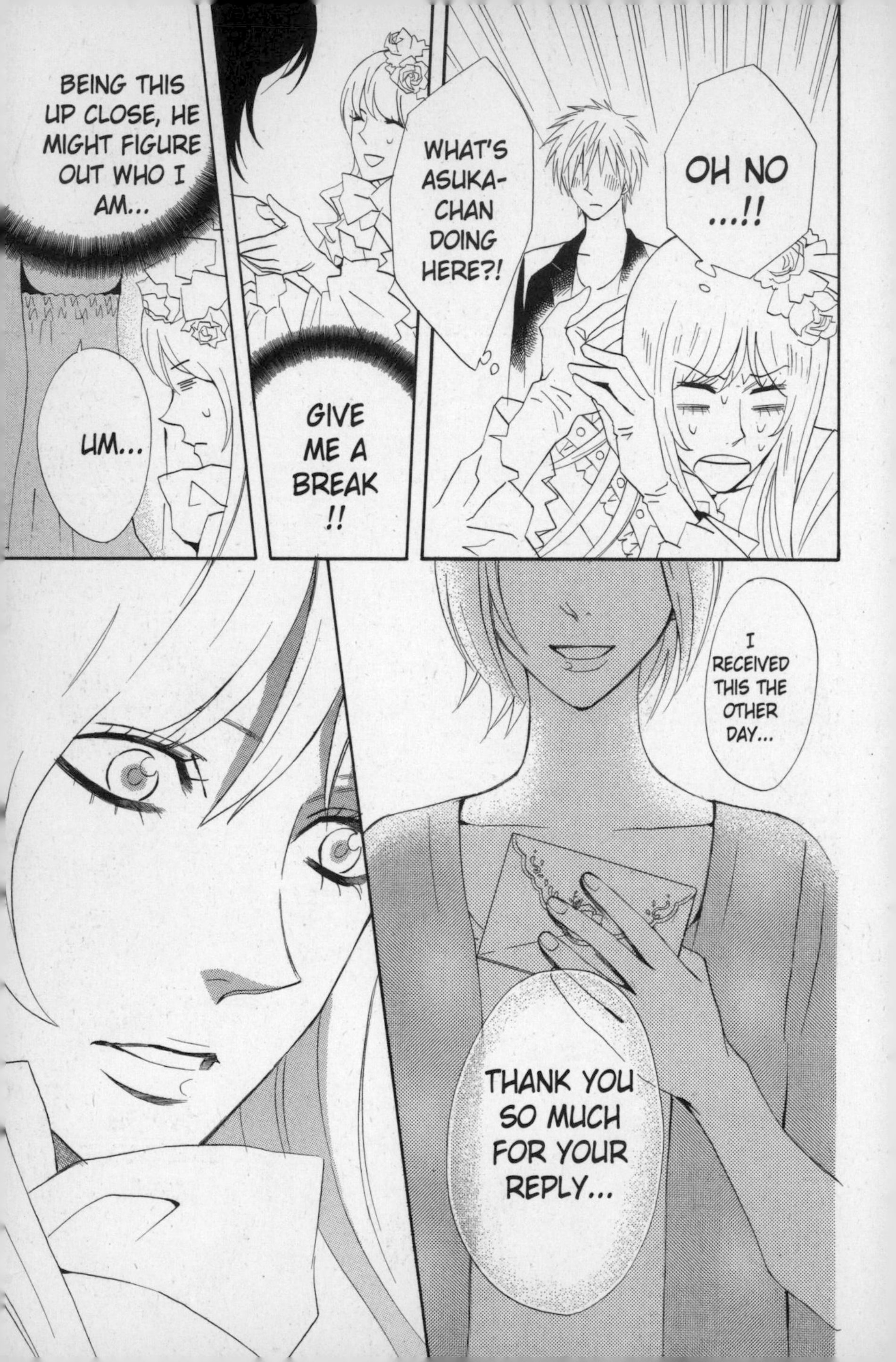
OH NO ...!!
WHAT'S ASUKA-CHAN DOING HERE?!
GIVE ME A BREAK !!
BEING THIS UP CLOSE, HE MIGHT FIGURE OUT WHO I AM...
UM...
I RECEIVED THIS THE OTHER DAY...
THANK YOU SO MUCH FOR YOUR REPLY...

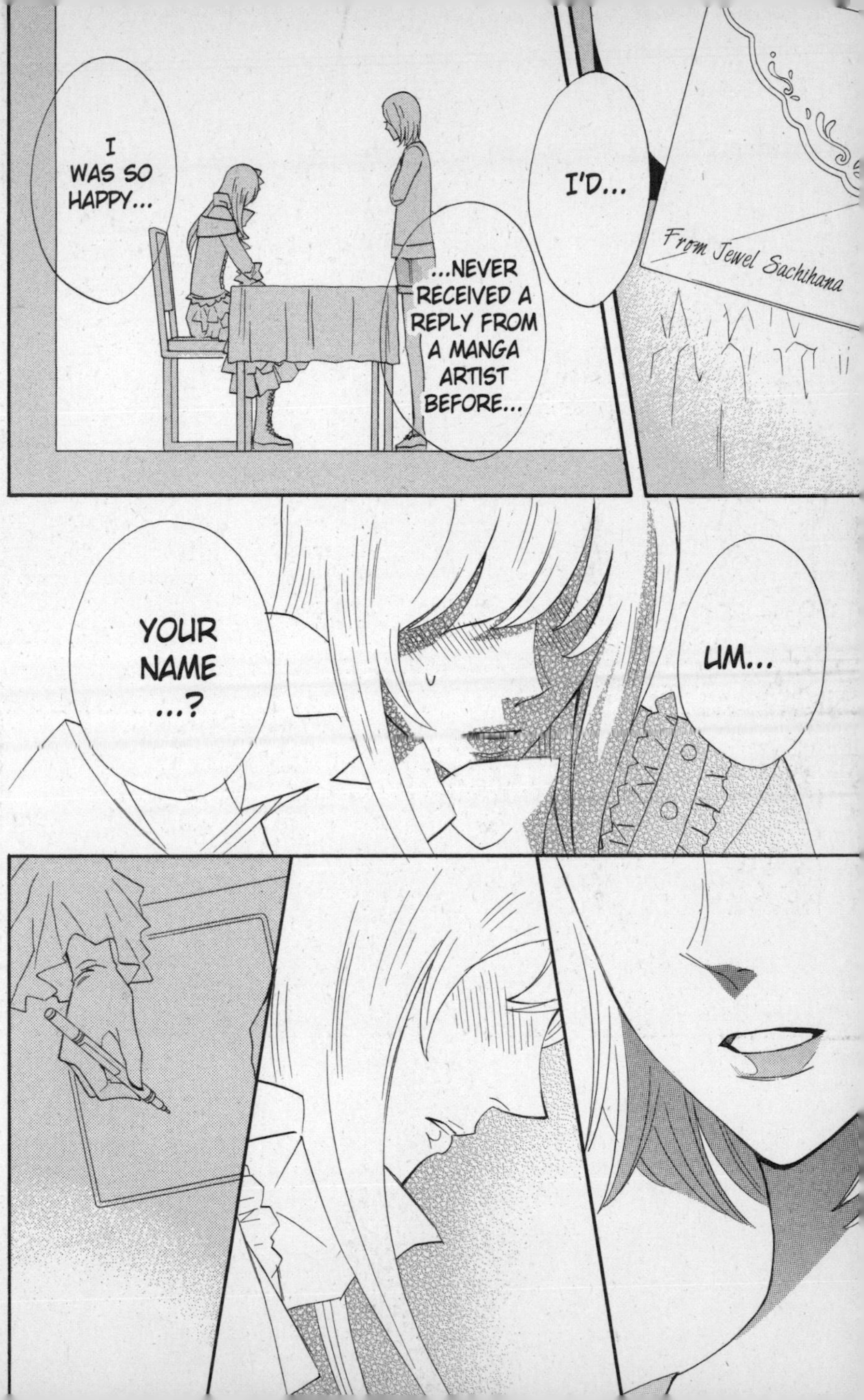
From Jewel Sachihana
I'D...
...NEVER RECEIVED A REPLY FROM A MANGA ARTIST BEFORE...
I WAS SO HAPPY...
UM...
YOUR NAME ...?

Shizuka Sakurai

LOVE CHICK
Jewel Sachihara

LOVE CHICK
Jewel Sachihara

LOVE CHICK
Jewel Sachihara

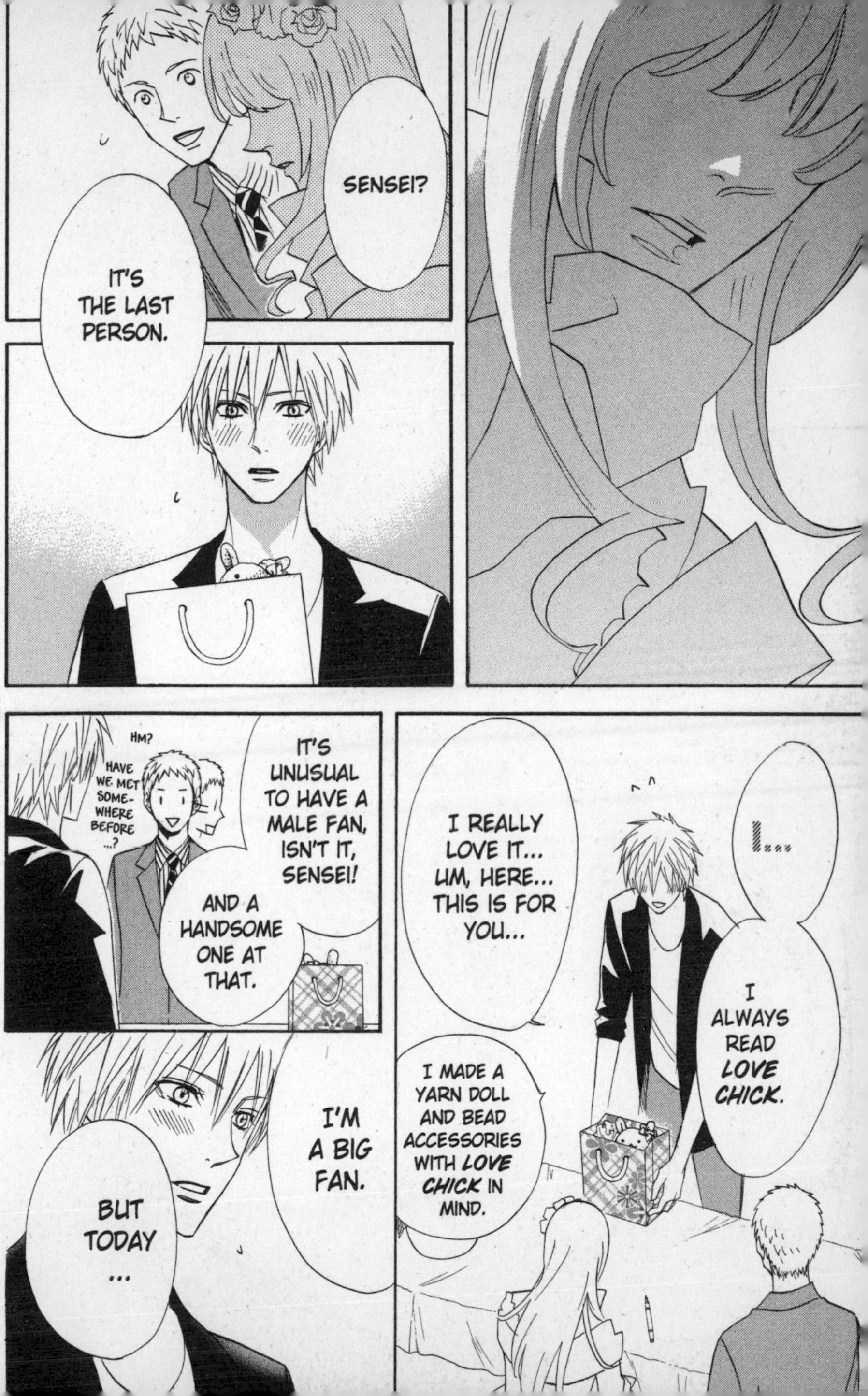
SENSEI?
IT'S THE LAST PERSON.
I...
I ALWAYS READ *LOVE CHICK*.
I REALLY LOVE IT... UM, HERE... THIS IS FOR YOU...
I MADE A YARN DOLL AND BEAD ACCESSORIES WITH *LOVE CHICK* IN MIND.
IT'S UNUSUAL TO HAVE A MALE FAN, ISN'T IT, SENSEI!
AND A HANDSOME ONE AT THAT.
HM?
HAVE WE MET SOME-WHERE BEFORE ...?
I'M A BIG FAN.
BUT TODAY ...

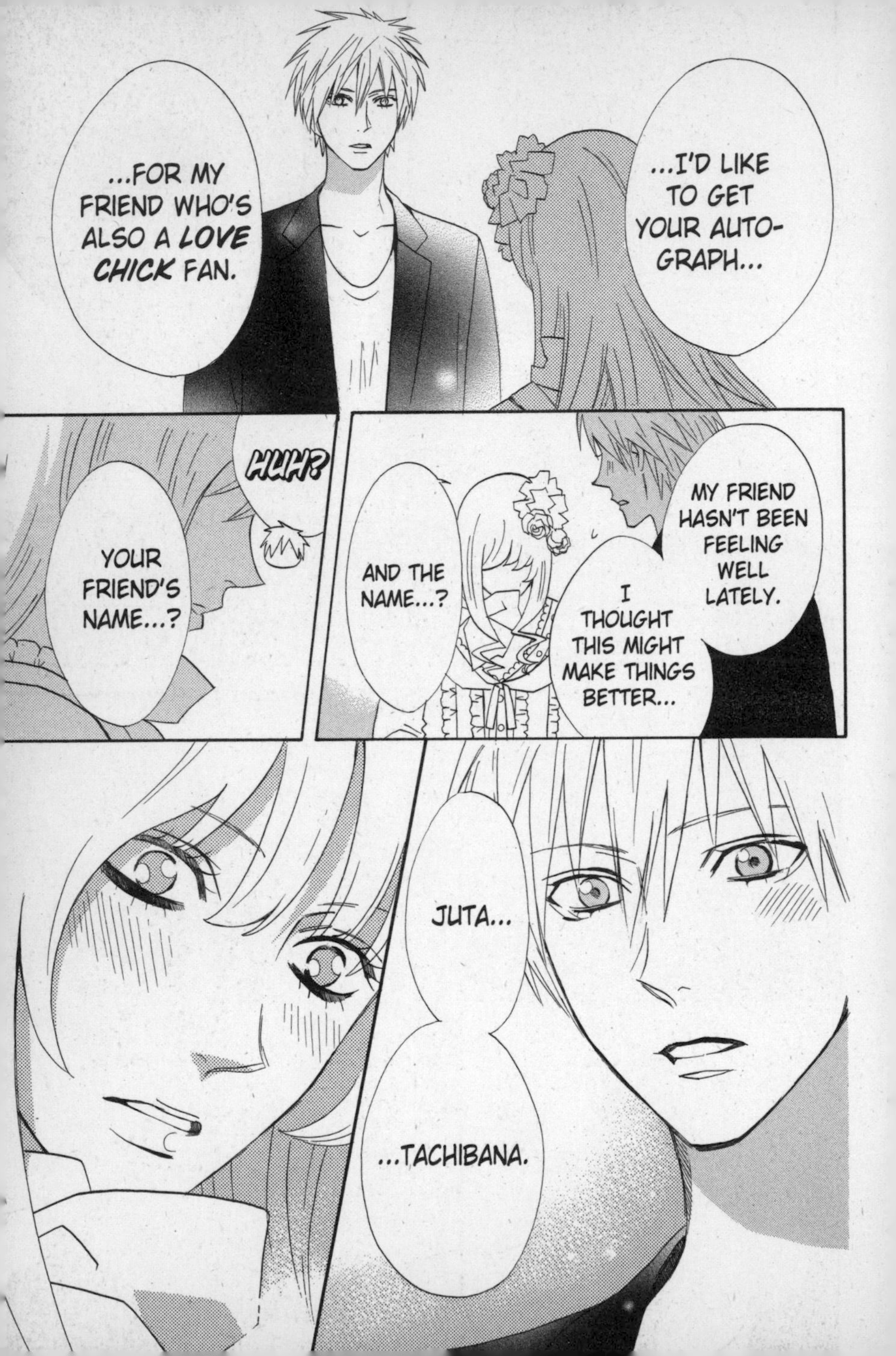
...I'D LIKE TO GET YOUR AUTO-GRAPH...
...FOR MY FRIEND WHO'S ALSO A *LOVE CHICK* FAN.
MY FRIEND HASN'T BEEN FEELING WELL LATELY.
I THOUGHT THIS MIGHT MAKE THINGS BETTER...
AND THE NAME...?
HUH?
YOUR FRIEND'S NAME...?
JUTA...
...TACHIBANA.

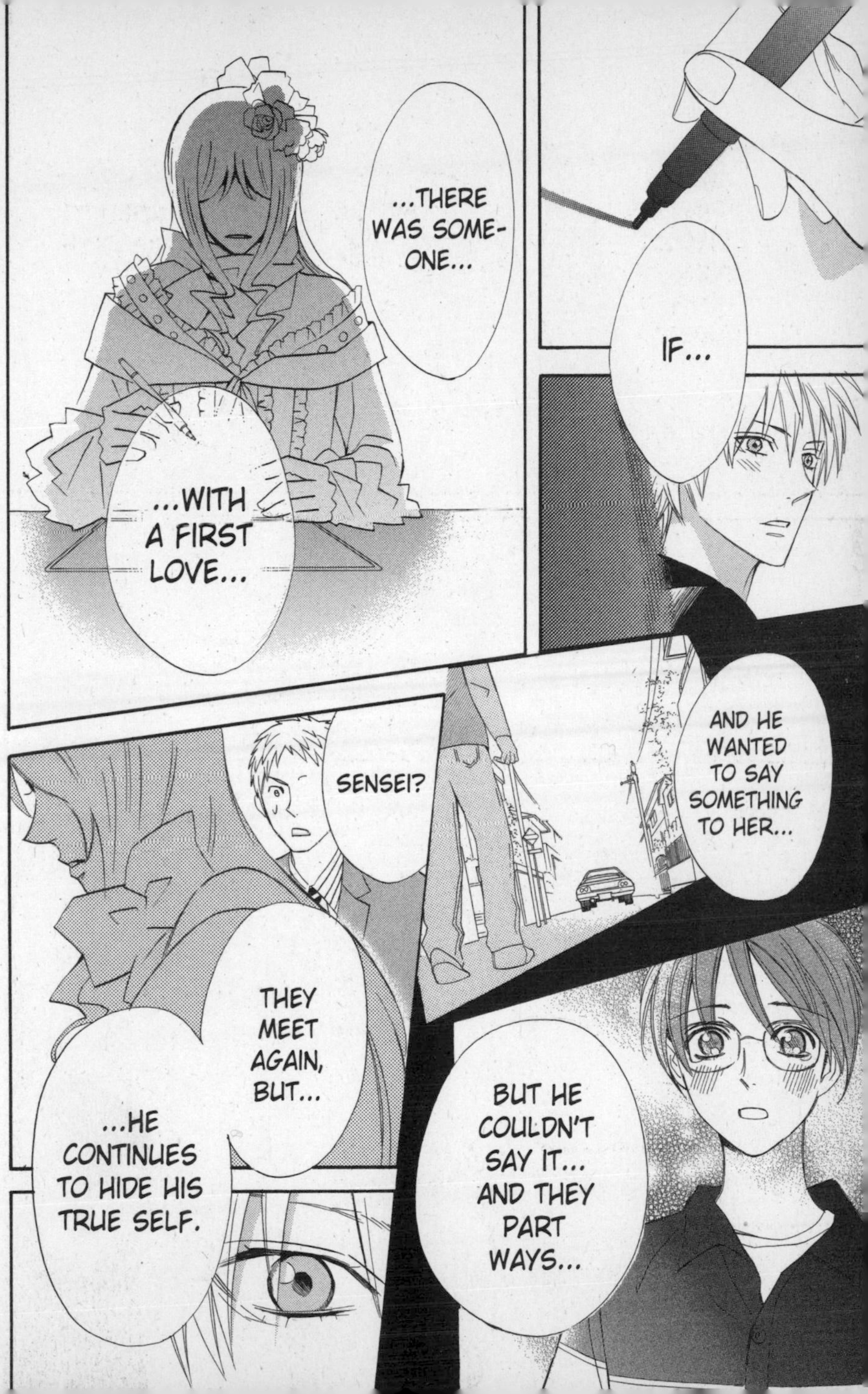
IF...
...THERE WAS SOME-ONE...
...WITH A FIRST LOVE...
AND HE WANTED TO SAY SOMETHING TO HER...
SENSEI?
BUT HE COULDN'T SAY IT... AND THEY PART WAYS...
THEY MEET AGAIN, BUT...
...HE CONTINUES TO HIDE HIS TRUE SELF.

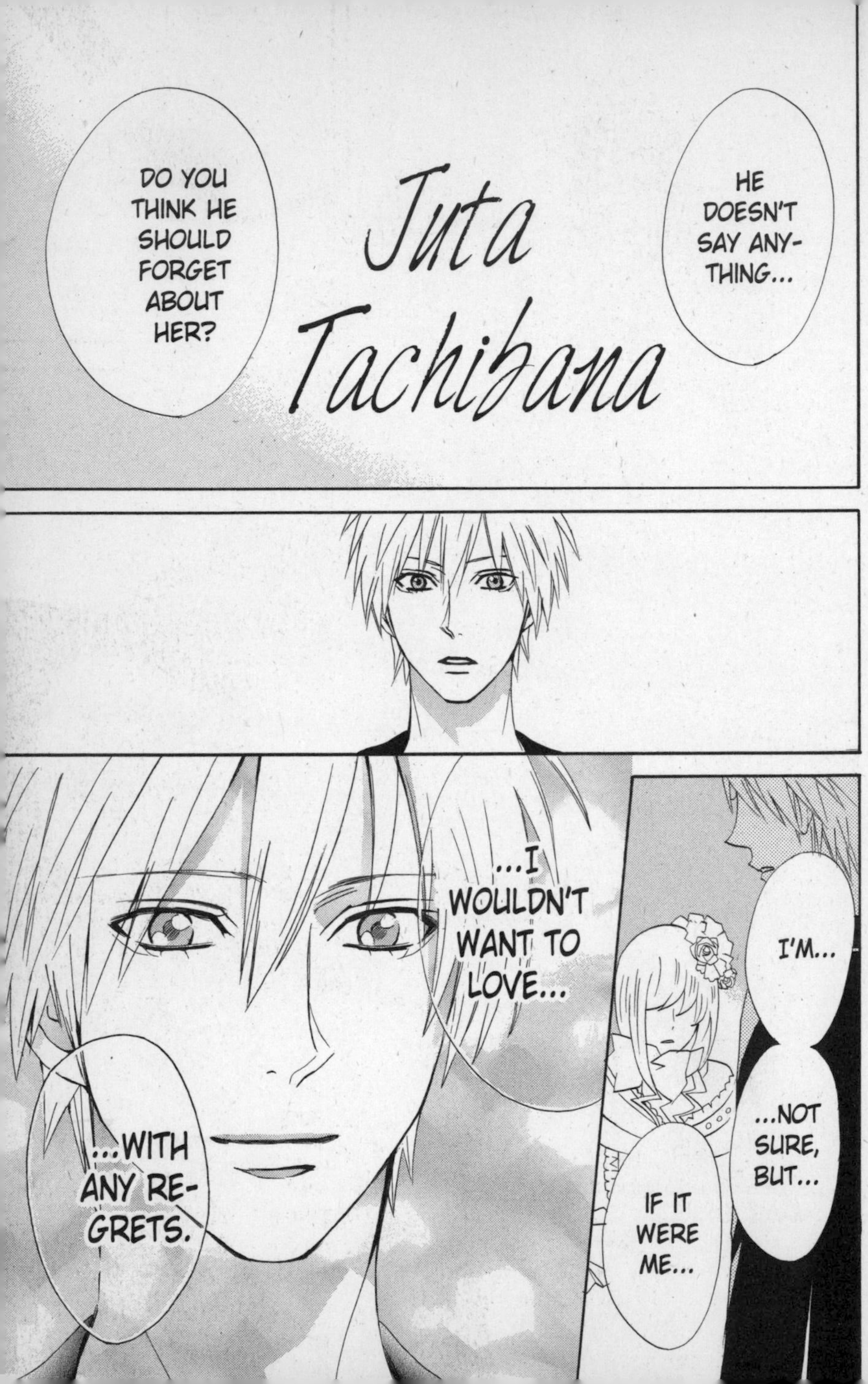
HE DOESN'T SAY ANYTHING...
Juta Tachibana
DO YOU THINK HE SHOULD FORGET ABOUT HER?
I'M...
...NOT SURE, BUT...
IF IT WERE ME...
...I WOULDN'T WANT TO LOVE...
...WITH ANY REGRETS.

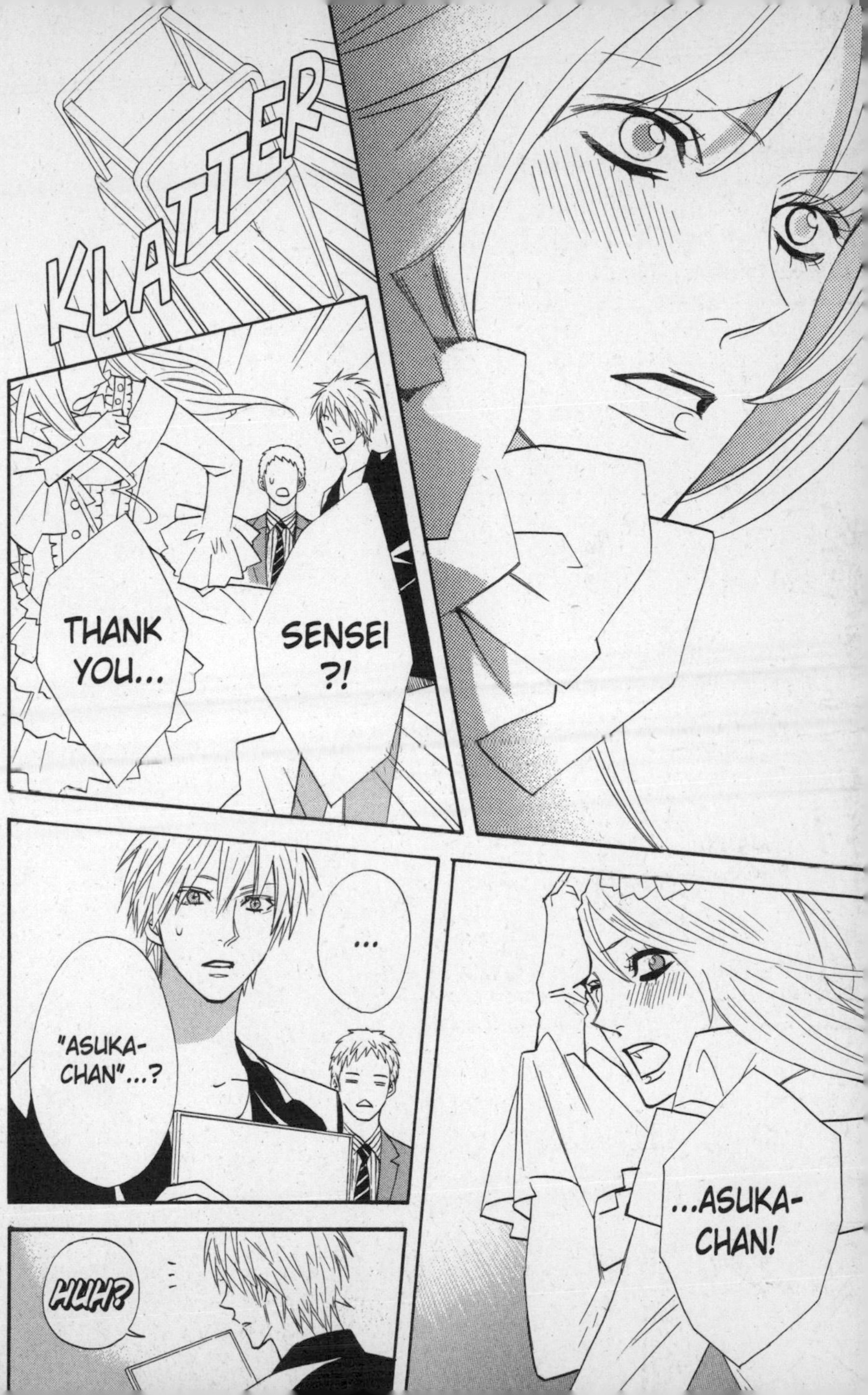
KLATTER
SENSEI ?!
THANK YOU...
...ASUKA-CHAN!
...
"ASUKA-CHAN"...?
HUH?

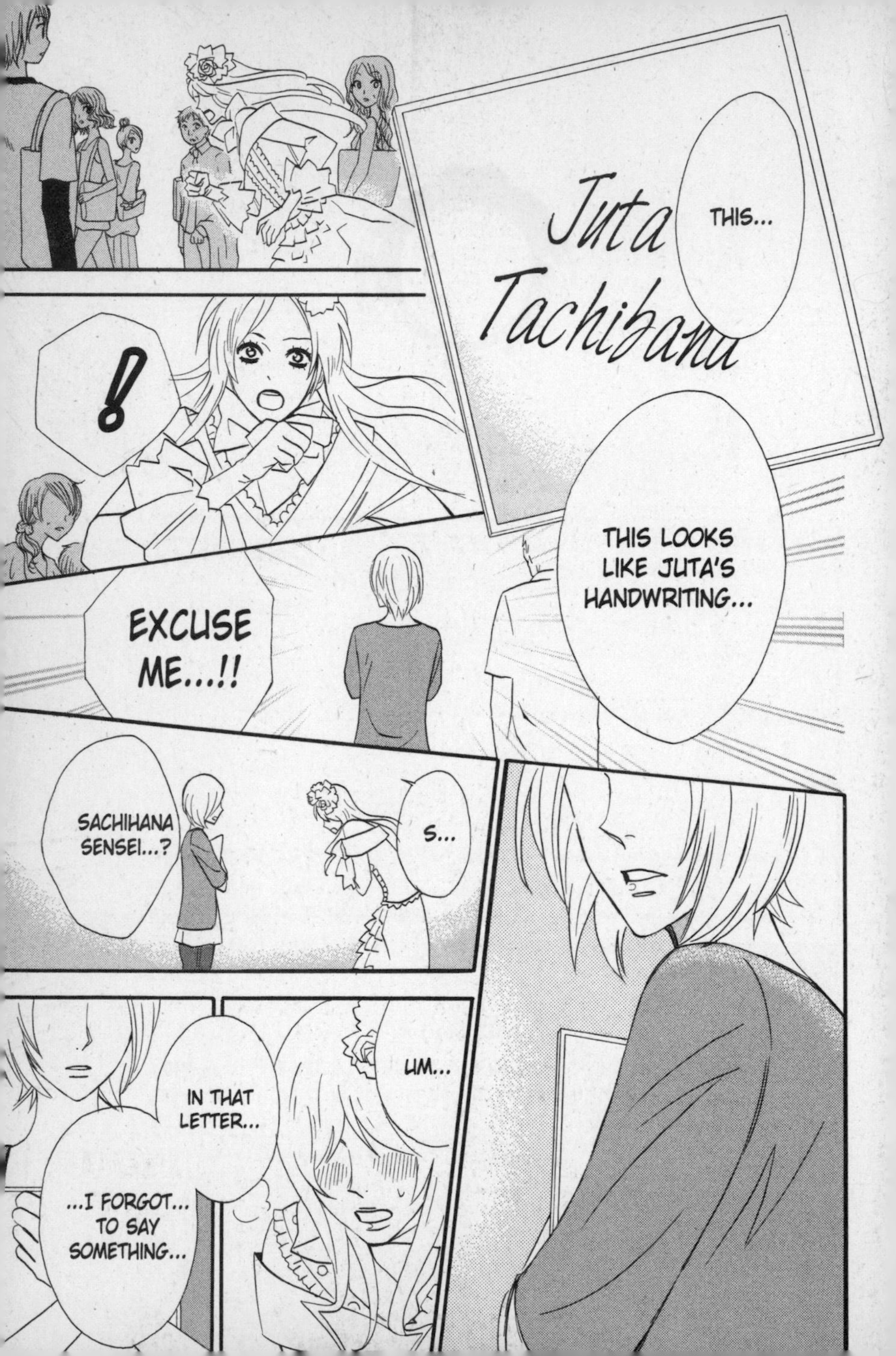
Juta Tachibana
THIS...
THIS LOOKS LIKE JUTA'S HANDWRITING...
!
EXCUSE ME...!!
S...
SACHIHANA SENSEI...?
UM...
IN THAT LETTER...
...I FORGOT... TO SAY SOMETHING...

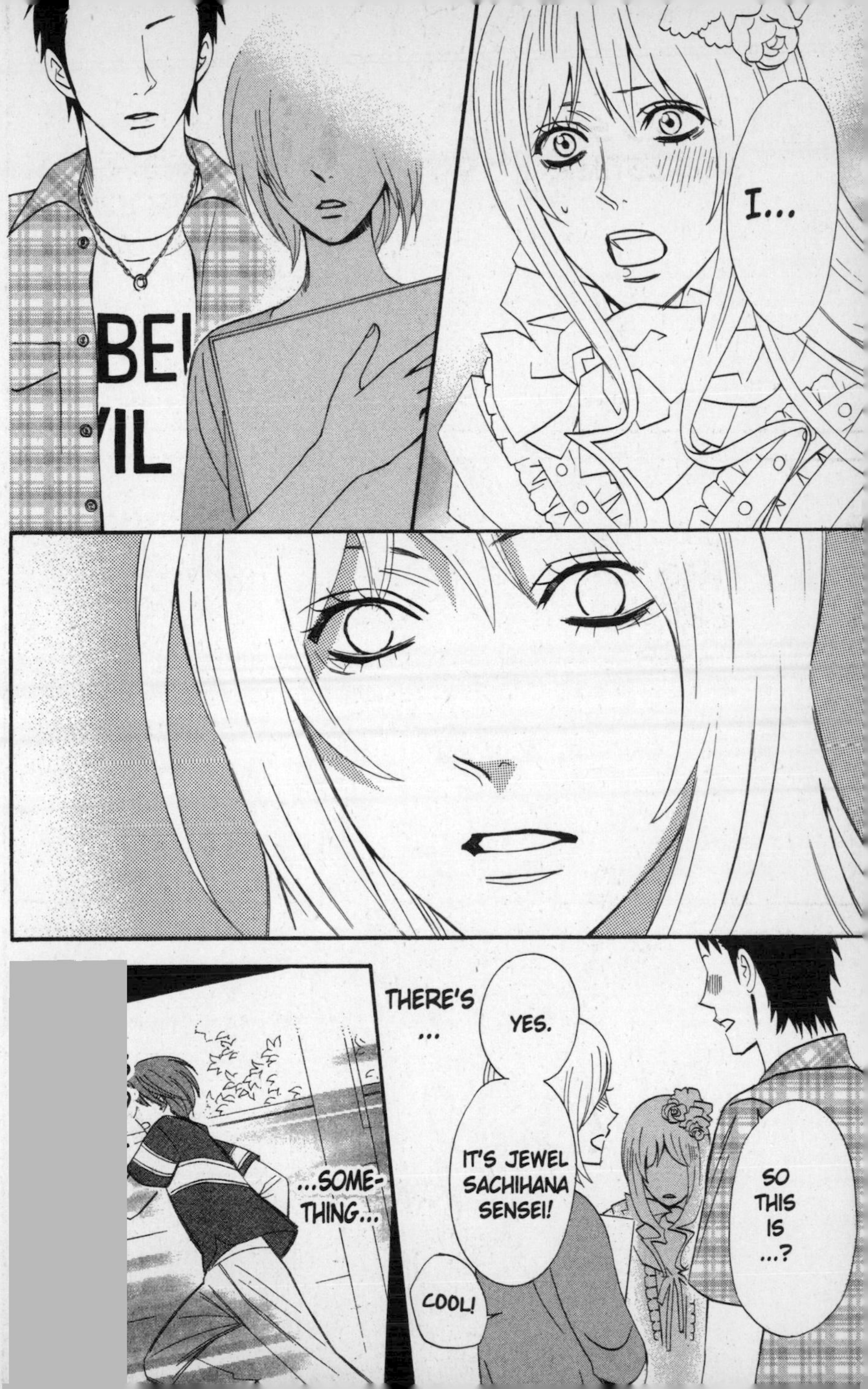
I...
SO THIS IS ...?
YES.
IT'S JEWEL SACHIHANA SENSEI!
COOL!
THERE'S ...
...SOME-THING...

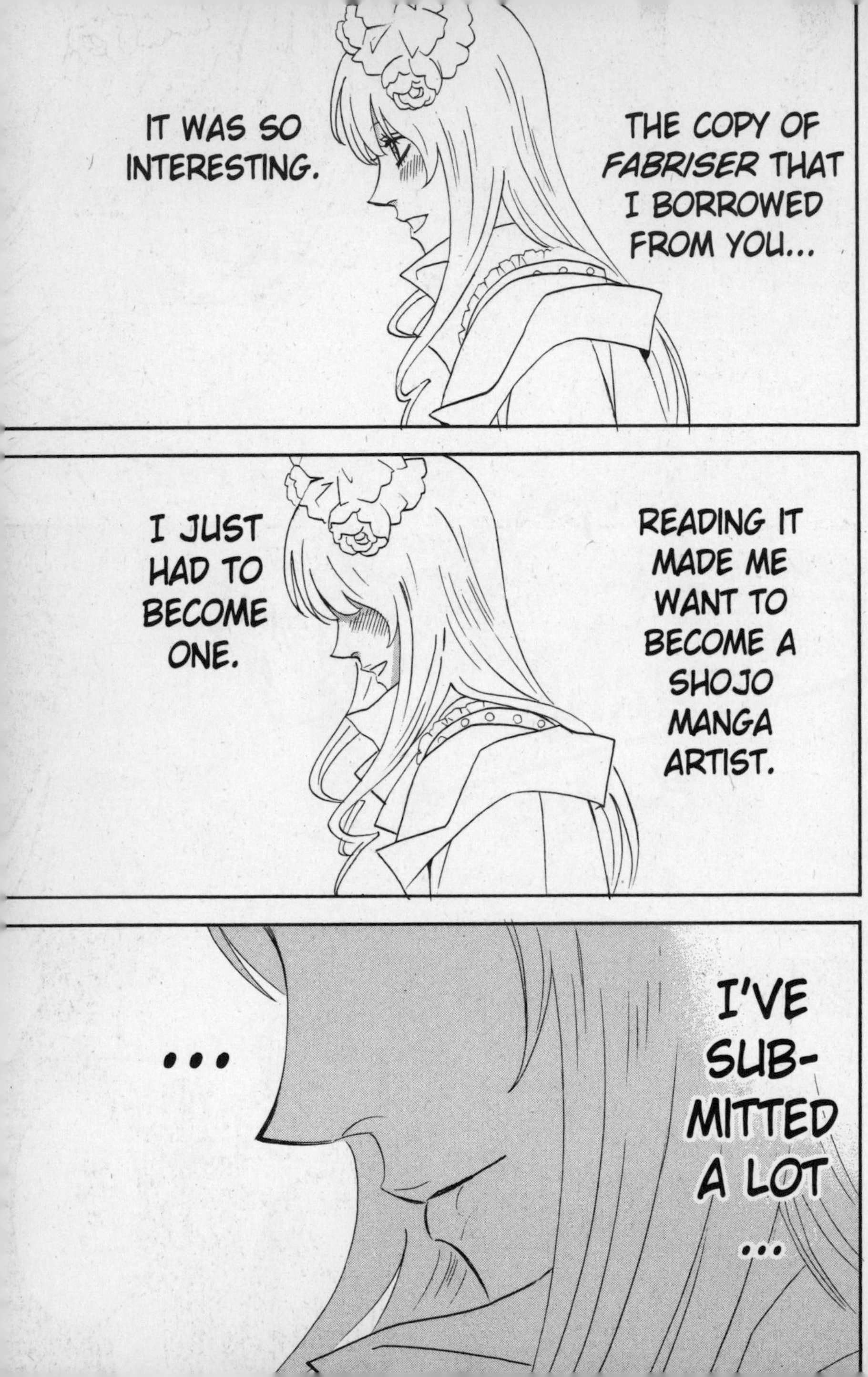
THE COPY OF *FABRISER* THAT I BORROWED FROM YOU...
IT WAS SO INTERESTING.
READING IT MADE ME WANT TO BECOME A SHOJO MANGA ARTIST.
I JUST HAD TO BECOME ONE.
I'VE SUB-MITTED A LOT ...
...

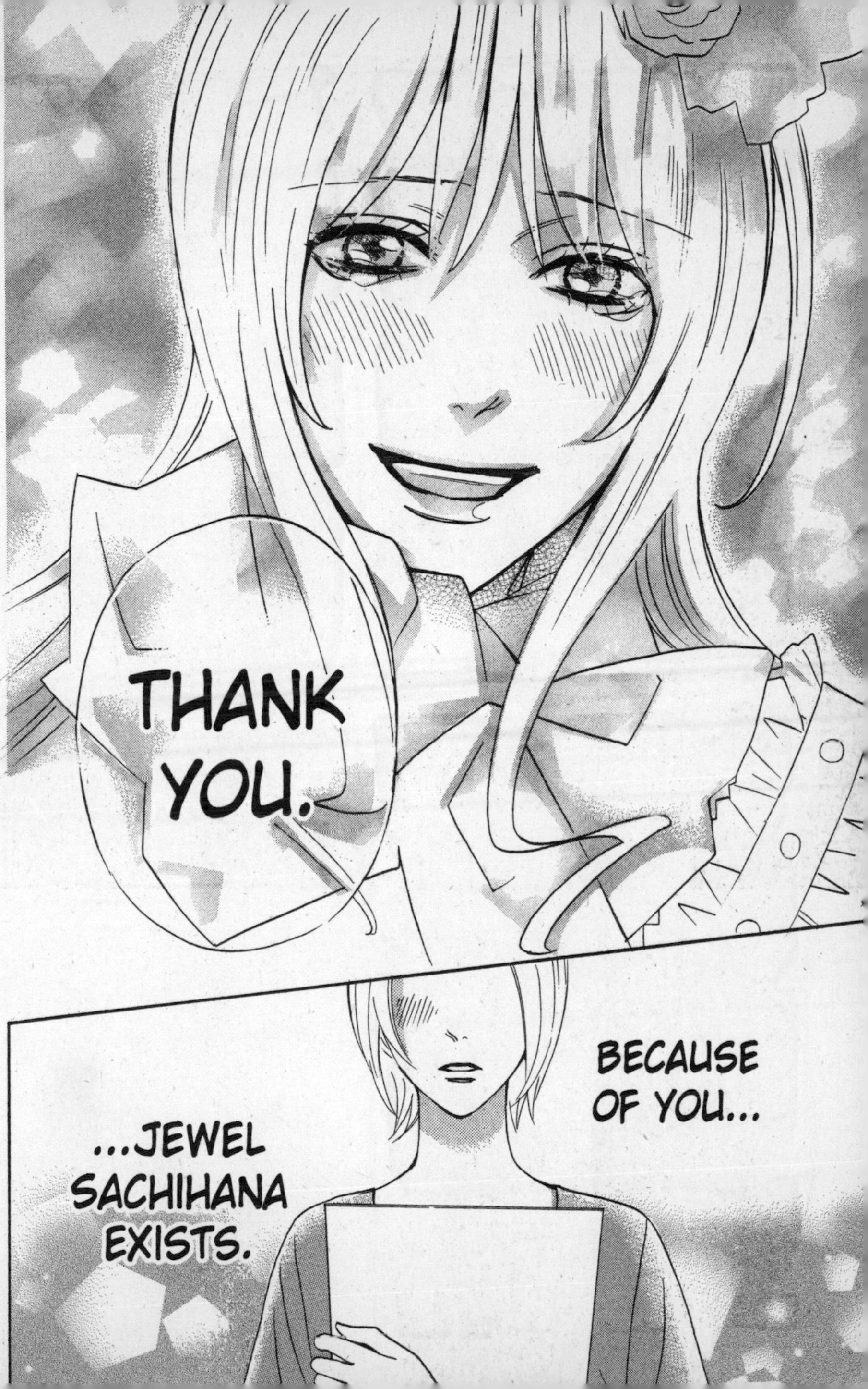
THANK YOU.
BECAUSE OF YOU...
...JEWEL SACHIHANA EXISTS.

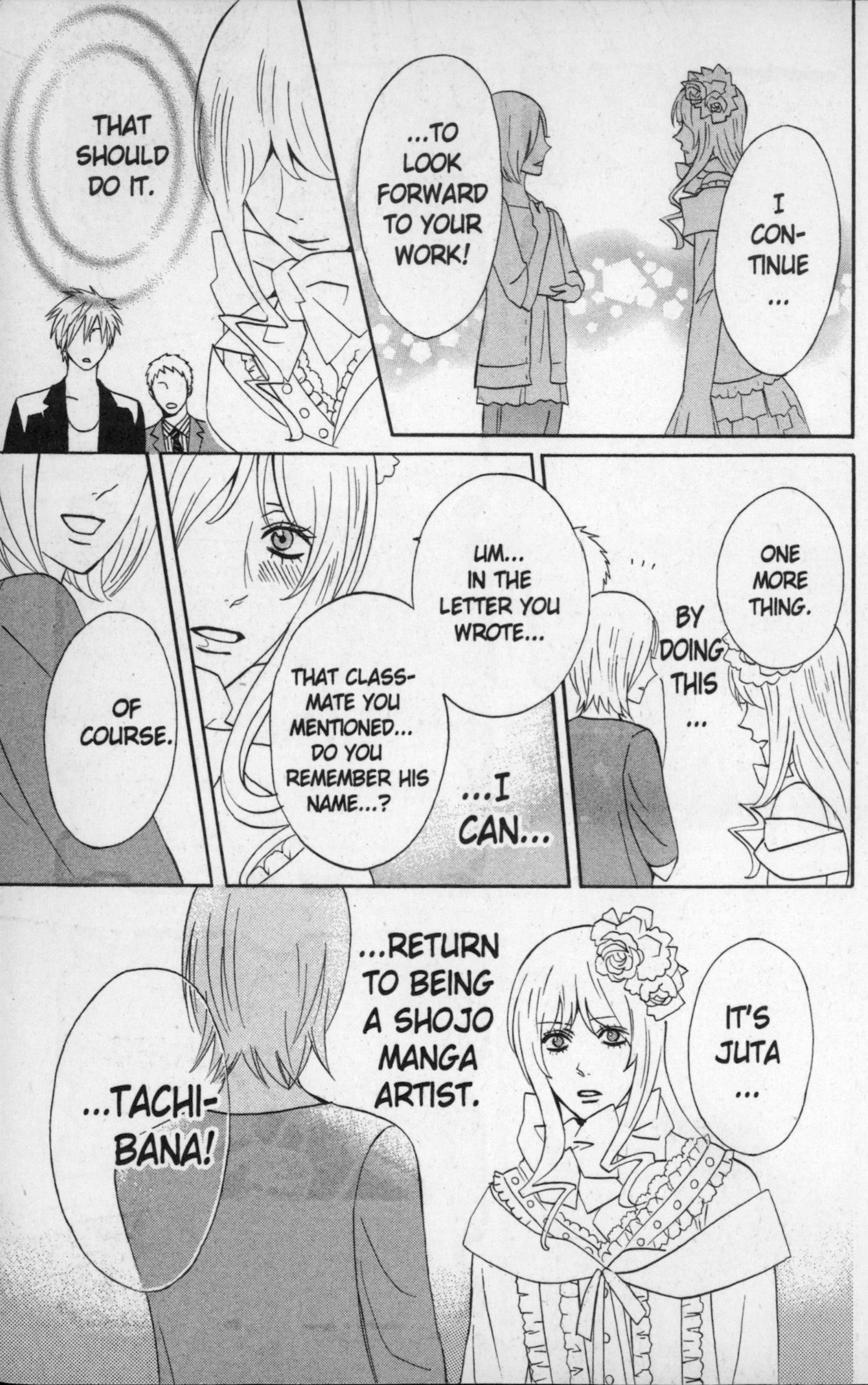
I CONTINUE ...
...TO LOOK FORWARD TO YOUR WORK!
THAT SHOULD DO IT.
ONE MORE THING.
BY DOING THIS ...
...I CAN...
UM... IN THE LETTER YOU WROTE...
THAT CLASSMATE YOU MENTIONED... DO YOU REMEMBER HIS NAME...?
OF COURSE.
IT'S JUTA ...
...RETURN TO BEING A SHOJO MANGA ARTIST.
...TACHIBANA!

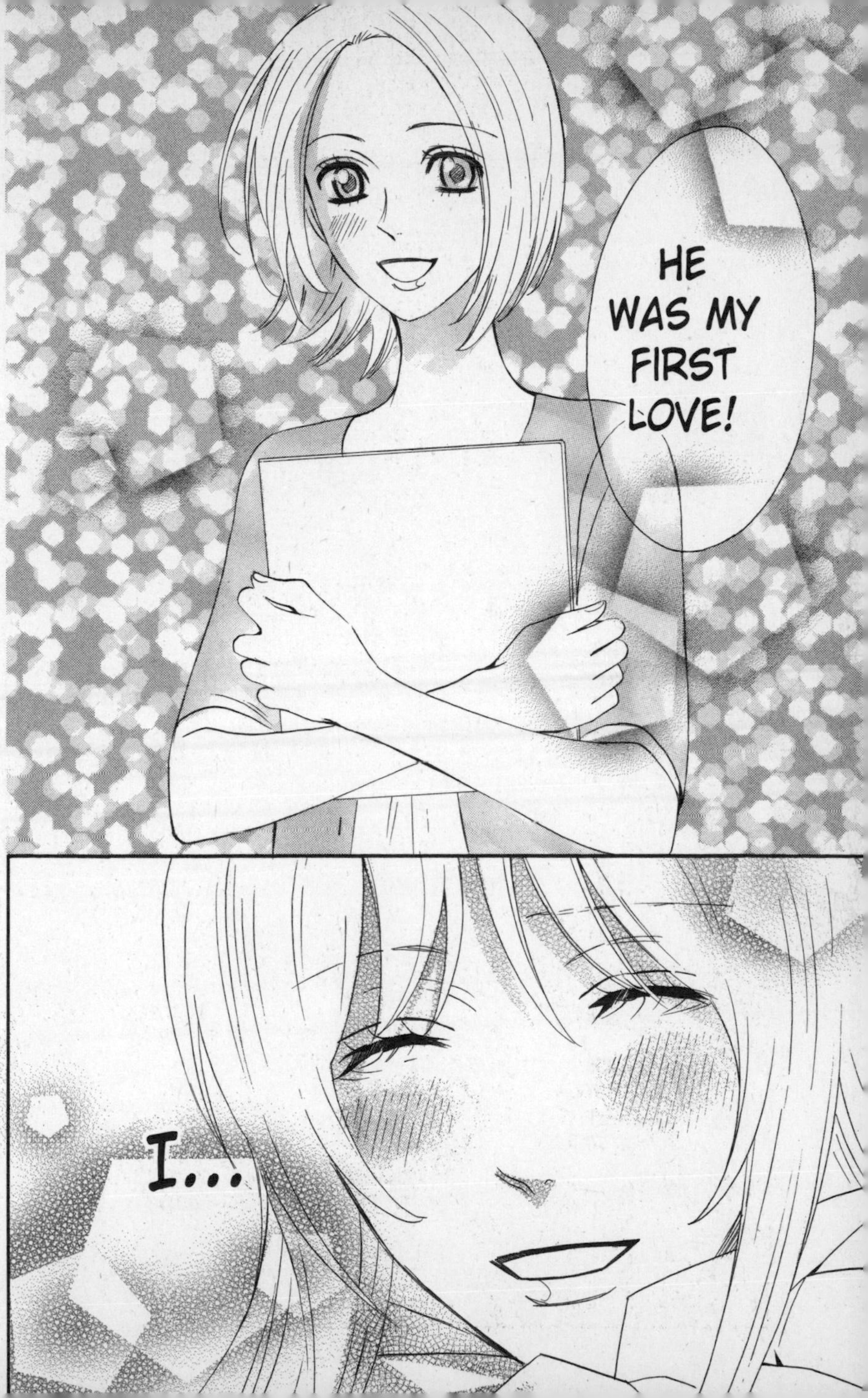
HE WAS MY FIRST LOVE!
I...

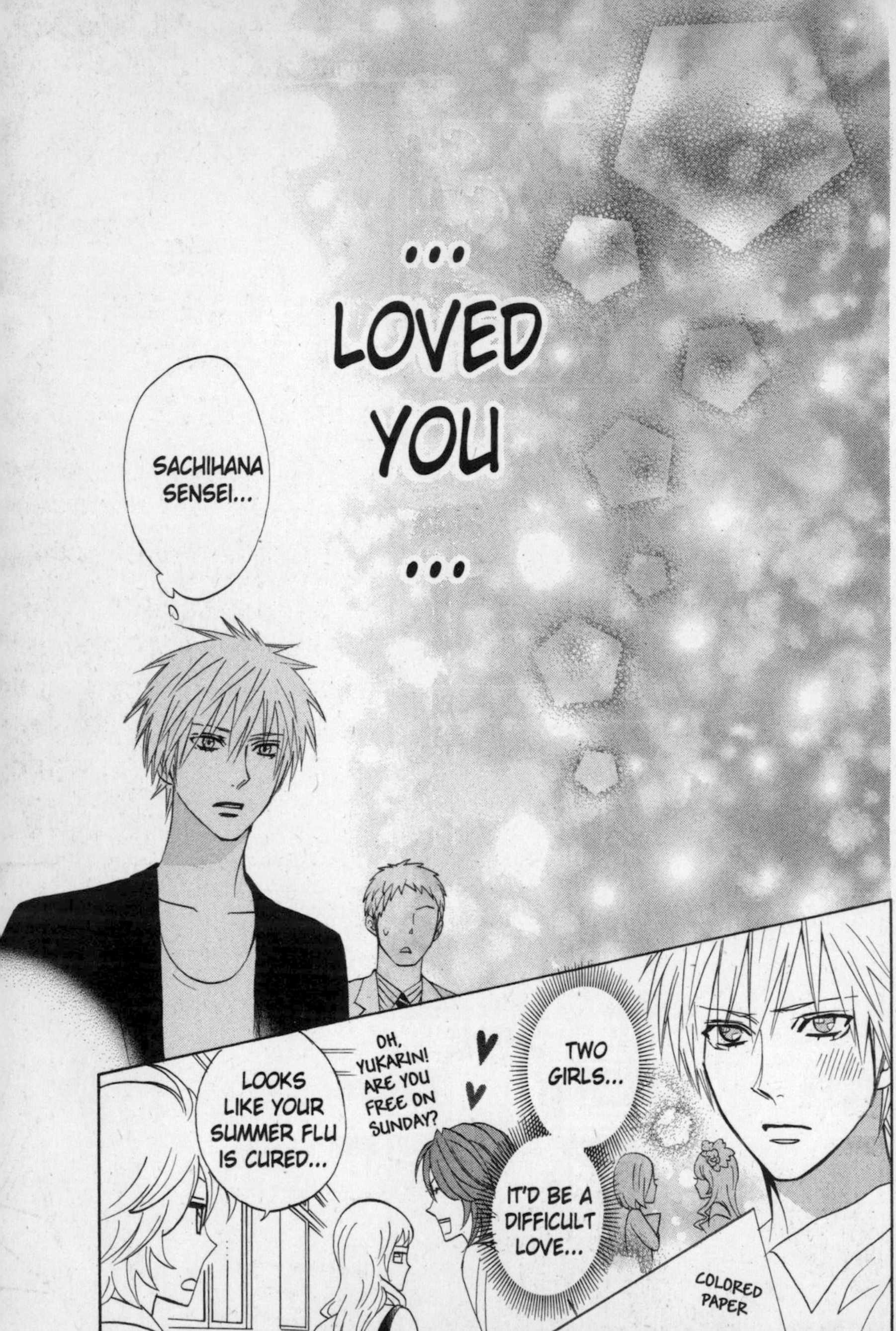
...
LOVED YOU
...
SACHIHANA SENSEI...
TWO GIRLS...
IT'D BE A DIFFICULT LOVE...
COLORED PAPER
OH, YUKARIN! ARE YOU FREE ON SUNDAY?
LOOKS LIKE YOUR SUMMER FLU IS CURED...

OTOMEN

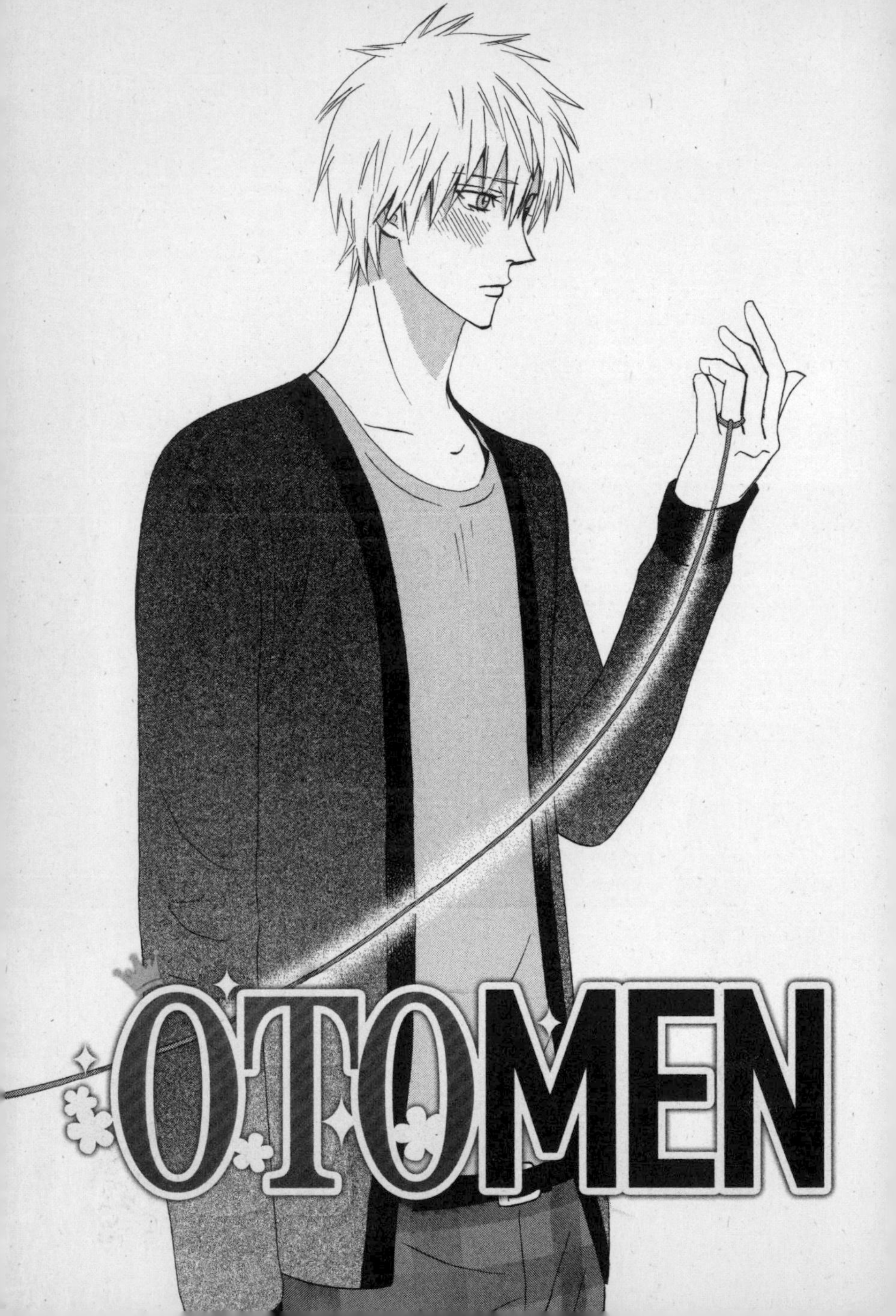
OTOMEN

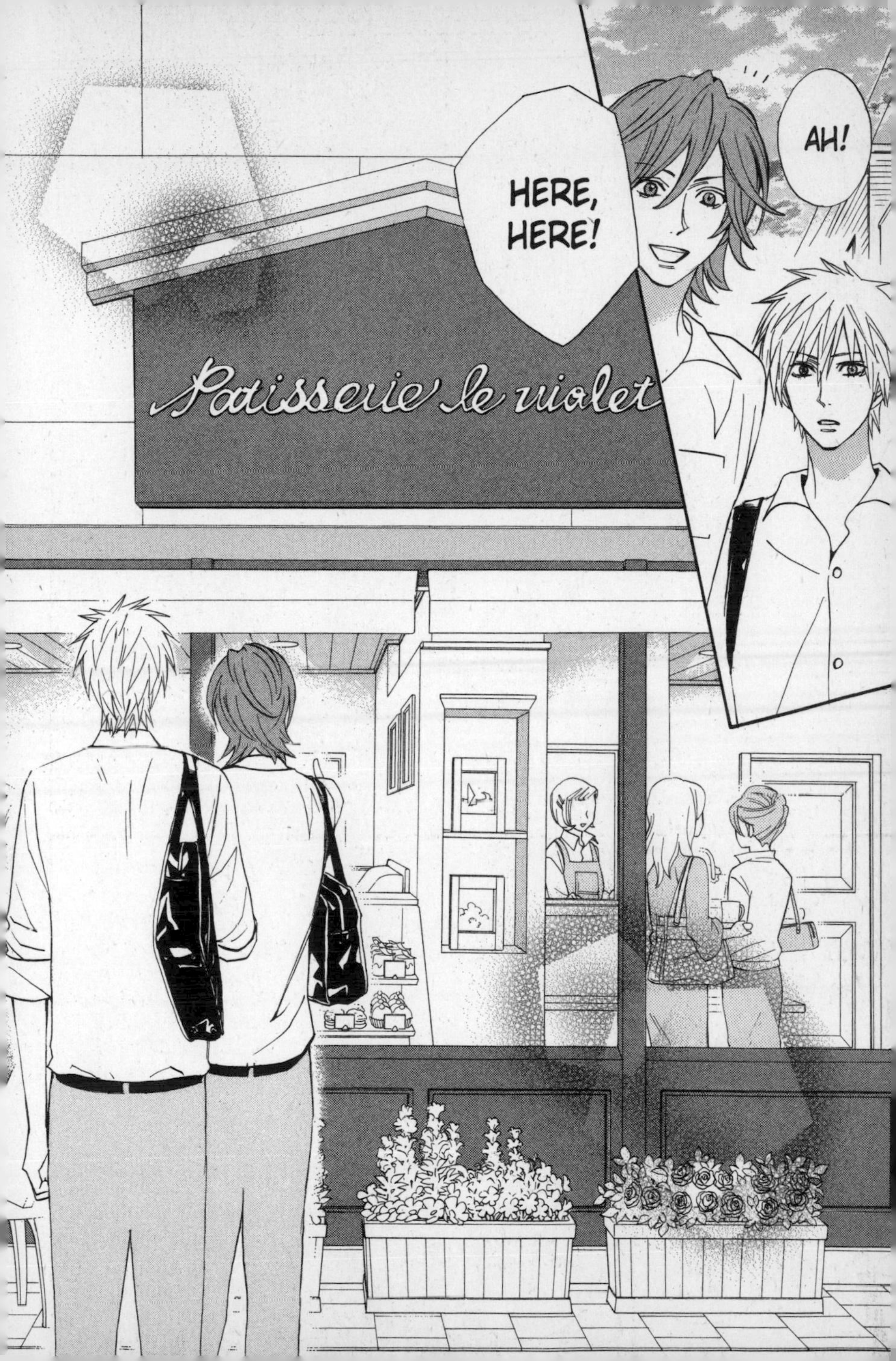
AH!
HERE, HERE!
Patisserie le violet

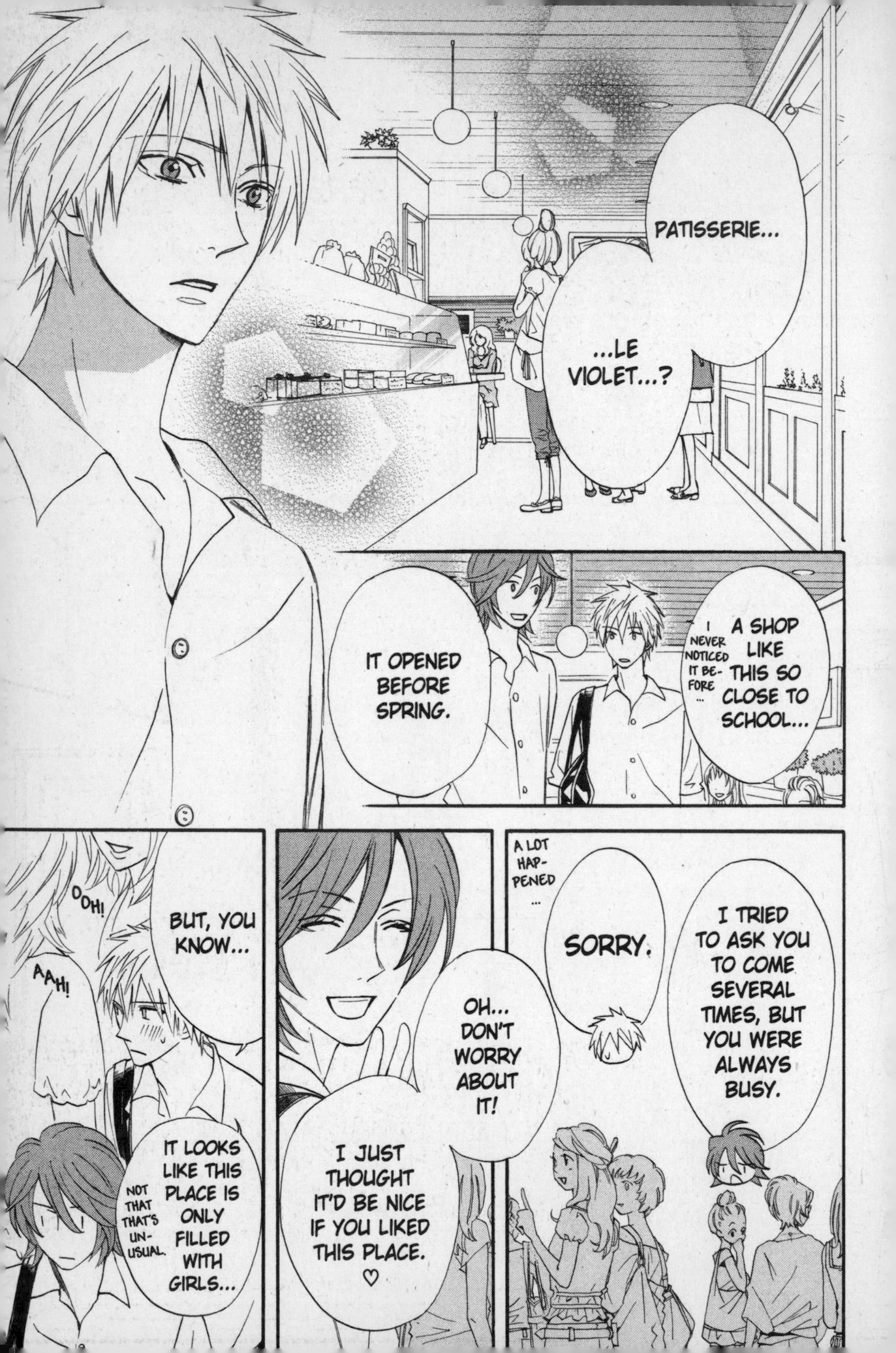
PATISSERIE...
...LE VIOLET...?
A SHOP LIKE THIS SO CLOSE TO SCHOOL...
I NEVER NOTICED IT BEFORE...
IT OPENED BEFORE SPRING.
I TRIED TO ASK YOU TO COME SEVERAL TIMES, BUT YOU WERE ALWAYS BUSY.
A LOT HAPPENED...
SORRY.
OH... DON'T WORRY ABOUT IT!
I JUST THOUGHT IT'D BE NICE IF YOU LIKED THIS PLACE. ♡
BUT, YOU KNOW...
OOH!
AAH!
IT LOOKS LIKE THIS PLACE IS ONLY FILLED WITH GIRLS...
NOT THAT THAT'S UNUSUAL.

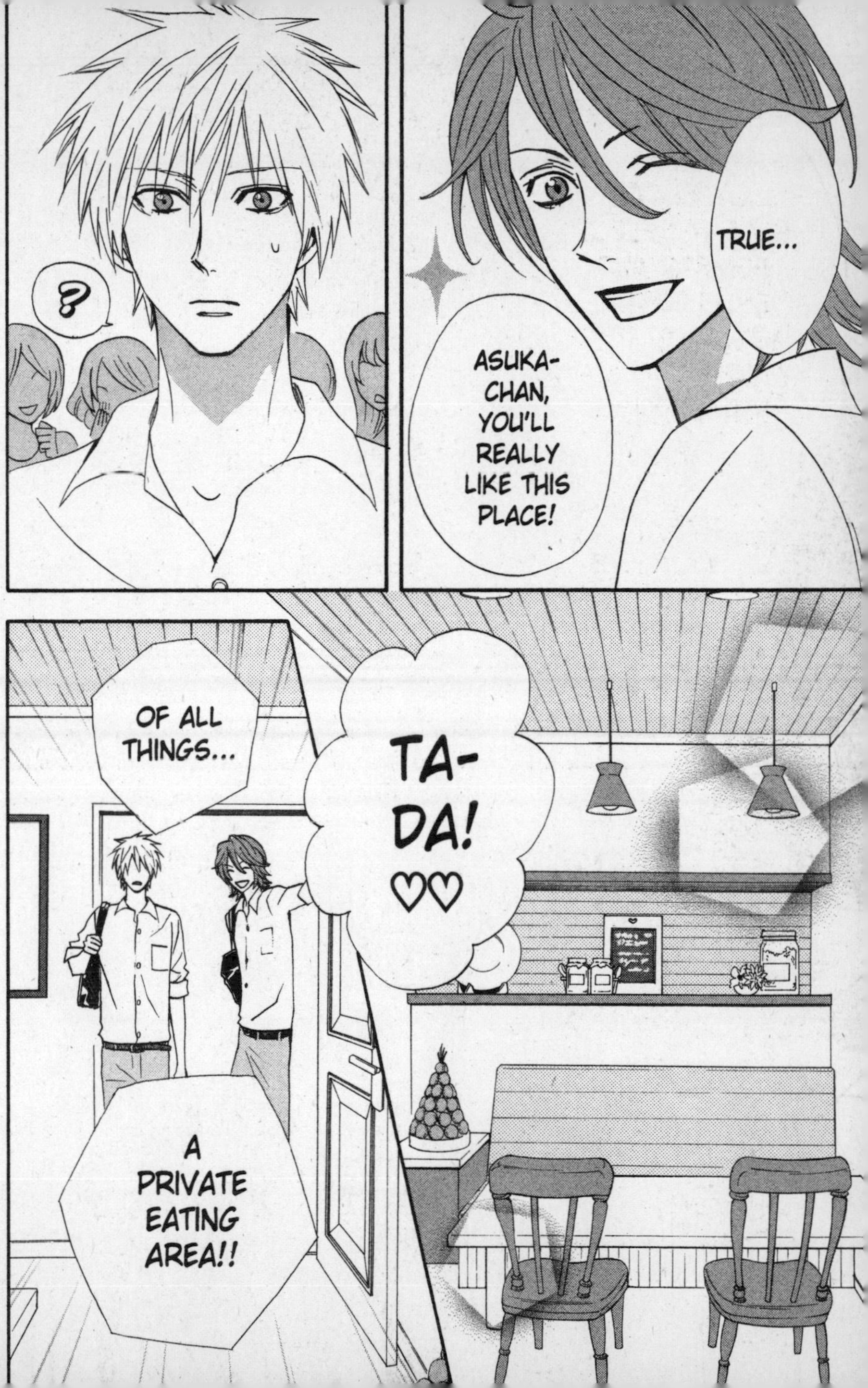
TRUE...
ASUKA-CHAN, YOU'LL REALLY LIKE THIS PLACE!
?
TA-DA! ♡♡
OF ALL THINGS...
A PRIVATE EATING AREA!!

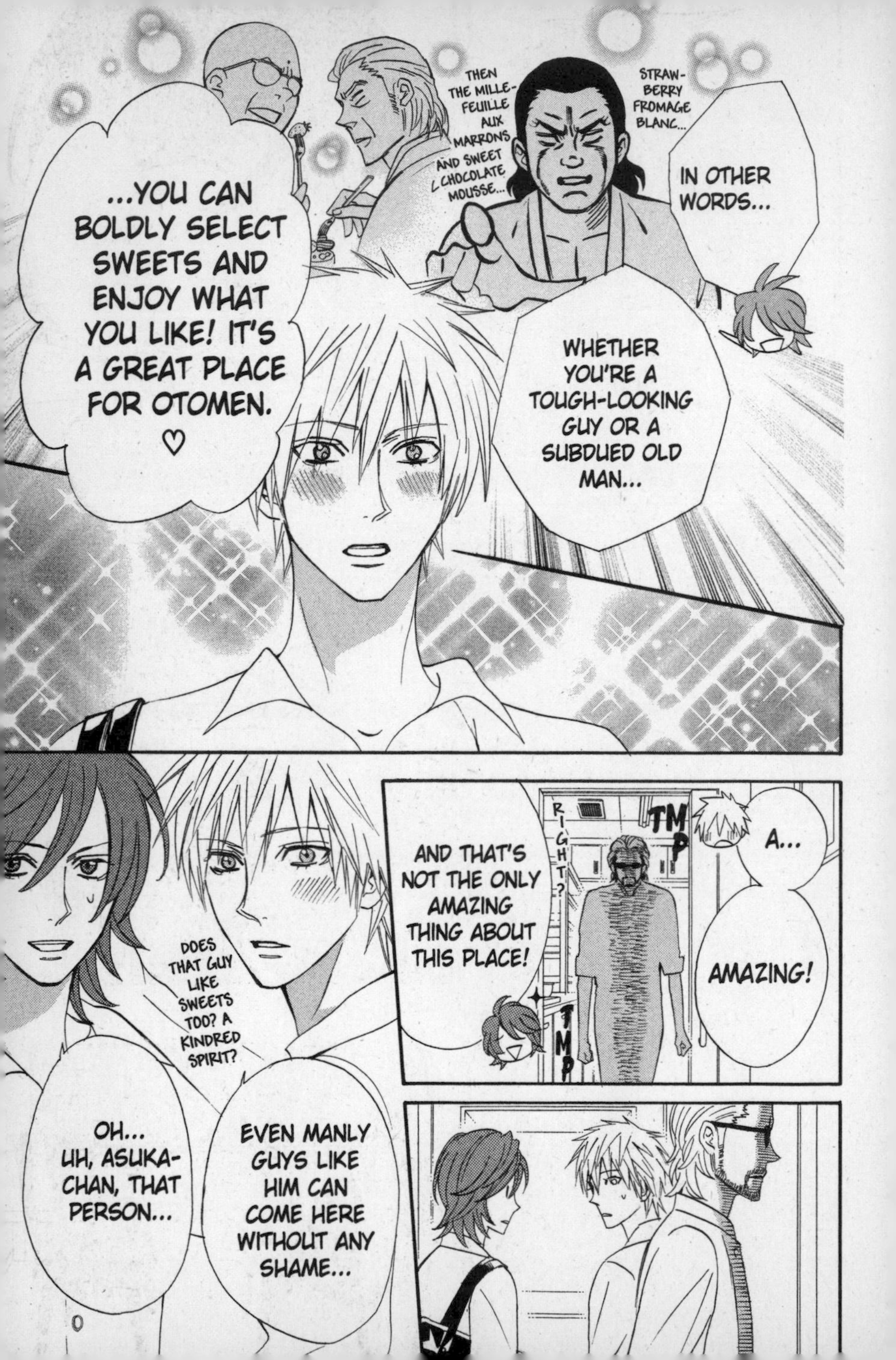
STRAW-BERRY FROMAGE BLANC...
IN OTHER WORDS...
THEN THE MILLE-FEUILLE AUX MARRONS AND SWEET CHOCOLATE MOUSSE...
WHETHER YOU'RE A TOUGH-LOOKING GUY OR A SUBDUED OLD MAN...
...YOU CAN BOLDLY SELECT SWEETS AND ENJOY WHAT YOU LIKE! IT'S A GREAT PLACE FOR OTOMEN. ♡
A...
AMAZING!
TMP
RIGHT?
AND THAT'S NOT THE ONLY AMAZING THING ABOUT THIS PLACE!
TMP
DOES THAT GUY LIKE SWEETS TOO? A KINDRED SPIRIT?
EVEN MANLY GUYS LIKE HIM CAN COME HERE WITHOUT ANY SHAME...
OH... UH, ASUKA-CHAN, THAT PERSON...

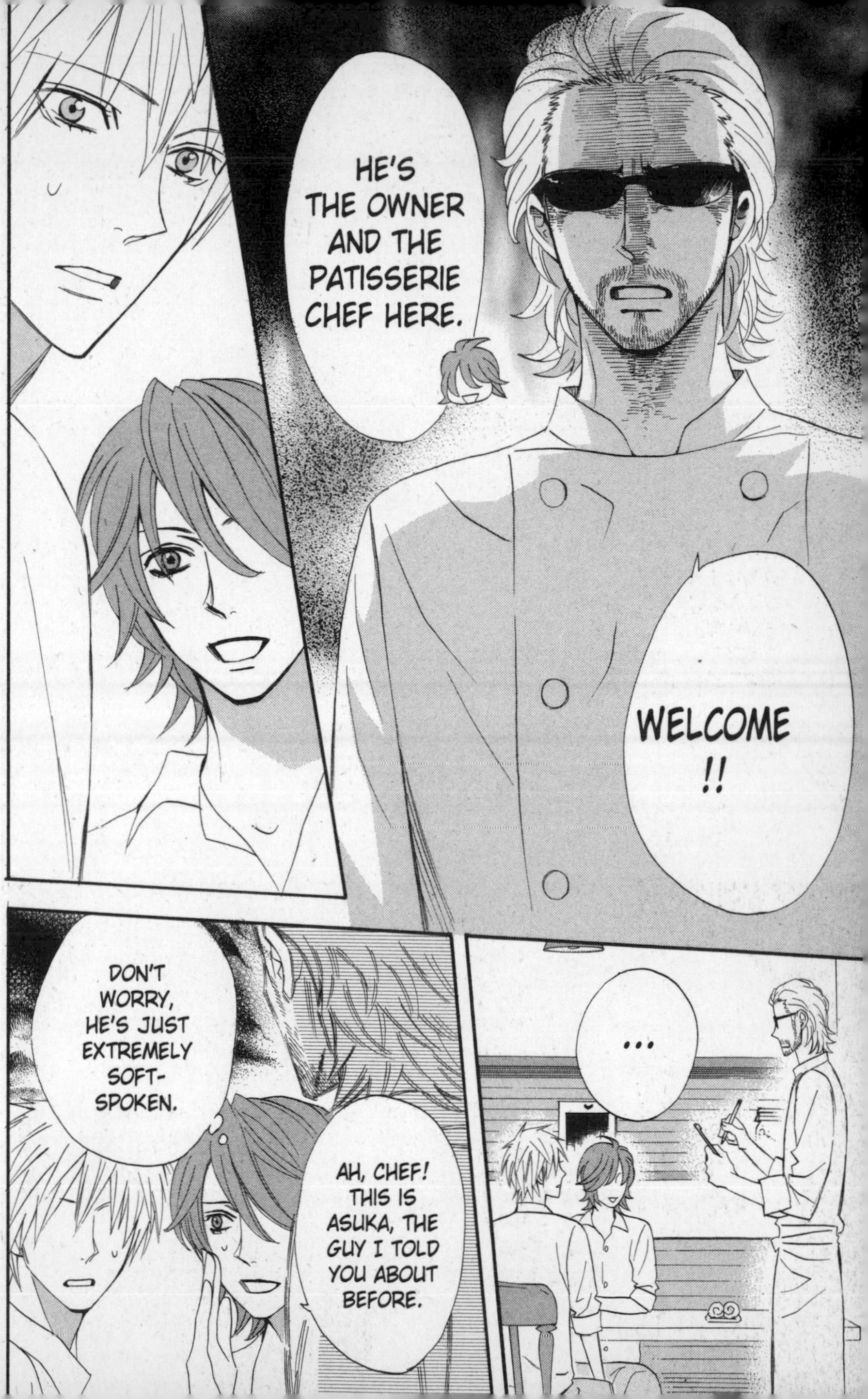
WELCOME !!
HE'S THE OWNER AND THE PATISSERIE CHEF HERE.
...
AH, CHEF! THIS IS ASUKA, THE GUY I TOLD YOU ABOUT BEFORE.
DON'T WORRY, HE'S JUST EXTREMELY SOFT-SPOKEN.

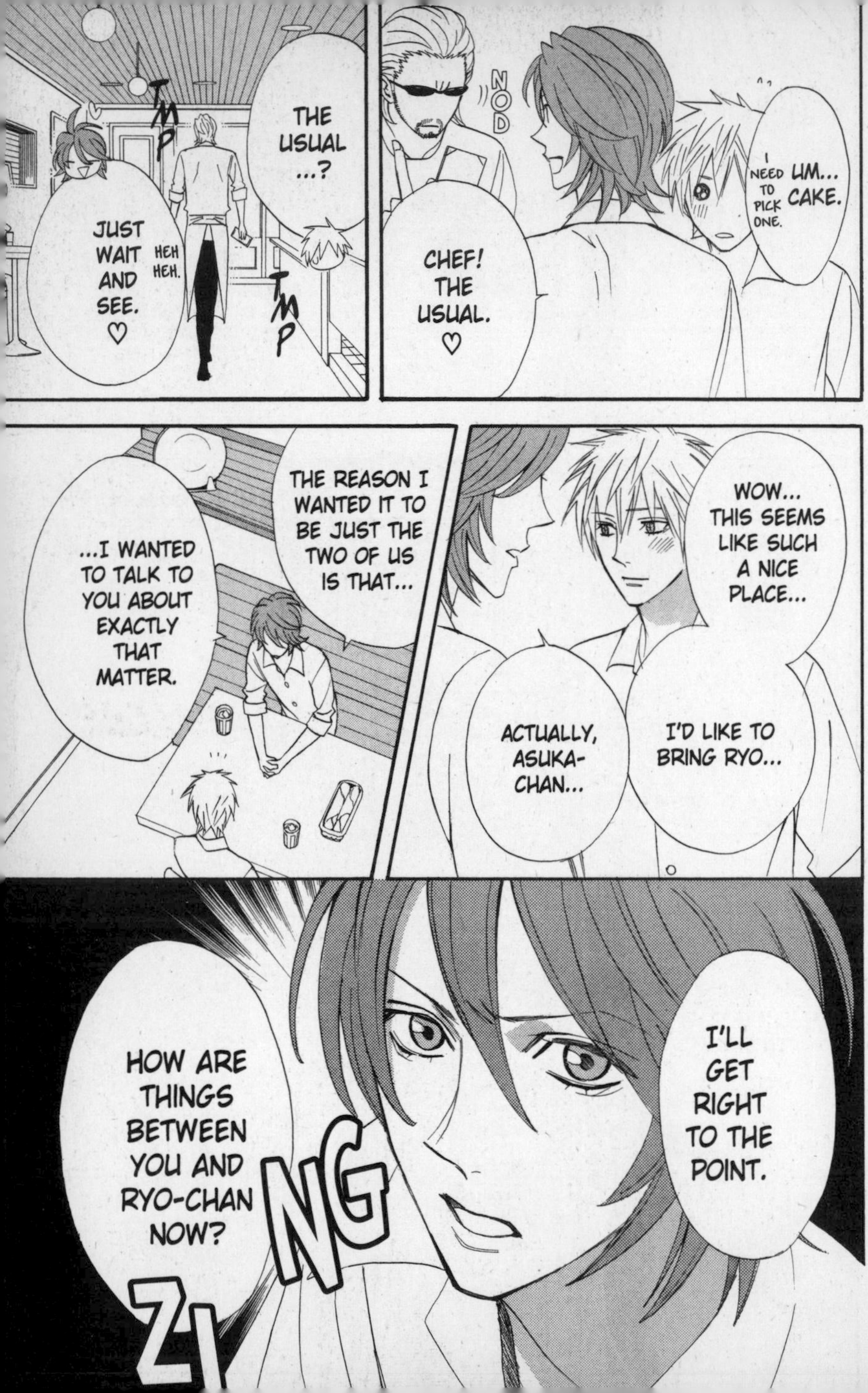
UM... CAKE.
I NEED TO PICK ONE.
NOD
CHEF! THE USUAL. ♡
THE USUAL ...?
TMP
TMP
JUST WAIT AND SEE. ♡
HEH HEH.
WOW... THIS SEEMS LIKE SUCH A NICE PLACE...
I'D LIKE TO BRING RYO...
ACTUALLY, ASUKA-CHAN...
THE REASON I WANTED IT TO BE JUST THE TWO OF US IS THAT...
...I WANTED TO TALK TO YOU ABOUT EXACTLY THAT MATTER.
I'LL GET RIGHT TO THE POINT.
ZI NG
HOW ARE THINGS BETWEEN YOU AND RYO-CHAN NOW?

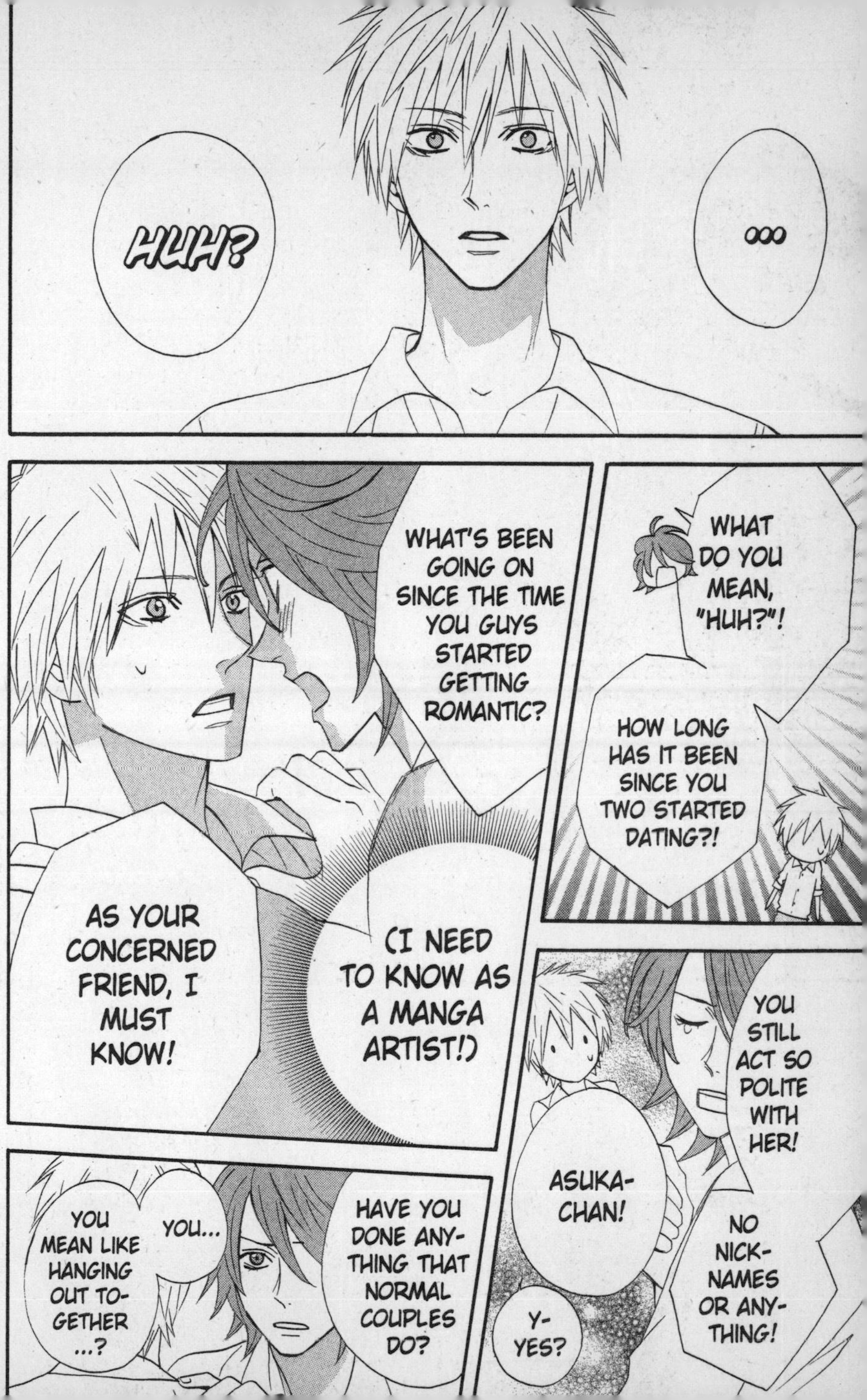
•••
HUH?
WHAT DO YOU MEAN, "HUH?"!
HOW LONG HAS IT BEEN SINCE YOU TWO STARTED DATING?!
WHAT'S BEEN GOING ON SINCE THE TIME YOU GUYS STARTED GETTING ROMANTIC?
(I NEED TO KNOW AS A MANGA ARTIST!)
AS YOUR CONCERNED FRIEND, I MUST KNOW!
YOU STILL ACT SO POLITE WITH HER!
NO NICK-NAMES OR ANY-THING!
ASUKA-CHAN!
Y-YES?
HAVE YOU DONE ANY-THING THAT NORMAL COUPLES DO?
YOU...
YOU MEAN LIKE HANGING OUT TO-GETHER ...?

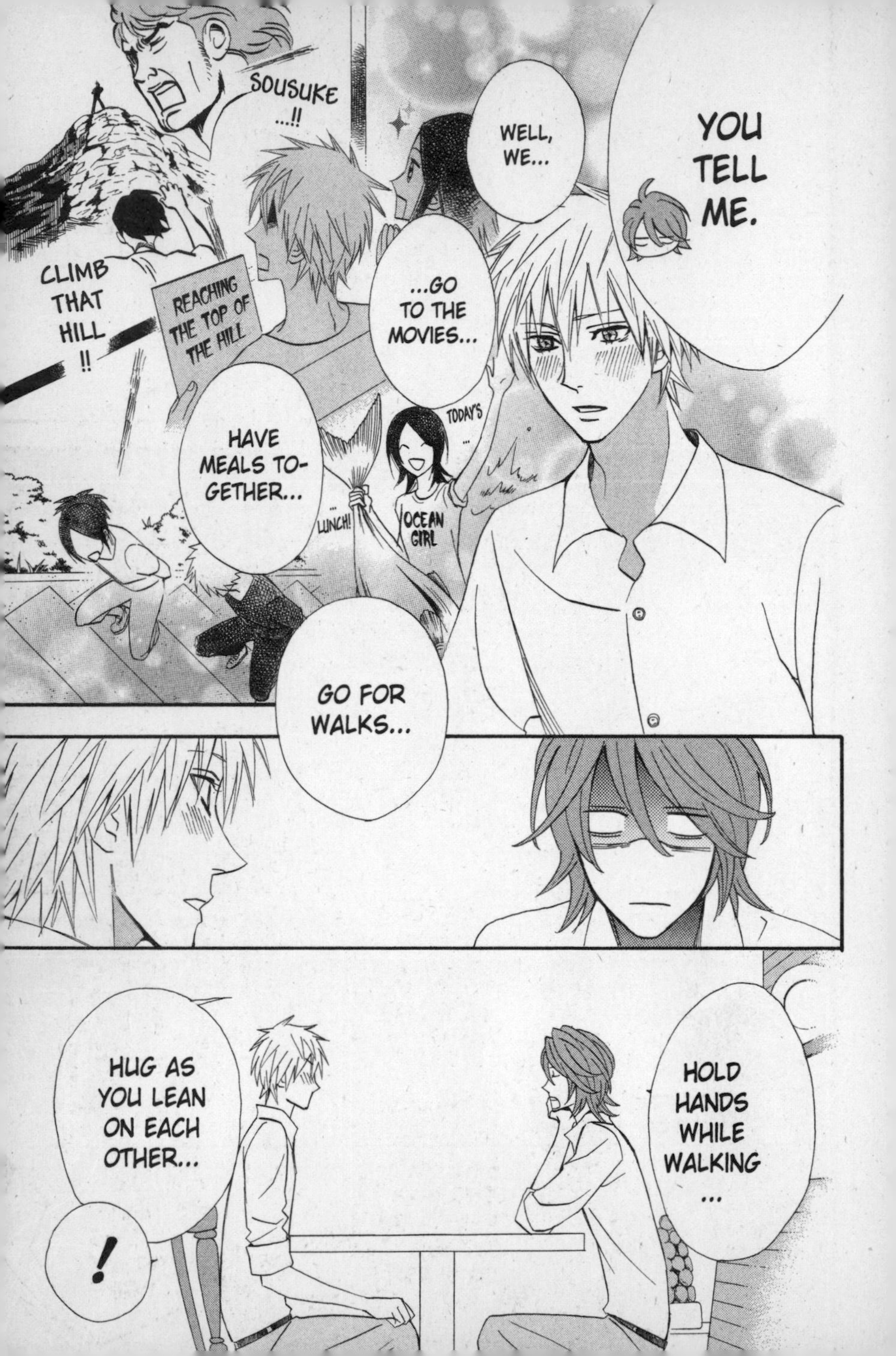
YOU TELL ME.
WELL, WE...
...GO TO THE MOVIES...
SOUSUKE ...!!
REACHING THE TOP OF THE HILL
CLIMB THAT HILL !!
TODAY'S ...
... LUNCH!
OCEAN GIRL
HAVE MEALS TO-GETHER...
GO FOR WALKS...
HOLD HANDS WHILE WALKING ...
HUG AS YOU LEAN ON EACH OTHER...
!

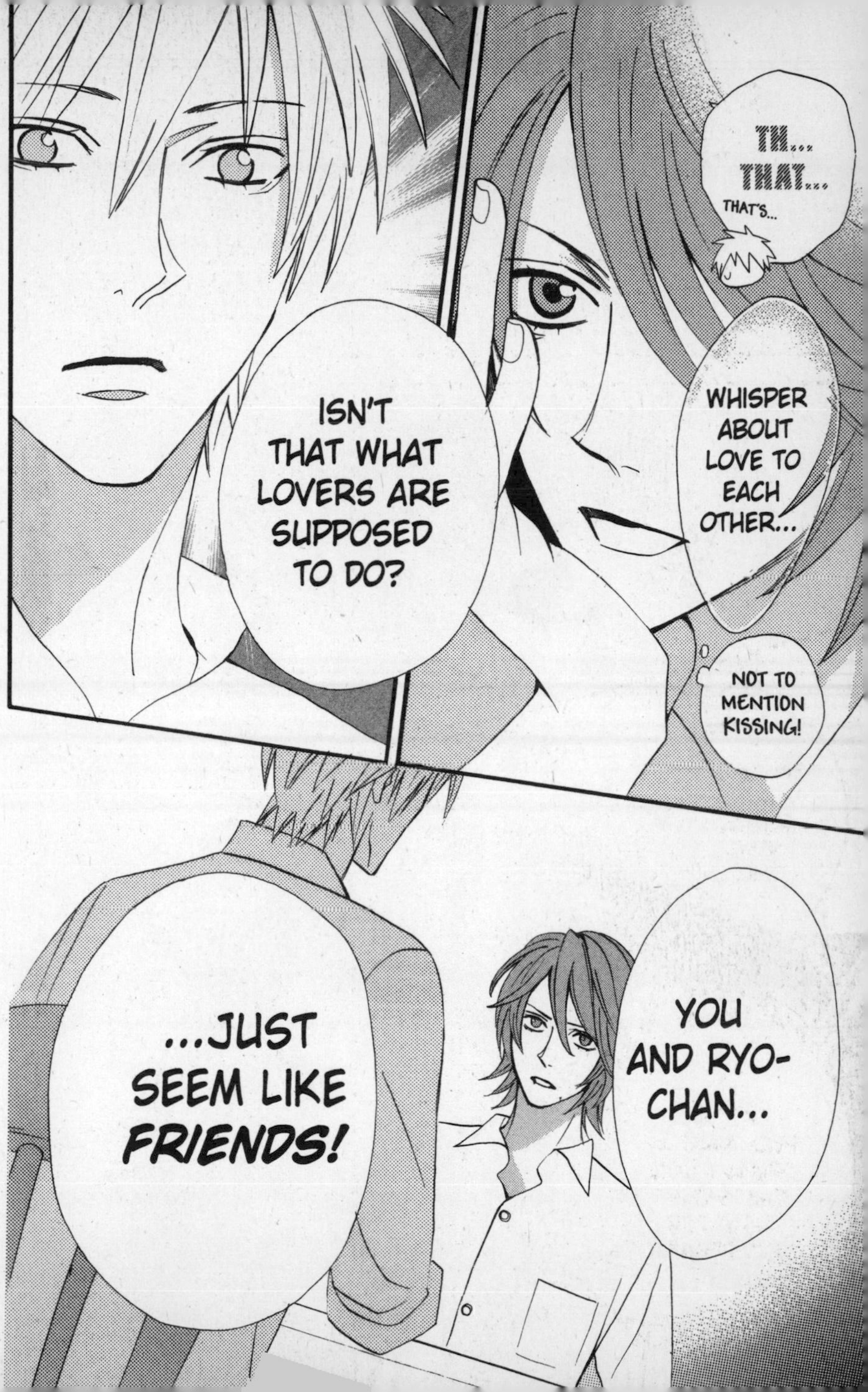
TH... THAT...
THAT'S...
WHISPER ABOUT LOVE TO EACH OTHER...
NOT TO MENTION KISSING!
ISN'T THAT WHAT LOVERS ARE SUPPOSED TO DO?
YOU AND RYO-CHAN...
...JUST SEEM LIKE *FRIENDS!*

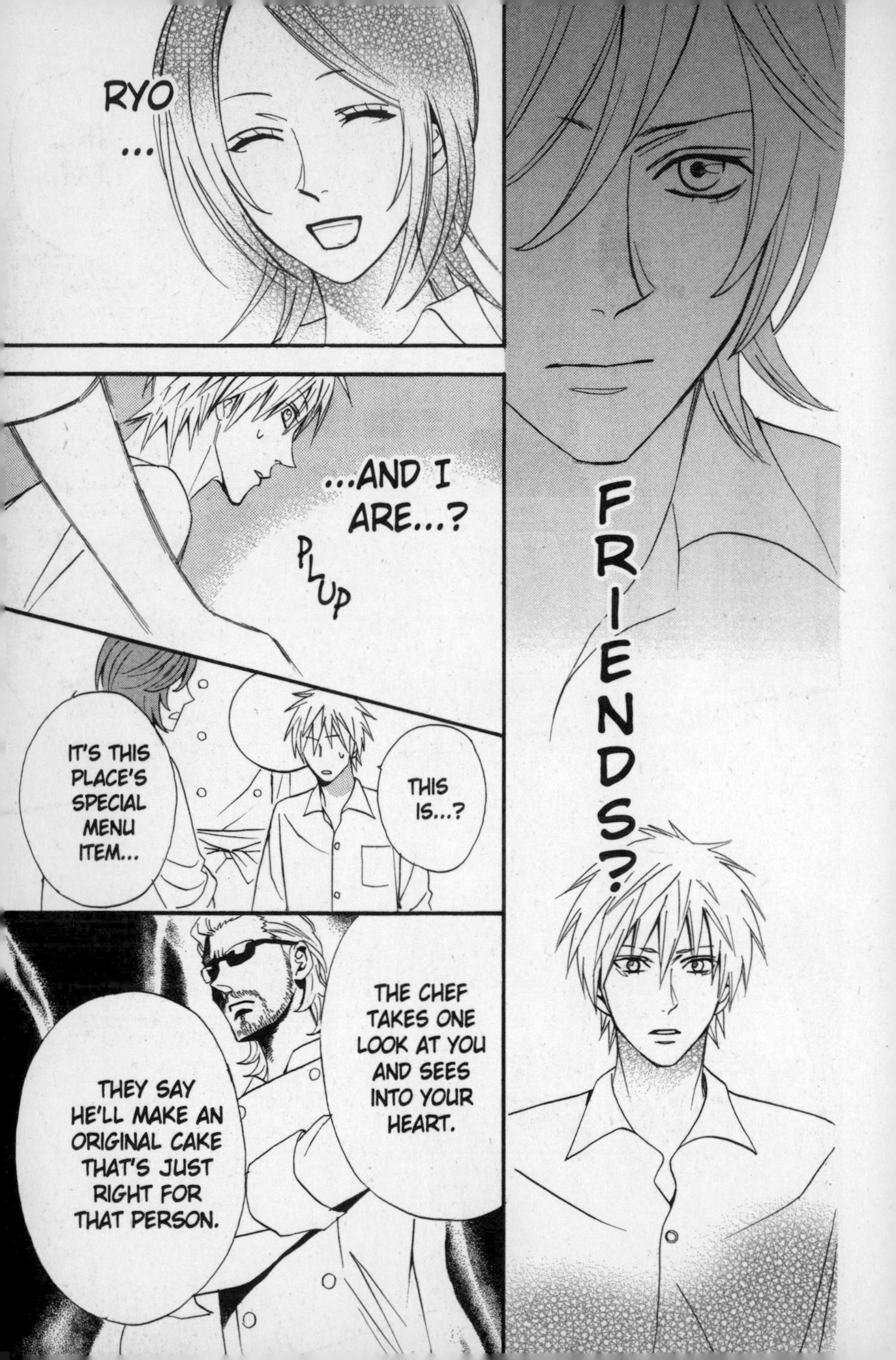
RYO
...
...AND I
ARE...?
PLUP
THIS IS...?
IT'S THIS PLACE'S SPECIAL MENU ITEM...
THE CHEF TAKES ONE LOOK AT YOU AND SEES INTO YOUR HEART.
THEY SAY HE'LL MAKE AN ORIGINAL CAKE THAT'S JUST RIGHT FOR THAT PERSON.
FRIENDS?

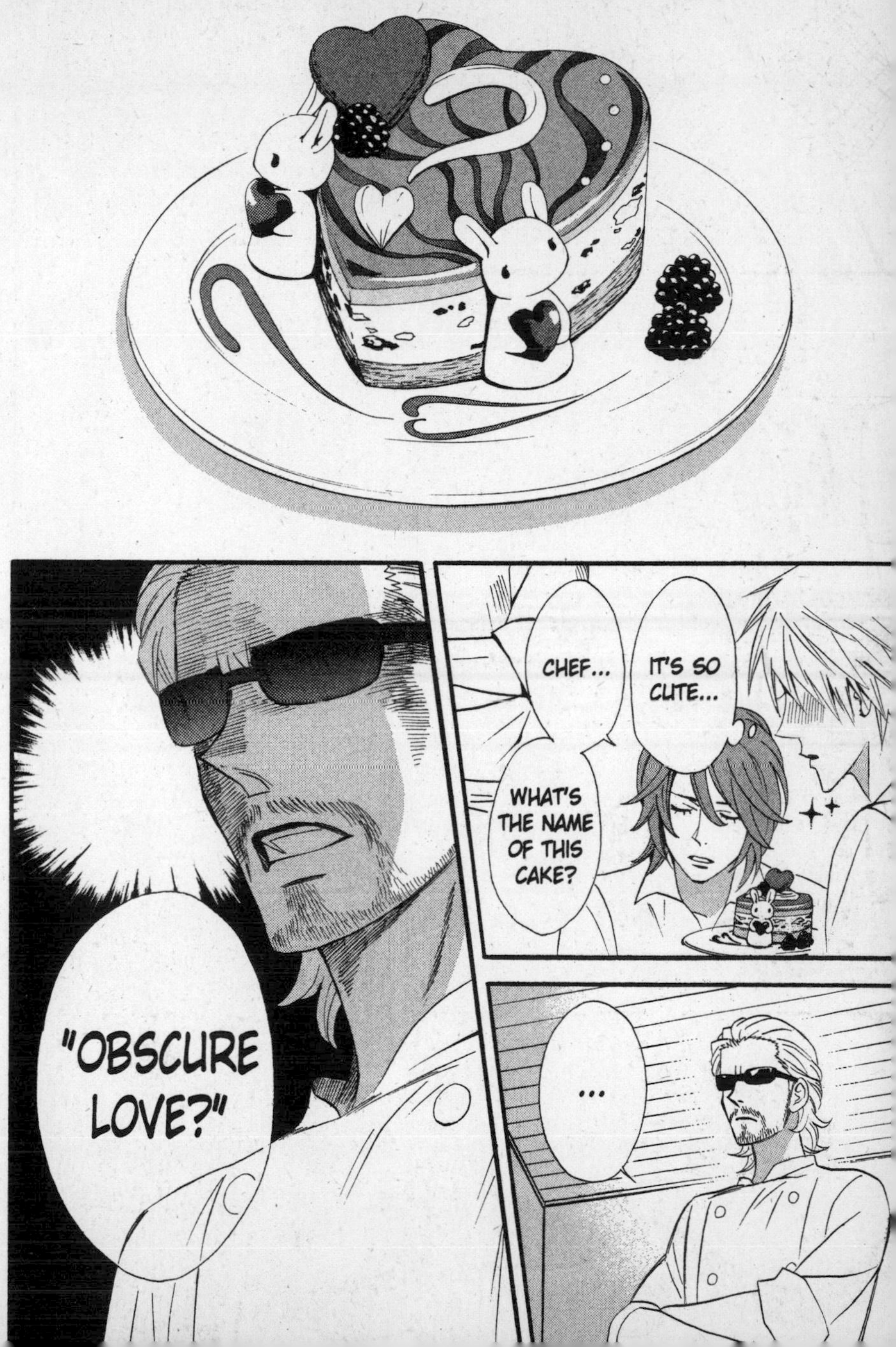
IT'S SO CUTE...
CHEF...
WHAT'S THE NAME OF THIS CAKE?
...
"OBSCURE LOVE?"

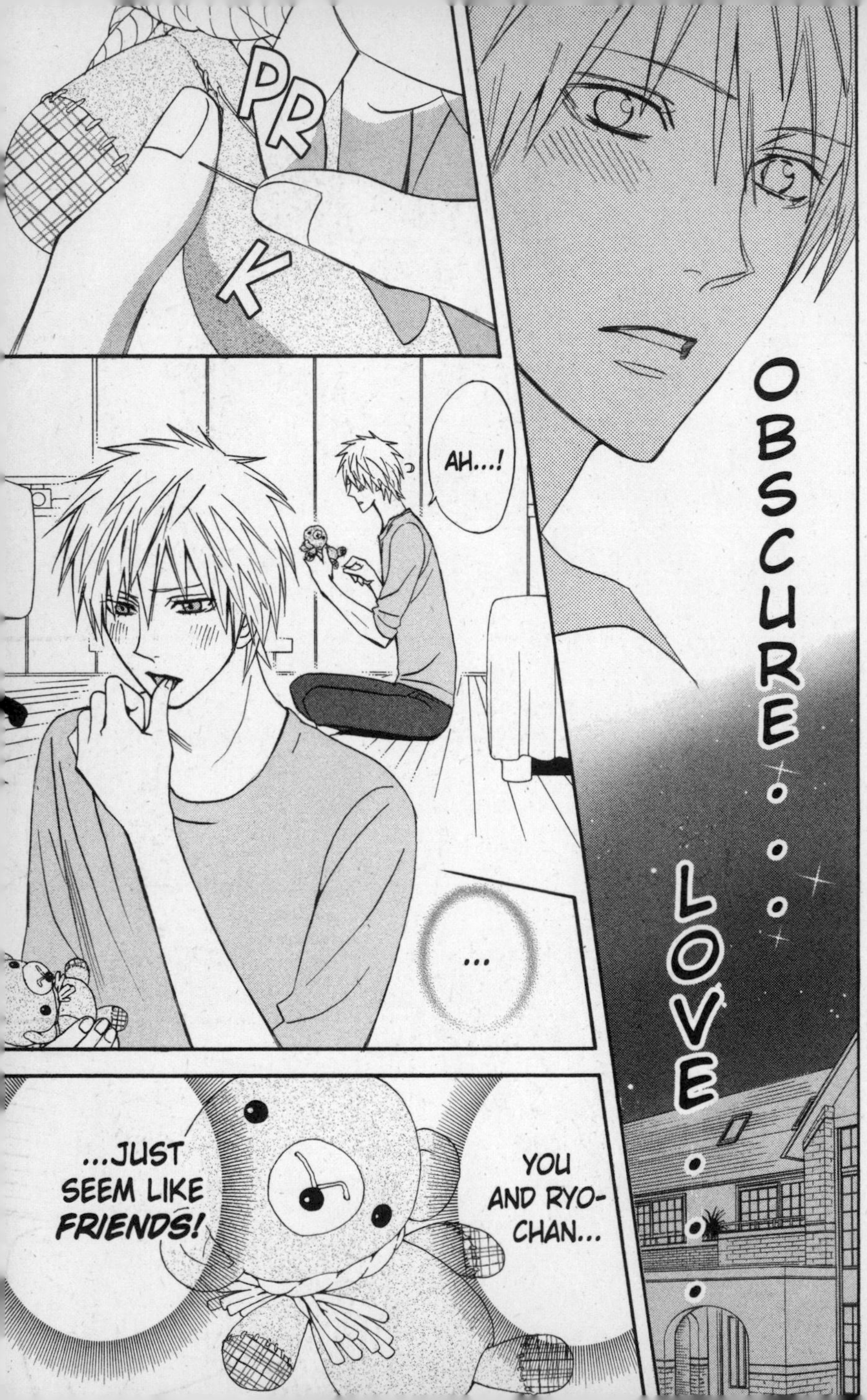
OBSCURE... LOVE...
PRK
AH...!
...
YOU AND RYO-CHAN...
...JUST SEEM LIKE FRIENDS!

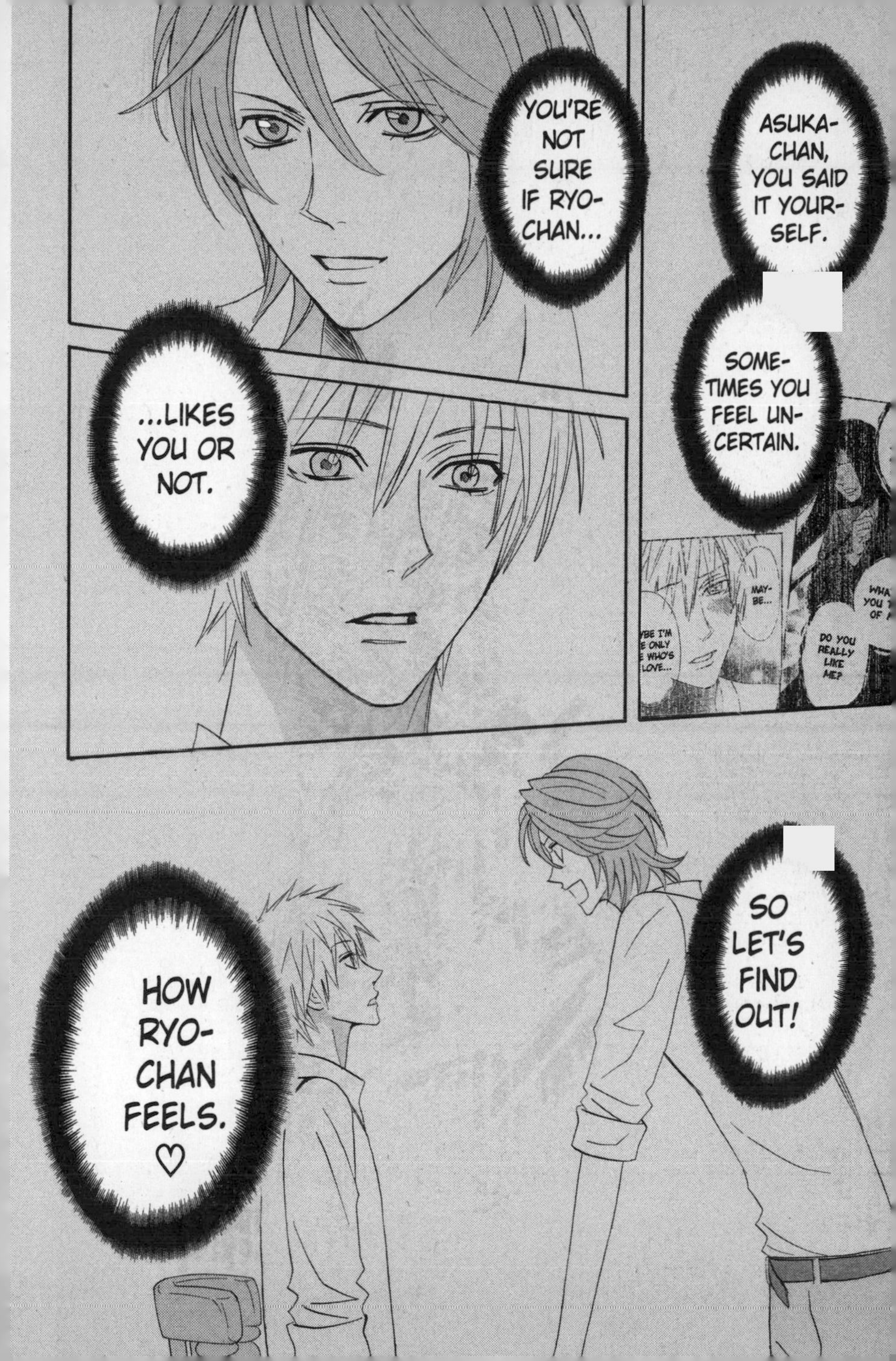
ASUKA-CHAN, YOU SAID IT YOURSELF.
SOMETIMES YOU FEEL UNCERTAIN.
DO YOU REALLY LIKE ME?
MAY-BE...
YOU'RE NOT SURE IF RYO-CHAN...
...LIKES YOU OR NOT.
SO LET'S FIND OUT!
HOW RYO-CHAN FEELS. ♡

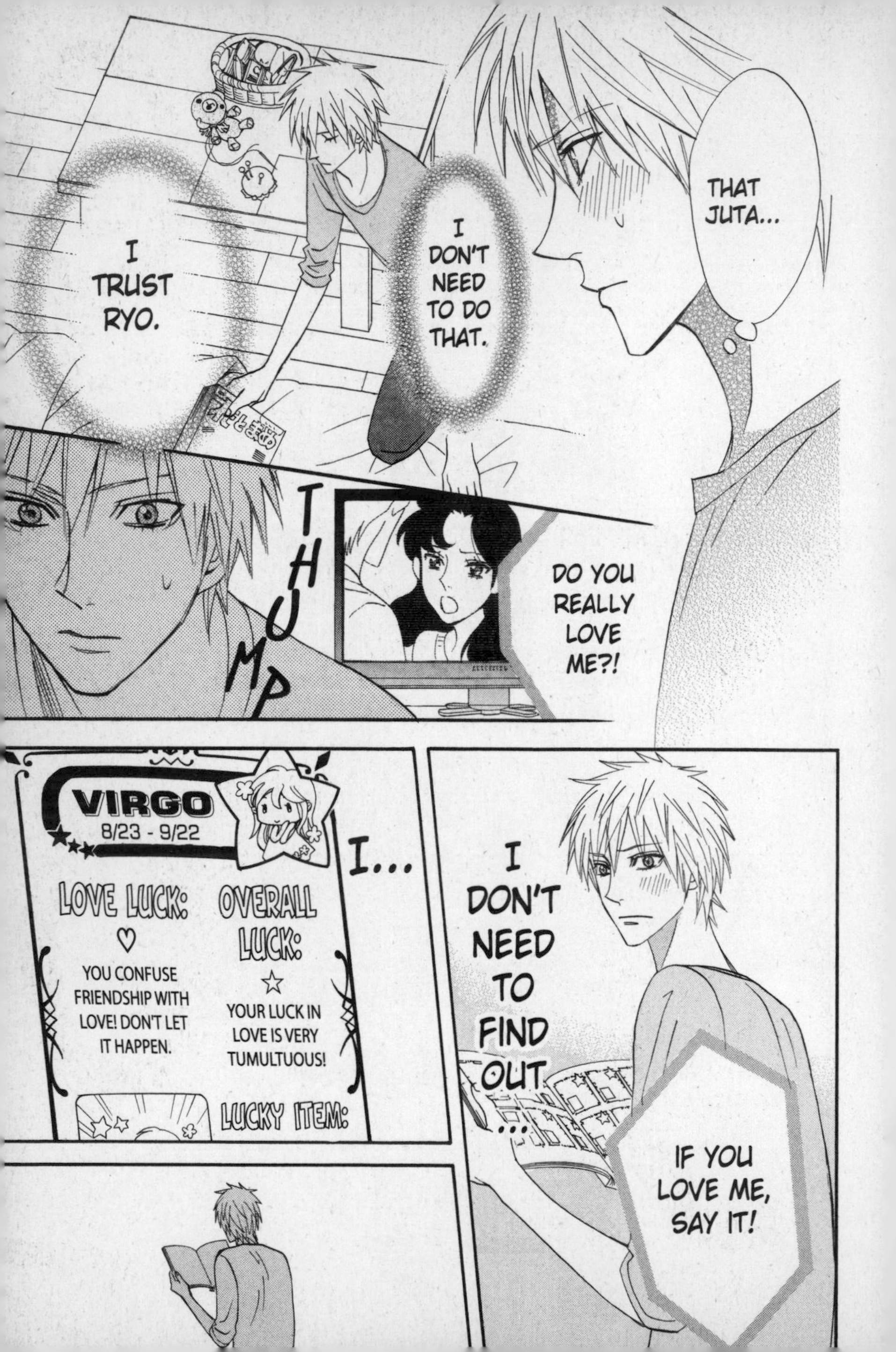
THAT JUTA...
I DON'T NEED TO DO THAT.
I TRUST RYO.
DO YOU REALLY LOVE ME?!
THUMP
I DON'T NEED TO FIND OUT...
IF YOU LOVE ME, SAY IT!
I...
VIRGO
8/23 - 9/22
LOVE LUCK:
♡
YOU CONFUSE FRIENDSHIP WITH LOVE! DON'T LET IT HAPPEN.
OVERALL LUCK:
☆
YOUR LUCK IN LOVE IS VERY TUMULTUOUS!
LUCKY ITEM:

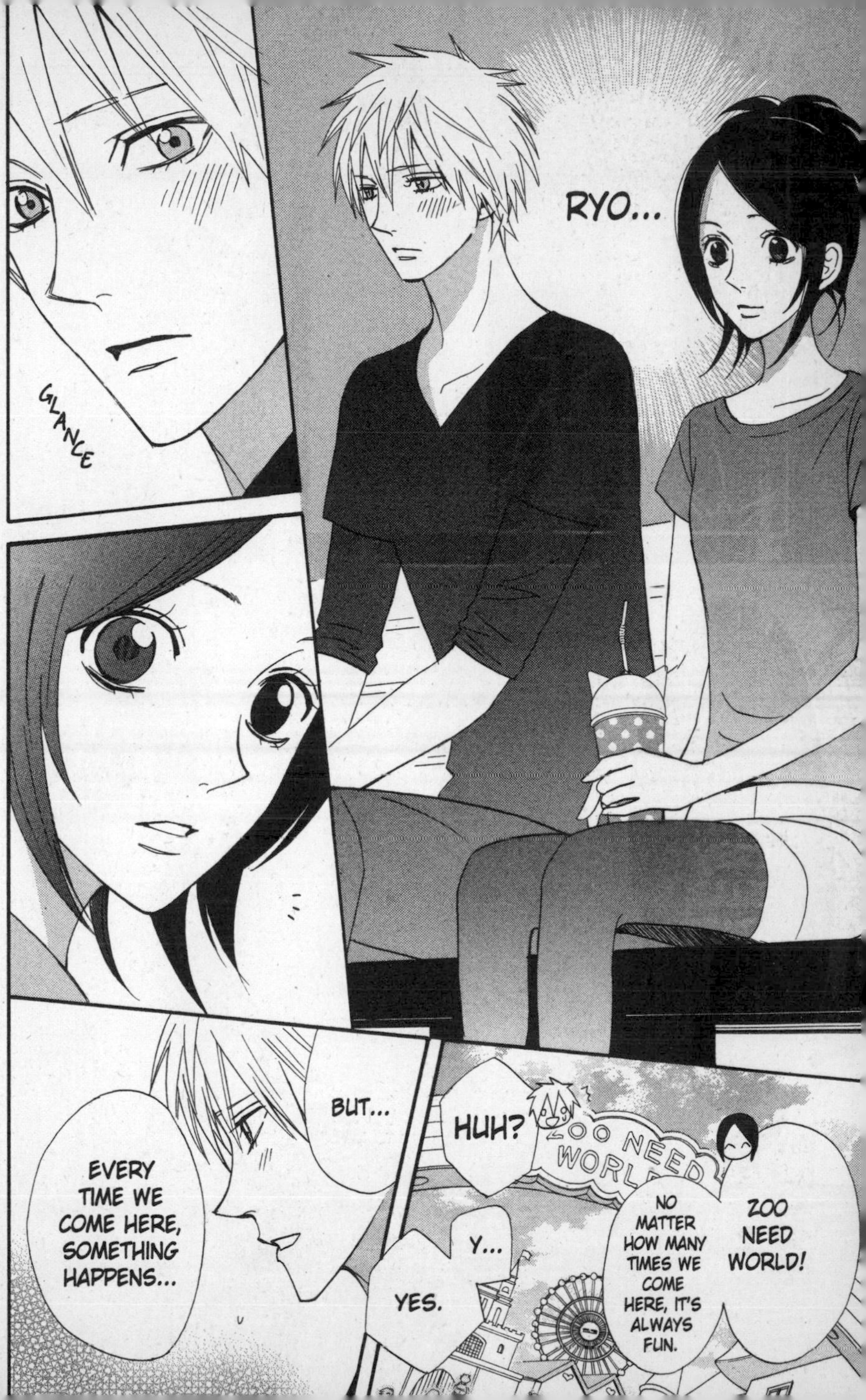
RYO...
GLANCE
ZOO NEED WORLD!
NO MATTER HOW MANY TIMES WE COME HERE, IT'S ALWAYS FUN.
HUH?
Y...
YES.
BUT...
EVERY TIME WE COME HERE, SOMETHING HAPPENS...

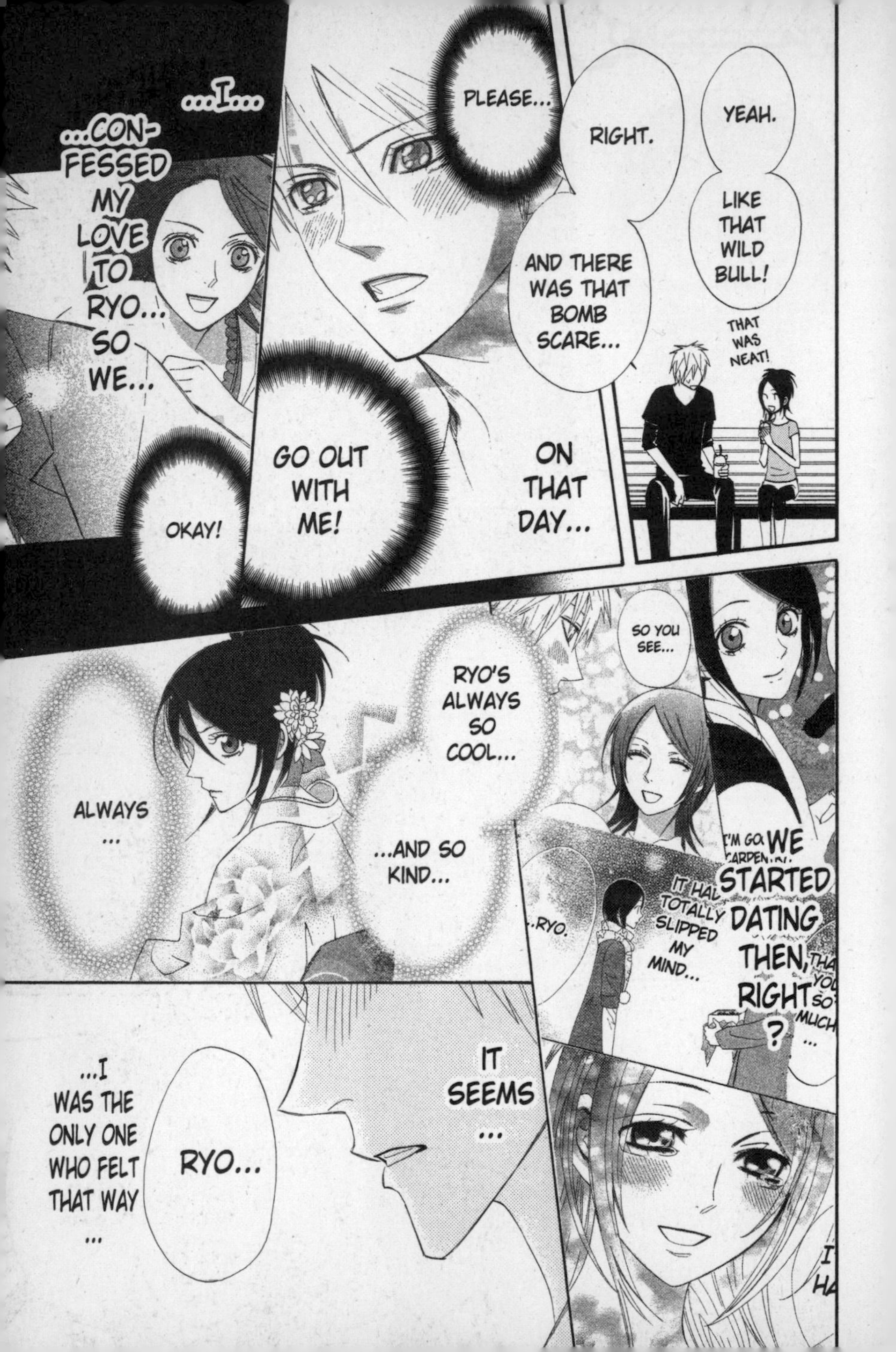
YEAH.
LIKE THAT WILD BULL!
THAT WAS NEAT!
RIGHT.
AND THERE WAS THAT BOMB SCARE...
ON THAT DAY...
PLEASE...
GO OUT WITH ME!
...I...
...CONFESSED MY LOVE TO RYO... SO WE...
OKAY!
SO YOU SEE...
WE STARTED DATING THEN, RIGHT?
TOTALLY SLIPPED MY MIND...
...RYO.
RYO'S ALWAYS SO COOL...
...AND SO KIND...
ALWAYS...
IT SEEMS...
RYO...
...I WAS THE ONLY ONE WHO FELT THAT WAY...

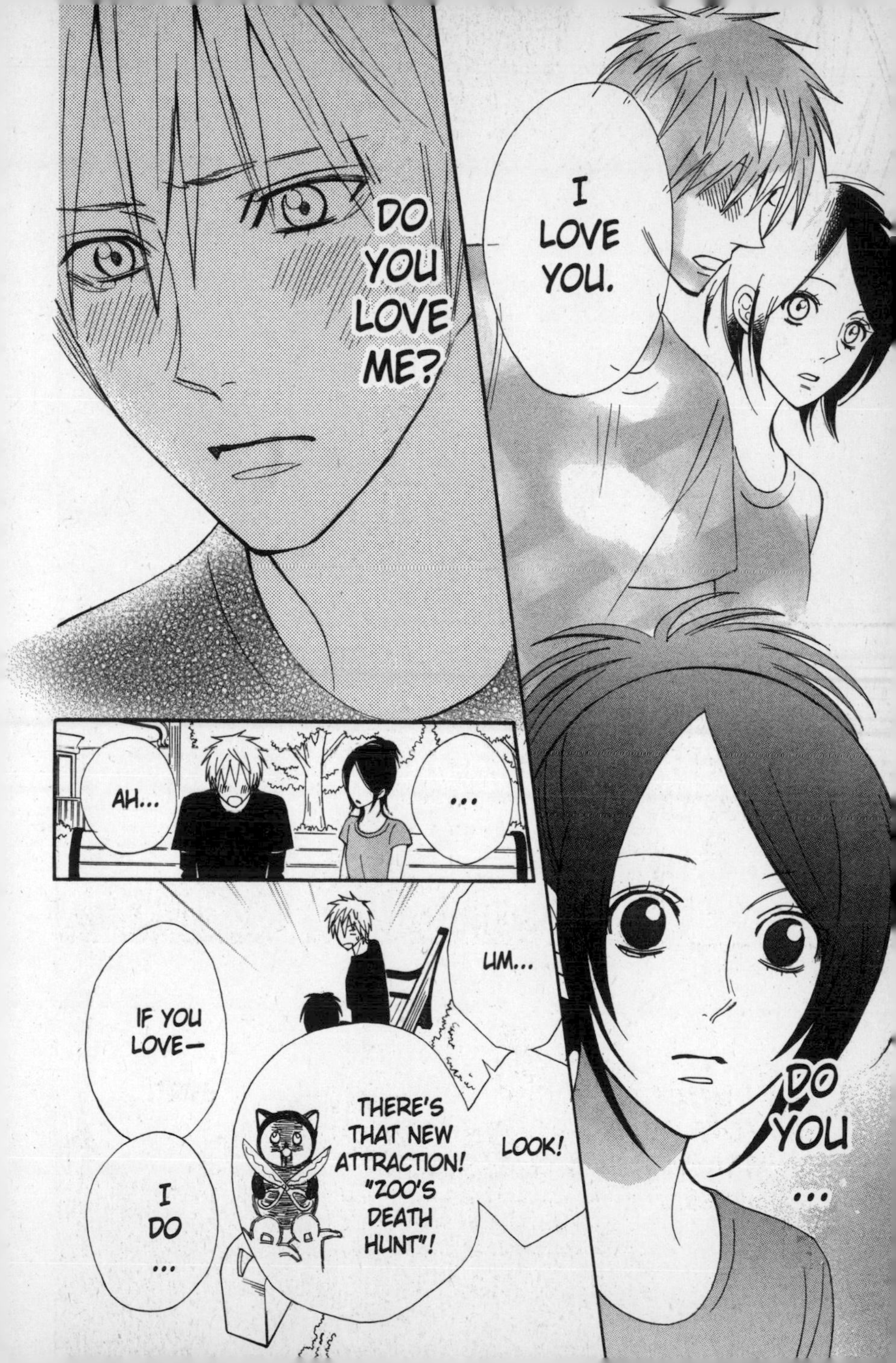
I LOVE YOU.
DO YOU LOVE ME?
DO YOU ...
...
AH...
UM...
IF YOU LOVE—
I DO ...
LOOK!
THERE'S THAT NEW ATTRACTION! "ZOO'S DEATH HUNT"!

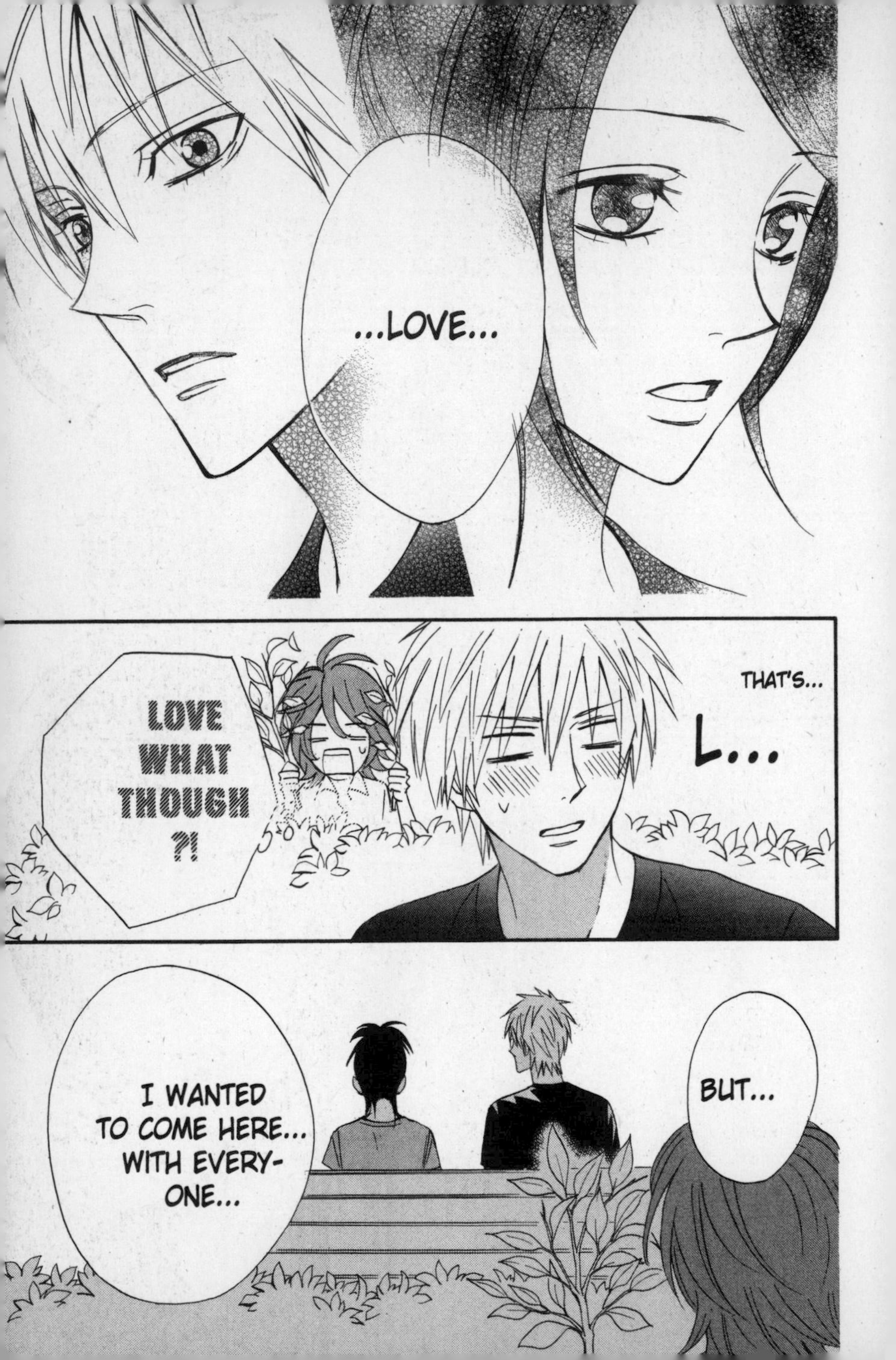
...LOVE...
THAT'S...
L...
LOVE WHAT THOUGH ?!
BUT...
I WANTED TO COME HERE... WITH EVERY-ONE...

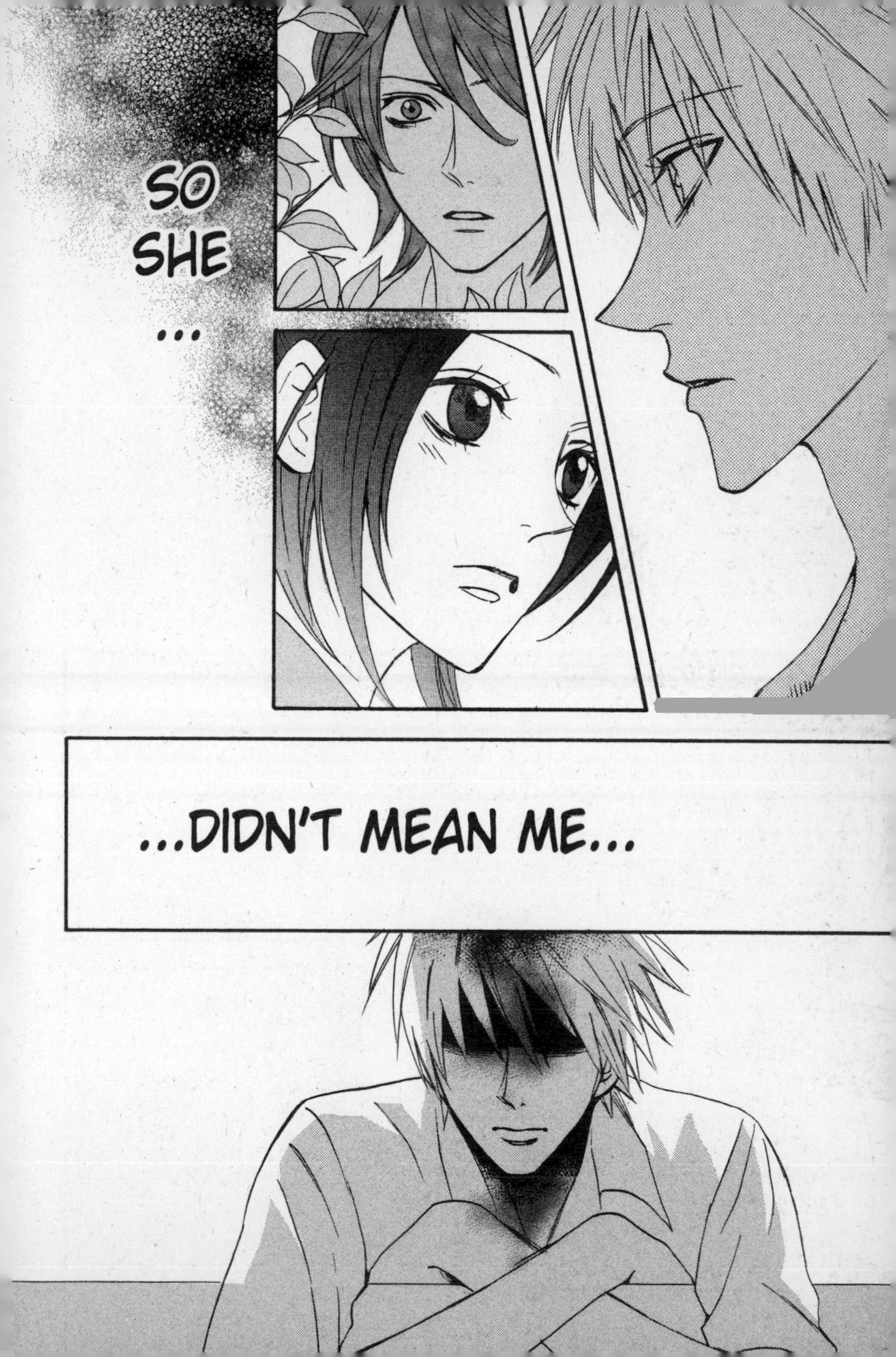
SO SHE ...
...DIDN'T MEAN ME...

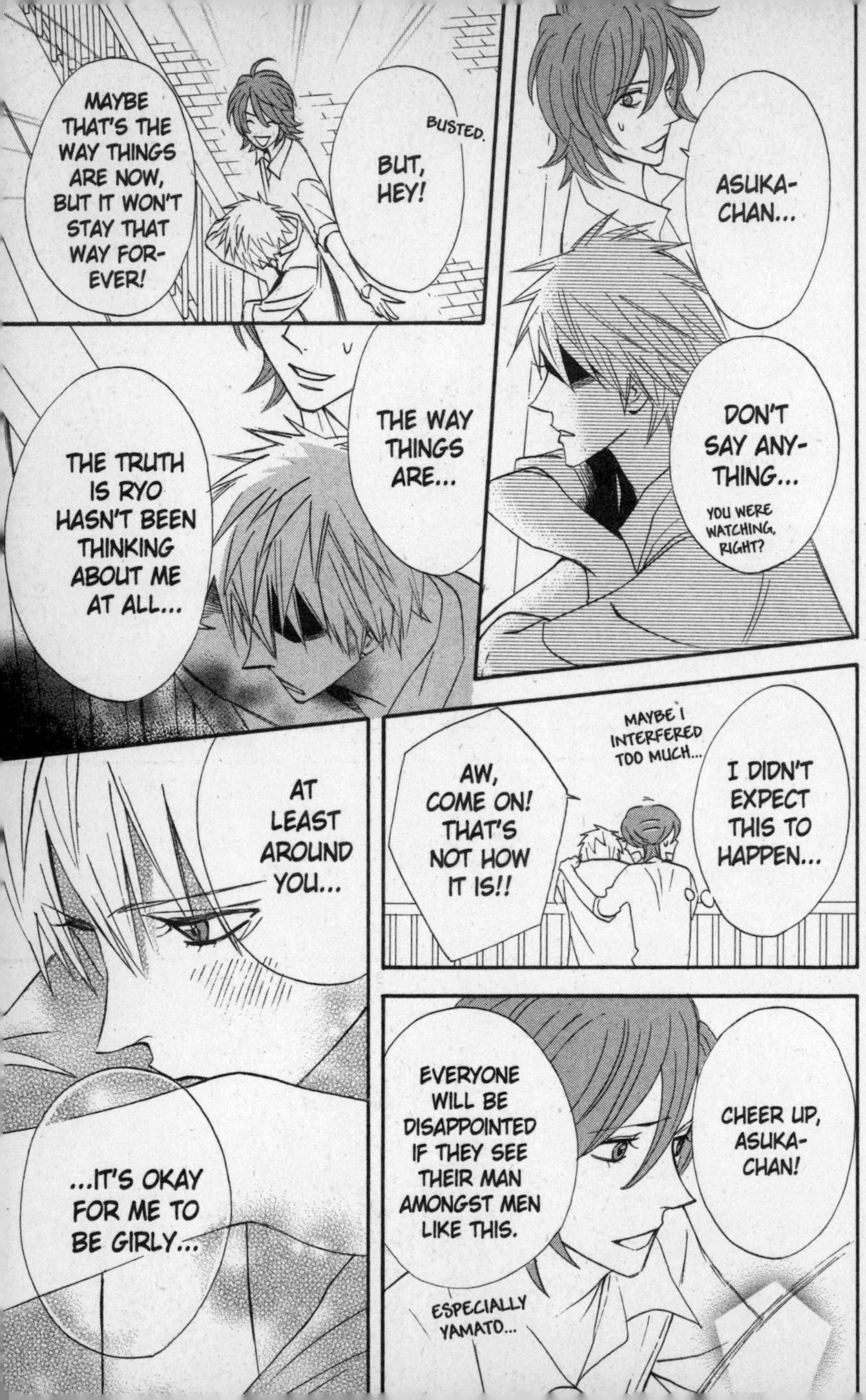

ASUKA-CHAN...
DON'T SAY ANYTHING...
YOU WERE WATCHING, RIGHT?
BUT, HEY!
BUSTED.
MAYBE THAT'S THE WAY THINGS ARE NOW, BUT IT WON'T STAY THAT WAY FOREVER!
THE WAY THINGS ARE...
THE TRUTH IS RYO HASN'T BEEN THINKING ABOUT ME AT ALL...
I DIDN'T EXPECT THIS TO HAPPEN...
MAYBE I INTERFERED TOO MUCH...
AW, COME ON! THAT'S NOT HOW IT IS!!
CHEER UP, ASUKA-CHAN!
EVERYONE WILL BE DISAPPOINTED IF THEY SEE THEIR MAN AMONGST MEN LIKE THIS.
ESPECIALLY YAMATO...
AT LEAST AROUND YOU...
...IT'S OKAY FOR ME TO BE GIRLY...

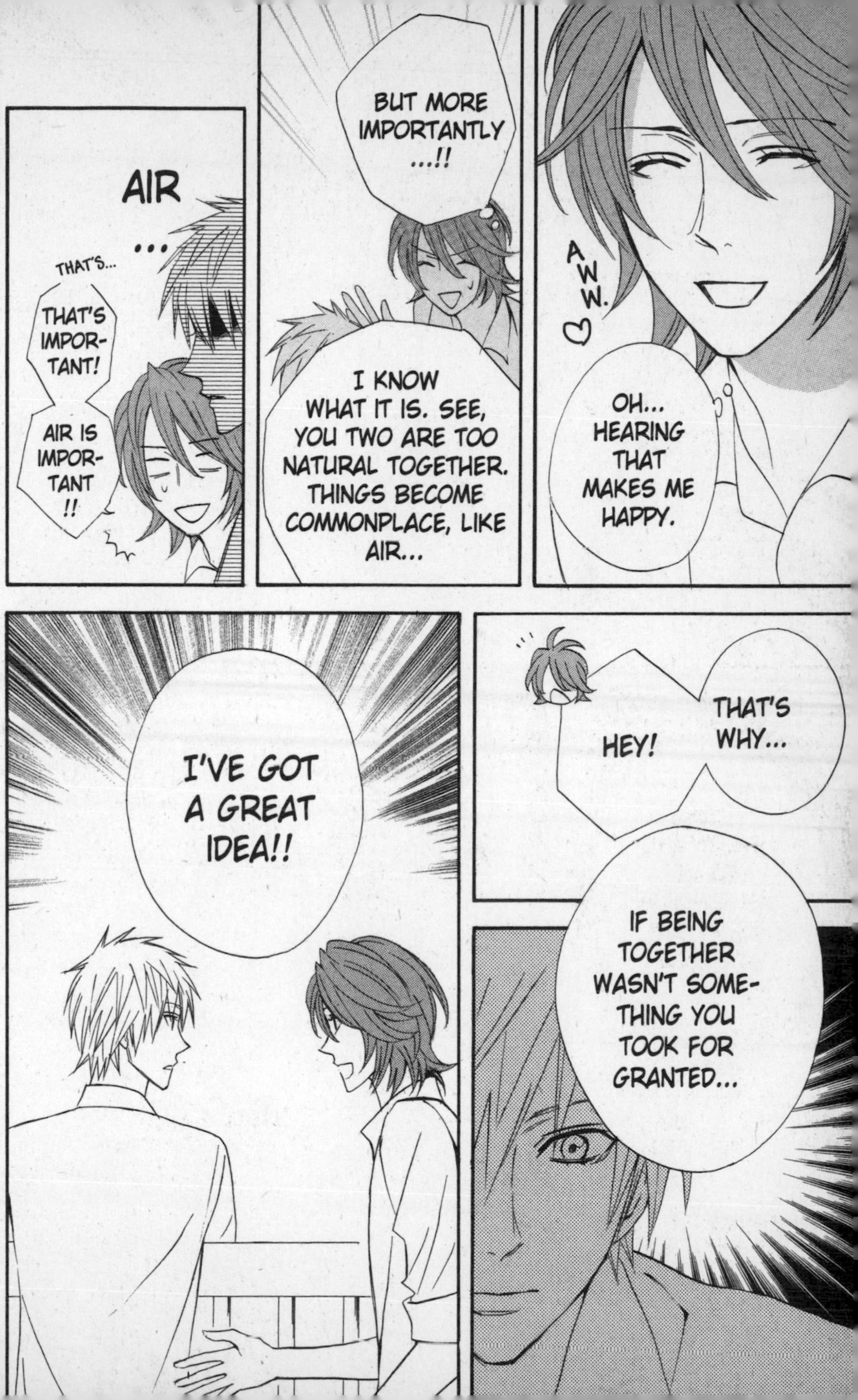
AWW. ♡
OH... HEARING THAT MAKES ME HAPPY.
BUT MORE IMPORTANTLY ...!!
I KNOW WHAT IT IS. SEE, YOU TWO ARE TOO NATURAL TOGETHER. THINGS BECOME COMMONPLACE, LIKE AIR...
AIR ...
THAT'S...
THAT'S IMPORTANT!
AIR IS IMPORTANT !!
THAT'S WHY...
HEY!
IF BEING TOGETHER WASN'T SOMETHING YOU TOOK FOR GRANTED...
I'VE GOT A GREAT IDEA!!

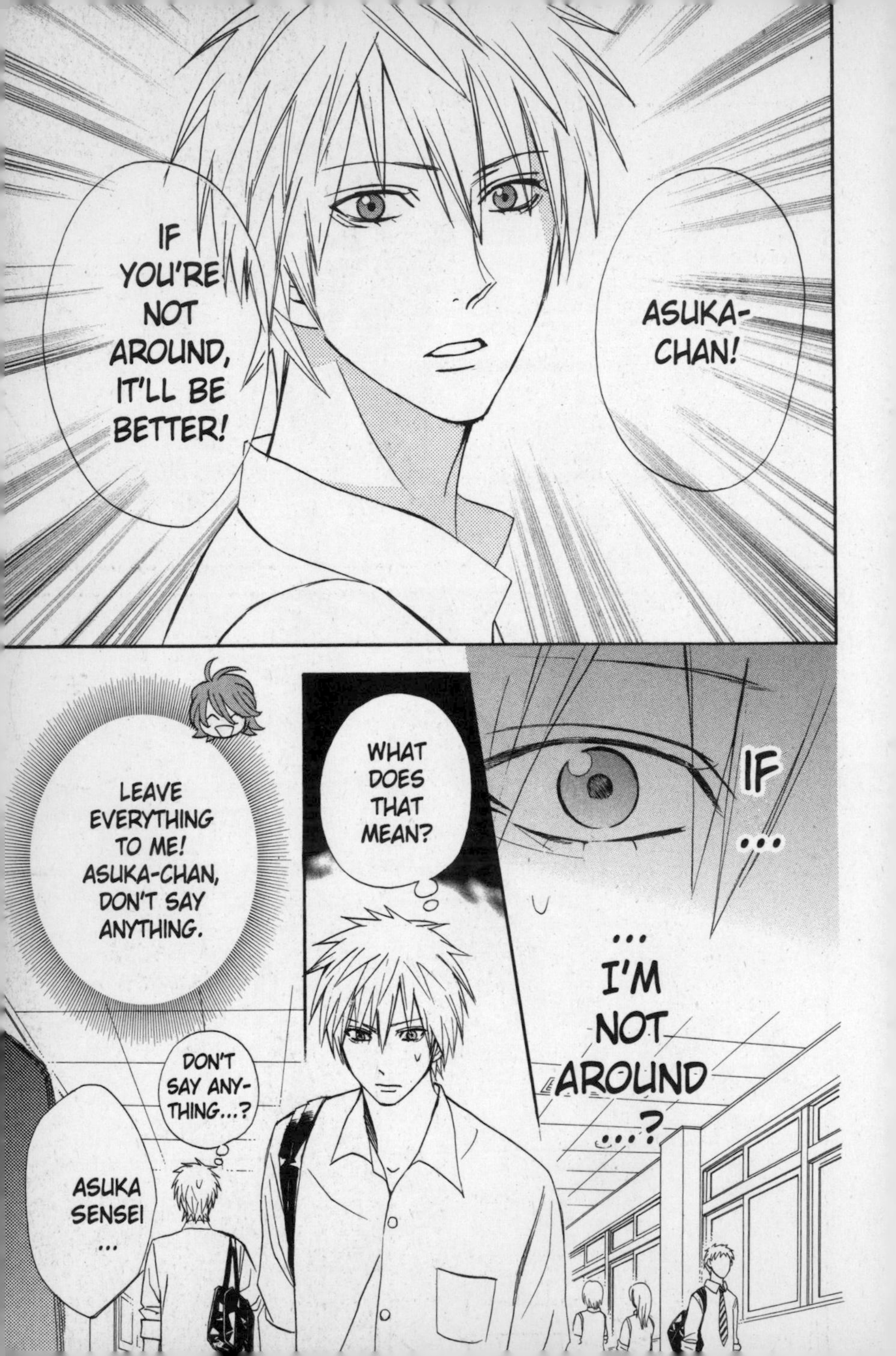
ASUKA-CHAN!
IF YOU'RE NOT AROUND, IT'LL BE BETTER!
IF...
...I'M NOT AROUND...?
WHAT DOES THAT MEAN?
LEAVE EVERYTHING TO ME! ASUKA-CHAN, DON'T SAY ANYTHING.
DON'T SAY ANY-THING...?
ASUKA SENSEI...

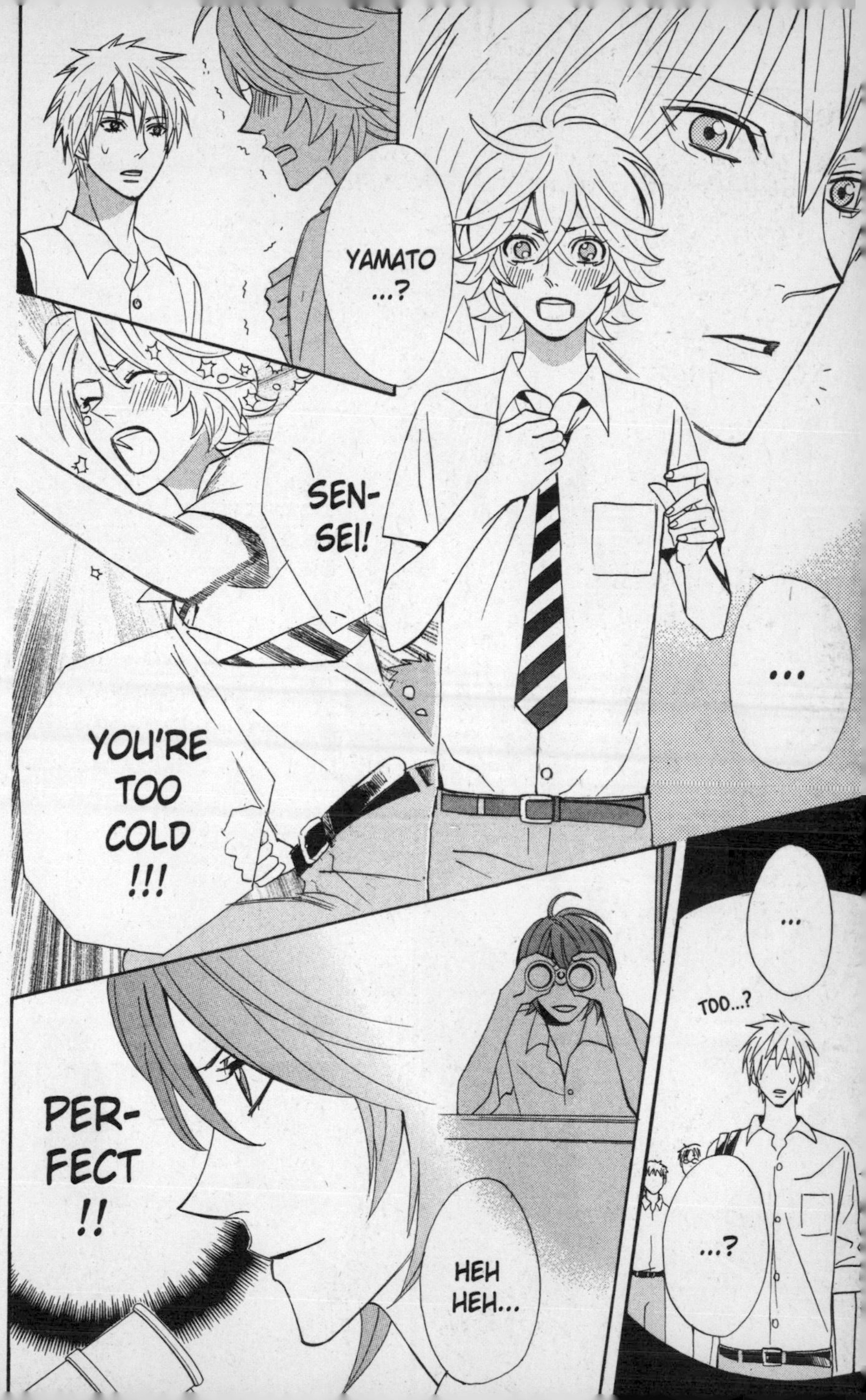
...
YAMATO ...?
SEN-SEI!
YOU'RE TOO COLD !!!
...
TOO...?
...?
HEH HEH...
PER-FECT !!

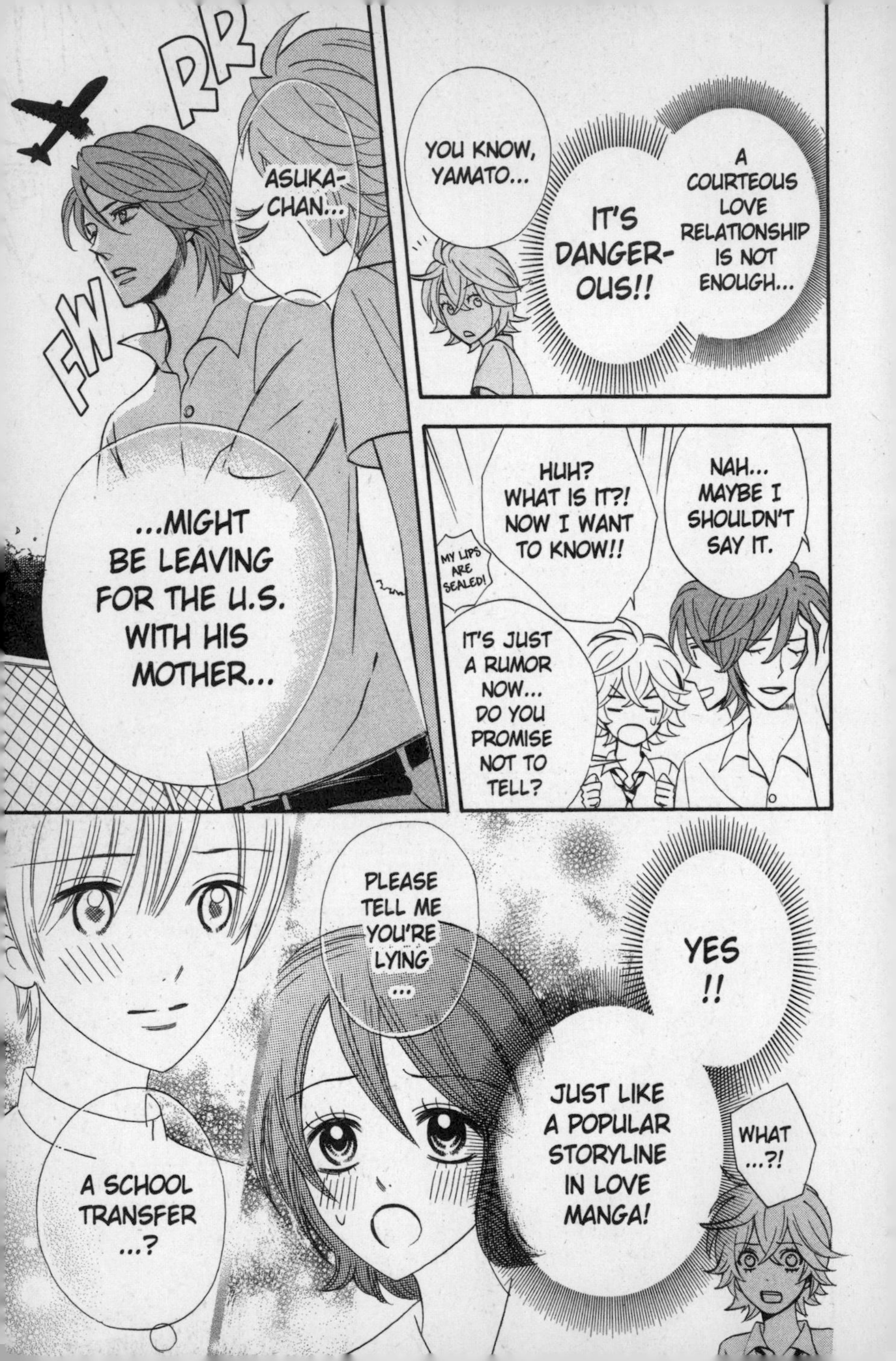

A COURTEOUS LOVE RELATIONSHIP IS NOT ENOUGH...
IT'S DANGER-OUS!!
YOU KNOW, YAMATO...
NAH... MAYBE I SHOULDN'T SAY IT.
HUH? WHAT IS IT?! NOW I WANT TO KNOW!!
MY LIPS ARE SEALED!
IT'S JUST A RUMOR NOW... DO YOU PROMISE NOT TO TELL?
RR
ASUKA-CHAN...
FW
...MIGHT BE LEAVING FOR THE U.S. WITH HIS MOTHER...
YES !!
WHAT ...?!
JUST LIKE A POPULAR STORYLINE IN LOVE MANGA!
PLEASE TELL ME YOU'RE LYING ...
A SCHOOL TRANSFER ...?

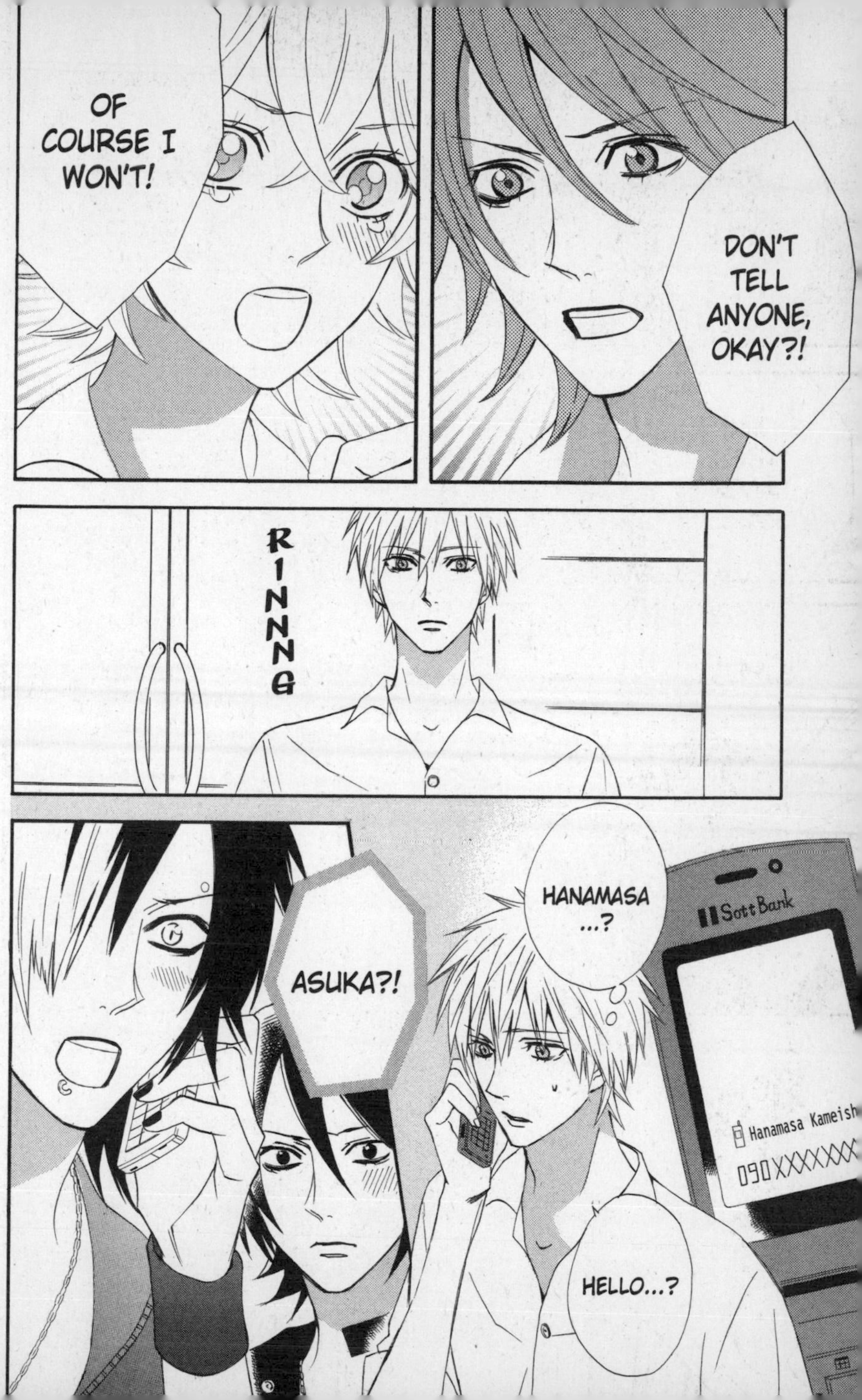
DON'T TELL ANYONE, OKAY?!
OF COURSE I WON'T!
RINNNG
HANAMASA ...?
Hanamasa Kameish
090XXXXXX
ASUKA?!
HELLO...?

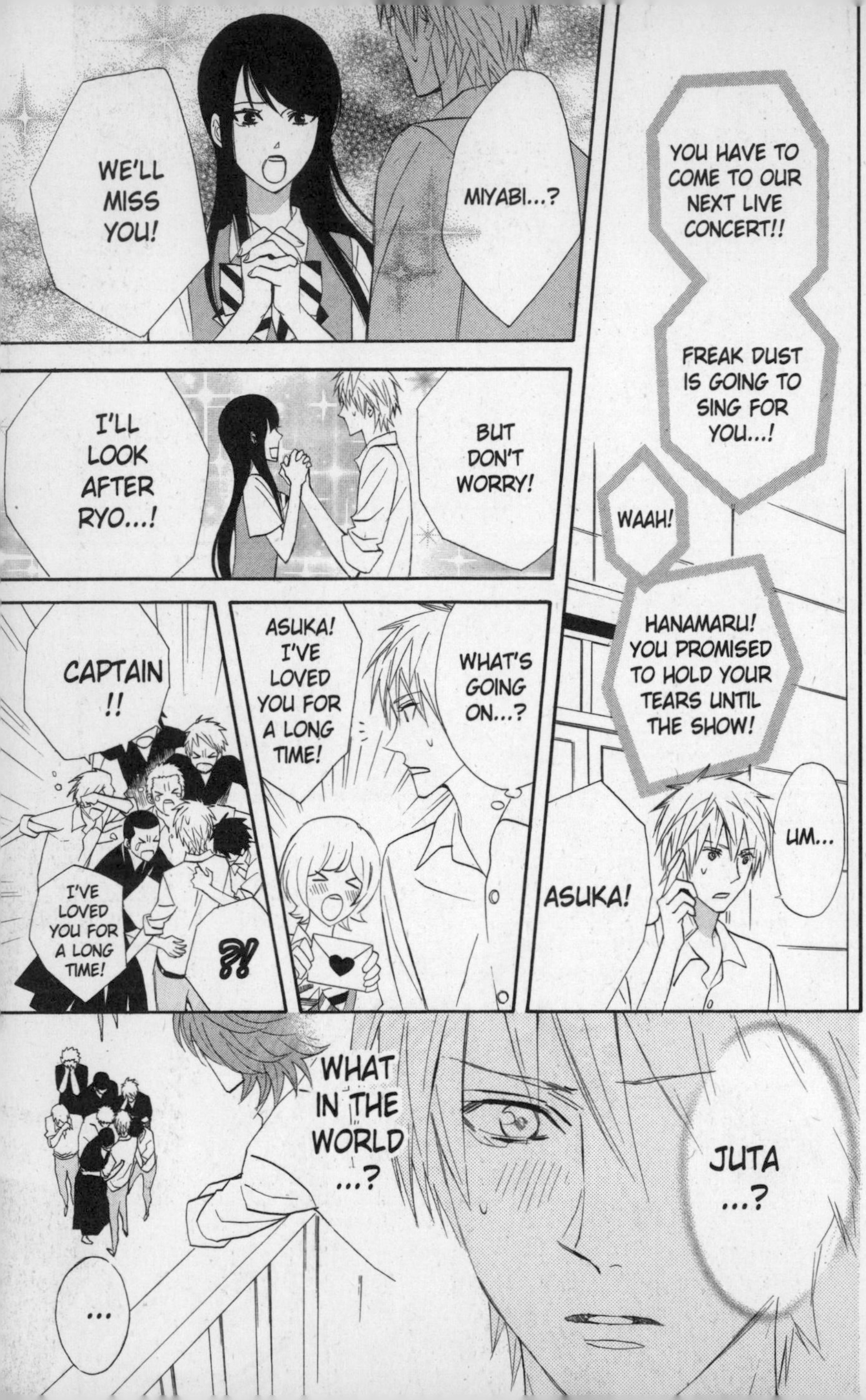
YOU HAVE TO COME TO OUR NEXT LIVE CONCERT!!
FREAK DUST IS GOING TO SING FOR YOU...!
WAAH!
HANAMARU! YOU PROMISED TO HOLD YOUR TEARS UNTIL THE SHOW!
UM...
ASUKA!
MIYABI...?
WE'LL MISS YOU!
BUT DON'T WORRY!
I'LL LOOK AFTER RYO...!
WHAT'S GOING ON...?
ASUKA! I'VE LOVED YOU FOR A LONG TIME!
?!
CAPTAIN !!
I'VE LOVED YOU FOR A LONG TIME!
JUTA ...?
WHAT IN THE WORLD ...?
...

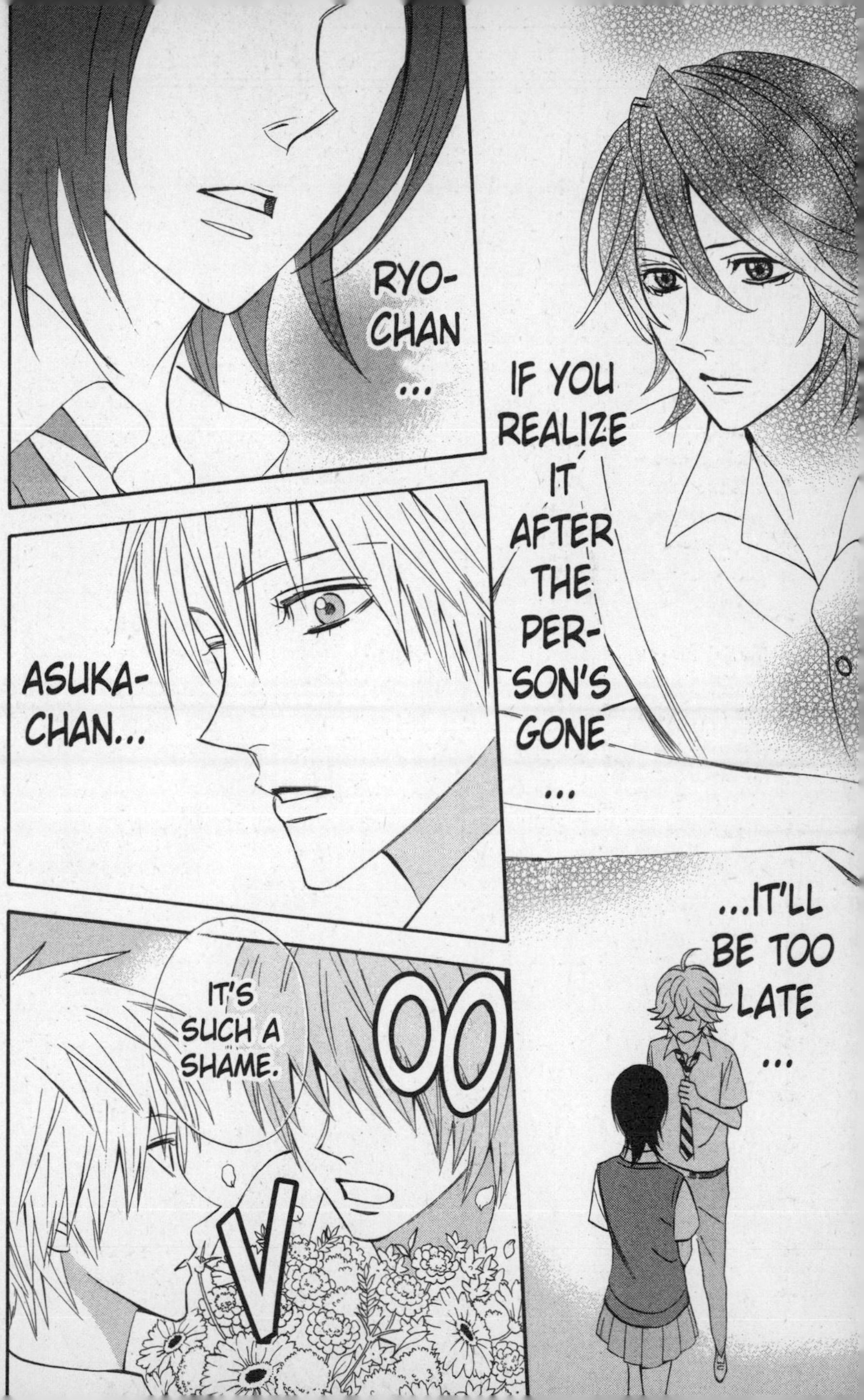
IF YOU REALIZE IT AFTER THE PER-SON'S GONE...
...IT'LL BE TOO LATE...
RYO-CHAN...
ASUKA-CHAN...
IT'S SUCH A SHAME.
OO
V

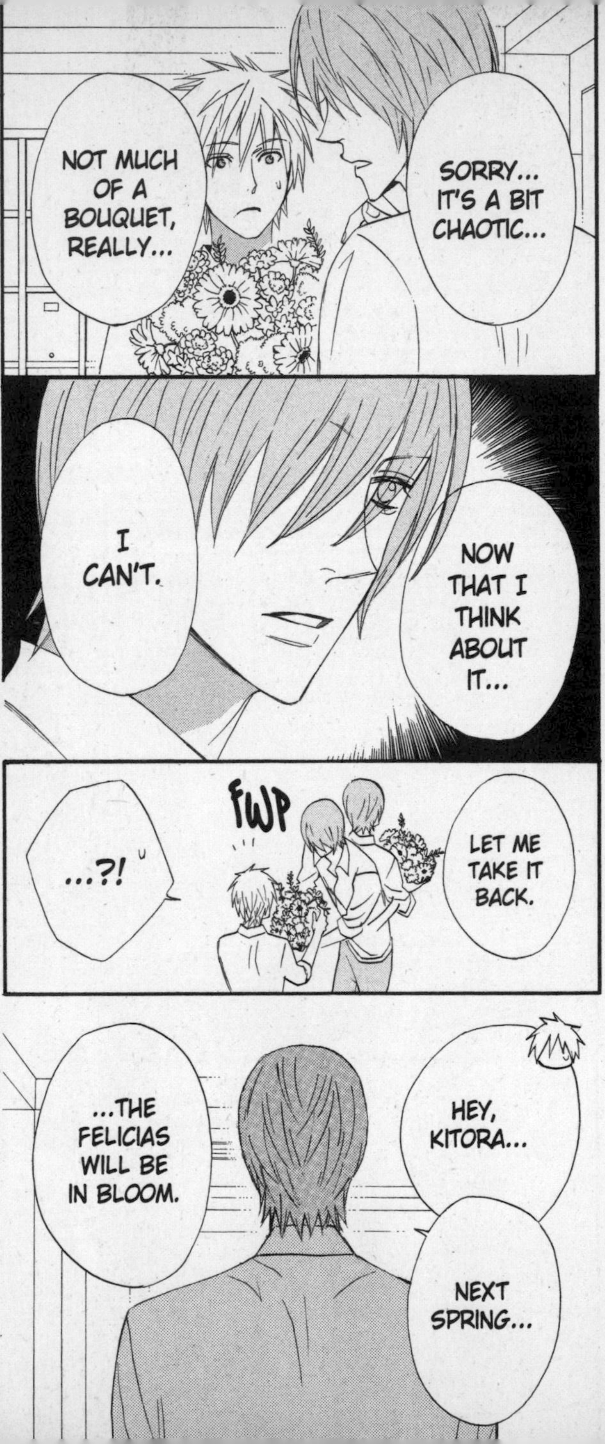
SORRY... IT'S A BIT CHAOTIC...
NOT MUCH OF A BOUQUET, REALLY...
NOW THAT I THINK ABOUT IT...
I CAN'T.
LET ME TAKE IT BACK.
FWP
...?!
HEY, KITORA...
NEXT SPRING...
...THE FELICIAS WILL BE IN BLOOM.

Production Assistance:

Shimada-san
Takowa-san
Kuwana-san
Kawashima-san
Sayaka-san
Tanaka-san
Nakazawa-san
Sakurai-san
Kaneko-san
Yoneyan
Nishizawa-san
Kuroda-san

Special Thanks:

Abe-san
All the Readers

Thank you so much for reading this series.

If you have any comments or suggestions, please write to:

Aya Kanno
c/o Otomen Editor
VIZ Media
P.O. Box 77010
San Francisco, CA
94107

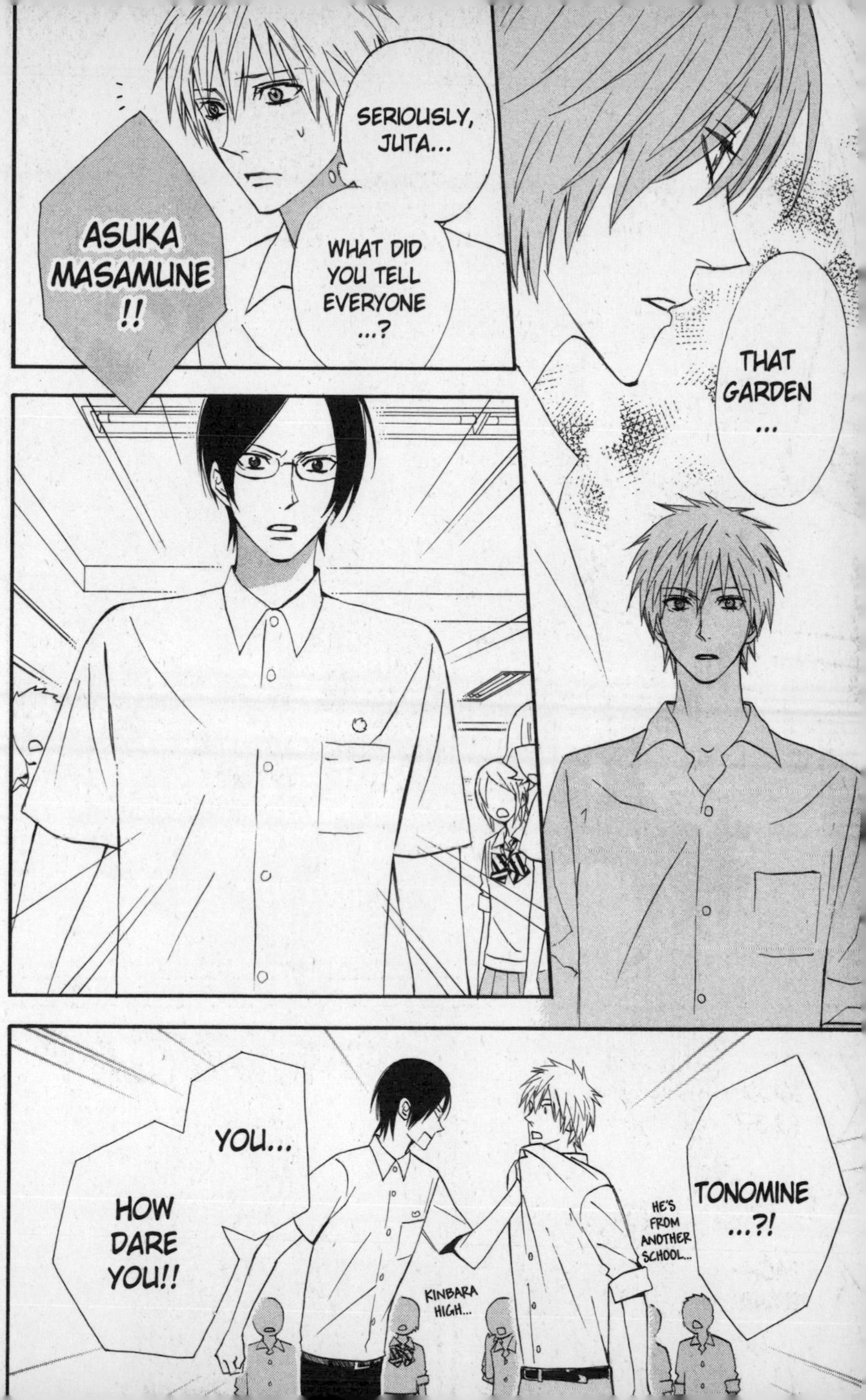
THAT GARDEN ...
SERIOUSLY, JUTA...
WHAT DID YOU TELL EVERYONE ...?
ASUKA MASAMUNE !!
TONOMINE ...?!
HE'S FROM ANOTHER SCHOOL...
KINBARA HIGH...
YOU...
HOW DARE YOU!!

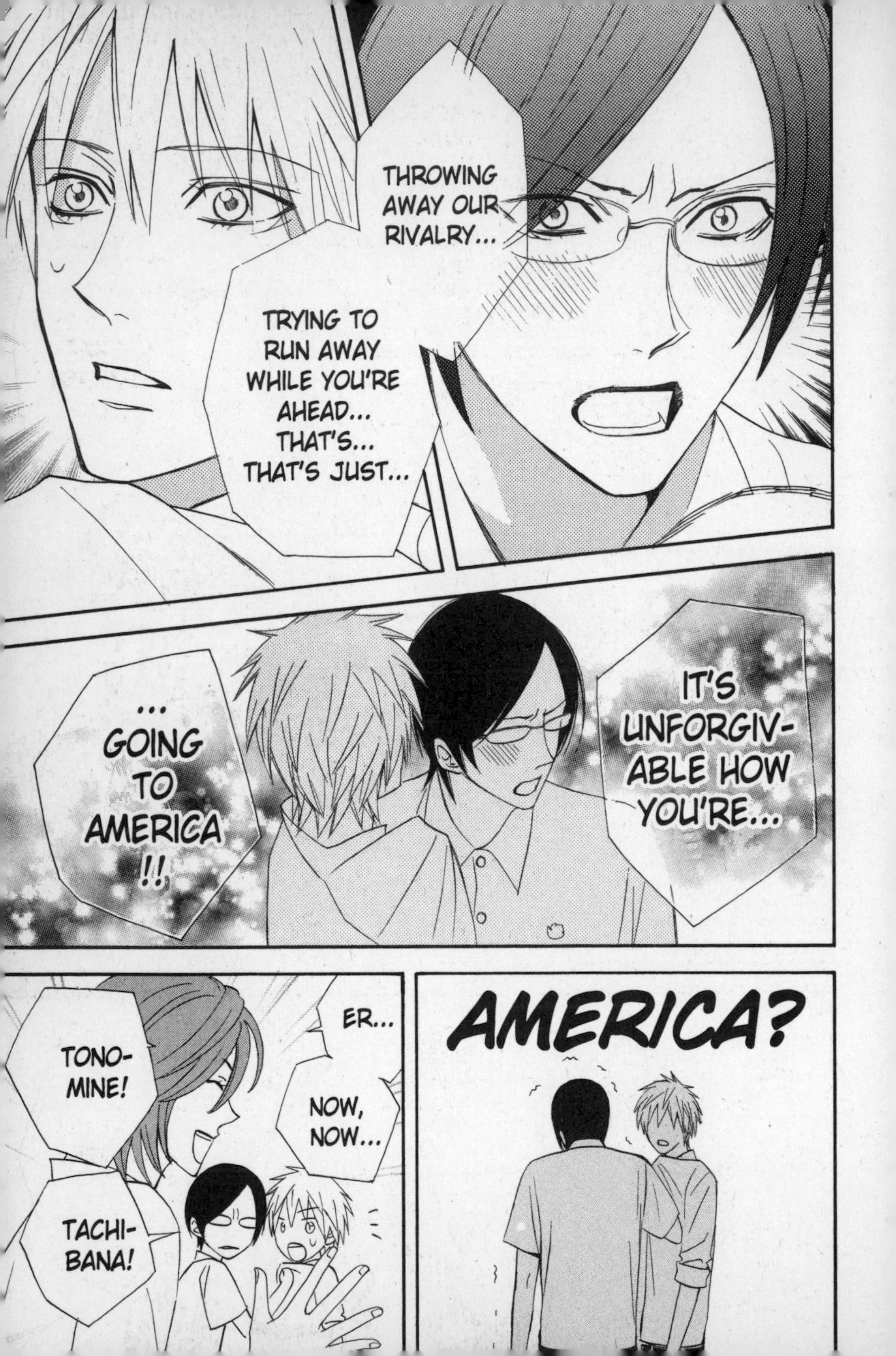
THROWING AWAY OUR RIVALRY...
TRYING TO RUN AWAY WHILE YOU'RE AHEAD... THAT'S... THAT'S JUST...
IT'S UNFORGIV-ABLE HOW YOU'RE...
... GOING TO AMERICA!!
AMERICA?
ER...
NOW, NOW...
TONO-MINE!
TACHI-BANA!

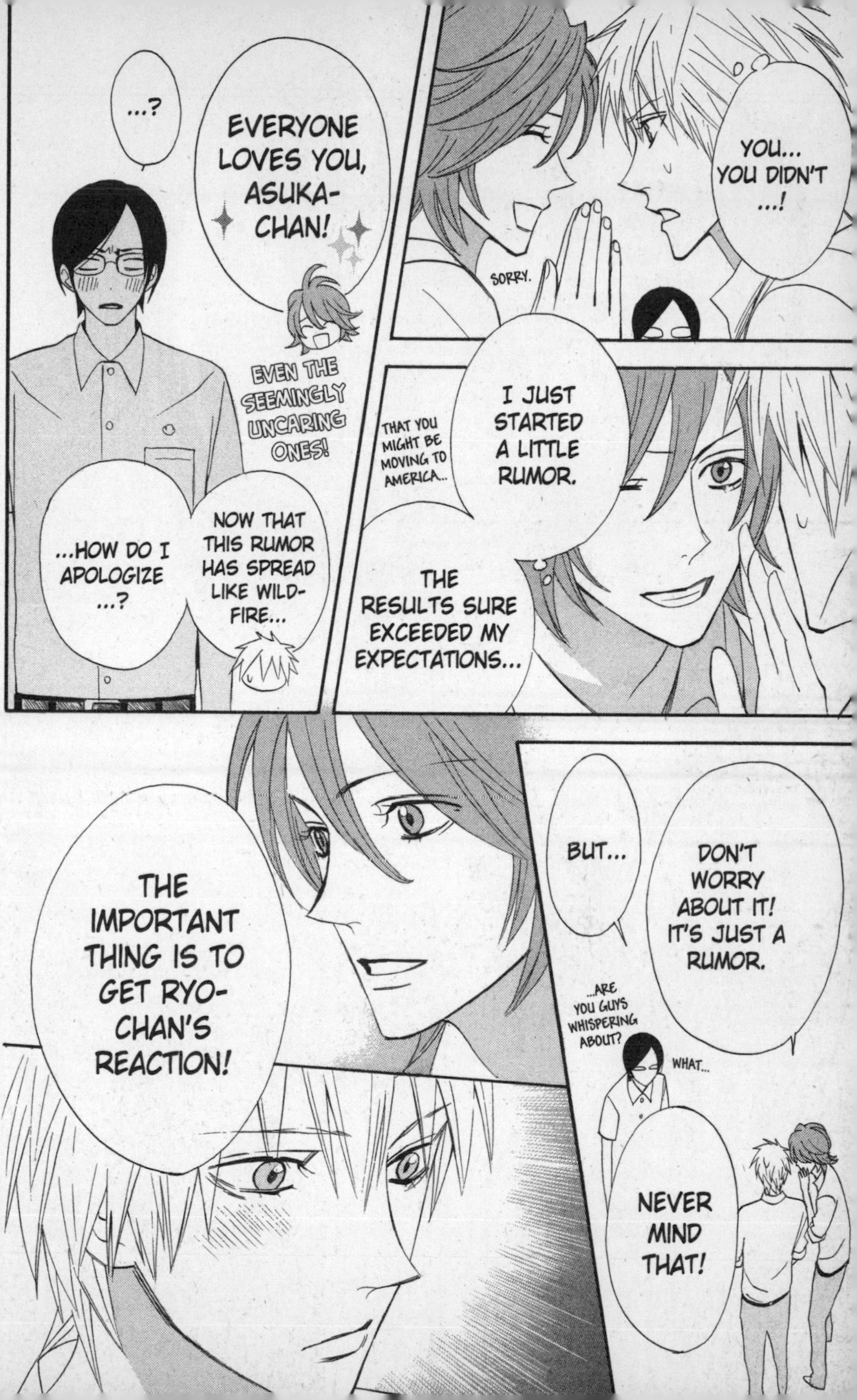
YOU... YOU DIDN'T ...!
SORRY.
I JUST STARTED A LITTLE RUMOR.
THAT YOU MIGHT BE MOVING TO AMERICA...
THE RESULTS SURE EXCEEDED MY EXPECTATIONS...
EVERYONE LOVES YOU, ASUKA-CHAN!
...?
EVEN THE SEEMINGLY UNCARING ONES!
NOW THAT THIS RUMOR HAS SPREAD LIKE WILD-FIRE...
...HOW DO I APOLOGIZE ...?
DON'T WORRY ABOUT IT! IT'S JUST A RUMOR.
BUT...
WHAT...
...ARE YOU GUYS WHISPERING ABOUT?
NEVER MIND THAT!
THE IMPORTANT THING IS TO GET RYO-CHAN'S REACTION!

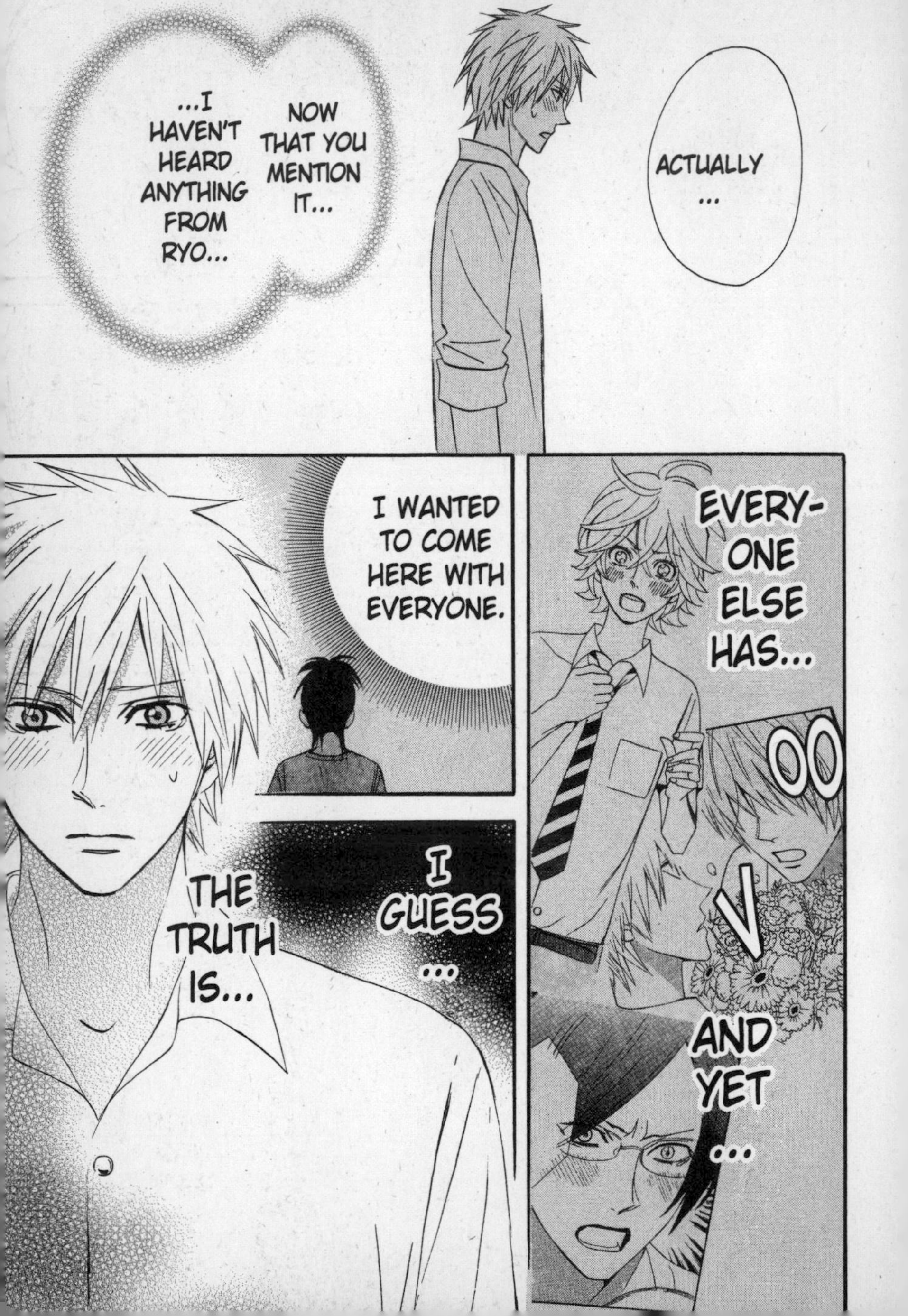
ACTUALLY...
NOW THAT YOU MENTION IT...
...I HAVEN'T HEARD ANYTHING FROM RYO...
EVERYONE ELSE HAS...
AND YET...
I WANTED TO COME HERE WITH EVERYONE.
I GUESS...
THE TRUTH IS...

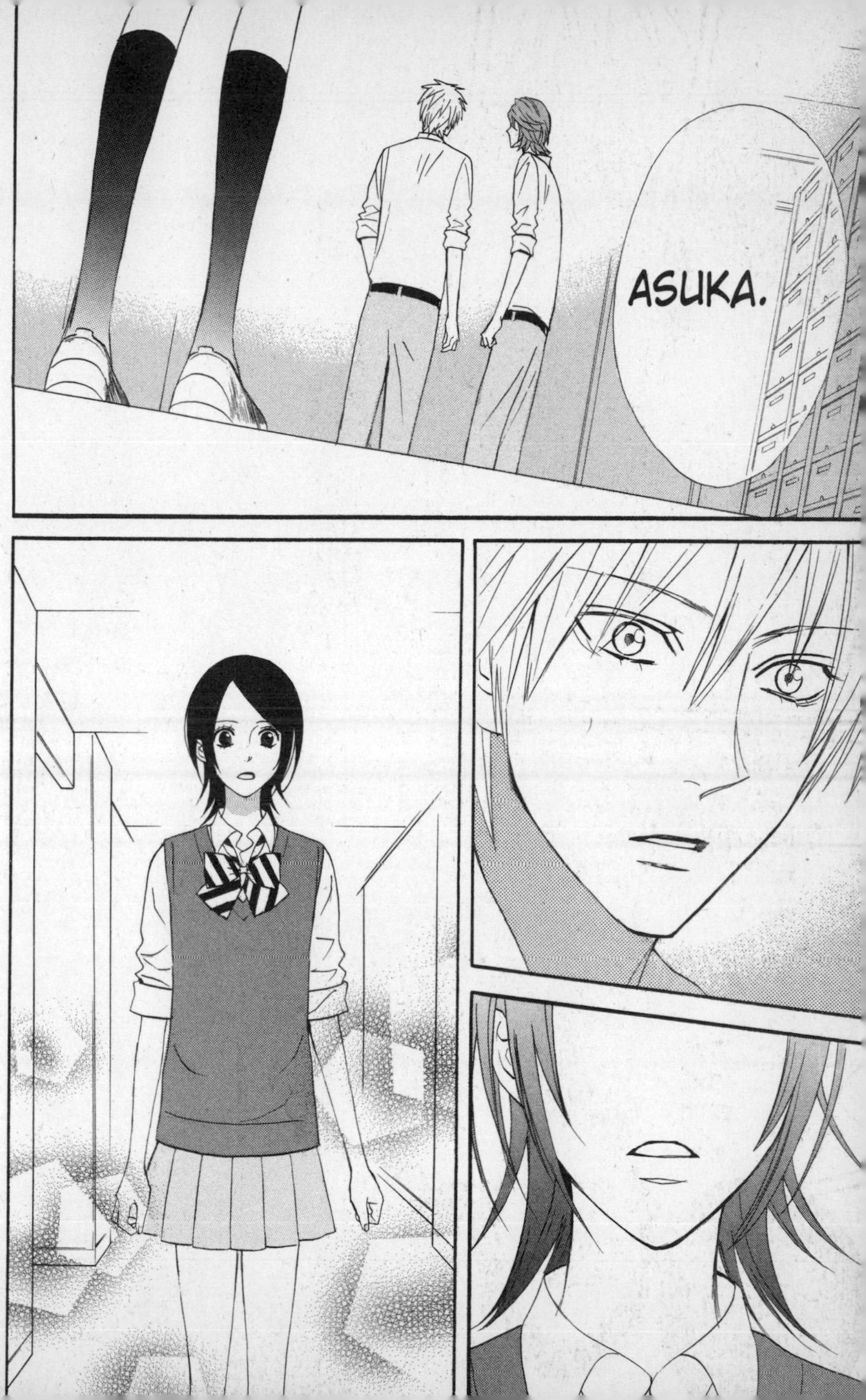
ASUKA.

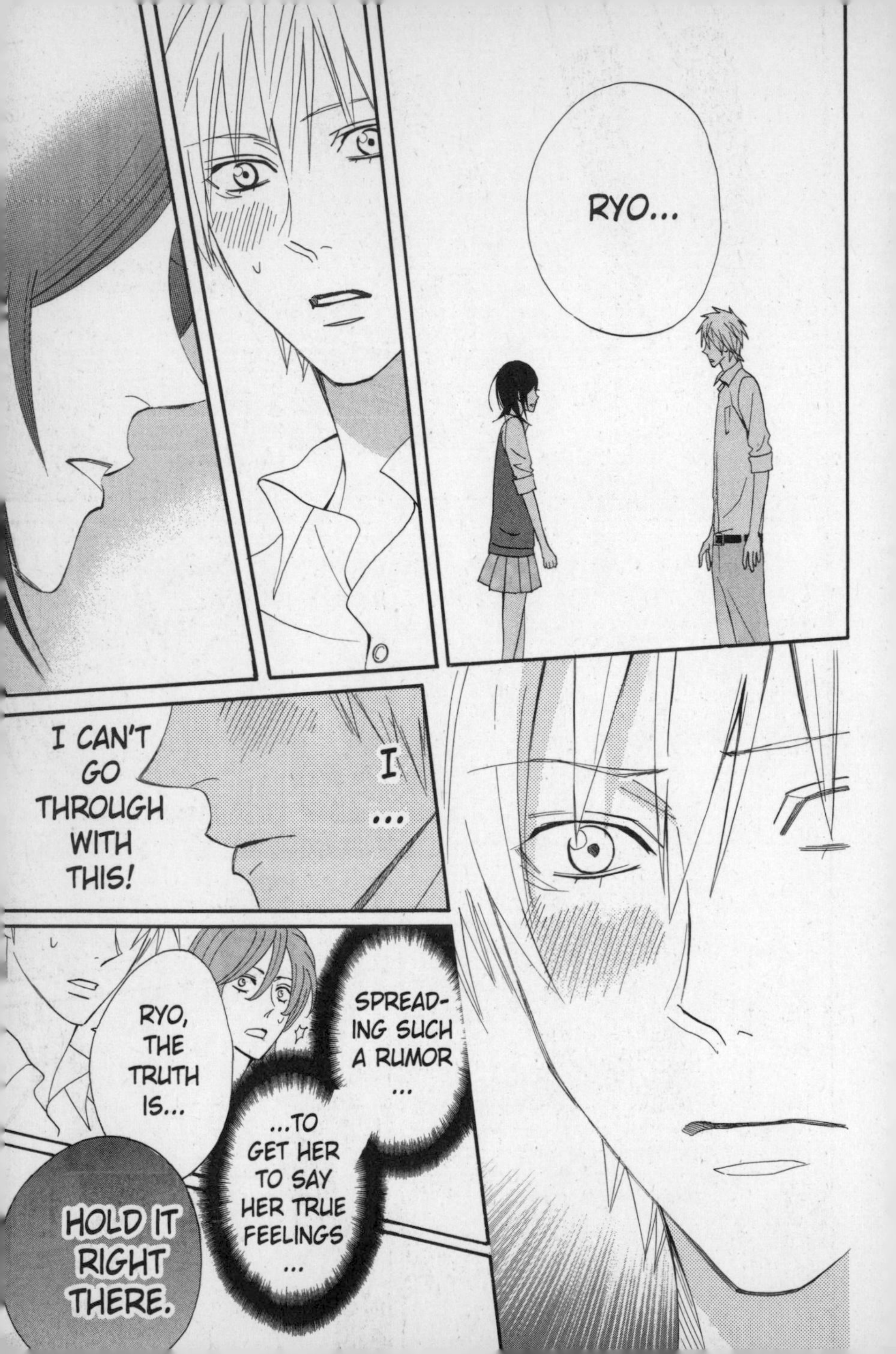
RYO...
I ...
I CAN'T GO THROUGH WITH THIS!
SPREAD-ING SUCH A RUMOR ...
...TO GET HER TO SAY HER TRUE FEELINGS ...
RYO, THE TRUTH IS...
HOLD IT RIGHT THERE.

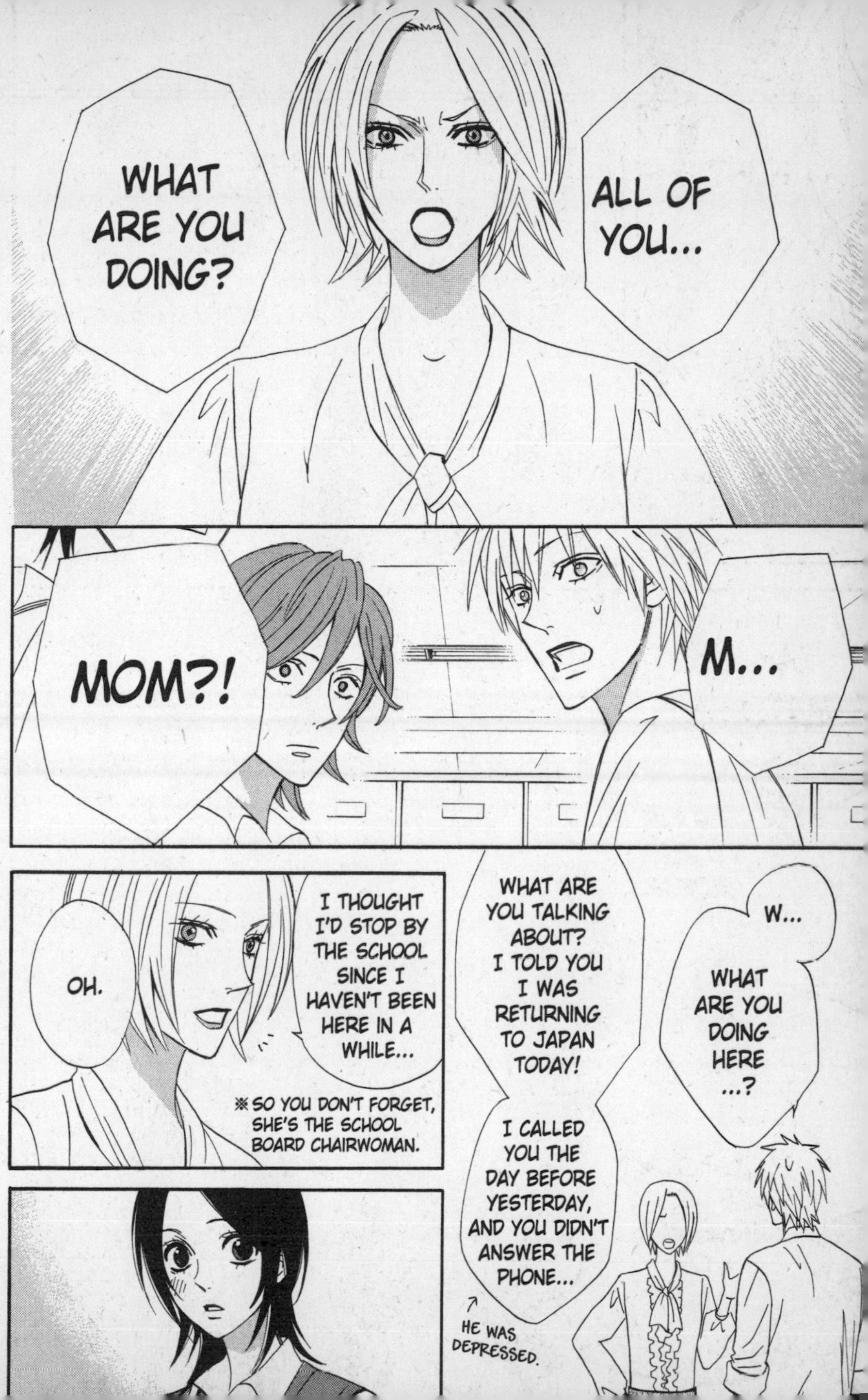
ALL OF YOU...
WHAT ARE YOU DOING?
M...
MOM?!
W... WHAT ARE YOU DOING HERE ...?
WHAT ARE YOU TALKING ABOUT? I TOLD YOU I WAS RETURNING TO JAPAN TODAY!
I CALLED YOU THE DAY BEFORE YESTERDAY, AND YOU DIDN'T ANSWER THE PHONE...
HE WAS DEPRESSED.
I THOUGHT I'D STOP BY THE SCHOOL SINCE I HAVEN'T BEEN HERE IN A WHILE...
OH.
※SO YOU DON'T FORGET, SHE'S THE SCHOOL BOARD CHAIRWOMAN.

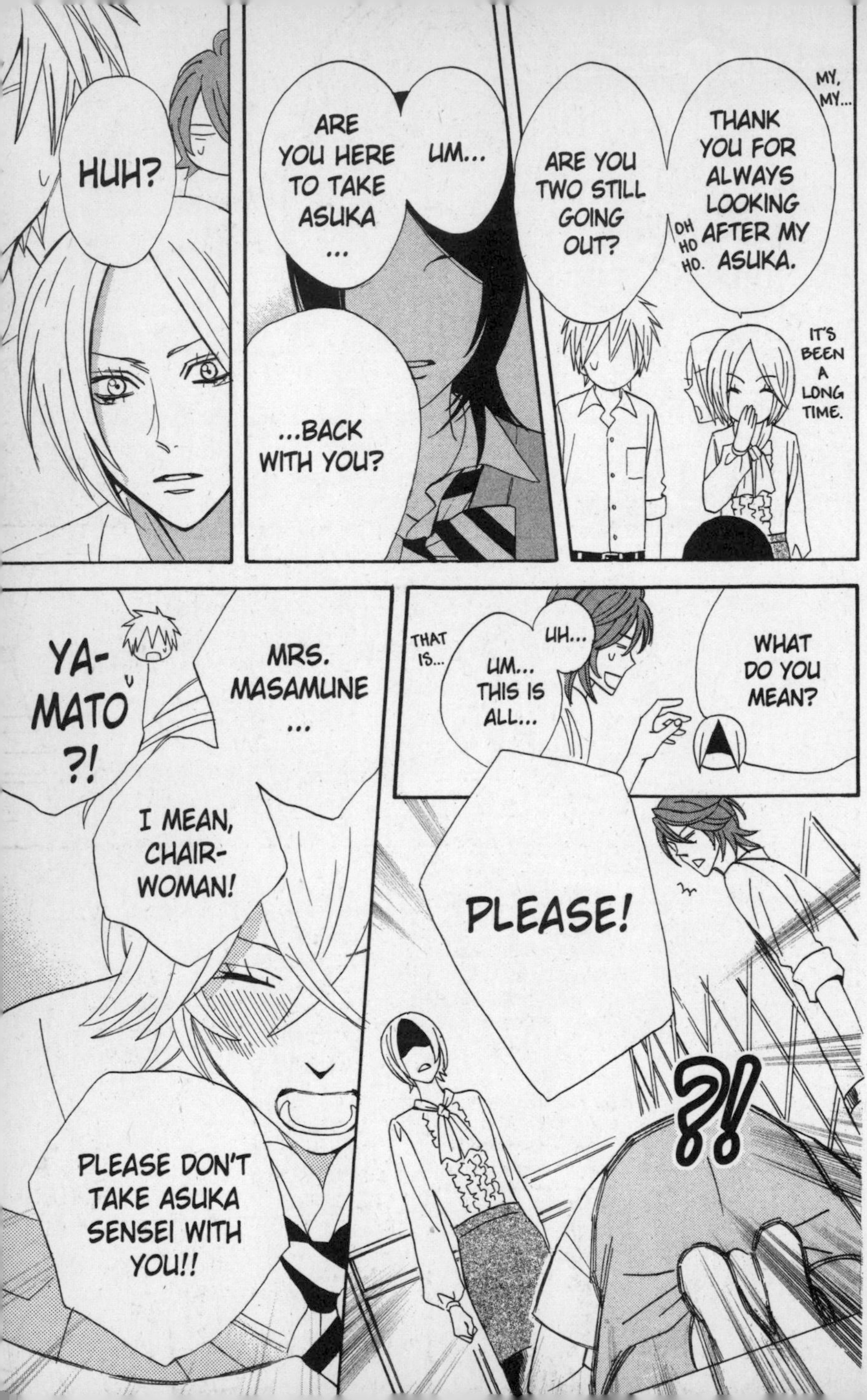
MY, MY...
THANK YOU FOR ALWAYS LOOKING AFTER MY ASUKA.
OH HO HO.
ARE YOU TWO STILL GOING OUT?
IT'S BEEN A LONG TIME.
UM...
ARE YOU HERE TO TAKE ASUKA...
...BACK WITH YOU?
HUH?
WHAT DO YOU MEAN?
UH...
THAT IS...
UM... THIS IS ALL...
PLEASE!
?!
YA-MATO?!
MRS. MASAMUNE...
I MEAN, CHAIR-WOMAN!
PLEASE DON'T TAKE ASUKA SENSEI WITH YOU!!

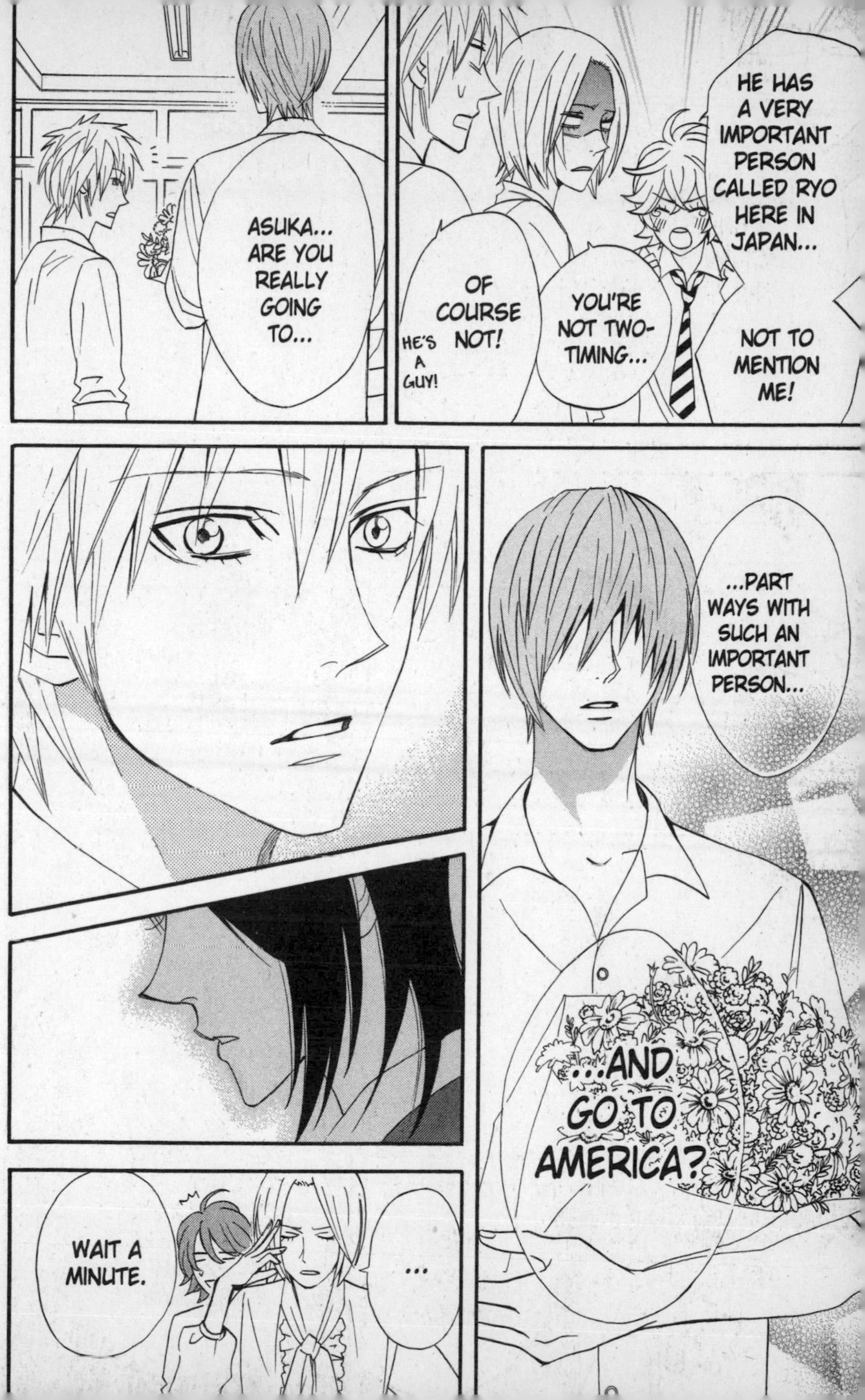
HE HAS A VERY IMPORTANT PERSON CALLED RYO HERE IN JAPAN...
NOT TO MENTION ME!
YOU'RE NOT TWO-TIMING...
OF COURSE NOT!
HE'S A GUY!
ASUKA... ARE YOU REALLY GOING TO...
...PART WAYS WITH SUCH AN IMPORTANT PERSON...
...AND GO TO AMERICA?
...
WAIT A MINUTE.

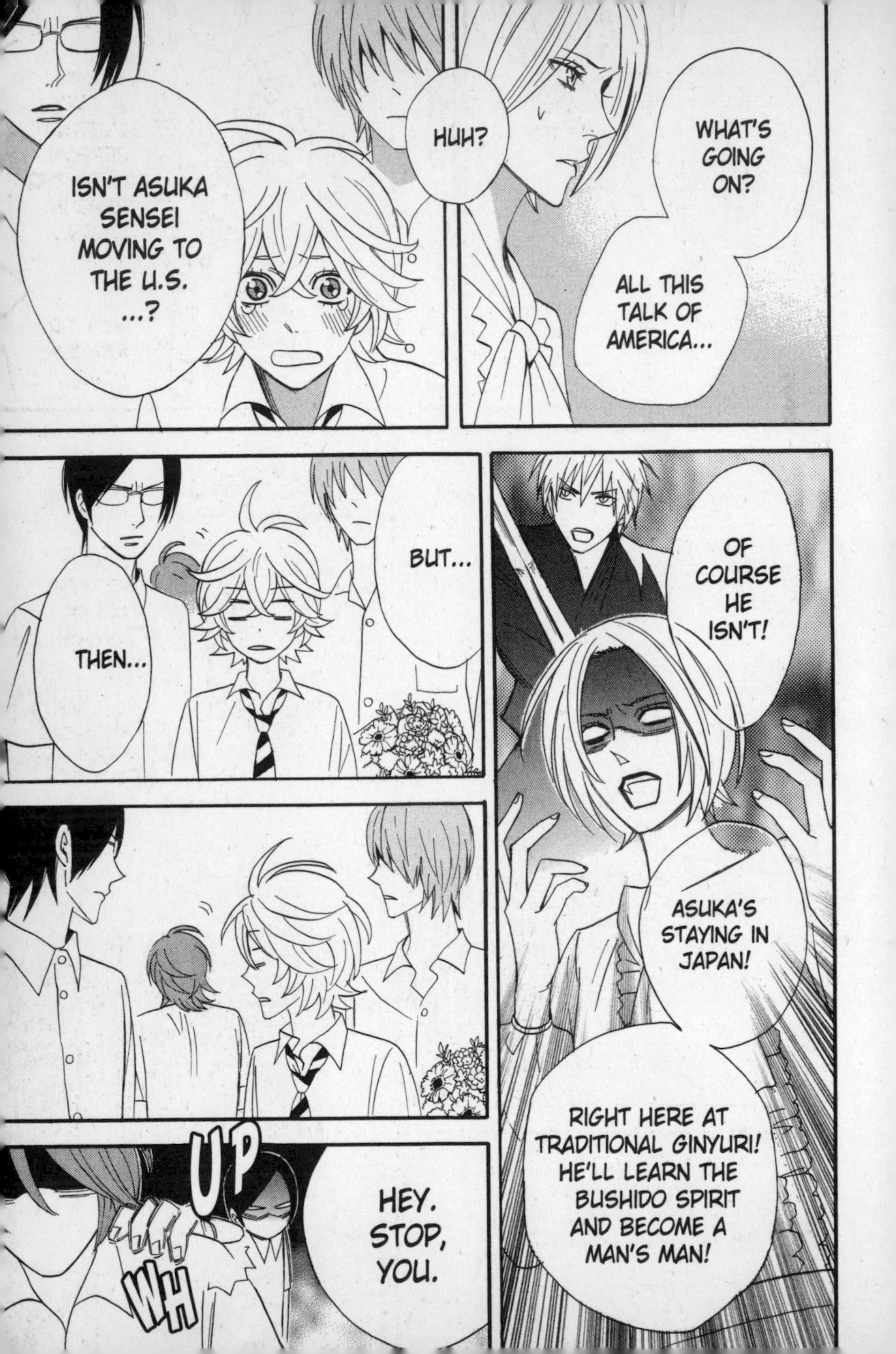
WHAT'S GOING ON?
ALL THIS TALK OF AMERICA...
HUH?
ISN'T ASUKA SENSEI MOVING TO THE U.S. ...?
OF COURSE HE ISN'T!
ASUKA'S STAYING IN JAPAN!
RIGHT HERE AT TRADITIONAL GINYURI! HE'LL LEARN THE BUSHIDO SPIRIT AND BECOME A MAN'S MAN!
BUT...
THEN...
UP
HEY. STOP, YOU.
WH

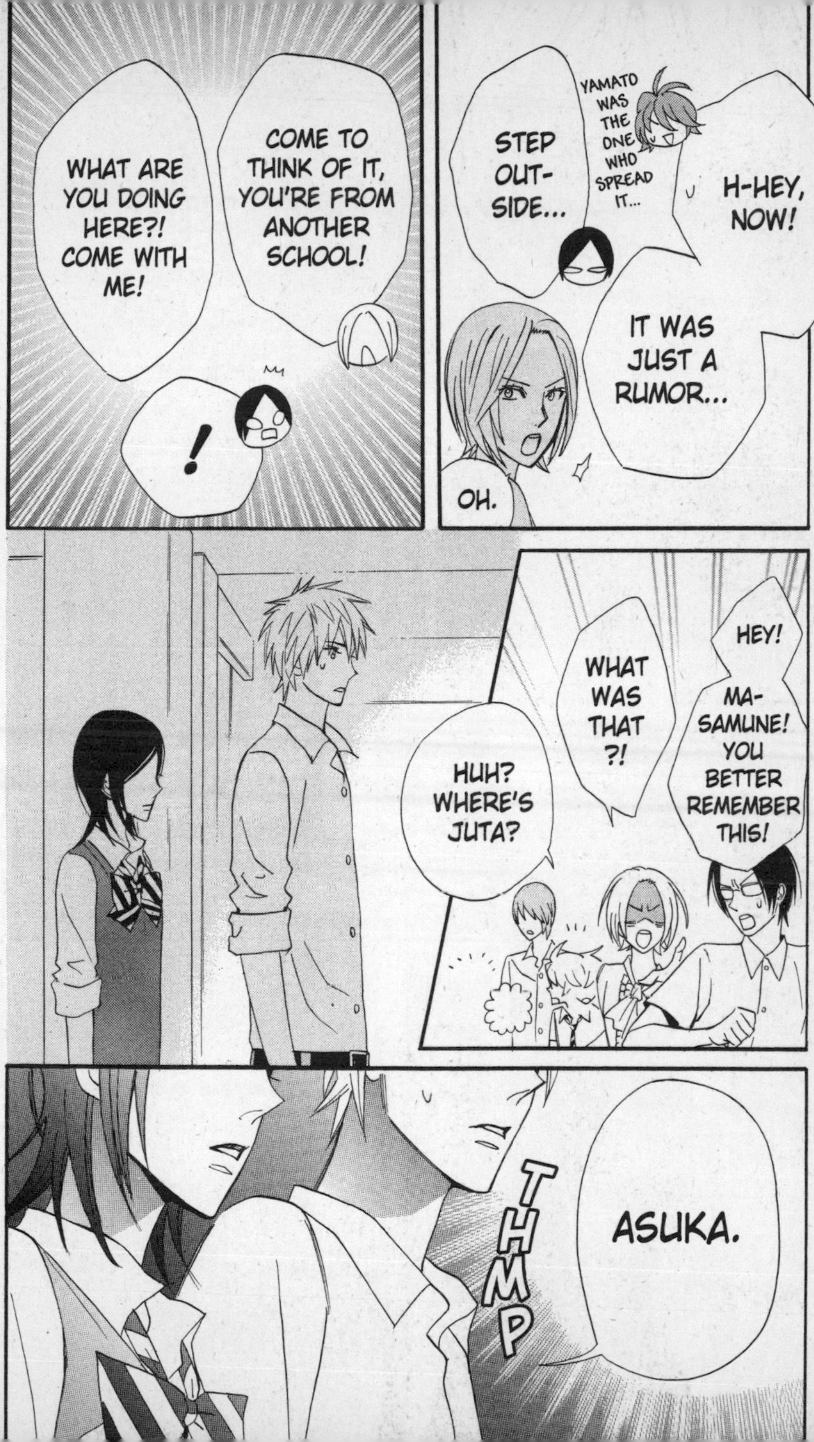
H-HEY, NOW!
YAMATO WAS THE ONE WHO SPREAD IT...
STEP OUT-SIDE...
IT WAS JUST A RUMOR...
OH.
COME TO THINK OF IT, YOU'RE FROM ANOTHER SCHOOL!
WHAT ARE YOU DOING HERE?! COME WITH ME!
!
HEY!
MA-SAMUNE! YOU BETTER REMEMBER THIS!
WHAT WAS THAT ?!
HUH? WHERE'S JUTA?
ASUKA.
THMP

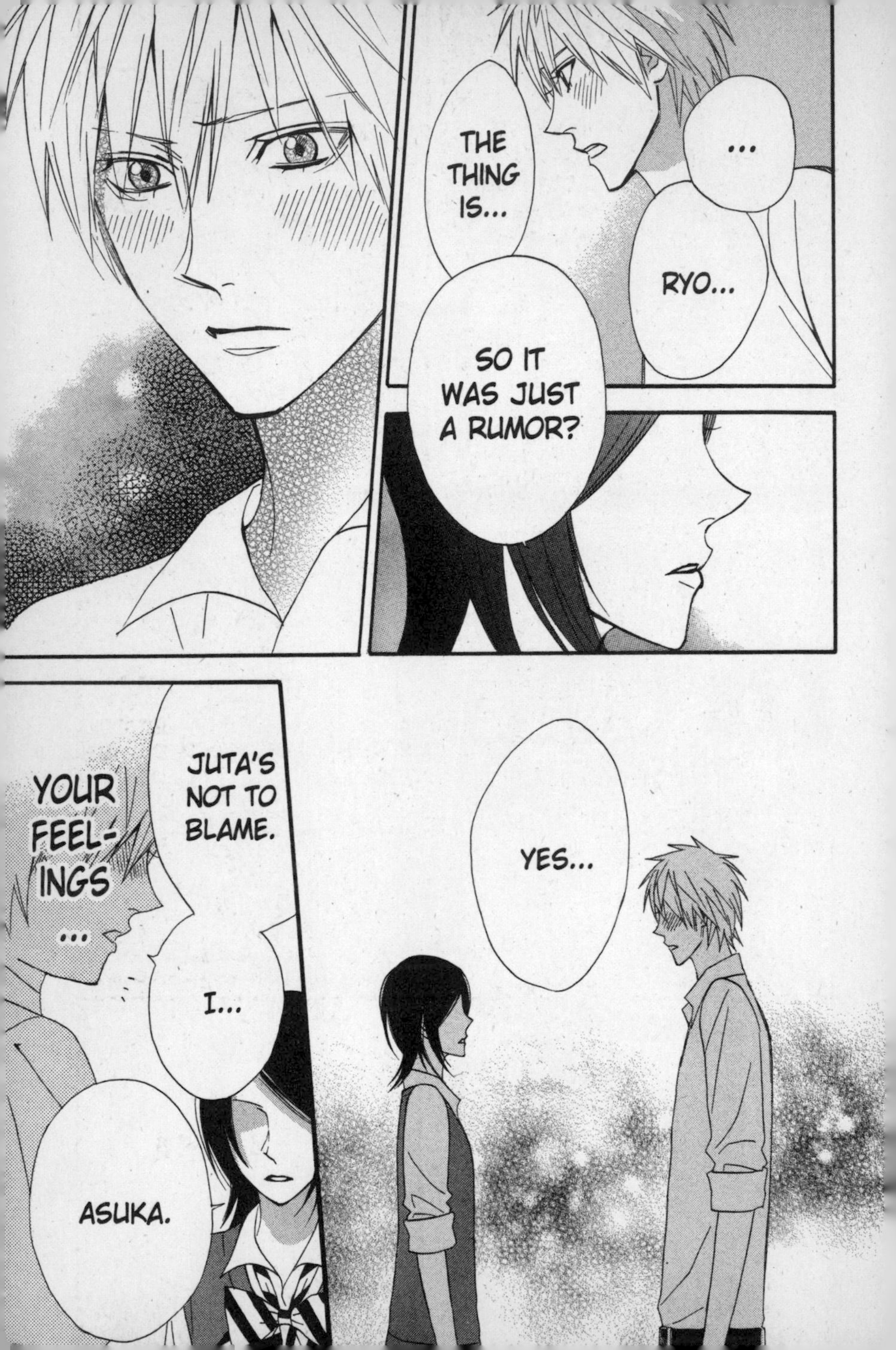
...
RYO...
THE THING IS...
SO IT WAS JUST A RUMOR?
YES...
JUTA'S NOT TO BLAME.
YOUR FEEL-INGS...
I...
ASUKA.

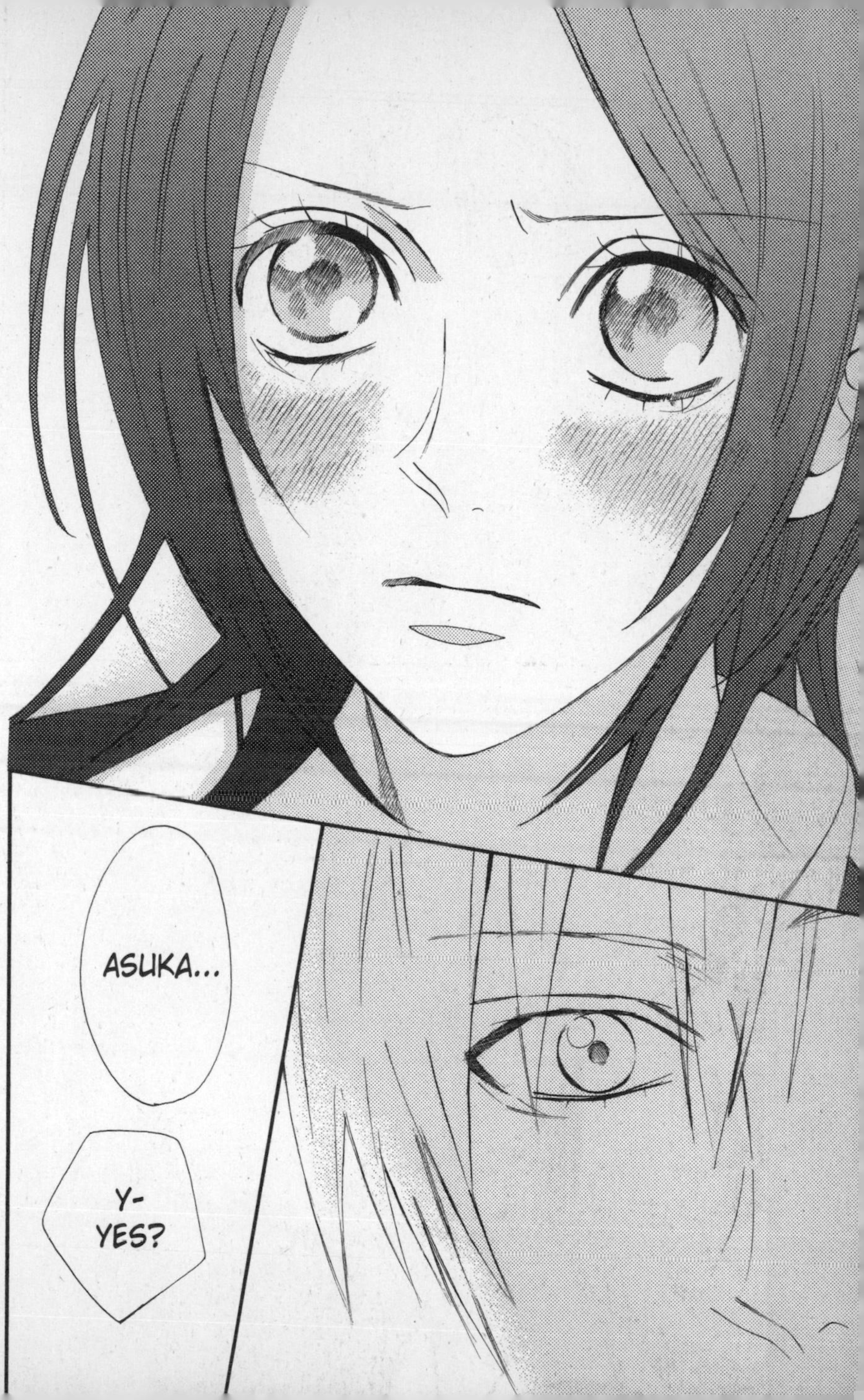
ASUKA...
Y-YES?

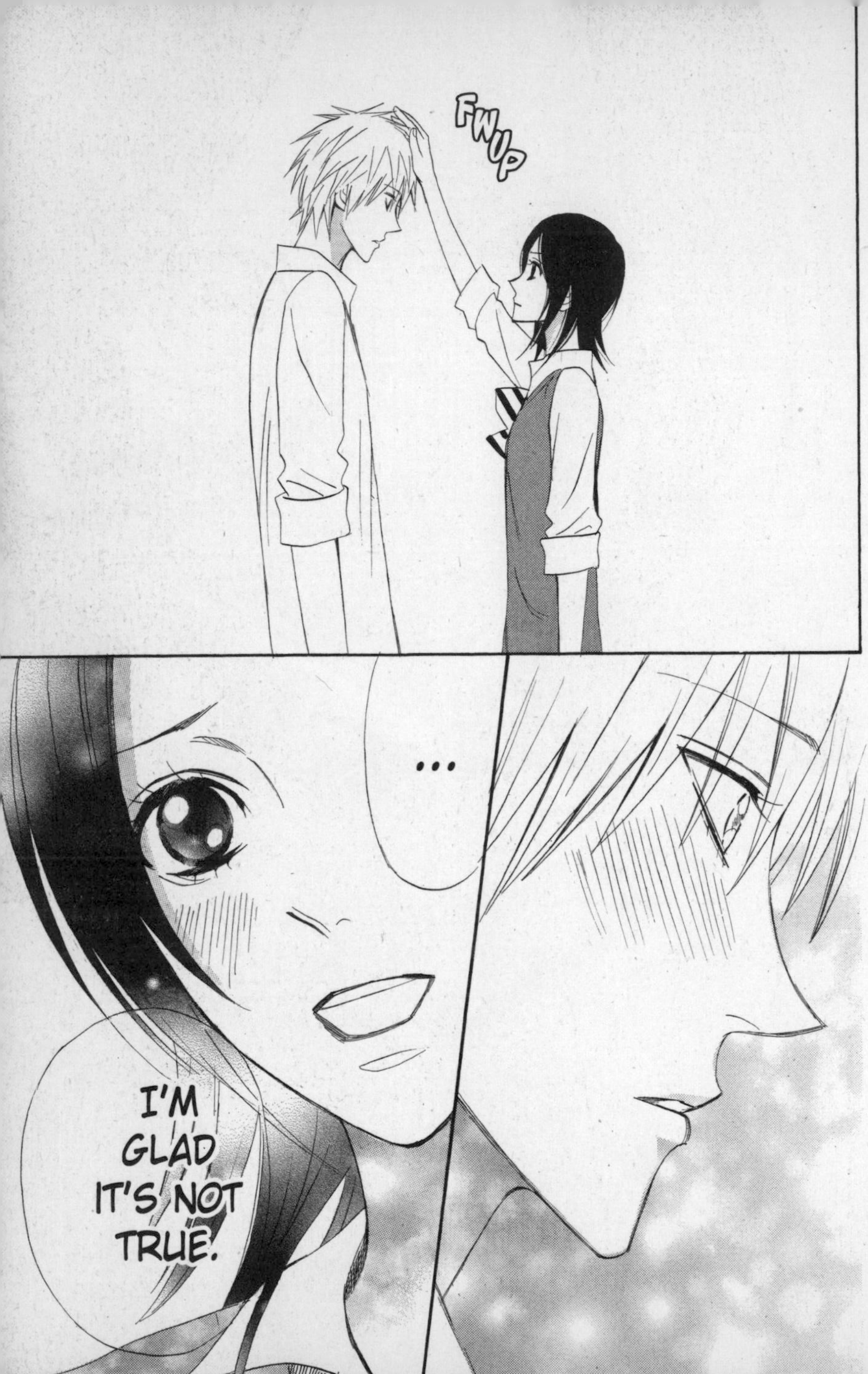
FWUP
...
I'M GLAD IT'S NOT TRUE.

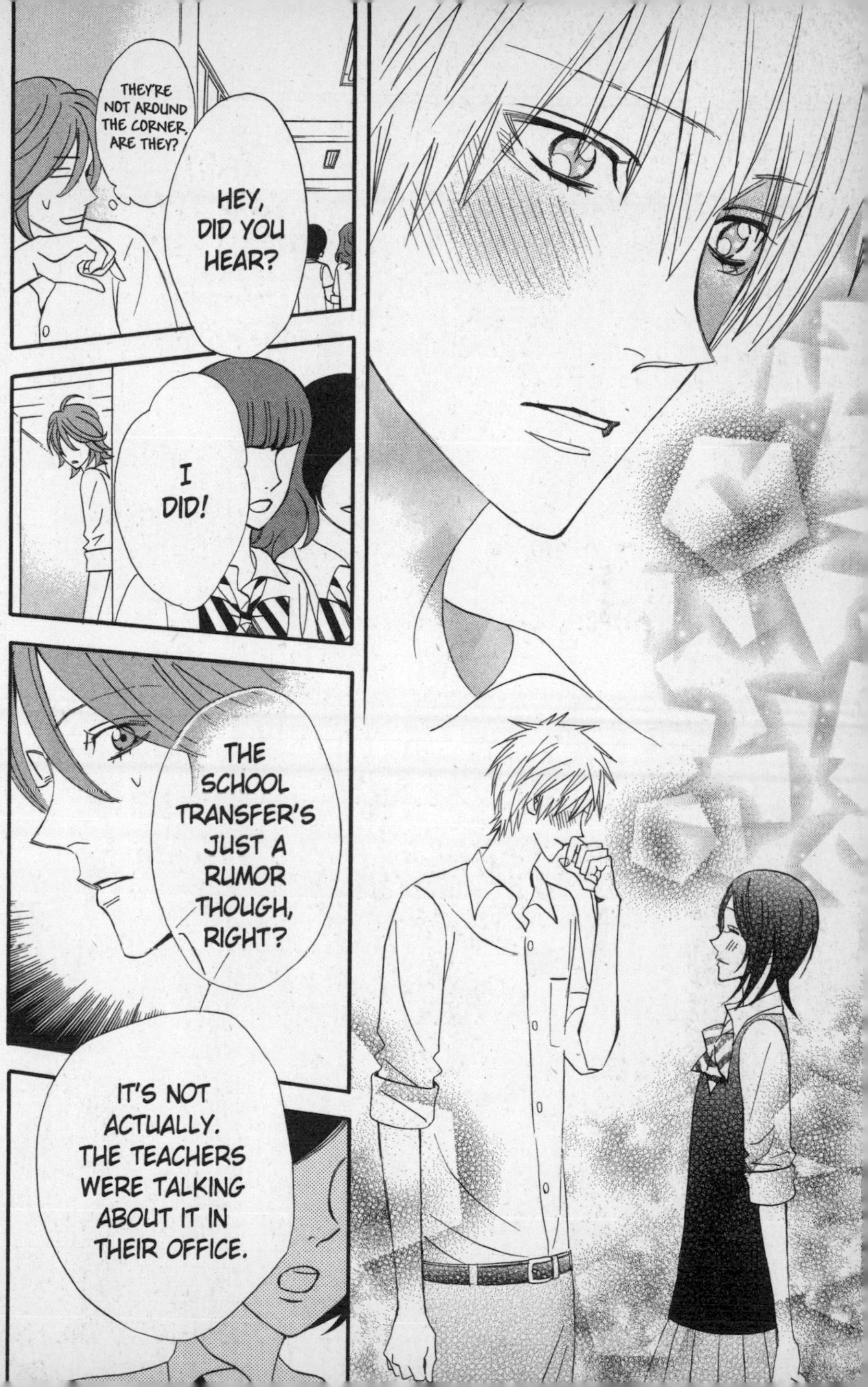
HEY, DID YOU HEAR?
THEY'RE NOT AROUND THE CORNER, ARE THEY?
I DID!
THE SCHOOL TRANSFER'S JUST A RUMOR THOUGH, RIGHT?
IT'S NOT ACTUALLY. THE TEACHERS WERE TALKING ABOUT IT IN THEIR OFFICE.

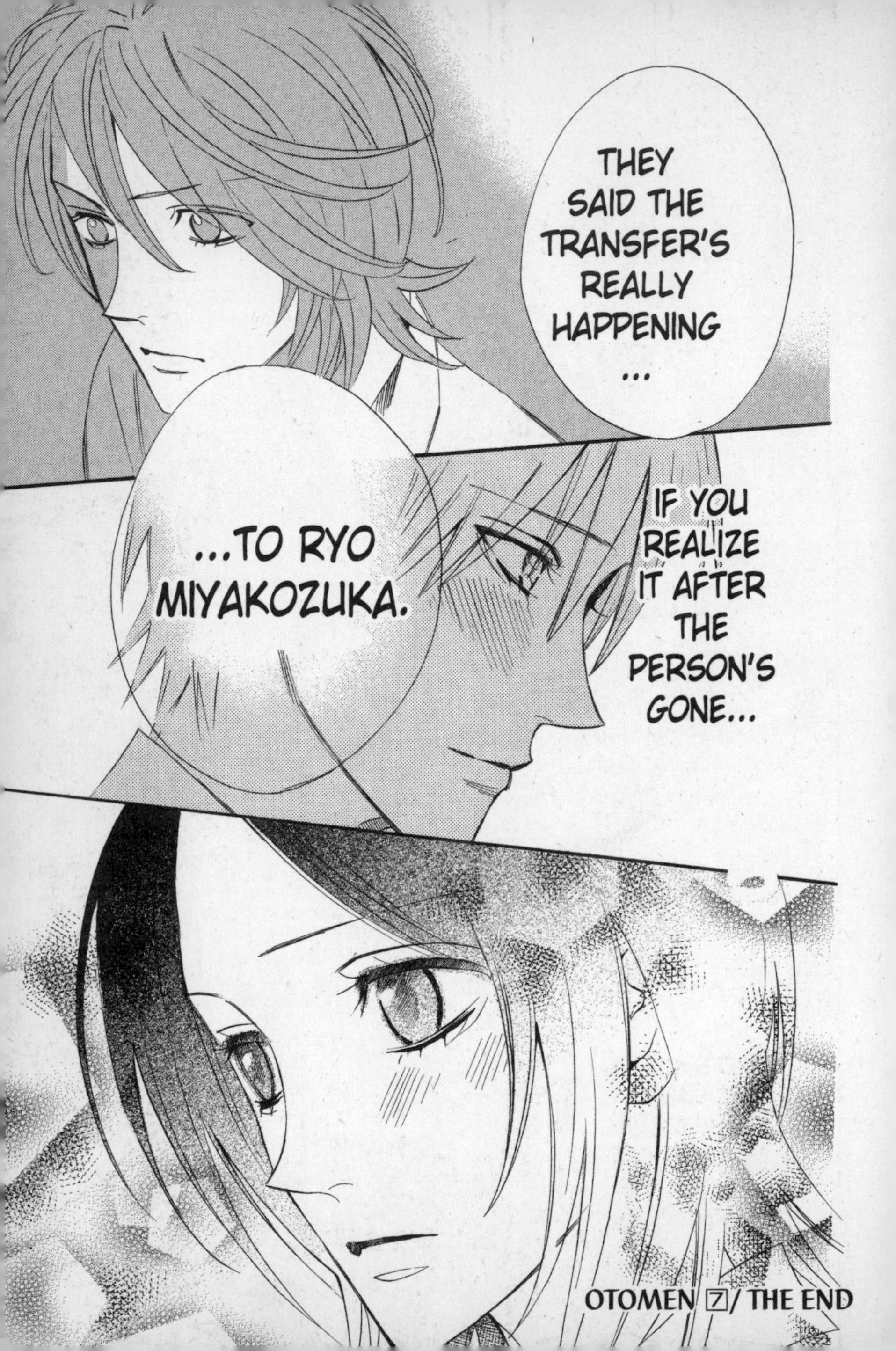
THEY SAID THE TRANSFER'S REALLY HAPPENING...
...TO RYO MIYAKOZUKA.
IF YOU REALIZE IT AFTER THE PERSON'S GONE...
OTOMEN 7 / THE END

OTOMEN

Confused by some of the terms, but too MANLY to ask for help?

Here are some **cultural notes** to assist you!

Chan – an informal honorific used to address children and females. *Chan* can also be used toward animals, lovers, intimate friends and people whom one has known since childhood.

San – the most common honorific title. It is used to address people outside one's immediate family and close circle of friends.

Sensei – honorific title used to address teachers as well as professionals such as doctors, lawyers and artists.

Sama – honorific used to address persons much higher in rank than oneself.

Page 3 | **Hana to Mame**
The name *Hana to Mame* (Flowers and Beans) is a play on the real shojo manga magazine *Hana to Yume* (Flowers and Dreams) published by Hakusensha.

Page 3 | **Tsun-sama**
Juta makes this word up by combining *tsundere* and *ore-sama*. *Tsundere* describes a character who is *tsuntsun* (cold or irritable) and later becomes *deredere* (affectionate or sentimental). *Ore-sama* describes a pompous and arrogant person, as it combines *ore* (me) with the honorific *sama*.

Page 31, panel 5 | **Kishidan**
A real-life Japanese band whose members sport the pompadour hairstyle similar to the man in this panel.

Page 72, panel 5 | **Shinai**
The bamboo sword used in kendo.

Page 83, panel 4 | **Eko Eko Azarak**
The opening phrase of a Wiccan chant. It is also the name of a Japanese horror manga from the '70s by Shinichi Koga.

Page 193 | **Jewel Sachihana's Signature**
The image here is Jewel Sachihana's signature. *Hana* means "flower" in Japanese, so *Sachi* is combined with the flower to read *Sachihana*.

Aya Kanno was born in Tokyo, Japan.
She is the creator of *Soul Rescue* and *Blank Slate*
(originally published as *Akusaga* in Japan's
BetsuHana magazine). Her latest work, *Otomen*,
is currently being serialized in *BetsuHana*.

OTOMEN

Vol. 7
Shojo Beat Edition

Story and Art by | **AYA KANNO**

Translation & Adaptation | **JN Productions**
Touch-up Art & Lettering | **Mark McMurray**
Design | **Fawn Lau**
Editor | **Amy Yu**

VP, Production | **Alvin Lu**
VP, Sales & Product Marketing | **Gonzalo Ferreyra**
VP, Creative | **Linda Espinosa**
Publisher | **Hyoe Narita**

Otomen by Aya Kanno © Aya Kanno 2009
All rights reserved. First published in Japan in 2009 by HAKUSENSHA, Inc., Tokyo.
English language translation rights arranged with HAKUSENSHA, Inc., Tokyo.

Printed in the U.S.A.

Published by VIZ Media, LLC
P.O. Box 77010
San Francisco, CA 94107

10 9 8 7 6 5 4 3 2 1
First printing, August 2010

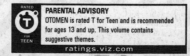

PARENTAL ADVISORY
OTOMEN is rated T for Teen and is recommended
for ages 13 and up. This volume contains
suggestive themes.
ratings.viz.com

www.viz.com

www.shojobeat.com

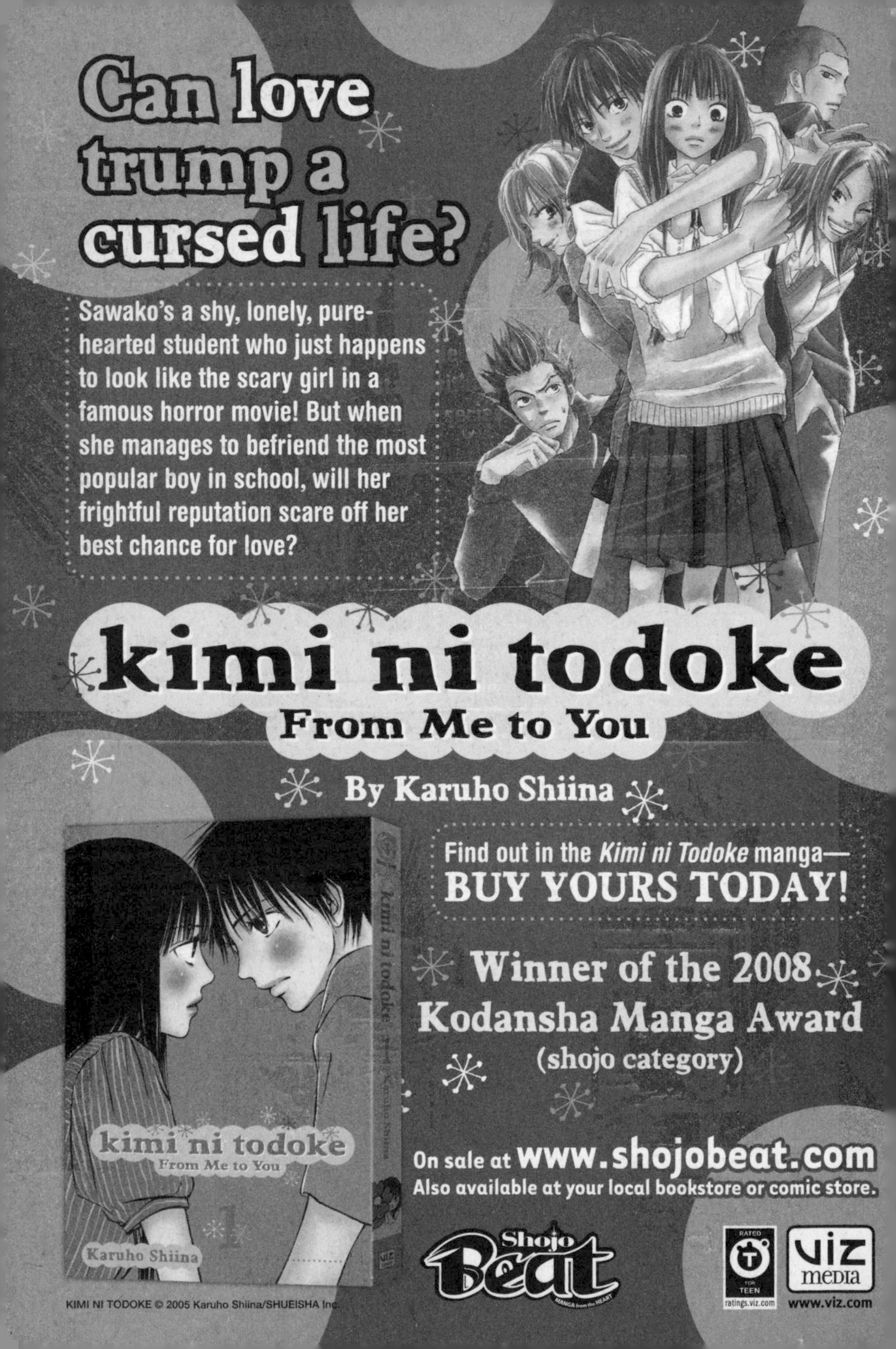
Can love trump a cursed life?
Sawako's a shy, lonely, pure-hearted student who just happens to look like the scary girl in a famous horror movie! But when she manages to befriend the most popular boy in school, will her frightful reputation scare off her best chance for love?
kimi ni todoke
From Me to You
By Karuho Shiina
kimi ni todoke
From Me to You
1
Karuho Shiina
Find out in the Kimi ni Todoke manga—
BUY YOURS TODAY!
Winner of the 2008
Kodansha Manga Award
(shojo category)
On sale at www.shojobeat.com
Also available at your local bookstore or comic store.
Shojo Beat
RATED T FOR TEEN
ratings.viz.com
VIZ media
www.viz.com
KIMI NI TODOKE © 2005 Karuho Shiina/SHUEISHA Inc.

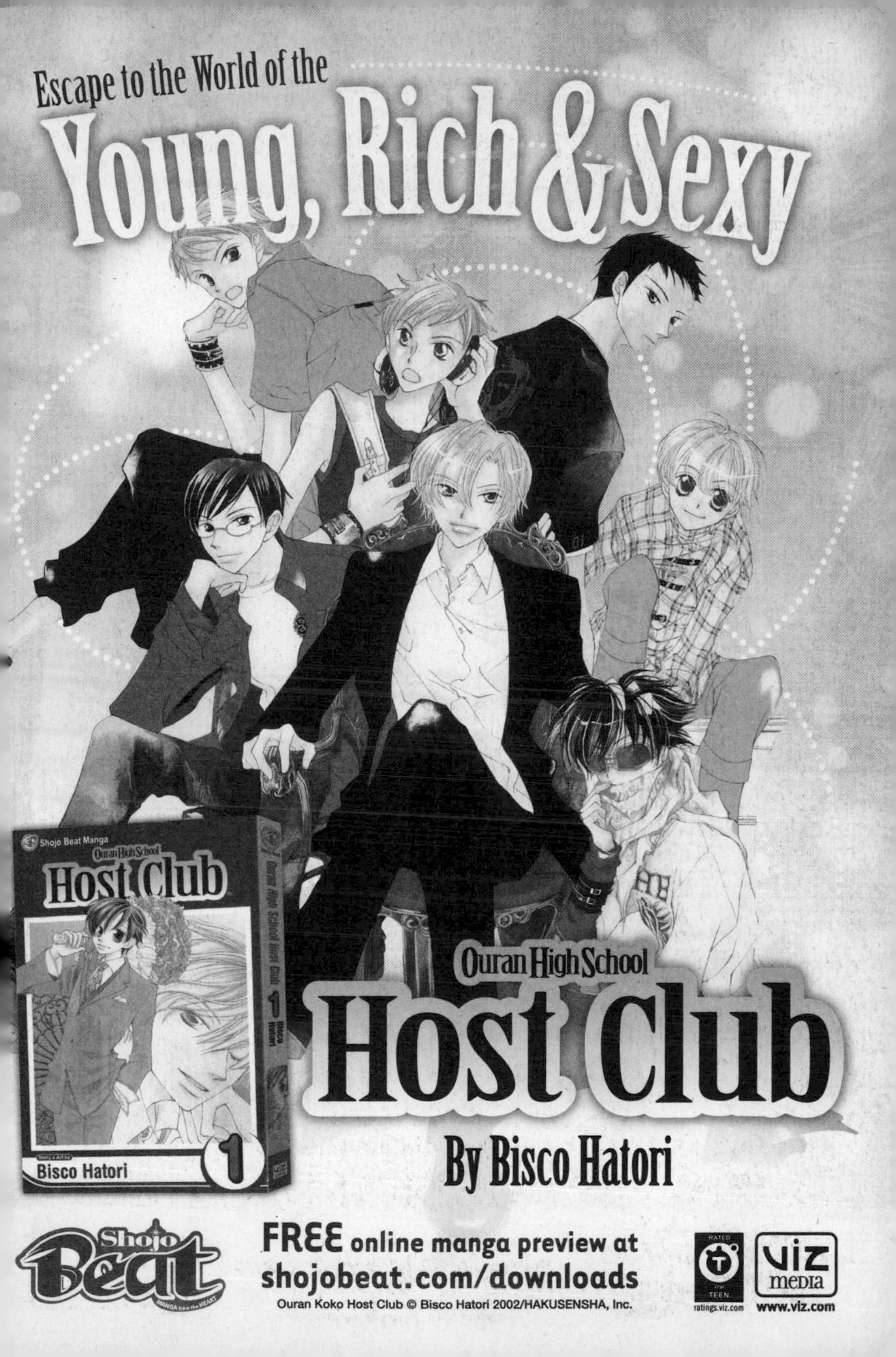
Escape to the World of the
Young, Rich & Sexy
Shojo Beat Manga
Ouran High School
Host Club
Ouran High School Host Club 1
Bisco Hatori
1
Ouran High School
Host Club
By Bisco Hatori
Shojo Beat
MANGA from the HEART
FREE online manga preview at
shojobeat.com/downloads
Ouran Koko Host Club © Bisco Hatori 2002/HAKUSENSHA, Inc.
RATED
T
TEEN
ratings.viz.com
VIZ media
www.viz.com